Reading and Writing for Research Papers

英语研究论文读写教程

丛书主编　张为民　张文霞

主　　编　庞红梅

编　　者　杨　莉　张为民

English Reading and Writing for General Academic Purposes

通用学术英语读写系列教材

清华大学出版社

北　京

内 容 简 介

  本书是"通用学术英语读写系列教材"中的第四部。教材以提高学生英语学术研究论文读写能力为目标，精心挑选阅读素材，巧妙安排各单元的写作重点，循序渐进帮助学生了解研究论文的基本框架、写作原则和写作技巧，最终使学生能独立完成以IMRD格式为标准框架、以APA格式为基本要求的英语研究论文写作任务。

  本教材根据研究论题进行分类，共包括四大主题：对剽窃的理解、语言学习中字典的使用、跨文化交际和EFL写作。每个主题包括主题导引、两篇相关论文和一个补充阅读。其中两篇论文是重点学习内容，每篇文章即为一个单元，各单元都设计了学习目标、论文阅读、词汇表、课后练习和写作重点五个部分。

图书在版编目（CIP）数据

英语研究论文读写教程/庞红梅主编. —北京：清华大学出版社，2013（2023.8 重印）
（通用学术英语读写系列教材）
ISBN 978-7-302-33227-5

Ⅰ.①英… Ⅱ.①庞… Ⅲ.①英语—论文—阅读教学—教材 ②英语—论文—写作—教材 Ⅳ.①H31

中国版本图书馆CIP数据核字（2013）第160402号

责任编辑：刘细珍
封面设计：傅瑞学
责任校对：王凤芝
责任印制：沈　露

出版发行：清华大学出版社
    网　　址：http://www.tup.com.cn, http://www.wqbook.com
    地　　址：北京清华大学学研大厦A座   邮　编：100084
    社 总 机：010-83470000   邮　购：010-62786544
    投稿与读者服务：010-62776969, c-service@tup.tsinghua.edu.cn
    质量反馈：010-62772015, zhiliang@tup.tsinghua.edu.cn

印 装 者：三河市龙大印装有限公司
经　　销：全国新华书店
开　　本：185mm×260mm 印　张：19 字　数：428千字
版　　次：2013年9月第1版   印　次：2023年8月第12次印刷
定　　价：76.00元

产品编号：052607-04

"通用学术英语读写系列教材"编委会

丛书主编：张为民　张文霞（清华大学）

编　　委：（按姓氏笔画排序）

王　哲（中山大学）

刘宇慧（北京工业大学）

刘泽华（华中科技大学）

江桂英（厦门大学）

余渭深（重庆大学）

吴树敬（北京理工大学）

张　莉（华北电力大学）

张彩华（中国农业大学）

李小红（哈尔滨工业大学）

杨连瑞（中国海洋大学）

汪火焰（武汉大学）

战　菊（吉林大学）

赵雪爱（西北工业大学）

秦明利（大连理工大学）

蒋学清（北京交通大学）

谢小苑（南京航空航天大学）

学术英语学习旨在培养学生的学术交流能力，满足学生使用英语进行专业学习和发展的需要。中小学阶段英语教学的重点一般是培养学生用英语进行一般交流的能力，即侧重于一般英语教学。学术英语与一般英语既有联系，又有自己的特点。学术英语的学习既可以提高学生专业发展所需的语言知识和技能，同时也可以提高其一般英语的能力；它很大程度上涵盖了一般英语的学习，同时又可看作英语学习的更高阶段。学术英语学习包括两个层面的内容：一是技能层面（English for Academic Purposes）（如参加学术讲座、进行学术阅读需要的记笔记能力，论文写作、学术发言需要的概括能力等）；二是语言层面（Academic English）（如用学术语言写研究报告、研究论文的能力等）。学术英语是本科生、研究生用英语进行专业文献学习及研究交流所需要掌握的基本能力。

"通用学术英语读写系列教材"（English Reading and Writing for General Academic Purposes）针对教育部在《大学英语课程教学要求》（2007）中提出的英语较高要求和更高要求而编写。根据较高要求和更高要求，大学英语教学要注重培养学生的学术交流能力，要求学生能阅读所学专业的英语文献和资料，能用英语撰写所学专业的报告和论文。同时，本系列教材的编写也迎合全球化国际大环境对大学英语教学由一般英语转向学术英语的需要。

本系列教材的设计与编写主要依据两大原则：语言学习规律和高等教育特点。根据语言学习规律，语言输入为语言产出的基础，语言产出需与语言输入相结合，外语学习尤其如此。因此，本系列教材采用了以读促写、读写结合的编写理念。同时，掌握一门语言的读写能力遵循一定的先后顺序，如先学组词、造句、写段落，然后是记叙文、说明文、议论文等。在此基础上，进行更高层次的读写学习，即综述读写、论文读写等。另外，高等教育在很大程度上是专业教育，培养与专业相关的学术素养（如综述、议论、思辨、研究规范等）对学生而言至关重要。因此，大学英语教育应该顺应和符合学生的专业发展需求。具体而言，本科和研究生英语教育均需培养学生用英语完成说明文、议论文、文献综述和研究论文等不同语体的读写能力。

鉴于此，本系列教材 1~4 册分别围绕高等教育中最常用的四个学术语体进行设计与编写，即说明文、议论文、文献综述、研究论文。同时，这四册教材又针对高等教育对学生的学术素养要求，专门就常用的学术读写能力进行训练，包括学术阅读技能、学术词汇扩展、学术语言特点、学术文本特点、学术写作技巧（如 paraphrasing）等。这些能力的训练贯穿于整个 1~4 册教材系列。

本系列教材是在教育全球化的新形势下为满足我国高校人才培养需求而开发的。教材

旨在为学生用英语顺利进行专业学习提供帮助和支撑，帮助学生掌握学术规范，提高学生的批判性和创造性思维，培养和提高学生的英语学术交流能力和专业学术素养，适用于本科生和研究生学习。我们相信，通过本系列教材的学习，学生不仅会进一步提高一般的英语交流能力，更能提高学术英语交流能力和跨文化学术素养。

感谢本系列教材的每一位编委专家为教材进行全面细致的审读，并提出宝贵的意见和建议，使得教材的编写更加契合广大院校培养优秀的研究型人才之目标，更加符合各高校英语教学向学术英语转型的要求。

丛书主编

2013 年 7 月

前 言

《英语研究论文读写教程》是"通用学术英语读写系列教材"中的第四部。教材强调以项目为基础学习研究论文的阅读和写作，帮助学生做好英语研究论文读写的准备；试图让学生理解研究论文写作的框架和各部分的写作原则，同时跨越专业之间的界限，完成以 IMRD 格式为标准框架、以 APA 格式为基本要求的论文写作。本教材希望在提高学生学术英语读写能力的同时，能给不同专业学生提供相关的研究论文写作实践机会。

一、教材对象

本教材针对有较好学术英语基础、同时有完成学术论文读写需要的本科生和研究生。教材内容与教学实践的各个环节密切结合，适合一个学期的完整教学。

二、教材特点

1. 本教材采用各学科通用的 IMRD 研究论文写作框架，让学生突破学科障碍完成真实的项目写作，同时可以让学生关注到各个学科之间写作实践中的细微差别。

2. 本教材阅读部分的研究论文选材于语言学和文化研究方面的国际性权威期刊，正文内容未经删改，体例和格式也保留了各自的风貌和特点，目的是尽可能让学生接触真实的研究论文。

3. 本教材论文选题接近学生的学术生活和英语学习，提高学生对研究论文的读写兴趣，同时与传统英语教学密切相关。

4. 本教材中论文选材注重多样化，既包括以英语为母语的学者所写作的论文，也包括以英语为第二语言写作的学者所著论文，让学生在了解以英语为通用语言写作规范的同时观察并提高写作中的文化意识。

5. 本教材安排注重写作过程。教材详细解释了研究论文写作的完整过程，包括从研究论文整体框架设计到讲述、展示论文的各个环节。

三、内容安排

1. 全书根据研究论题进行分类，共包括 4 大主题，分别是对剽窃的理解、语言学习中字典的使用、跨文化交际和 EFL 写作，选题紧贴学生的英语学习和学术要求。

2. 每个主题包括主题导引、两篇相关论文和一个补充阅读。主题导引帮助学生了解主题，引入相关论文的阅读。两篇论文是重点学习内容，学生在了解相关主题的同时熟悉研究论文写作的基本规律和技巧。补充阅读旨在让学生更好地了解这一主题，也可以为学生自己的项目实践提供参考文献。

3. 同时，全书又按写作重心，共分 8 个单元，每单元包括以下 4 个部分。

A. 本单元学习目标展望。帮助学生树立明确、可行的目标，使学习更有针对性。

B. 论文阅读以及相关词汇表。

C. 课后练习。包括两大部分：Discussion Ideas（针对论文中的内容）；Vocabulary and Language Learning Skills（针对论文中的词汇）。其中词汇部分的练习包括两个重点方向：第一个习题强调学生对词汇意义的认知，旨在提高学生研究论文的阅读能力；第二个习题强调对词汇常见搭配的使用，旨在提高学生研究论文的写作水平。

D. 写作重点。按照研究论文写作的规范，每个单元分别详尽介绍了研究论文写作和展示的各个组成部分，包括研究论文框架、绪论、文献综述、研究方法、研究结果、讨论、标题页、摘要、展示等。每单元写作讲解后，安排了针对本单元的写作重点训练。

本教材是清华大学外文系教学团队在多年教学科研实践的基础上不断积累经验所进行的大胆尝试。因时间仓促，书中难免会有错误和不当之处，热忱欢迎读者批评指正。

编者

2013 年 3 月于清华园

Contents

Plagiarism

Anticipating the Issue

Discuss your answers to the following questions.

1. What is your definition of plagiarism? What should you do to avoid plagiarism?

2. Which of the following would be considered as plagiarism?

   a) Not providing a reference when you have used somebody's idea.

   b) Giving the reference but not using quotation marks when you take a sentence from another writer's article.

   c) Presenting the results of your own research.

   d) Copying a few sentences from an article on the Internet without giving a reference.

   e) Not giving a reference when you use commonly accepted ideas.

3. Here's the ORIGINAL text, from page 1 of *Lizzie Borden: A Case Book of Family and Crime in the 1890s* by Joyce Williams et al.:

   The rise of industry, the growth of cities, and the expansion of the population were the three great developments of late nineteenth century American history. As new, larger, steam-powered factories became a feature of the American landscape in the East, they transformed farm hands into industrial laborers, and provided jobs for a rising tide of immigrants. With industry came urbanization the growth of large cities (like Fall River, Massachusetts, where the Bordens lived) which became the centers of production as well as of commerce and trade.

Following are three paraphrases. Are they acceptable or unacceptable? What makes it/them plagiarism?

   a) The increase of industry, the growth of cities, and the explosion of the population were three large factors of nineteenth century America. As steam-driven companies became more visible in the eastern part of the country, they changed farm hands into factory workers and provided jobs for the large wave of immigrants. With industry came the growth of large cities like Fall River where the Bordens lived which turned into centers of commerce and trade as well as production.

   b) Fall River, where the Borden family lived, was typical of northeastern industrial cities of the nineteenth century. Steam-powered production had shifted labor from agriculture to manufacturing, and as immigrants arrived in the US, they found work in these new factories. As a result, populations

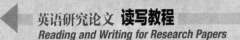
grew, and large urban areas arose. Fall River was one of these manufacturing and commercial centers (Williams, 1).

c) Fall River, where the Borden family lived, was typical of northeastern industrial cities of the nineteenth century. As steam-powered production shifted labor from agriculture to manufacturing, the demand for workers "transformed farm hands into industrial laborers", and created jobs for immigrants. In turn, growing populations increased the size of urban areas. Fall River was one of these hubs "which became the centers of production as well as of commerce and trade" (Williams, 1).

Selections

Unit 1   Exploring University Students' Perceptions of Plagiarism: A Focus Group Study

Unit 2   Exploring Staff Perceptions of Student Plagiarism

Supplementary Reading   How College Freshmen View Plagiarism?

Exploring University Students' Perceptions of Plagiarism: A Focus Group Study

Learning Objectives

- What is a research paper?
- How to read a research paper?
- Features of academic language

Exploring University Students' Perceptions of Plagiarism: A Focus Group Study

Judith Gullifer[*] and Graham A. Tyson

School of Social Sciences and Liberal Studies, Charles Sturt University, NSW, Australia

Plagiarism is perceived to be a growing problem and universities are being required to devote increasing time and resources to combating it. Theory and research in psychology show that a thorough understanding of an individual's view of an issue or problem is an essential requirement for successful change of that person's attitudes and behaviour. This pilot study explores students' perceptions of a number of issues relating to plagiarism in an Australian university. In the pilot study, focus groups were held with students across discipline areas, year and mode of study. A thematic analysis revealed six themes of perceptions of plagiarism: confusion, fear, perceived **sanctions**, perceived seriousness, academic consequences and resentment.

Keywords:

academic integrity; college students; plagiarism; student ethics; university student

Introduction

Since the 1960s, and particularly in today's technologically advanced society, academic dishonesty (for example, cheating, **collusion** and plagiarism) continues to attract considerable attention from the media, academics, administrators and students (Ashworth, Bannister, and Thorne, 1997; Ashworth, Freewood, and Macdonald, 2003;

---

* Corresponding author. Email: jgullifer@csu.edu.au

Franklyn-Stokes and Newstead, 1995; McCabe, Trevino, and Butterfield, 2001; Petress, 2003). Plagiarism, a type of academic dishonesty, is often conceived as fraudulent behaviour that diminishes the intellectual property of the original author and rewards plagiarists for their work. Indeed, Petress (2003) describes plagiarism as a 'plague on our profession' (624) that, arguably, **obliterates** rewarding the ethic of hard work, eroding the moral value of honesty, whilst devaluing the role of assessment items within our educational establishments.

This characterisation of plagiarism is partly due to its historical roots, positioning plagiarism within a legal discourse, suggesting that plagiarism refers to an act of theft of the individual ownership of intellectual work (Ashworth, Freewood, and Macdonald, 2003; Steams, 1992; Sutherland-Smith, 2005). This construction of plagiarism assumes that knowledge has a history and that past authors must be acknowledged. Without due acknowledgement, it has been argued that one severs the ties between the creator of the work and the creation (Stearns, 1992). Indeed, Athanasou and Olasehinde (2002, 2) assert that 'The essence of cheating is fraud and deception', arguably a simple and direct characterisation of plagiarism.

At a broader social level, Marsden, Carroll, and Neil (2005) stress that the costs to the public through inadequately trained graduates could pose a threat to public safety, welfare and financial decisions through inaccurate advice, the **ramifications** of which **tarnish** universities' reputations and increase media scrutiny. Moreover, it has been suggested that academic dishonesty is growing, requiring universities to devote increasing time and resources to combat it (Carroll, 2005a; Franklyn-Stokes and Newstead, 1995; James, McInnis, and Devlin, 2002; Johnston, 1991; O'Connor, 2003; Park, 2003). In particular, the **onus** is on the academic managing the subject to correctly identify plagiarism and refer the matter to appropriate university processes (Sutherland-Smith, 2005).

My (Gullifer's) experience of identifying and managing instances of plagiarism occurred in the first semester of my appointment as an associate lecturer. Whilst the number of cases was low, I felt an overwhelming sense of disappointment and frustration. Two issues were evident: firstly, investigating an **allegation** of plagiarism requires time and effort that can take a few hours of work to locate the original sources and cross-reference with the student assignment, and longer to process the allegation and any subsequent misconduct **panel** and/or appeals. Secondly, and more importantly, good academic writing is **contingent** on developing sound skills in both research and writing, critically reading and comprehending appropriate sources, careful note-taking, paraphrasing, **judicious** use of quotations and **giving credit to** authors for their ideas and writing (Burton, 2007). As a consequence of plagiarism, students deny themselves an opportunity to master these skills, making academic writing increasingly difficult as they progress through their degree.

As psychologists, we are aware that, when attempting to modify people's attitudes or behaviours, it is necessary to have a good understanding of the target person's perceptions of, and attitudes towards, the issue. In therapeutic situations, for instance, it is regarded as essential to obtain the client's perception and understanding of the issue or problem before **commencing** therapy. This insight, or lack of, is likely to influence the individual's responsiveness to different therapeutic approaches (Cochran and Cochran, 2005; Egan, 2007; Kanfer and Schefft, 1988; Prochaska and Norcross, 2007). Similarly, when exploring attitudes and beliefs towards plagiarism, we can apply the same principles to gain a better understanding of student perceptions, and then develop appropriate strategies with an increased probability of effectiveness.

Likewise, literature from **forensic** psychology suggests that having some understanding of an offender's perspective and motivation is important in order for positive change to occur, and **recidivism** to decrease. For example, Byrne and Trew (2005) argue, 'to be effective, interventions that aim to reduce or prevent offending behaviour need to be based on a sound understanding of what leads people to offend, and what leads people to stop offending' (185). Comparable sentiments are expressed by Ashworth, Bannister, and Thorne (1997) in relation to plagiarism. They argue that 'understanding the student perspective on...plagiarism can significantly assist academics in their efforts to communicate appropriate norms' (187).

From this, we argue that there is merit in understanding students' perspectives regarding plagiarism in order to develop successful strategies to promote academic integrity and thereby prevent plagiarism. McCabe and Trevino (1993) identified a significant relationship between academic dishonesty and how students perceived both student and faculty understanding of institutional policy. Higher levels of dishonesty were associated with lower levels of understanding. Another study by Roig (1997) clearly demonstrated that more than half of the students in their study could not identify clear examples of plagiarism, indicating that, whilst policy may exist, students have little knowledge or understanding of it.

It is apparent, therefore, that universities can benefit from learning about their own students' perceptions of plagiarism in order to develop appropriate strategies to promote academic integrity. In the light of this, the aim of our research program is to systematically examine students' understandings of, and attitudes towards, plagiarism, with the intention of informing the institution on approaches that might promote a greater awareness of plagiarism and, therefore, prevent its occurrence. This study is exploratory in nature and will form part of a larger investigation.

Literature review

There is abundant literature on academic misconduct, most of which has been published during the last two decades. The literature on plagiarism offers many different reasons for student plagiarism. These include, but are not limited to, time to complete tasks (poor time management), perceived **disjuncture** between award (grade) and effort required, too much work to complete over too many subjects, pressure to do well, perceptions that students will not get caught, **anomie**, motivation, and individual factors (age, grade point average, gender, personality type) (Anderman, Griesinger, and Westerfield, 1998; Anderman and Midgley, 1997; Calabrese and Cochran, 1990; Caruana, Ramaseshan, and Ewing, 2000; Davis, Grover, and Becker, 1992; Kibler, 1993; Love and Simmons, 1998; Newstead, Franklyn-Stokes, and Armstead, 1996; Park, 2003 ; Perry et al., 1990; Roig and Caso, 2005; Sheard, Carbone, and Dick, 2003; Whitley, 1998). These studies tend to focus on individual student characteristics.

Focusing on individual student characteristics can be problematic, as the emphasis is then placed on the individual behaviour change process, with little attention to socio-cultural and physical environmental influences on behaviour. McCabe and Trevino (1997) examined both individual characteristics and contextual influences on academic dishonesty. Their results indicated that decision-making relating to academic dishonest behaviour is not only influenced by individual characteristics (e.g. age, gender and grade point average), but also contextual influences (e.g. the level of cheating among peers, peer disapproval of cheating, membership of societies for male and female students [**fraternity/sorority**], and the perceived severity of penalties for cheating). Therefore, to better understand student perceptions of plagiarism, we need to **take into account** not only individual student characteristics but also broader contextual factors.

Only a few studies have been conducted to explore students' perceptions of plagiarism, and these tend to focus on the reasons why students **plagiarise** (Ashworth, Bannister, and Thorne, 1997; Devlin and Gray, 2007; Marsden, Carroll, and Neill, 2005), or **utilise** attitude scales that are developed with the assumption that all relevant stakeholders share the same meaning frame of how plagiarism is understood (Brimble and Stevenson-Clarke, 2005; Franklyn-Stokes and Newstead, 1995; Hasen and Huppert, 2005; Lim and See, 2001). The assumption that the term plagiarism has shared meaning is due to the institution's reliance on university policy to be an instrument to both define what plagiarism is and the possible consequences if **breached**.

It has been argued, therefore, that having a good understanding of institutional policy reduces the risk of engaging in plagiarism. Jordan (2001) found that students classified as non-cheaters reported greater understanding of institutional policy than did cheaters. The apparent lack of knowledge of institutional policy is further compounded by contradictory and often ambiguous information delivered by academic staff, as they also struggle to enforce an accepted and clear definition of plagiarism (McCabe, Butterfield, and Trevino, 2003). For instance, in a study conducted by Burke (1997), over half of the academics surveyed not only reported a lack of familiarity with the university's policy on plagiarism, but also did not refer to the policy when dealing with incidents. As Carroll (2005a) suggests, it is this lack of clarity about plagiarism that influences how students perceive plagiarism.

In order to both understand how students perceive plagiarism, and develop and evaluate learning materials aimed at educating students about plagiarism, Breen and Maassen (2005) conducted a two-phase research project, that firstly explored student perceptions of plagiarism and then developed learning materials to be embedded within courses. This was done by utilising four focus groups, consisting of 13 under-graduate psychology students across the first, second and third years. Their findings suggest that, apart from a clear understanding of **verbatim** use of other people's work without referencing, students had difficulty comprehending 'grey' areas (e.g. ability to comprehend and paraphrase work with due citation). The lack of familiarity with what required citation was, in part, due to the inability to source adequate 'information regarding the subtlety of paraphrasing, inconsistency between staff and the fear of **inadvertent** plagiarism. They also found that students reported an increasing under-standing of plagiarism as a function of year level, with the associate skill development to complete assignments. Students also made suggestions for course improvement to focus on proactive strategies, **as opposed to** the reactive nature of dealing with plagiarism once discovered.

Whilst Breen and Maassen (2005) aimed to explore students' understanding of plagiarism, their main focus was to develop resource material to embed within their courses. Consequently, only a small sample pool of 13 psychology students was utilised, and questions centred specifically on students' ability to define and avoid plagiarism. Though Breen and Maassen were able to elicit some understanding of student perceptions, based on how students define plagiarism and then avoid it, the current study aims to extend and build upon their work. It is proposed in this study to sample across disciplines and **delve** deeper into student understandings of plagiarism.

McCabe and Trevino (1993) argued for a shift in our conceptualisation and examination of plagiarism, from one focused on individual factors that may inform an individual's **propensity** to plagiarise, to one of examining situational or contextual variables that can be utilised towards an integrated institutional response. Despite this **exhortation**, relatively little systematic research has been done on the topic of understanding student perceptions of what plagiarism is, and most has been conducted in the USA or the UK. The aim of the present study is to develop a better understanding of how students construct plagiarism by using group discussion to explore the range of opinions regarding students' perceptions of plagiarism.

Method

Design

This is a focus group study, where our aim was to collect **qualitative** data by engaging groups of students in an informal group discussion 'focused' on their perceptions of plagiarism. Our study aimed to place students (who are typically aware of the rhetoric surrounding plagiarism) in the position of experts, whose knowledge and experience is essential to advance the theoretical discussion on student perceptions of plagiarism. It was intended, as suggested by Madriz (2000), that the interaction among group participants would reduce the interaction between the **moderator** and the individual members of the group. In this way, the role of the moderator was to actively facilitate discussion among the participants, by encouraging students to discuss their views with each other as opposed to directing them to the facilitator.

Participants

The participants were students recruited from a regional Australian university. A total of 41 students (25 women and 16 men), who were either in their first or third year of study, took part across seven focus groups. Each focus group was **homogeneous** with regard to discipline and year, as issues **pertinent** to understanding plagiarism may be discipline or faculty specific (e.g. referencing formats and emphasis placed on plagiarism), and would therefore impact on how students perceive plagiarism. The participants brought a rich variety of backgrounds to the discussions and represented four different discipline areas of psychology, policing, public relations and advertising. Wilkinson (2008) states that a focus group can involve as few as two or as many as a dozen participants, with the norm being between four and eight. The composition of each focus group is illustrated in Table 1.

Materials

An interview schedule was developed to provide an overall direction for the discussion. The schedule followed a semi-structured, open-ended format to enable the participants to set their own agenda (Wilkinson, 2008). Each focus group was asked the following questions:

    (1) What is plagiarism?

    (2) What are the causes of plagiarism?

    (3) How common is plagiarism?

    (4) How serious is plagiarism?

    (5) What are the chances of being caught?

Table 1. Focus group participants

Focus group	Participants	Year/Discipline
Group 1 (pilot group)	3 students: 2 men, 1 woman (all mature age[*])	1 st year psychology
Group 2	9 students: 8 women, 1 man (1 woman was a mature age student)	1 st year psychology
Group 3	8 students: 7 women, 1 man (mature age man).	1 st year psychology
Group 4	8 students: 6 men, 2 women (all mature age)	1 st session police students
Group 5	7 students: 5 men, 2 women (all mature age)	1 st session police students
Group 6	3 students: 2 women, 1 man (no mature age students)	3 rd year public relations students
Group 7	3 women students (no mature age students)	3 rd year advertising students

* Mature age refers to students who enrol at university and are over 21 years of age.

The guide provided moderators with topics and issues to be covered at some point during the group discussion. Questions that were more important to the research agenda were presented early in the session.

Procedure

Following ethics committee approval, piloting the interview schedule occurred with Group 1. Following guidelines by Wilkinson (2008), our aim was to explore if the schedule was likely to engage the students in discussion, and whether the questions themselves flowed logically and allowed for a variety of viewpoints. We felt satisfied that students were engaged with the structure of the interview schedule, and were quite willing to openly discuss issues **deemed** relevant to them. Consequently, only minor changes were made to the wording of some of the questions so that they were more open and less ambiguous.

Potential participants were initially sought by contacting the subject coordinators for **consent** to approach students during tutorial sessions. This was followed by a small presentation at the beginning of each class, or relayed by the subject coordinators. Interested students contacted the research assistant, who then organised a convenient time and place for the group to meet. Four moderators (who were all employed by the university) were used in total, to ensure that students were not familiar with the

moderator, thereby reducing any possible power dynamics within the focus groups. The duration of each focus group session was no more than 75 minutes. Each focus group discussion began with an introduction to explain the purpose and ground rules, and convey the expectation that everyone would contribute, all contributions would be valued and remain confidential, and the session would be digitally recorded. At the completion of each focus group, the moderator/s **debriefed** and noted initial impressions. The recording was then **transcribed**, **pseudonyms** assigned and preliminary ideas recorded.

Data analysis

As suggested by Hayes (2000), each transcript was read several times to identify content topics, that is, similar threads interwoven throughout all the transcripts. This coding of the data continued for each transcript until no new categories were found. After this initial **trawl**, patterns and commonalities among the categories were identified, and grouped into proto-themes. Hayes (2000) states that proto-themes represent the beginning of a theme and 'will develop and change as the analysis proceeds' (176).

Once an initial definition of a proto-theme was decided, the transcripts were re-examined for material relevant to that theme. The term 'theme' in this article refers to the patterns that repetitively occur, both within each transcript and across the focus groups. Once completed, the theme's final form was constructed, named and defined. This was done by referring back to the literature, deriving information that would allow inferences to be made from the focus groups. A technique used to increase confidence in the results was the use of credibility checks (Willig, 2001) within the research team, to see whether the analysis and interpretation of the data was credible. In this process the first author (Gullifer) conducted the initial data analysis. Once completed, the second author (Tyson) and research assistant also read the transcripts and met to discuss the credibility of the six themes generated.

Analysis/discussion

From the focus group discussions, we identified six themes relating to the perceptions of plagiarism: confusion, fear, perceived sanctions, perceived seriousness, academic consequences and resentment. Each theme is discussed in turn.

Confusion

There is evidence that, except for the verbatim copying of text, many participants were confused as to what behaviour constitutes plagiarism. This theme suggests that participants acknowledged an existence of a concrete and agreed upon definition of plagiarism somewhere 'out there', and were able to express some understanding of the more obvious instances of plagiarism. This is evidenced in the following discussion among two students:

P3: Simply, taking the words...like for example in an essay format, taking word for word out of paragraphs things that have been published, and not referencing it, and saying it's your own. Not referencing something basically, and just putting it in an essay.
P5: Passing off somebody else's work as your own.
P3: Exactly, that's it. (Group 4, 98-105)

However, whilst the discussion between students did demonstrate some basic understanding of the behaviours that constitute plagiarism, there was also a degree of misunderstanding. This confusion appeared to extend on a continuum from some misunderstanding to total misunderstanding, as indicated in these two data extracts:

If you get someone else to do your assignment for you, because you are not doing the work for yourself, someone else is doing it for you. (P7, Group 5, 370)
Paying someone to do your assessments? (P4, Group 5, 375)

From an institutional perspective, it was clear from the focus groups that, despite our belief that students **have access to** detailed information regarding plagiarism — within subject outlines, the academic misconduct policy (held online) and online plagiarism guidelines—this access was not utilised by the participants. Amongst academics, there appears to be an assumption that, by merely providing access to the academic misconduct policy and plagiarism guidelines, students would utilise these resources and, therefore, have a good understanding of plagiarism. But this was not the case, as demonstrated in the following discussion between three participants, who are not only confusing the act of collusion as an instance of plagiarism, but indicating that even the act of collusion is poorly understood:

P7: There's also things under plagiarism, a thing about you are not allowed to show your assignment to another person in your class or something like that, because...
P1: Like you can work together on it, but you're not allowed to...
P2: You're not allowed to show it to anyone else.
P7: In your class.
P2: Before you write it. (Group 3, 1190)

The under-utilisation of resources that provide information regarding plagiarism was apparent across all seven focus groups. Moreover, participants believed that academic writing was a learning process that needed to **encompass** not only having access to resources but also learning about plagiarism. According to the discussion between students, limited exposure to learning about plagiarism may contribute to unintentional plagiarism:

> Not fully understanding what plagiarism is, what are the different areas of plagiarism, and, therefore, they'll do it inadvertently, just because they don't understand what plagiarism is. (Group 5, 521)
>
> The main thing is that we aren't really getting a lot of feedback from our tutors to say that we're bordering... (P5)
>
> We are or we aren't, yeah. (P4, Group 5, 710)

There was generally a clear understanding that downloading complete essays or copying large chunks of material without citing the source was not appropriate, but similar to findings in Ashworth, Bannister, and Thorne (1997), we also found that students were confused about what the term plagiarism actually encompassed. Consequently, there was great confusion over the 'grey area', as indicated in the following data extract that was **endorsed** by all the other members of the group:

> Well, listen, I'm terribly confused what it actually means—I mean, that might sound stupid; there's a policy that...the wholesale copying is obviously quite obvious, but there's a hell of a lot of grey area in between that I really still don't even understand—today's moved that fence further to one side than it ever was before. (P1, Group 1, 45)
>
> [Participants all begin to talk over each other and nod in agreement]

Research by Carroll (2005b) found that students experience difficulty in defining their own ideas, and being able to discriminate between common knowledge and knowledge that requires citation, as expressed in the following data extract:

> But I reckon that confuses me, because all my ideas come from other people's ideas, so you can't have just say...'I have an idea'. (P6, Group 3, 271)
>
> P6: But then there's...I don't know how to actually quote a work.
>
> P2: I think that really worries me as well, because what if I am doing an assignment and I'm...what if I think is my brilliant idea...do I have to actually go some where and check whether I have stolen it from someone else? (Group 3, 278)

Moreover, even when participants could identify instances of when appropriate citation would be required, there was a lack of knowledge on the conventions of citation. The following discussion was echoed throughout the seven focus groups, regardless of year or discipline:

> P2: It's plagiarism if you don't reference the person. If you take someone else's knowledge, because it's not your knowledge that you're taking, you're taking someone else's knowledge, and rewording it...you didn't know it, it has come from them, so you need to reference it.
>
> P6: It's not word for word.
>
> P2: It doesn't even matter whether it's not word for word.
>
> P5: If you had no knowledge and the knowledge you're getting is from somewhere else...
>
> P2 ...exactly, you have to reference it if that is the case. (P2)
>
> P6 ...in an essay, do we then have to reference every sentence? (P6)
>
> P5: Well, that's it. How many times can you rewrite something? Every five or so words?

(Group 4, 153-172)

Within this theme it was evident that participants were unclear on the university policy on academic misconduct. Examining the current practice at the university, students report being provided with online links to the academic misconduct policy, via an electronic message sent to every student at the commencement of each semester. However, since a formal induction or transition into the scholarship of academic writing is not available to students, the onus is on the student to search for relevant information **pertaining** to plagiarism, or each academic to ensure that students understand academic integrity.

Fear

The theme of fear represents the anxiety expressed by students regarding the possibility of committing unintentional acts of plagiarism. This fear appears to flow from the discussion threads on confusion. Similar findings in Ashworth, Bannister, and Thorne (1997) and Breen and Maassen (2005) suggest that a combination of university expectations and sanctions, the difficulty in finding clear guidelines on minimising plagiarism, along with the mistaken belief that the most minor errors could result in an allegation of plagiarism increase students' level of anxiety. Central to the fear is the belief that unintentional plagiarism results in the same consequences as intentional plagiarism:

> There are people that intentionally plagiarise, like stealing others' work instead of doing their own...and then there are people who just haven't referenced it properly, or done something the wrong way, so it is considered plagiarism but they didn't mean to... (P3, Group 3, 101)

Arguably, this anxiety can be traced back to when students commence university, and are overloaded with new information in their first week at university (McGowan 2005):

> The concept's OK. The concept sits up and says not to use other people's work without giving them their due credit...it does become a bit of a complex issue. When you first start to study, you, you are given the booklet, you're given the directions, and you're, you know, put under... it becomes a bit of a fear factor about, 'boy, I need to pick this up pretty quickly'. (P3, Group 1, 60)

Moreover, participants report that 'education' about plagiarism is often presented as a set of rules and warnings that results in a 'sense of doom', which can be attributed to the legalistic discourse that positions plagiarism in a 'language of crime and punishment'. This is demonstrated in the following extract:

> I have realised how broad and real it is...like just using someone else's concept without even realising can be plagiarism, like there's so many...you can plagiarise so easily without even realising. It's pretty scary. (P5, Group 3, 82)
> I think it is scary though because it is always in the background though—it's always in the back of our minds, it is scary because it is something that I know I don't have a complete grasp on. (P3, Group 7, 422)

There appeared to be little understanding of scholarship, and the relevance of citation and attribution in developing a position built on a sound foundation of evidence; rather the participants report focusing on the conventions of citation:

> I was sitting there the other day thinking if I reference it right, I spend more time referencing than anything else in the assignment. Like the assignment is really difficult to research, but just the formatting and the referencing at the end can take so long, so I am just worried that if I put the wrong thing in there then I will get a 'oh she's trying to get away with this', when really I just forgot it to include to cite it really. (P3, Group 6, 259)

Similar to Ashworth, Bannister, and Thorne (1997), the participants indicated that despite making every effort to avoid plagiarism, there was a very real fear of inadvertent plagiarism. This was evident across all our focus groups, regardless of year of study or discipline. The participants perceived a relationship between the expressed fear and writing confidence, as expressed by the following participant:

> Yeah I quote way too much, like you are scared, I am scared to write my own words in case they are someone else's but I didn't know about it. (Pl, Group 7, 215)

The loss of confidence implicit here may form a poor basis for learning. For instance, research investigating the impact of self-efficacy in learning indicates that students who exhibit confidence and self-esteem are much more likely to be successful at mastering the academic conventions (Archer, Cantwell, and Bourke, 1999; Ingleton and Cadman, 2002). Conversely, having a poor understanding of plagiarism may create some uncertainty regarding the academic conventions of writing. Rumours appear to provide a source of information to the recipient, despite their inaccuracies, which may increase the perception of some control to avoid the threat of perceived sanctions. Fiske (2004) argues that, in times of uncertainty, humans are motivated to try to control the environment in order to act effectively. Students report doing this by actively working towards avoiding plagiarism at all costs, even if it means resorting to poor writing strategies, as demonstrated in the following extract:

> I think a lot of the time you have to, like we had to do an assignment last year on this practice in community events. So basically I had a whole heap of references saying this is the best practice...and I had actually done community events so I knew what they told me, but I felt like my whole essay was just quoting other people and other people's ideas. And I thought, because traditionally quotes don't contribute to your word count, so my two thousand word essay was probably five hundred words in my own words, because it was just jam-packed with so many quotes because they were everybody else's ideas, and I didn't want to, say yeah this is what I think you should do because I hadn't actually done it. So I didn't really know ... so I was just getting this information off other people. (P2, Group 7, 204)

Whilst fear appeared to be very strongly evident across all of our focus groups, the literature on plagiarism only gives this **scant** regard. Moreover, the fear expressed by the participants may have been **augmented** by an overestimation of the severity of sanctions.

Perceived sanctions

Sanctions for plagiarism were often compared against sanctions for some types of criminal activity. This is not surprising given the legal discourse that frames plagiarism:

> P4:   At the end of the day, it is copying five or six words, as opposed to getting done for
>   DUI [driving under the influence of...]...
>   [participants talking over each other]
> P5:   That's the problem with this place, they...all they focus on is doing the wrong thing,
>   it's just a small thing. (Group 5,785)

Explicit in this is that, relative to some criminal offences, plagiarism is perceived to be relatively minor. Therefore, if the sanctions of engaging in plagiarism are considered to be disproportionately severe, a student may be less likely to engage in it. For instance, the following participants openly expressed their fear of possible sanctions:

> Well, I've been at university for a long, long time, I think it's certainly become more prevalent
> now, and since I've been doing this course, which is two years, it's pushed all the time, and
> if you don't do this, you'll be—I don't know—hung, drawn, quartered, thrown out, and you
> think—blimey! (Pl, Group 1, 224)
> Plagiarism is sold under [the] one verse, and that is that you are basically dealt with, with the
> sword hand. So, it's a very worrying concept that's chortling along in the background. (Group
> 1,251)

Arguably, the fear expressed by participants not only related to inadvertent plagiarism, but also to the often incorrect understanding of the penalties involved in the university academic misconduct policy. Noticeably, in the current study, fear was more apparent m disciplines where plagiarism would not only lead to academic sanctions, but also to sanctions that resulted in exclusion from career pathways, as in the case of police officer training:

> Coming from a fire job, I have given up so much to be here, I've got a wife and two kids at
> home, 15-week old baby, if I went back to them and got booted out for plagiarism, which I
> know myself...I'm not trying to prove anything to anyone...but I would never do. You know, I
> want to graduate and do it myself, I'd just be shattered. I'd be absolutely shattered. You know,
> the disappointment would be just unbelievable. (P4, Group 5,676)

Associated with the perception of severe consequences, there is also the perception that there is a high likelihood of being caught:

> Moderator: What are the chances of being caught at plagiarism?
> P2   A hundred percent.
> Moderator: A hundred percent?
> P1:   seems to be...
> P2:   Apparently, they all know the sources really, really well. (Group 3, 1002)

These student statements hint to a possible factor underlying and influencing students' perceptions, and that is rumour:

> Everyone keeps going on about how the lecturers know exactly what they are teaching, and they will just be able to tell straightaway. (P2, Group 2, 367)

Rumours can have a very important influence on behaviour, and could be **aggravating** the confusion and fear expressed by the participants. The rumours regarding plagiarism could be perceived by the students to be ambiguous and potentially threatening.

Consequently, instead of helping students reduce the confusion surrounding the term, such rumours tend to **exacerbate** their anxiety, as shown in the following quotes:

> And because this place is a beehive of rumours, right, and hype, that adds to your fear. You know, it adds to your fear, because you know what happens, a situation might happen, and it is this big...by the time it goes through two or three hundred people, it is that big. (P4, Group 5, 1029)
>
> P5: People will get caught, eventually, even if it is three years later when they put it through the system before we graduate. So there is a chance of getting caught in the next three years.
>
> P1: Imagine that!
>
> P5: [laughs] You're going to worry about it for three years that you have accidentally plagiarised! (Group 5, 1011)

It has been suggested that the content of rumours acts as 'impoverished news' when there is a lack of reliable information (DiFonzo and Bordia, 2007). Consequently, as a collective group, students may try to make sense of plagiarism, and the threat of unintentional plagiarism, by trying to determine the evidential basis of the information sourced. Unfortunately, evident within discussions in the focus groups, much of the 'information' obtained regarding plagiarism is presented as factual, creating uncertainty and fear, as demonstrated in the following extract:

> P1: So, is that really the consequence of plagiarism—you get **expelled**?
>
> P3: It can...well, that's what's stated.
>
> (P1: yeah, that's...)
> It's stated that if it's proven, that's the end of your career at this establishment. That's my understanding of it.
>
> P1: Is that correct [looking at moderator], or is that...? I mean, you mightn't be able to answer that. (Group 1,595)

The nature of the rumours appears to have some implications regarding students obtaining clear information concerning plagiarism, adding to the inaccurate knowledge of the sanctions applied. Consequently, the perceived sanctions only add to the fear expressed.

Perceived seriousness

Participants in the focus groups reported that, unless a student had intentionally plagiarised, the perceived penalties for plagiarism were considered to be too severe. For example, the following quote reflects the participants' perceptions that the act of plagiarism (in this instance limited by their own definitions) is not as serious as the university treats it:

> I don't believe it's as serious as people make out, I think it's a bit of a beat-up. Provided you're not wholesale copying. (Pl, Group 1, 485)

Brimble and Stevenson-Clarke (2005) found evidence to suggest that students view academic dishonesty less seriously than academic staff, and tend to underestimate the prevalence of student dishonesty. There was some evidence of this among participants:

> ...in uni they are very particular if you put a comma in the wrong spot then you are in trouble. You lose marks on referencing and that is frustrating because it doesn't...if they wanted to look it up they could still they can still see who wrote it, what article it came from, what year it was written, the commas don't matter. But a lot of people [academics] are pedantic about it. (Pl, Group 6,150)

Ashworth, Bannister, and Thorne (1997) found similar views expressed by their interviewees and concluded, 'plagiarism is a far less meaningful concept for students than it is for academic staff, and it ranks relatively low in the student's system of values' (201). In the following quote the mismatch of expectations is evident:

> I should imagine most of the plagiarism errors are errors, not purposely done, so it's a rather...**draconian** for not understanding some rules and regulations. Sure enough, if they're wholesale just cut and copy, that's fair enough, but if it's just a lack of understanding of really what it means. It does appear to be a bit severe, what you...the impression that you've got that will happen if you are caught for plagiarism. That's my impression. (P1, Group 1, 224)

These findings are also consistent with Franklyn-Stokes and Newstead (1995), who found that, in terms of academic dishonesty, plagiarism is perceived by students to be the least serious form. Moreover, McCabe and Trevino (1996) also found that copying without citation, and collusion were not considered serious offences. Relative to this past research, our findings suggest that the penalties associated with plagiarism were perceived to be draconian, whilst the act of plagiarism itself is not perceived as serious (a 'beat up') relative to other **deviant** acts. This may be augmented by a rumour mill operating, and not based on factual evidence.

Resentment

The final two themes appear to reflect important consequences resulting from the four thematic areas discussed. Participants in all seven focus groups expressed resentment

towards the institution's management of plagiarism, and the impact that this may be having on their ability to write an academic paper in the form of decreased self-efficacy.

Participants articulated an inadequate understanding of plagiarism, hence the worrying possibility of inadvertently plagiarising. Moreover, they perceived the sanctions for plagiarism to be too draconian, which was **incongruent** with the low level of seriousness placed on plagiarism by them. Therefore, the participants believed that the university treated plagiarism too seriously. As a result, they expressed resentment toward the institution, and the academic staff whom they believed monitored plagiarism. This is expressed in the following quotes:

> The problem with universities is that they are all at a higher level of education, and they are going to speak to people like...and that's how it should be. We're coming along as police officers, not as doctors or solicitors or anything, we're at the bottom level of all that. Make it easy for us to understand. (Pl, Group 4, 1034)

> I don't know...I kind of see it as the lecturers taking it almost personally, like 'oh these people have tried to plagiarise and they think that I am really ignorant and don't realize that it is happening', that is what I get from the plagiarism speeches they give us. So yeah. (Pl, Group 6, 310-13)

In both quotes participants perceive themselves as victims of institutional anti-plagiarism 'laws' that focus on stylistic requirements to be able to reference correctly.

Consequently, plagiarism was perceived to be more about the mechanics of writing than about due acknowledgement to the creator of a piece of work:

> Yeah, but that's stupid, everything I've done at uni is to do with referencing! (P3, Group 4, 420)
> You don't even feel like you are getting your own work marked, it is all about whether you can piece together other people's works. (P2, Group 7, 237)

Ashworth, Bannister, and Thorne (1997) found similar sentiments expressed among their interview participants. They claimed that students were unaware of a broader discourse of scholarship in which they are important stakeholders. Within a community of scholars, participation requires the ability to correctly attribute sources of knowledge. Interestingly, this discourse is perceived to be shared amongst academics, but lies in contrast to the plagiarism discourse that is constructed by the participants. Some of the expressed resentment could be linked to the inability to generalise the importance of scholarship to the external work environment that students are working towards. The policing students, in particular, voiced some resentment towards the relevance of academic work to their future career. For example, the following extract was endorsed by all the students in the focus group:

> I mean we are not going to be going and writing theses and all sorts of academic stuff, we are going to be writing reports, so I am not sure how plagiarism comes into that. (Group 5, 754)

[students nodding and agreeing]

Much of the expressed resentment was manifested in the students' verbal and nonverbal language. Many of the students became quite animated in discussions, particularly with exchanges that centred on inadvertent plagiarism. Voices often became quite raised, and students spoke rapidly. They tried to speak over each other to get their points across, whilst others became quite silent and still. It could be argued that the focus group method may have heightened the participants' anxiety and resentment.

Academic consequences

The theme of academic consequences manifested as a form of academic learned helplessness, reported as a decrease in confidence to write an academic paper:

> But...I'm just wondering, with all this...is how much our creativity is cut down by all this? And...in some papers that I've written in the past that I've wanted some licence to move...to really express stuff, and I've been that fearful to do it, because of the...that I worry about, is that I wonder how marks are going sometimes, in the respect of...because we're all very cautious. (P3, Group 1, 337)

Implicit within this quote, and within the participants' discussion, was expressed fear that is arguably **reminiscent** of Seligman's theory of learned helplessness (Seligman 1975), which McKean (1994) has applied to the academic situation. McKean suggested that learned helplessness can lead to negative academic consequences such as **procrastination** and poor performance. Certainly the students in the focus groups seemed to recognise some of these negative consequences, as described in the following quotes:

> Sometimes we do the assignments, worry about the plagiarism, and we forget about the issue in the assignment. (P2, Group 1, 649)
>
> P3: And I guess, in the end, are we spending too much time concerned about referencing and plagiarism than the actual outcome of the assessment?
>
> P7: Mmm. It's like, what is it, 5% of your mark is the referencing but you probably spend 40% of your time on it, and worry about it. (Group 3, 702)

This indicates that participants were concerned about inadvertent plagiarism, and, as discussed previously, believed that this may result in **punitive** measures instead of remedial intervention. For example, students expressed concern that despite their best efforts there was a distinct probability of accidentally using a phrase or sentence from a book, lecture or journal without acknowledgement. These beliefs were also evident in other studies (Ashworth, Bannister, and Thorne, 1997; Breen and Maassen, 2005). Consequently, participants reported a loss of confidence:

> P2: There's no real encouragement. There's no positive...

P7:   Your confidence is just shot, like I would go home and say I'm going to fail, and then I get an assignment back and it is a good result and I'm really happy. The whole thing about you're going to fail, it's not good enough, you need to get 20 references for this, it sort of makes you lose your confidence about what you're doing? You're sitting there going…like with our essay, I am sure everybody had it, you don't feel like you are putting in anything of you…oh, I've just got to get 20 references and it's really difficult to get a high mark if you want to be critical of it and you want to put your own opinion into it. (Group 5, 842-57)

The perceived loss of confidence was evident within all seven focus groups, with the fear of failure being attributed to not understanding what the word 'plagiarism' meant:

P1:   No one really knows what it [plagiarism] is…
P3:   I think all the **rigmarole**, is with the issue. I reckon with people, about plagiarism, it is sort of like a dirty word. (Group 7, 569)

It could be argued that students may eventually give up trying to write a 'good' academic paper and, as a result, may not invest as much effort or no effort at all, as predicted in the learnt helplessness model. There appeared to be evidence that some students felt an inhibition of learning that impacted on their ability to fully and freely express their ideas:

And then they expect you to reference it. People…I think that dumbs people down at the same time. It really, really does. It doesn't allow people to express their own creativity; it doesn't allow people to express their own ideas, their own feelings, their own thought processes about a specific idea, a process, a methodology…anything. It inhibits a person's understanding, it really does. (Group 5, 584)

Whilst we expected students to have some difficulty with clear and explicit definitions of plagiarism, we were not prepared for the level of anxiety expressed or the amount of resentment. As previously discussed, this may have been an artefact of the focus group process. Nevertheless, students across the seven focus groups shared similar perceptions of plagiarism, with the participants in the policing focus group demonstrating more extreme reactions. This could be due to the **dire** consequences of plagiarism for policing students, who believe they will be dismissed from the police officer training.

Conclusion

It is evident that the university's approach towards plagiarism is not effective. Whilst students were able to clearly define cases of plagiarism, where verbatim text was inserted in a student assignment without due acknowledgement, they were unable to **discern** the more subtle aspects of attribution of ideas and paraphrasing of text. This confusion appeared to increase the fear of inadvertent plagiarism, which arguably appears to be related to the students' confusion. This fear appeared to be augmented by an overestimation of the severity of sanctions, along with the perception that the university treats the act of plagiarism very seriously in contrast to how students perceive plagiarism. The other concerning aspect was that students reported negative academic consequences that manifested as a form of academic learned helplessness. This was reported as a decrease in confidence to write an academic paper.

In order to address some of these issues, we can turn to McGowan (2005), who argues for a system that is twofold, and focuses on the intent of the writer. Penalties for deliberate academic misconduct are recognised as an important **deterrent**. However, she recognises a need to change the way that we talk about plagiarism, or bypass the term altogether and instead focus on academic integrity. Her recommended strategy is to acculturate students into university culture through a process of **apprenticeship**, thereby giving students the appropriate skills of academic writing. Our research would clearly support such a strategy, and is one recognised by our own participants:

> P1:   ...it's a bit like something's a crime, some things you go to jail for life, and some things you go to jail for a year—you know, not all crimes are equal, not all plagiarism is equal. I think that's going to be...
>
> P3   ...and then there's magistrate's discretion. Yeah, you're right, I mean, there are variables within...within the process. It's not...it's not as fully cut-and-dried, as one would like to have it down pat, probably understanding. (Group 1, 507)
> But then also if you get caught, if I get caught doing it accidentally, I want to know what I did wrong, because it is not intentional, I want to learn and do it right. (P7, Group 3, 1112)

As a way forward, the institution may overcome some of the issues highlighted in the themes by exploring a holistic university-wide approach, where the onus of responsibility on academic integrity is shared by all stakeholders of the institution. A system is required where students are exposed to the principles of academic integrity that encompass the development of scholarship: learning about the principles of academic writing, the development of the authorial voice and, with it, the place of attribution.

It has been evident from this research, therefore, how important it is for institutions to develop an understanding of the perceptions of university students' understanding of plagiarism. We cannot presume to know that students entering university come with an understanding of the conventions of academic writing. Furthermore, we need to work toward an orientation to university culture that encompasses academic integrity that is not done in the **haphazard** or **piecemeal** manner reported by participants:

> Yeah, on one...in one hand, you're forced or pushed in the direction, you've got to read masses of things, you've got to quote lots of things, you're not to use your own work, you're nearly forced into using a lot of that work, and then how you use it correctly is the problem, I find. Obviously, not as correctly as one should have done, in the past, but...so there's that sort of contra. (Pl, Group 1, 84)

Drawing from Breen and Maassen's (2005) study, information on plagiarism needs to be specifically covered as a unit in the first semester of study in the first year at university. The students in Breen and Massens' study also recognised that skill development in time management, critical reading, note-taking, paraphrasing, writing and referencing were also required to prevent academic misconduct. Skill development was also identified by our participants as an important factor to reduce the possibility of plagiarising:

> It also comes down to...this is a learning institution and if you can't learn how to actually do an essay and do it...therefore they've got to give you some **leniency**, and show you...point you in the direction of where've you got that information from? Oh, I got it from here. Oh, but you didn't reference that. So, it's a learning experience as well. (P1, Group 5, 620)

Finally, while the results do provide a greater understanding of how students perceive plagiarism and the consequences of those beliefs, caution is needed in drawing strong conclusions due to the study's exploratory nature. We do not seek to generalise our findings as one would do in a representative survey, given that the only data collection method within this study was a set of one-time focus groups with a relatively small sample of self-selected students in one Australian university. It is proposed that further studies would extend this research, building on the six themes found.

Acknowledgements

This research was made possible through a Scholarship in Teaching Fund awarded through Centre for Enhancing Learning and Teaching (CELT), Charles Sturt University, Australia. The authors thank Kate Seymour and Jennifer Greig for their valued assistance.

References

Anderman, E. M., T. Griesinger, and G. Westerfield. 1998. Motivation and cheating during early adolescence. *Journal of Educational Psychology* 90: 84–93.

Anderman, E. M., and C. Midgley. 1997. Changes in achievement orientations, perceived academic competence, and grades across transition to middle-level schools. *Contemporary Educational Psychology* 22: 269–98.

Archer, J., R. Cantwell, and S. Bourke. 1999. Coping at university: An examination of achievement, motivation, self-regulation, confidence, and method of entry. *Higher Education Research & Development* 18, no. 1: 31–54.

Ashworth, P., P. Bannister, and P. Thorne. 1997. Guilty in whose eyes? University students' perceptions of cheating and plagiarism in academic work and assessment. *Studies in Higher Education* 22, no. 2: 187–203.

Ashworth, P., M. Freewood, and R. Macdonald. 2003. The student lifeworld and the meanings of plagiarism. *Journal of Phenomenological Psychology* 34, no. 2: 257–78.

Athanasou, J. A., and O. Olasehinde. 2002. Male and female differences in self-report cheating. *Practical Assessment, Research & Evaluation* 8, no. 5. http://PAREonline.net/ getvn.asp?v=8&n=5 (accessed June 16, 2007).

Breen, L., and M. Maassen. 2005. Reducing the incidence of plagiarism in an undergraduate course: The role of education. *Issues in Educational Research* 15, no. 1: 1–16.

Brimble, M., and P. Stevenson-Clarke. 2005. Prevalence of and penalties for academic dishonesty: Perceptions of Australian accounting students. Paper presented at the Conference of the Accounting and Finance Association of Australia and New Zealand, July 3–5, in Melbourne.

Burke, J. L. 1997. Faculty perceptions of and attitudes toward academic dishonesty at a two year college. Unpublished doctoral dissertation, University of Georgia.

Burton, L. J. 2007. *An interactive approach to writing essays and research reports in psychology.* 2nd ed. Milton: John Wiley & Sons.

Byrne, C. F., and K. F. Trew. 2005. Crime orientations, social relations and involvement in crime: Patterns emerging from offenders' accounts. *The Howard Journal of Criminal Justice* 44, no. 2: 185–205.

Calabrese, R. L., and J. T. Cochran. 1990. The relationship of alienation to cheating among a sample of American adolescents. *Journal of Research and Development in Education* 23, no. 2: 65–72.

Carroll, J. 2005a. Institutional issues in deterring, detecting and dealing with student plagiarism. http://www.jisc.ac.uk/index.cfm?name'pub_plagiarism (accessed April 5, 2007).

Carroll, J. 2005b. Handling student plagiarism: Moving to mainstream. *Brookes eJournal of Learning and Teaching* 1, no. 2. http://bejlt.brookes.ac.uk/voll/volumelissue2/perspective/carroll.html (accessed April 10, 2007).

Caruana, A., B. Ramaseshan, and M. T. Ewing. 2000. The effect of anomie on academic dishonesty among university students. *International Journal of Educational Management* 14, no. 1: 23–30.

Cochran, J. L., and N. H. Cochran. 2005. *The heart of counseling: A guide to developing therapeutic relationships.* Belmont: Wadsworth.

Davis, S. F., C. A. Grover, and A. H. Becker. 1992. Academic dishonesty: Prevalence, determinants, techniques, and punishments. *Teaching of Psychology* 19, no. 1: 16.

Devlin, M., and K. Gray. 2007. In their own words: A qualitative study of the reasons Australian university students plagiarize. *Higher Education Research & Development* 26, no. 2: 181–98.

DiFonzo, N., and P. Bordia. 2007. Rumor, gossip and urban legends. *Diogenes* 54, no. 1: 19–35.

Egan, G. 2007. *The skilled helper: A problem-management and opportunity-development approach to helping.* 8th ed. Belmont: Thomson/Brooks/Cole.

Fiske, S. T. 2004. *Social beings: A core motives approach to social psychology.* Hoboken: John Wiley & Sons.

Franklyn-Stokes, A., and S. E. Newstead. 1995. Undergraduate cheating: Who does what and why. *Studies in Higher Education* 20, no. 2: 159–72.

Hasen, M., and M. Huppert. 2005. The trial of damocles: An investigation into the incidence of plagiarism at an Australian university. Paper presented at the Australian Association for Research in Education (AARE) Annual Conference, November 27–December 1, in Parramatta, NSW.

Hayes, N. 2000. *Doing psychological research.* Philadelphia: Open University Press.

Ingleton, C., and K. Cadman. 2002. Silent issues for international postgraduate research students: Emotion and agency in academic success. *Australian Educational Researcher* 29, no. 1: 93–114.

James, R., C. McInnis, and M. Devlin. 2002. *Assessing learning in Australian universities: Ideas, strategies and resources for quality in student assessment.* Melbourne: Centre for the Study of Higher Education.

Johnston, D. K. 1991. Cheating: Reflections on a moral dilemma. *Journal of Moral Education* 20, no. 3: 283–91.

Jordan, A. E. 2001. College student cheating: The role of motivation, perceived norms, attitudes, and knowledge of institutional policy. *Ethics & Behavior* 11, no. 3: 233–47.

Kanfer, F. H., and B. Schefft. 1988. *Guiding the process of therapeutic change*. Champaign: Research Press.

Kibler, W. L. 1993. Academic dishonesty: A student development dilemma. *National Association of Student Personnel Administrators, Inc. (NASPA) Journal* 30, no. 4: 252–67.

Lim, V. K., and S. K. B. See. 2001. Attitudes toward and intentions to report: Academic cheating among students in Singapore. *Ethics & Behavior* 11, no. 3: 261–74.

Love, P. G., and J. Simmons. 1998. Factors influencing cheating and plagiarism among graduate students in a college of education. *College Student Journal* 32, no. 4: 539–50.

Madriz, E. 2000. Focus groups as feminist research. In *Handbook of qualitative research*, ed. N. Denzin and Y. Lincoln, 835–50. Thousand Oaks: Sage.

Marsden, H., M. Carroll, and J. T. Neill. 2005. Who cheats at university? A self-report study of dishonest academic behaviours in a sample of Australian university students. *Australian Journal of Psychology* 57, no. 1: 1–10.

McCabe, D. L., K. D. Butterfield, and L.K. Trevino 2003. Faculty and academic integrity: The influence of current honor codes and past honor code experiences. *Research in Higher Education* 44, no. 3: 367–85.

McCabe, D. L., and L. K. Trevino. 1993. Academic dishonesty: Honor codes and other contextual influences. *Journal of Higher Education* 64, no. 5: 522–38.

McCabe, D. L., and L. K. Trevino. 1996. What we know about cheating in college. *Change* 28, no. 1: 28–33.

McCabe, D. L., and L. K. Trevino. 1997. Individual and contextual influences on academic dishonesty: A multicampus investigation. *Research in Higher Education* 38, no. 3: 379–96.

McCabe, D. L., L. K. Trevino, and K.D. Butterfield. 2001. Cheating in academic institutions: A decade of research. *Ethics & Behavior* 11, no. 3: 219–32.

McGowan, U. 2005. Plagiarism detection and prevention: Are we putting the cart before the horse? In *Higher Education Research and Development Society of Australasia (HERDSA) conference: Higher education in a changing world*. Sydney: HERDSA.

McKean, K. J. 1994. Using multiple risk factors to assess the behavioral, cognitive, and affective effects of learned helplessness. *Journal of Psychology* 128, no. 2: 177–83.

Newstead, S. E., A. Franklyn-Stokes, and P. Armstead. 1996. Individual differences in student cheating. *Journal of Educational Psychology* 88: 229–41.

O'Connor, S. 2003. Cheating and electronic plagiarism—Scope, consequences and detection. Paper presented at the Educause in Australia Conference, May 6–9, in Adelaide, Australia.

Park, C. 2003. In other (people's) words: Plagiarism by university students—literature and lessons. *Assessment & Evaluation in Higher Education* 28, no. 5: 471–88.

Perry, A. R., K. M. Kane, K. J. Bernesser, and P. T. Spicker. 1990. Type A behavior, competitive achievement–striving, and cheating among college students. *Psychological Reports* 66, no. 2: 459–65.

Petress, K. 2003. Academic dishonesty: A plague on our profession. *Education* 123, no. 3: 624–27.

Prochaska, J. O., and J. C. Norcross. 2007. *Systems of psychotherapy: A transtheoretical analysis*. 6th ed. Belmont: Wadsworth.

Roig, M. 1997. Can undergraduate students determine whether text has been plagiarized? *Psychological Record* 47, no. 1: 113–23.

Roig, M., and M. Caso. 2005. Lying and cheating: Fraudulent excuse making, cheating, and plagiarism. *Journal of Psychology* 139, no. 6: 485–94.

Seligman, M. E. P. 1975. *Helplessness: On depression, development, and death.* San Francisco: W. H. Freeman.

Sheard, J., A. Carbone, and M. Dick. 2003. Determination of factors which impact on students' propensity to cheat. In *Australasian Computing Education Conference*, ed. T. Greening and R. Lister. Adelaide: Conferences in Research and Practice in Information Technology (CRPIT).

Stearns, L. 1992. Copy wrong: Plagiarism, process, property, and the law. *California Law Review* 80, no. 2: 513–53.

Sutherland-Smith, W. 2005. Pandora's box: Academic perceptions of student plagiarism in writing. *Journal of English for Academic Purposes* 4, no. 1: 83–95.

Whitley, B. E. 1998. Factors associated with cheating among college students. *Research in Higher Education* 39, no. 3: 235–74.

Wilkinson, S. 2008. Focus groups. In *Qualitative psychology: A practical guide to research methods*, ed. J. Smith. London: Sage.

Willig, C. 2001. *Introducing qualitative research in psychology.* Buckingham: Open University Press.

New Words

aggravate	['ægrəveit]	*vt.*	加重（剧），使恶化；激怒，使恼火
allegation	[ˌælə'geiʃn]	*n.*	（无证据的）指控
anomie	['ænəmi]	*n.*	社会的反常状态，混乱
apprenticeship	[ə'prentiʃip]	*n.*	学徒身份，学徒期
augment	[ɔ:g'ment]	*vt.*	增强，加强，增加
breach	[bri:tʃ]	*n./vt.*	破坏，破裂，违反
collusion	[kə'lu:ʒn]	*n.*	勾结，串通
commence	[kə'mens]	*v.*	开始
consent	[kən'sent]	*n./vi.*	准许，同意，赞成
contingent	[kən'tindʒənt]	*a.*	视条件而定的
debrief	[ˌdi:'bri:f]	*vt.*	向……询问情况，汇报情况
deem	[di:m]	*v.*	认为，视为
delve	[delv]	*v.*	深入探究，钻研
deterrent	[di'terənt]	*a.*	威慑的，制止的
deviant	['di:viənt]	*a.*	越出常规的，反常的
dire	['daiə]	*a.*	可怕的
disjuncture	[dis'dʒʌŋktʃə]	*n.*	分离，分裂
discern	[di's3:n]	*v.*	看出，理解，了解
draconian	[drə'kəuniən]	*a.*	严峻的，苛刻的

encompass	[in'kʌmpəs]	vt.	包围，包含或包括某事物
endorse	[in'dɔ:s]	vt.	赞同；签名于……背面
exacerbate	[ig'zæsəbeit]	vt.	加重，恶化
exhortation	[ˌegzɔ:'teiʃn]	n.	敦促，极力推荐
expel	[ik'spel]	vt.	把……开除；驱逐，放逐；排出，喷出
forensic	[fə'rensik]	a.	法庭的，辩论的
fraternity	[frə'tɜ:nəti]	n.	兄弟会，大学生联谊会，友爱
haphazard	[hæp'hæzəd]	a.	偶然的，随意的，任意的
homogeneous	[ˌhɔmə'dʒi:niəs]	a.	同种类的，同性质的，有相同特征的
inadvertent	[ˌinəd'vɜ:tənt]	a.	非故意的
incongruent	[in'kɔŋgruənt]	a.	不一致的
judicious	[dʒu:'diʃəs]	a.	明智的
leniency	['li:niənsi]	n.	宽大，仁慈
moderator	['mɔdəreitə]	n.	调解人，仲裁人
obliterate	[ə'bli:təreit]	vt.	涂去，擦掉，使消失
onus	['əunəs]	n.	义务，责任
panel	['pænl]	n.	面，板；专门小组
pertain	[pə'tein]	vi.	（to）从属，有关
pertinent	['pɜ:tinənt]	a.	有关系的，相关的
piecemeal	['pi:smi:l]	a.	逐渐的，零碎的
plagiarise	['pleidʒəraiz]	vt.	剽窃，抄袭（别人学说、著作）
procrastination	[prəuˌkræsti'neiʃn]	n.	耽搁，拖延
propensity	[prə'pensəti]	n.	癖好
pseudonym	['sju:dənim]	n.	假名，笔名
punitive	['pju:nətiv]	a.	处罚的
qualitative	['kwɔlitətiv]	a.	（性）质上的，定性的
ramification	[ræmifi'keiʃn]	n.	结果，后果
recidivism	[ri'sidəˌvizəm]	n.	再犯，累犯（行为或倾向）
reminiscent	[ˌremi'nisnt]	a.	（of）使人想起……的；怀旧的
rigmarole	['rigmərəul]	n.	冗长无聊的废话
sanction	['sæŋkʃn]	n.	批准；约束力
scant	['skænt]	a.	不足的，缺乏的
sorority	[sə'rɔrəti]	n.	妇女联谊会，女学生联谊会
tarnish	['tɑ:niʃ]	v.	（使）失去光泽；玷污，败坏

transcribe	[træn'skraib]	vt.	抄写，转录
trawl	[trɔ:l]	vt.	查阅（档案等）
utilise	['ju:tilaiz]	vt.	利用
verbatim	[vɜ:'beitim]	a.	（完全）照字面的，逐字的

Phrases

give credit to	认可
take into account	考虑到，顾及到
as opposed to	与……对比，相对于
have access to	进入（某物）；接近（某人）

Discussion Ideas

1. Identify the linguistic characteristics of a Research Paper.

2. What is a "focus group study"? What are the advantages and limitations of a "focus group study"?

3. What is the aim of the present study?

4. What is a pilot study? Why is a pilot study necessary?

5. What is the function of a "Literature review"? Why should it be obligatory?

6. What is "qualitative data"?

7. How were the participants recruited in this study? Why were they put into different focus groups?

8. What is "credibility check"?

9. What do you think might be the implications or applications of the present study?

Vocabulary and Language Learning Skills

1. Recognizing Word Meanings

Match the definitions in Column B with vocabulary items in Column A.

Column A	Column B
1. literature	a. advantage
2. assumption	b. use, adopt, apply
3. merit	c. sum up, recapitulate

(continued)

Column A	Column B
4. abundant	d. a proposition that is taken for granted
5. utilise	e. publish sources
6. anxiety	f. prudence
7. caution	g. adequate, plentiful
8. generalise	h. worry, concern

2. Making a Collocation

Use the vocabulary items in the box to complete the sentences. Make changes if necessary.

identify	assert	recruit
arguably	conceive	address
in the light of	consistent with	attribute to

1) Learning itself, however, is not something they _____ as an intentional pursuit; they see it as a natural consequence of carrying out appropriate learning activities.

2) _____ the most important advance in biology in decades has been the discovery that RNA molecules can regulate the expression of genes.

3) We propose a novel use of mobile communications to permit individuals to _____ a preference for privacy from video surveillance.

4) The study tried to _____ and explain the relationship between parental mediation and children's aggression.

5) Social values in relation to personal needs are discussed _____ this experiment.

6) The process used to locate and _____ participants in a qualitative study is important for efficiently obtaining a representative sample.

7) Using the 1994 NHIS data, cost of lost productivity _____ obesity was $3.9 billion and reflected 39.2 million days of lost work.

8) It was found that few managers exhibited behaviour _____ what is described in the literature.

9) The book covers well the range of issues which must be _____ by those wanting to conduct research using the in-depth interviewing method.

Writing Focus

Overview of the Research Paper

Most research papers are subdivided into the following sections: Title, Authors and Affiliation, Abstract, Introduction, Methods, Results, Discussion, Acknowledgments, and References. The sections appear in a research paper in the following prescribed order:

Experimental Process	Section of Paper
What did I do in a nutshell?	Abstract
What is the problem?	Introduction
How did I solve the problem?	Methods
What did I find out?	Results
What does it mean?	Discussion
Who helped me out?	Acknowledgments (optional)
Whose work did I refer to?	References
Extra Information	Appendices (optional)

The research paper typically follows the four-part IMRD format (Introduction, Methods, Results, and Discussion).

Introduction (I)	The main purpose of the Introduction is to provide the rationale for the paper, moving from general discussion of the topic to the particular question or hypothesis being investigated. A secondary purpose is to attract interest in the topic—and hence readers.
Methods (M)	The Methods section describes, in various degrees of detail, methodology, materials, and procedures. This is the narrowest part of the research paper.
Results (R)	In the Results section, the findings are described, accompanied by variable amounts of commentary.
Discussion (D)	The Discussion section offers an increasingly generalized account of what has been learned in the study. This is usually done through a series of "points", at least some of which refer back to statements made in the Introduction.

The following diagram gives a useful indication of the out-in-out or general-specific-general movement of the typical research paper.

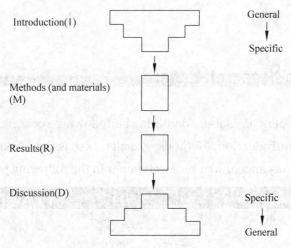

Overall shape of a research paper

As a result of the different purposes, the four sections have taken on different linguistic characteristics. The linguistic characteristics are summarized in the following table.

	Introduction	Methods	Results	Discussion
Present tense	high	low	low	high
Past tense	mid	high	high	mid
Passive voice	low	high	variable	variable
Citation/references	high	low	variable	high
Qualification	mid	low	mid	high
Commentary	high	low	variable	high

Task One

Here's an example of a research article that MIGHT have been written (a short version). This article is meant as an example of a research paper in psychology. It's written for educational purposes. Identify the four sections of the paper and summarize the linguistic characteristics of each section.

Part	Tense	Voice
Introduction		
Methods		
Results		
Discussions		

Behavioral Study of Obedience

by [*author*], [*University*]

Abstract

There is little literature on the role of obedience when doing evil actions up until now (2008). Most theories suggest that only very disturbed people do horrible actions if they are ordered to do so. Our experiment tested people's obedience to authority. The results showed that most obey all orders given by the authority-figure. The conclusion is that when it comes to people harming others, the situation a person's in is more important than previously thought. In contrary to earlier belief, individual characteristics are less important.

Introduction

Current theories focus on personal characteristics to explain wrong-doing and how someone can intentionally harm others. In a survey, professionals such as doctors, psychologists and laymen thought that very few out of a population (1–3%) would harm others if ordered to do so.

In the recent war trial with Adolph Eichmann, he claims to "only have been following orders". The author wanted to test whether this is true, or just a cheap explanation. Can people harm others because they obey the orders? Are good-hearted people able to do this?

The experiment will test whether a person can keep giving electric shocks to another person just because they are told to do so. The expectation is that very few will keep giving shocks, and that most persons will disobey the order.

Methods

Participants

There were male 30 participants participating. They were recruited by an advertisement in a newspaper and were paid $4.50.

Instruments

A "shock generator" was used to trick the participants into thinking that they gave shock to another person in another room. The shock generator had switches labeled with different voltages, starting at 30 volts and increasing in 15-volt increments all the way up to 450 volts. The switches were also labeled with terms which reminded the participant of how dangerous the shocks were.

Procedures

The participant met another "participant" in the waiting room before the experiment. The other "participant" was an actor. Each participant got the role as a "teacher" who would then deliver a shock to the actor ("learner") every time an incorrect answer was produced. The participant believed that he was delivering real shocks to the learner.

The learner was a confederate who would pretend to be shocked. As the experiment progressed, the teacher would hear the learner plead to be released and complain about a heart condition. Once the 300-volt level had been reached, the learner banged on the wall and demanded to be released. Beyond this point, the learner became completely silent and refused to answer any more questions. The experimenter then instructed the participant to treat this silence as an incorrect response and deliver a further shock.

When asking the experimenter if they should stop, they were instructed to continue.

Results

Of the 40 participants in the study, 26 delivered the maximum shocks. 14 persons did not obey the experimenter and stopped before reaching the highest levels. All 40 participants continued to give shocks up to 300 volts.

Discussion/Conclusion

Most of the participants became very agitated, stressed and angry at the experimenter. Many continued to follow orders all the time even though they were clearly uncomfortable. The study shows that people are able to harm others intentionally if ordered to do so. It shows that the situation is far more important than previously believed, and that personal characteristics are less important in such a situation.

Task Two

Here are 8 sentences from a research paper entitled "Studying in a Second Language: the Experiences of Chinese Students in Canada". Based on your knowledge, can you guess from which of the sections they come? Mark each one I, M, R, D. There are two sentences from each section.

_____ 1. In contrast, subjects in the text absent condition of Study 2 appeared to apply planning and organizational strategies more directly.

_____ 2. Similarly, Yee (1989) reported that Asian university students commonly respond to the intense pressure for academic achievement by adopting memorization strategies, and this may be particularly true for such students in English-speaking universities.

_____ 3. This supports the argument made earlier in this paper that a reasonable level of fluency provides a basis for higher level processes.

_____ 4. The text used in Study 2 consisted of a five-page article about nurses' management of children's pain, typical of texts read in an undergraduate course; no glossary was provided.

_____ 5. However, several patterns were apparent in the results and these deserve some comments.

_____ 6. It is now common for students from virtually every country in the world to either study English at home, or to study abroad in an English-speaking country.

_____ 7. Not only did subjects in Study 1 appear heavily dependent on the overall structure of the text, they also were reliant in the way it expressed ideas.

_____ 8. The students selected were adult, native-Chinese speakers from mainland China, studying in Canada.

Task Three

Identify and analyze the structure of the research paper in Unit 1.

Unit 2

Exploring Staff Perceptions of Student Plagiarism

Learning Objectives

- What are three moves in the Introduction?
- Language patterns in Introduction
- How to write the Introduction of a research paper?

Exploring Staff Perceptions of Student Plagiarism

Abbi Flint[*], Sue Clegg and Ranald Macdonald

Sheffield Hallam University, UK

This paper presents analysis of qualitative data from a research project looking at staff perceptions of plagiarism at a post-1992 university. Twenty-six members of staff from departments and academic schools from across the university took part in open and semi-structured interviews. Analysis shows that variable definitions of plagiarism exist; both regarding student activities that constitute plagiarism and the way in which plagiarism is perceived to be related to cheating. The factors underlying these personal definitions are unclear, but the analysis suggests that values perceived to **underpin** higher education may play an important role. This paper provides new empirical data on staff perceptions of student plagiarism, which complement previous research on student perceptions. The potential implications of different perceptions of plagiarism, and a mismatch between staff and student understandings is highlighted as an area for further consideration.

Introduction

Plagiarism is a **contentious** issue in higher education (HE), frequently the subject of 'colourful' **rhetoric** (Park, 2003, p. 472). Plagiarism amongst university students is perceived, by many, to be widespread and increasing (Roberts & Toombs, 1993; Larkham & Manns, 2002). Whether this reflects real increases in the rate of plagiarism, the rate of detection, or increases due to greater student numbers is unclear (Larkham, 2003),

---

* Corresponding author. The Learning and Teaching Institute, City Campus, Sheffield Hallam University, Sheffield S1 1WB, UK. Email: A.L.Flint@shu.ac.uk

but the fact that there is perceived to be an increase is an important issue in itself (Dordoy, 2002). Increased access to and use of the Internet is also thought to create new opportunities for plagiarists (Underwood & Szabo, 2003), and problems associated with **massification** of HE and increasing numbers of 'non-traditional' students create challenges to the way students are educated about acceptable academic practices (Lillis, 1997). The Quality Assurance Agency (QAA) advises higher education institutions (HEIs) to ensure that 'assessment policies and practices are responsive and provide for the effective monitoring of the validity, equity and reliability of assessment' (QAA, 2000). As part of this they suggest that universities provide students with: 'definitions of academic misconduct in respect of assessment, such as plagiarism, collusion, cheating, impersonation and the use of inadmissible material (including material downloaded from the internet)' (QAA, 2000).

In order to deal with issues of plagiarism effectively and **equitably**, it is necessary for staff, students and departments to be working from the same definitions and interpretations (Stefani & Carroll, 2001). At the institutional level a brief survey of the plagiarism/cheating policies and guidelines of a selection of HEIs shows that, whilst definitions of plagiarism are consistent with general dictionary definitions,[1] they stress different aspects of this definition. For example, Liverpool Hope University frame their definition in terms of referencing techniques and writing skills (our emphasis).

> Plagiarism is defined as: The use of material which is not acknowledged to its source and also the direct use of material, referenced or unreferenced, without a clear indication that the material is taken verbatim from its source. (Liverpool Hope University College, 2003)

In contrast, Pyer's definition locates plagiarism more in terms of personal ownership of work and academic integrity, with a more general allusion to referencing skills (our emphasis).

> Every piece of written coursework submitted to the department must be accompanied by a *Declaration of Academic Integrity which you sign, affirming that the work is your own* and does not contain material from unacknowledged sources. ...Plagiarism is simply theft. It is taking the words, ideas and labour of other people and giving the impression that they are your own. (Pyer, 2000)

The relationship between cheating and plagiarism, and the constituent student activities which make up these categories, may also vary. Furthermore, some institutions have central procedures to be followed by all departments whereas others have a more general central definition which departments/subject areas can interpret in their own way (see University of Leeds, 2003).

Previous research on student understandings of plagiarism suggests that a diverse range of definitions are held, which may differ from staff and institutional views (Franklyn-Stokes & Newstead, 1995; Macdonald & Freewood, 2002; Ashworth *et al.*, 2003). Recent research at the University of Northumbria, for example, has highlighted differences between staff and students in the way the scale of plagiarism is perceived, the seriousness of offences and reasons why students cheat (Dordoy, 2002). Whilst it is important for educators to understand why and how students cheat (Harris, 2002), it is not within the scope of this paper to provide a comprehensive view of research on this subject (instead see Park, 2003).

In contrast to the wealth of studies exploring the student perspective there has been less research looking at staff perceptions of plagiarism. Borg's (2002) study at the University of Northumbria suggests staff definitions are influenced by personal views and disciplinary context, resulting in 'local' interpretations. Furthermore, staff recognized that other definitions and interpretations exist both within and between disciplines (Borg, 2002). Roig's (2001) study, asking educators to paraphrase extracts and assess examples of paraphrasing, suggests that the distinction between acceptable paraphrasing and plagiarism is not clear for all staff. Some staff paraphrased in a way which would be **construed** by others as plagiarism (Roig, 2001). Staff may have different levels of concern over notions of equity to students when detecting and dealing with plagiarism (Larkham, 2003) and perceptions of the seriousness of offences varies (Larkham & Manns, 2002). A review of the attitudes of Australian college and high school staff (Morgan, 1996) indicated that disciplinary differences may be linked to the type of assessment used. For instance, tutors in maths and science placed more emphasis on students' choice of material and getting answers correct whereas staff from humanities and social sciences were more concerned with students being able to use their own words (Morgan, 1996). Dordoy (2002) found that 90.7% of the staff interviewed in his study had experience of detecting plagiarism, but whilst some form of action was taken in the majority of cases, not all of these instances were taken through formal institutional procedures. Other studies indicate that staff may be **disillusioned** with formal procedures (Borg, 2002), see it in a negative light (Larkham & Manns, 2002), or disagree with the **penalties** it **imposes** (Osborn, 2000). Morgan's (1996) study found a range of reasons for not engaging in the formal process, from reluctance to take on the extra workload of a plagiarism enquiry, to concerns that policy is not applied across the board and may therefore result in some students being penalized more than others. Keith-Spiegel *et al.*'s (1998) exploration of why psychology lecturers may choose not to raise issues of plagiarism found that it was often framed in negative emotions. Staff were concerned about the personal **repercussions** of confrontations with students, they did not always feel protected by university procedures, and felt real sympathy for the possible impact of sanctions on students (Keith-Spiegel *et al.*, 1998). Case studies of informal dealings with plagiarism indicate staff may choose to do this to avoid **detrimental** impacts on students' future studies or careers (Shapira, 1993), and to engage students with the moral issues involved (Johnston, 1991). In these cases staff used their professional academic judgement to determine a course of action. 'Whatever his decision, he would have to take account of his own strong feelings about cheating the effect on [the student's] career, and the effect on other students' **morale**' (Shapira, 1993, p. 31).

The three perspectives on plagiarism discussed (student, staff and institutional) should not be seen as three alternative and mutually exclusive categories. On the contrary, although there is scope for interpretative difference, interpretations are typically dynamic and there are areas of common concern. For example, a number of articles stress the fact that, left unchallenged, plagiarism threatens the reputation of HEIs and devalues qualifications and educational experience (Lupton & Chapman, 2002; Johnston, 2003). Recent research with students suggests that, similarly, they felt tutors who did not act on detected plagiarism undermined the quality of their education (Freewood *et al.*, 2003). However, the differences between student, staff and institutional policy-led definitions do have important implications for the **implementation** of policy and the way in which discourse about plagiarism is framed.

Rationale

The research project was stimulated by the recognition of a need to explore the relationship between academic policy and how it is put into practice by teaching staff. Sheffield Hallam introduced new institutional procedures for dealing with academic misconduct over the 2003–2004 academic period, as part of the approach to broader issues of assessment and quality enhancement. The new procedures involve a streamlined process which reflects the relative seriousness of cases. Minor cases can be dealt with through a 'lighter touch' single stage process by staff within courses/programmes with a common reporting and monitoring process to ensure consistency and fairness. For more serious cases the outcome of the two stage process is considered by academic conduct panels. Although a programme of briefing events and workshops were held to inform staff of changes and involve them in dialogue about these issues, it was felt that more investigation was needed to uncover the interpretative framework staff use when dealing with plagiarism. It was hoped that this would enable us to unpack some of the complex issues around how policy is used in practice. It also complements previous research carried out by the Learning and Teaching Institute into student perceptions of plagiarism

(Ashworth *et al.*, 1997, 2003; Freewood *et al.*, 2003).

Twenty-six interviews of around 45 minutes each were undertaken by the researcher. Initially, the academic lead on the project identified eight participants, selected for particular interest or knowledge of plagiarism issues. The issues arising from these open interviews were used to develop the semi-structured interview schedule, used in the second round of interviews. For the second round 18 further members of staff were strategically selected from different departments and schools to ensure a broad range of teaching experience; including staff from postgraduate, undergraduate, part time, HND, distance learning, and sandwich courses. The transcripts were coded using Nvivo software and the context of each participant's disciplinary area, level of teaching and the make up of the student body was recorded and compared. For the purposes of analysis the participants were grouped into three different disciplinary areas; art and design, humanities and science. These categories were decided by the researcher and do not reflect any self-**ascription** by participants or institutional organization. The interviews yielded a wealth of qualitative data, some of which has been reported elsewhere (Flint *et al.*, 2005), and analysis is ongoing. The quotes used in this paper are from a selection of the interview data and represent the range of views held by participants.

Staff perceptions of plagiarism

There was considerable variation in the way that participants conceptualized student plagiarism, and many felt it was problematic to define. Interestingly, initial analysis suggests that this variation is not linked to disciplinary context but more tied to individual, personal interpretations and understandings.

A number of practices were considered to constitute plagiarism by staff across disciplinary areas. Most commonly cited was copying verbatim, or poorly paraphrasing, material from published sources without appropriate acknowledgement. Published sources included the Internet, books, journals, other published reports and less frequently broadcasting media (science) and unpublished material from placement employers (humanities). The types of activities described were linked to personal experience and therefore to a certain extent were connected with the disciplinary context. For instance, participants from art and design talked about plagiarism in terms of appropriation of ideas and design more than those from science and humanities. There was less consensus about other activities. For instance, falsifying research data was considered to be plagiarism by two participants, whereas another felt this belonged to a broader category of cheating. One participant felt that cheating in a test or exam constitutes plagiarism. Activities which involved another party, such as copying and **collaboration** amongst students, created considerable diversity of opinion. Although copying from other students was included in most definitions of plagiarism, for some participants from humanities and science, this was considered to be a different kind of cheating. Different types of collusion were described, from students working together on assignments or problems, to individuals getting help from other people. Not all staff agreed that collusion should be considered a form of plagiarism and many felt the boundaries between acceptable levels of collaboration and undue collusion were not clear for staff or students. Common understandings of these terms cannot be assumed.

> I think there are some very, very difficult dividing lines between plagiarism and peer groups helping each other, and that's a really big problem for staff and students…And it can be very difficult for me to define where the dividing line is. And if I'm having trouble, students are having trouble. (Interview 1, science)

Staff used their judgement to decide when the students had actually crossed the line into plagiarism. Many talked about the intention, extent and scale of the offence being linked to the severity of punishment, and for some the incorporation of a 'small amount' of others' work was acceptable. In summary, most participants recognized that the definition of plagiarism was complex and varied between individual staff members and students, and could take one or a variety of forms.

> It can be un-attributed copying, lifting stuff from texts without indicating the author, which is where it's partly about poor referencing techniques. It can be undue collaboration among students, it can be getting other people, parents, friends, relatives, other people paid to do the work for them, or lifting stuff from the Web. So it can take a variety of forms, it can also be falsifying data. (Interview 8, humanities)

Relationship between cheating and plagiarism

Figure 1 illustrates, in very simple form, the kind of conceptions participants held about the relationship between cheating and plagiarism. Model A represents the view that cheating and plagiarism are **synonymous**: 'It's cheating isn't it?…I think if the intention is to cheat in an exam, or copying someone else's work, then it's the same crime effectively, don't you think? Same offence' (Interview 18, humanities).

Model B indicates cheating and plagiarism are different **discrete** activities:

> Cheating to me is, is where you're copying off someone…you're getting information in a more illicit way, whereas plagiarism is where you're actually either sharing information or taking it directly from…an open source, and it's not so underhand if you know what I mean. I think that would be the distinction, one's more overt than the other. (Interview 11, science)

Model C recognizes that there is some **overlap** but also some significant differences between cheating and plagiarism:

> There is the issue to do with how you use references and how you use other people's thinking in developing your own. And the other issue is to do with cheating. I'm not saying that these can't sort of meld into each other because I'm afraid they sometimes do. (Interview 17, humanities)

Model D suggests that plagiarism is a **subsidiary** category of cheating: 'I think all plagiarism is cheating, but not all cheating is plagiarism' (Interview 14, science).

All of these conceptions were present in the data from humanities, all but D from science, and all but A from art and design. The most common view from all disciplines was that plagiarism and cheating share some common characteristics but also have essential differences (C). Although the models provide a useful summary of the range of conceptions, in reality staff appeared to hold different conceptions in different situations rather than holding one fixed model. Many found it difficult to explain how they perceived the relationship between cheating and plagiarism. Most indicated there were both similarities and differences, and the nature, intentionality and scale of the offence often dictated the closeness of the relationship.

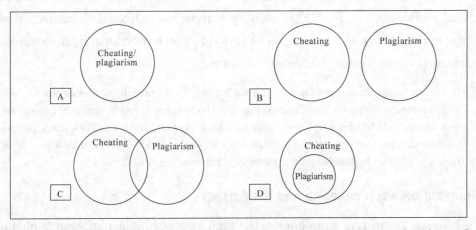

Figure 1. Different ways of conceptualizing the relationship between cheating and plagiarism (inspired by diagram in Carroll, 2002)

Similarities between plagiarism and cheating were often linked with intent. Plagiarism was much more likely to be seen as cheating if it was perceived to be intentional, in which case 'both [plagiarism and cheating are] trying to gain advantage by unfair means' (Interview 1, science). Some staff made distinctions between cheating and plagiarism in relation to the form of assessment; with cheating linked to exams and plagiarism to coursework.

Copying from other students was seen by many as a form of plagiarism synonymous with cheating. This was perceived as more serious than incorporating small pieces of unacknowledged published text.

> When they copy off each other, then yes, I would call that cheating...But sometimes when

they're using the literature without proper referencing I don't think they're deliberately setting out to fool us, in which case it's not cheating as such. (Interview 6, humanities)

Those who shared this view felt that cheating was more serious than plagiarism. Indeed one participant pointed out that the penalties for cheating were often more serious than the sliding scale applied to those who plagiarized. However, there were a few participants who felt that plagiarism was more serious than other forms of cheating and should be punished accordingly. 'Plagiarism is more serious. It is probably the most serious form of cheating, at least academically I think' (Interview 3, art and design).

For these the idea that student work should be original and individually completed was seen as one of the core values of HE. Plagiarism was framed in terms of personal ownership, describing it as 'using other people's ideas' or submitting something 'when it wasn't really your own work', rather than copying from inanimate sources. By **contravening** this core academic value, plagiarism raised strong emotions for some staff. Furthermore, some saw it as symptomatic of increased instrumentalism in students, which was perceived to be exacerbated by the massification and commercialization of HE.

Also it becomes more of a situation when you've got that many students where it becomes like, 'Well I'm just in a sausage factory...what difference does it make?...and if to get through this unit means cobbling an essay off the internet then I'll do that'. And I think it's those kind of situations that produce the cynicism that's basically plagiarism. (Interview 16, art and design)

The kind of conceptions that the participants held of plagiarism were not always consistent with policy. In fact one participant explicitly stated that they had a highly personal definition. 'It all depends on whether we are talking about the technical definition of plagiarism and what I would consider to be plagiarism in students' (Interview 10, art and design).

Sheffield Hallam's (2003) assessment regulations and procedures place plagiarism firmly inside the broader category of cheating (consistent with Model D), whereas the staff we interviewed held multiple models depending on their situation. The procedures recognize that plagiarism can take a variety of forms and describe these in detail as: complete plagiarism, partial plagiarism, self-plagiarism/**duplication**, and collusion. Although self-plagiarism is explicitly described in the procedures, only one participant included this in their own definition. Other dishonest activities such as falsifying data, impersonation, dishonest practice, and irregular behaviour relating to exams are considered to be different types of cheating.

Discussion

The analysis presented creates a number of challenges for HEIs. It is clear from the data that staff hold differing perceptions of plagiarism, and the relationships between cheating and plagiarism, which are not always consistent with institutional policy definitions. Whilst we acknowledge that there are issues with the definition of some terms used in discussion about plagiarism, such as 'unintentional plagiarism', it is not our intention to debate the validity of those definitions here.

Differences in the way staff, students and institutions define plagiarism can influence the implementation of policy in a number of ways. Firstly, the fact that staff have internalized definitions means that all instances of plagiarism are **mediated** by these before consulting policy. This may result in inconsistent application of policy and differential treatment of students. Our data suggest this occurs both within and between particular subject groups or schools. Furthermore, when staff recognize differences between their own and policy led definitions this can lead to conflicting viewpoints, which may not always be resolved. For instance, our data revealed some staff felt that, because their experience of the formal process did not match their personal understandings of how instances of plagiarism should be dealt with, they would be more inclined to deal with plagiarism at an individual and informal level. Furthermore, many staff place considerable value on academic professional judgement and may perceive centralized policy to pose a threat to this.

> Such codes, though, can quickly come to resemble little more than a rulebook to prevent unlawful or unethical conduct taking away the need for a lecturer to make a professional judgement in the process. The assumption at the heart of a detailed code of conduct is that professionals (or employees) cannot be trusted to act in the right way. (Macfarlane, 2004, p. 35)

The danger is that informal dealings, or personal and local interpretations of policy, may act to negate the aims of centralized policy, i.e., ideas of equity and consistency, in dealing with plagiarism (Borg, 2002). For example, at Sheffield Hallam one of the principles underpinning the university's action on cheating and plagiarism is that the process should be fair, transparent, and consistent; clearly informal dealings cannot ensure these attributes.

This also has implications for how we educate students about plagiarism. Individual students may receive conflicting information on definitions of plagiarism and the boundaries between acceptable and unacceptable practice from different module tutors. More than one participant from our data set expressed concern about inconsistency in the way staff educate students about plagiarism.

The fact that individual understandings of the core values of academia were used to frame their definitions of plagiarism and how it is dealt with also has implications for how students are educated about plagiarism. Common understandings of these core values cannot be assumed for all members of the academic community (including students). The notion of intellectual integrity and originality being **paramount** to academic achievement is inherent in HE (Macfarlane, 2004) and **perpetuated** by external processes such as the Research Assessment Exercise (RAE), which rates single authorship journal articles as the highest form of academic output (Larkham & Manns, 2002). As such, plagiarism can be seen as an attack on the principles of scholarship (Freewood *et al.*, 2003), rather than a **transgression** of rules. It is important to bear in mind that ideas of the importance of originality are not objective but stem from the particular cultural context of western and European academic institutions (Larkham, 2003). Haggis has suggested that some students may have problems with the concepts involved in academic literacy rhetoric, such as 'argument' and 'evidence', and in the process of 'concretizing' these **abstractions** may commit plagiarism (Haggis, 2003). The challenge of academic writing can be **daunting** and confusing for students (Johnston, 2003). Clearly this creates challenges for the way we develop student skills and the expectations we have of students at university level. Routes into HE are diverse, meaning that institutions cannot make assumptions about the sorts of preparation students receive prior to university, or their motivation or understandings of HE. This diversity of routes into HE means that academic institutions need to make explicit the expectations the university has of students. Furthermore, we need to think carefully about how we engage students with ideas of academic integrity, and induct them into a culture where plagiarism would not occur to, nor be tolerated by any members of the academic community.

Previous research on student understandings of plagiarism at Sheffield Hallam (Ashworth *et al.*, 1997; Macdonald & Freewood, 2002) indicates that student perceptions may differ from those of staff. For example, some students differentiated between plagiarism of published material and copying from or colluding with another student, with copying and collusion not always considered to be plagiarism (Macdonald & Freewood, 2002). Some students did not feel that the emphasis staff placed on issues around plagiarism was justified, especially regarding plagiarism in undergraduate essays (Ashworth *et al.*, 1997). This attitude may be indicative of the fact that many students do not engage with the idea that plagiarism is associated with core values of academia, such as academic integrity, although this is how many staff understand it. Furthermore, differences between individual staff members' perceptions of plagiarism may have implications for the student experience. Students noticed and were affected by inconsistent staff approaches to plagiarism, and in some cases did not feel they clearly understood the definitions or guidelines provided by the university (Ashworth *et al.*, 1997; Macdonald & Freewood, 2002). 'Students wanted a much more consistent approach by tutors in explaining what it is, providing the appropriate training such as in referencing and then dealing with it' (Macdonald & Freewood, 2002, p. 5).

Clearly these issues need to be considered when designing and implementing institutional policy. The new procedures for dealing with academic misconduct at Sheffield Hallam, described in the rationale, were informed by the research undertaken with students. One of the principles underlying the procedures is that they are 'fair, transparent and consistent' (SHU, 2003), and it is hoped that the new procedures for dealing with minor cases of plagiarism will enable this consistency.

Conclusion

Data from the 26 interviews with teaching and departmental staff carried out during this study suggest that staff have highly personalized definitions of plagiarism. Whilst these are undoubtedly influenced by their experience of plagiarism issues within HEIs, they are not always consistent with institutionally **espoused** policy definitions. The disjunction between these definitions creates problems for the implementation of centralized university policy. Previous work on student perceptions suggests there is potential for a mismatch between staff and student understandings of plagiarism.

For some staff, definitions are influenced by notions of assumed core values of HE; specifically, ideas of individual intellectual ownership of work and academic integrity. These abstract concepts may not be shared with students, and raise challenges for the way we involve students in a dialogue about plagiarism.

The challenge ahead is to consider how staff, student, and institutional perspectives can be **reconciled** or unified, as well as balancing them with the QAA Code of Practice and maintaining the reputation of the university as one that values high academic principles. The next stage is to use the data from the staff interviews to develop further guidelines and staff development activities to engage staff without **alienating** them. This fits with an approach of using research to inform policy and practice (Clegg *et al.*, 2004), as well as developing a better understanding of the issue and sharing this with others.

Note

1. According to the *Concise Oxford Dictionary*, to plagiarise is to take '(the work or an idea of someone else) and pass it off as one's own' (Pearsall, 2001).

References

Ashworth, P. Bannister, P. & Thorne, P. (1997) Guilty in whose eyes? University students' perception of cheating and plagiarism in academic work and assessment, *Studies in Higher Education*, 22(2), 187–203.

Ashworth, P., Freewood, M. & Macdonald, R. (2003) The student lifeworld and the meanings of plagiarism, *Journal of Phenomenological Psychology*, 34(2), 257–278.

Borg, E. (2002) Northumbria University lecturers' experience of plagiarism and collusion, Proceedings from The First Northumbria Conference 2002: Educating for the future. Available online at: http://online.northumbria.ac.uk/LTA/media/docs/Conference%20 Publication%202002/ (accessed 11 February 2004).

Carroll, J. (2002) *A handbook for deterring plagiarism in higher education* (Oxford, Oxford Centre for Staff and Learning Development).

Clegg, S., Macdonald, R., Smith, K., Bradley, S. & Glover, S. (2004) Using research evidence to inform policy and practice—the Sheffield Hallam University model, Paper presented at The Higher Education Academy Third Mike Daniel Symposium for Institutional Research UMIST, 7 July.

Dordoy, A. (2002) Cheating and plagiarism: student and staff perceptions at Northumbria, Proceedings from The First Northumbria Conference 2002: Educating for the future. Available online at: http://www.jiscpas.ac.uk/apppage.cgi?USERPAGE–7509 (accessed 10 March 2006).

Flint, A., Macdonald, R. & Clegg, S. (2005) Emotion, practice, and plagiarism: exploring the staff perspective, in: A. Peden Smith & F. Duggan (eds.) Plagiarism: Prevention, Practice and Policy Conference, 29–30 June 2004, Proceedings (Newcastle, Northumbria University Press) 65–72.

Franklyn-Stokes, A. & Newstead, S. E. (1995) Undergraduate cheating: who does what and why?, *Studies in Higher Education*, 20(2), 159–172.

Freewood, M., Macdonald, R. & Ashworth, P. (2003) Why simply policing is not the answer, in: C. Rust (ed.) *Improving student learning: theory and practice—ten years on* (Oxford, Oxford Centre for Staff and Learning Development).

Haggis, T. (2003) Constructing images of ourselves? A critical investigation into 'approaches to learning' research in higher education, *British Educational Research Journal*, 29 (1), 89–104.

Harris, R. (2002) Anti-plagiarism strategies for research papers. Available online at: www. virtualsalt. com/antiplag. htm (accessed 12 May 2004).

Johnston, K. (1991) Cheating: reflections on a moral dilemma, *Journal of Moral Education*, 20(1), 283–292.

Johnston, W. (2003) The concept of plagiarism, *Assessment Paper*, 2 (1) (Manchester Metropolitan University, Learning and Teaching Unit).

Keith-Spiegel, P., Tabachnick, B. G., Whitley, B. E. J. & Washburn, J. (1998) Why professors ignore cheating: opinions of a national sample of psychology instructors, *Ethics & Behaviour*, 8(3), 215–227.

Lancaster University (2003) University rules. Available online at: www.lancs.ac.uk/users/acadreg/ rules/rules2003.htm (accessed 12 May 2004).

Larkham, P. J. (2003) Exploring and dealing with plagiarism: traditional approaches. Available online at: http://online.northumbria.ac.uk/faculties/art/information_studies/Imri/Jiscpas/site/pubs_goodprac_larkham.asp (accessed 8 June 2004).

Larkham, P. J. & Manns, S. (2002) Plagiarism and its treatment in higher education, *Further & Higher Education*, 26(4), 339–349.

Lillis, T. (1997) New voices in academia? The regulative nature of academic writing conventions, *Language & Education*, 11(3), 182–199.

Liverpool Hope University College (2003) Undergraduate modular scheme (awards of the University of Liverpool)—appendices. Available online at: www.hope.ac.uk/compass/ Registry/UMS%20 University%20of%20Liverpool%20Awards%202003-2004.pdf (accessed 19 May 2004).

Lupton, R. A. & Chapman, K. J. (2002) Russian and American college students' attitudes, perceptions and tendencies towards cheating, *Educational Research*, 44 (1), 17–27.

Macdonald, R. & Freewood, M. (2002) Dealing with plagiarism: using research to develop an holistic approach, in: A. Goody, J. Herrington & M. Northcote (eds.) *Proceedings of the 2002 Annual International Conference of the Higher Education Research and Development Society of Australasia (HERDSA)*. Available online at: www.ecu.edu.au/conferences/herdsa/main/ papers/ nonref/pdf/RanaldMacdonald.pdf (accessed 10 March 2006).

Macfarlane, B. (2004) *Teaching with integrity: the ethics of higher education practice* (London, Routledge Falmer).

Morgan, K. (1996) Plagiarism: does it matter? Available online at: www.canberrac.act.edu.au/plagiarism. htm (accessed 9 June 2004).

Osborn, E. (2000) Punishment: a story for medical educators, *Academic Medicine*, 75 (3), 241–244.

Park, C. (2003) In other (people's) words: plagiarism by university students—literature and lessons, *Assessment & Evaluation in Higher Education*, 28(5), 471–488.

Pearsall, J. (ed.) (2001) *The concise Oxford dictionary* (10th edn.) (Oxford, Oxford University Press). Available online at: www.oxfordreference.com/views/SEARCH_RESULTS. html?y=13&q=plagia rism&category=t23&x=5&ssid=356918411&scope=book&time=0.464284462812731 (accessed 23 April 2004).

Pyer, H. S. (2000) Plagiarism. Available online at: http://online.northumbria.ac.uk/faculties/art/ information_studies/Imri/Jiscpas/docs/external/student_plagiarism_advice.pdf(accessed 30 September 2003).

QAA (2000) Code of practice for the assurance of academic quality and standards in higher education. Available online at: www.qaa.ac.ukpublic/Cop/COPaosfinal/contents.htm (accessed 13 May 2004).

Roberts, D. M. & Toombs, R. (1993) A scale to assess perceptions of cheating in examination-related situations, *Educational & Psychological Measurement*, 53, 755–762.

Roig, M. (2001) Plagiarism and paraphrasing criteria of college and university professors, *Ethics & Behaviour*, 11(3), 307–323.

Shapira, G. (1993) Did she or did she not?, in: P. Schwartz & G. Webb (eds.) *Case studies on teaching in higher education* (London, Kogan Page), 29–35.

Sheffield Hallam University (2003) Assessment regulations and procedures: cheating procedures for undergraduate and taught postgraduate courses. Internal policy document.

Stefani, L. & Carroll, J. (2001) Assessment: a briefing on plagiarism. *Assessment series, No. 10* (York, LTSN Generic Centre).

Underwood, J. & Szabo, A. (2003) Academic offences and e-learning: individual propensities in cheating, *British Journal of Educational Technology*, 34(4), 467–477.

University of Leeds (2003) Taught students handbook 2003–2004. Available online at: www.leeds.ac.uk/ students/handbook/SECTIONS.htm#cheat (accessed 12 May 2004).

New Words

abstraction	[æb'strækʃn]	n.	抽象化；抽象过程
alienate	['eiliəneit]	vt.	使疏远，离间；使转移，放弃
ascription	[ə'skripʃn]	n.	归属
collaboration	[kə,læbə'reiʃn]	n.	合作，协作；勾结
construe	[kən'stru:]	vt.	分析，解释
contentious	[kən'tenʃəs]	a.	好辩的，喜争吵的
contravene	[,kɔntrə'vi:n]	vt.	违反
daunting	['dɔ:ntiŋ]	a.	令人畏惧的，令人气馁的
detrimental	[,detri'mentl]	a.	有害的，不利的
discrete	[di'skri:t]	a.	分离的，不相关联的
disillusion	[,disi'lu:ʒn]	vt.	使不再抱幻想，使理想破灭
duplication	[,dju:pli'keiʃn]	n.	复制；副本
equitably	['ekwitəbli]	adv.	公正地
espouse	[i'spauz]	vt.	支持，拥护
implementation	[,implimen'teiʃn]	n.	生效，履行，实施
impose	[im'pəuz]	vt.	强加于
massification	[,mæsifi'keiʃn]	n.	扩大化，大规模化
mediate	['mi:dieit]	vt.	经调停解决
morale	[mə'rɑ:l]	n.	士气，斗志
overlap	[,əuvə'læp]	n.	重叠部分，相交
paramount	['pærəmaunt]	a.	最重要的，主要的
penalty	['penəlti]	n.	处罚，惩罚，罚金
perpetuate	[pə'petʃueit]	vt.	使永存，使不朽
rationale	[,ræʃə'nɑ:l]	n.	理论的说明，基本原理，依据
reconcile	['rekənsail]	vt.	使和解，调停，排解
repercussion	[,ri:pə'kʌʃn]	n.	（不良的）影响，反响，后果
rhetoric	['retərik]	n.	修辞学
subsidiary	[səb'sidiəri]	a.	辅助的，附设的
synonymous	[si'nɔniməs]	a.	同义的，同义词的
transgression	[træns'greʃn]	n.	违反，违法，罪过
underpin	[,ʌndə'pin]	vt.	加固（墙等）的基础，加强⋯⋯的基础

Discussion Ideas

1. Identify the different sections of the present study.

2. What is a "rationale"? What is the function of it?

3. A qualitative paradigm has been chosen for this study. Why is it appropriate for this study?

4. Is there a "pilot study" in this study?

5. In this study, the participants took part in the open and semi-structured interviews. What do you think might be the benefits of open interviews and semi-structured interviews? Are there any other kinds of interviews?

6. What do you think might be the implications of the present study?

Vocabulary and Language Learning Skills

1. Recognizing Word Meanings

Choose the appropriate synonyms from the text to replace the underlined words.

1) Some teachers are insufficiently sensitive and can underestimate a child's intellectual abilities or wrongly <u>regard</u> a child as lazy.

2) Teachers often use questions to ensure that students are attentive and <u>involved</u>, and to assess students' understanding.

3) These suggestions <u>show</u> how cultural values can be used to generate hypotheses about work-related variables.

4) Plagiarism is a <u>controversial</u> issue in higher education, frequently the subject of colourful rhetoric.

5) The <u>bottom-line</u> difference between economic activity inside the firm and economic activity in the "market" is that the former is carried on within an administrative organization, while the latter is not.

6) <u>In agreement with</u> Darwin's evolutionary perspective, Freud observed that intense anxiety was prevalent in most psychiatric disorders.

7) For some time now, I have been deeply concerned about the growing <u>separation</u> between legal education and the legal profession.

2. Making a Collocation

Use appropriate words to complete the sentences. Make changes if necessary.

although	strategy	in contrast to	whilst
incline	stimulate	common	distinct

1) The case study research must _____ select a case that will allow the subject to be investigated fully.

2) Most people believe that plagiarism and cheating share some _____ characteristics but also have essential differences.

3) The research project was _____ by the recognition of a need to explore the relationship between academic policy and how it is put into practice by teaching staff.

4) _____ to the wealth of studies exploring the student perspective there has been less research looking at staff perceptions of plagiarism.

5) _____ there have been some interesting surveys of the incidence of academic dishonesty among students in both high school and college, I have not been able to find any studies that examine college students' conceptions of why it is wrong to plagiarize.

6) _____ it is important for educators to understand why and how students cheat, it is not within the scope of this paper to provide a comprehensive view of research on this subject.

Writing Focus

Introduction

Function

The purpose of an introduction section is to acquaint the reader with the rationale behind the work, with the intention of defending it. It places your work in a theoretical context, and enables the reader to understand and appreciate your objectives. The function of the Introduction is to:

- Establish the context of the work being reported. This is accomplished by discussing the relevant primary research literature (with citations) and summarizing your current understanding of the problem you are investigating;

- State the purpose of the work in the form of the hypothesis, question, or problem you investigated;

● Briefly explain your rationale and approach and, whenever possible, the possible outcomes your study can reveal.

Style

The introduction sections of research papers typically follow the Create-a-Response-Space (or CARS) model in response to two kinds of competition: competition for research space and competition for readers.

Moves in Research Paper Introductions

Move 1	Establishing a research territory	a. by showing that the general research area is important, central, interesting, problematic, or relevant in some way. (optional) b. by introducing and reviewing items of previous research in the area. (obligatory)
Move 2	Establishing the motivation for the study	a. by indicating a gap in the previous research, raising a question about it, or extending previous knowledge in some way. (obligatory)
Move 3	Making an offer to fill the gap	a. by outlining purposes or stating the nature of the present research. (obligatory) b. by announcing principal findings. (optional) c. by indicating the structure of the research paper. (optional)

Language Focus

1. Showing importance and rationale:

The increasing interest in…has heightened the need for…

Recently, there has been a growing interest in…

The possibility of…has generated wide interest in…

The development of…has led to the hope that…

The…has become a favorite for analysis…

Knowledge of…has a great importance for…

The study of…become an important aspect of…

A central issue in…is…

The…has been extensively studied in recent years.

Many investigators have recently turned to…

The relationship between…has been investigated by many researchers.

Many recent studies have focused on…

The rationale for the selection of…as the focus of the study is two-fold.

2. Indicating purposes:

The aim of the present paper is to give…

This paper reports on the results obtained…

In this paper we give preliminary results for…

The main purpose of the experiment reported here was to…

This study was designed to evaluate…

The present work extends the use of the last model by…

We now report the interaction between…

The primary focus of this paper is on…

The aim of this investigation was to test…

It is the purpose of the present paper to provide…

3. Secondary aims or features (Optional):

In addition, an effort is made to…

Additionally, …

A secondary aim of the present paper is to…

A further reason for…

4. Stating value (Optional):

In this way, we offer a solution to a long-standing problem in…

It is hoped that this study will revive interest in a long-neglected feature of…

The information presented should be useful to…

5. Outlining the structure of the text (Optional):

The plan of this paper is as follows.

Section II describes…

In Section III a theoretical model is constructed which is designed to…

…are then tested in Section IV.

Finally, Section V offers some suggestions for the modification of the current…

Task One

Read the following Introduction section to a mini-RP and carry out the tasks that follow.

The Position of Sentence Connectors in Academic English

Author

Introduction

Many commentators have noted that sentence connectors (e.g., *however*) are an important and useful element in expository and argumentative writing. Frequency studies of their occurrence in academic English extend at least as far back as Huddleson (1971). ESL writing textbooks have for many years regularly included chapters on sentence connectors (e.g., Herbert, 1965). Most reference grammars deal with their grammatical status, classification, meaning, and use. Some attention has also been given to the position of sentence connectors in clauses and sentences. Quirk and Greenbaum (1973) observe (a) that the normal position is initial; (b) that certain connectors, such as *hence* and *overall,* "are restricted, or virtually restricted, to initial position" (p.248); and (c) that medial positions are rare for most connectors, and final positions even rarer. The only attempt known to us to explain differences in position on semantic grounds is an unpublished paper by Salera (1976). The Salera paper deals only with adversative like *however* and suggests that initial position reflects something contrary to expectation, while medial position reflects a contrast that is not necessarily unexpected. However, neither of these studies provides any descriptive evidence of the actual positions of sentence connectors in academic texts. In the present paper, we report on a preliminary study of sentence connector position in a sample of twelve published articles.

1. Divide the text into the three basic moves.

2. What word signals that Move 1 has ended and Move 2 has started? What other words or expressions could also indicate this shift?

3. What do you think the next sentence is going to be?

Task Two

Below is a textual outline draft that lacks variety. Can you rewrite it?

The rest of the paper is organized as follows. Section 2 presents the theoretical concept. Section 3 presents the empirical specification, the implementation of the model. Section 4 presents the results of statistical and other computational analyses. Section 5 summarizes the findings and provides a brief discussion concerning the shortcomings of the methods employed. Finally, an appendix presenting the detailed algebraic works is presented at the end of the paper.

Task Three

Identify the different parts of the Introduction section of the study in Unit 2.

Supplementary Reading

College freshmen (75 men and 75 women) at Indiana University completed a questionnaire designed to elicit their reasoning about, and attitudes toward, plagiarism. Students wrote their own explanations of why it is wrong to plagiarize, rated five standard explanations that were based on different ethical orientations, and responded to a series of statements about the seriousness and consequences of plagiarizing. Analyses revealed that these students took the matter of plagiarism rather seriously, and that they tended to construe plagiarism in terms of three major issues: fairness to authors and other students, the responsibility of students to do independent work, and respect for ownership rights.

How College Freshmen View Plagiarism?*

Barry M. Kroll

Indiana University

Most schools and colleges have institutional policies that are designed to curb plagiarism and other forms of academic dishonesty. Although such policies are important, someone still has to assume the task of explaining the nature and significance of plagiarism to students, as well as teaching them how to avoid committing it. That task has traditionally been given to composition teachers. Consequently, in the field of composition studies much of the professional literature on plagiarism consists of advice about ways to prevent, detect, or respond to student cheating (e.g., Bjaaland & Lederman, 1973; Carroll, 1982; Daniels, 1960; Drum, 1986; Martin, 1971; Sauer, 1983;Waltman, 1980). When authors of composition textbooks discuss the topic, usually in a brief section in a chapter on research writing, they typically explain why plagiarism is a serious offense and then offer strategies for properly documenting one's use of source materials.

What is conspicuously missing in most discussions, however, is any consideration of how students conceptualize the issue of plagiarism. We can probably assume that most college freshmen have been told that plagiarism is wrong. But what reasons have they been given for why it is wrong? What do students understand about the nature and meaning of academic dishonesty? We know very little, I suspect, about why our students think plagiarism is wrong, despite the fact that it would seem logical to consider college students' own moral frames of reference when explaining the ethics of plagiarism.

* *Written Communication*, Vol. 5 No. 2, April 1988 203-221 © 1988 Sage Publications, Inc.

Although there have been some interesting surveys of the incidence of, and attitudes toward, academic dishonesty among students in both high school (Dant, 1986; Schab, 1980) and college (Baird, 1980; Hawley, 1984; Nuss, 1984), I have not been able to find any studies that examine college students' conceptions of why it is wrong to plagiarize. Thus my purpose in this study was to investigate what a sample of college freshmen thought about plagiarism, exploring the reasons they thought it was wrong, as well as examining some of their beliefs and attitudes about plagiarizing college papers.

Method and analysis of data

Participants

I drew the participants in the study from students enrolled in 12 sections of freshman composition at Indiana University (a pool of 286 students) during fall semester 1985. A number of students in these sections did not meet my criteria for inclusion in the study. Because I wanted to study "typical" freshmen at the beginning of their college experience, I eliminated students who were classified as something other than first-semester freshmen (24 of them), any significantly "older" students (defined as over 22 years of age—there were only 4 of them), and all nonnative speakers of English (6) on the assumption that their conceptions of plagiarism might be somewhat different from those of students in our culture. I also eliminated students who failed to complete some sections of the questionnaire that I administered (29), as well as students who indicated that they either didn't understand all the questions or weren't certain they had answered them thoroughly and honestly (31). (At the end of the questionnaire I asked students to indicate whether they had understood the questions and answered them thoroughly and honestly: 27 students said they weren't certain they had understood the questions, and 4 weren't certain they had answered them thoroughly and honestly.)

After disqualifying these students, I had 75 men and 117 women who met all my criteria. Because I wanted to include an equal number of responses from the two sexes, I chose a random sample of 75 women from those who qualified for the project, creating a final sample of 150 first-semester freshmen.

The questionnaire

Students in the 12 sections of freshman composition were asked to complete, during part of a class period in the first two weeks of classes (and before the instructor mentioned plagiarism), a questionnaire on the subject of plagiarism. The first two pages introduced the project, defined plagiarism, and explained how to complete the questions. Students were given the following rationale for the questionnaire:

> As part of the English department's effort to improve instruction in composition courses, we're asking freshmen to complete this questionnaire about plagiarism. As you probably know, plagiarism involves presenting another person's words or ideas as if they were your own, without acknowledging the source. We want to find out what freshmen know and how they feel about the matter of plagiarism. Please answer the questions in this booklet as fully and honestly as you can. Since you don't have to put your name on the questionnaire, you can be sure that your responses are completely anonymous. We hope anonymity makes you feel free to say what you really think on the issue of plagiarism—not what you've been told to think, and not what you think you should say to make yourself look good.

This rationale was followed with a section requesting information about gender, age, native language, and enrollment status. The remainder of the introduction explained and illustrated the types of questions that students would find in the booklet.

The first type of question asked students to respond by writing several sentences to explain why plagiarism was wrong. Then they were instructed to go back over their response and to bracket each separate reason they had written. Finally, they were told to number the bracketed reasons from the most important (number 1) to the least important. The second type of question contained a statement followed by a 5-point rating scale. Students were given an example of how to place a check on this kind of scale to indicate a particular level of agreement with a statement. When they completed each section, students were instructed to go on to the next page but not to return to a previous section.

Why is plagiarism wrong? The first question in the booklet asked students to write a short explanation in response to the following statement:

> The Indiana University "Policy on Academic Dishonesty" states the following:
> Plagiarism: A student must not intentionally adopt or reproduce ideas, words, or statements of another person without acknowledgment.
> Most people would agree that it is "wrong" to plagiarize. But why is it wrong? Please write your response in the space below.

At the bottom of the page were these instructions:

> If you mentioned more than one reason, please put brackets around each separate reason and number each to indicate how important that reason is in explaining why plagiarism is wrong (starting with 1 for the most important reason). Put the number at the beginning of each bracketed reason, inside each left-hand bracket. (If you're uncertain about how to do this bracketing, look back at the instructions on page 2.)

I normally followed the students' bracketing to decide what would count as separate reasons. However, I discovered that I could not always rely on the accuracy of students' bracketing of reasons; sometimes students did not bracket any reasons, and in other instances their bracketing did not seem to account for all the different reasons in their explanations. Therefore, in those cases where clearly different reasons were grouped together or two identical responses were bracketed separately, I adjusted the students' bracketing to reflect more accurately the reasons in their explanations. I then classified each bracketed reason according to a set of categories that emerged during the process of examining the responses and formulating categories that accounted for the majority of reasons students gave. I used six principal categories: Individual Responsibility, Fairness, Ownership, Honesty, Laziness, and Crime and Punishment. (I will explain and illustrate these categories later.) When assigning reasons to categories I followed the rule that at most one response from each student could be placed in each primary category. I also used two categories for reasons that didn't fit elsewhere: Miscellaneous and Unclassifiable. Reasons were assigned to the Miscellaneous category when they were legitimate but uncommon responses that did not fit into any other categories (e.g., saying that plagiarism would cause accumulated knowledge to shrink, or that plagiarism involves an invasion of privacy). Reasons were assigned to the Unclassifiable category when they were tautological (e.g., saying that plagiarism was "morally wrong") or when I couldn't understand the meaning or relevance of the response (e.g., saying "I don't know", or claiming that plagiarism isn't that bad). Unlike the rule for the primary categories, more than one reason from each student could be placed in these categories. (Out of a total of 279 reasons, 25 were placed in the Miscellaneous category and 17 were designated as Unclassifiable.)

While many of the students' responses fit clearly into a particular category, in some cases students' reasons were ambiguous and more difficult to classify. For example, one student wrote only this reason: "It is not your thoughts or ideas." Does this statement reveal an orientation to ownership rights or an orientation to the individual's responsibility to do his or her own work?

To get an estimate of how consistent and reliable my ratings were, I selected a random sample of 38 explanations (25% of the total) and asked a rater who was untrained and unfamiliar with the project to use a scoring guide to identify reasons and then assign them to categories. We were in exact agreement on 68% of the assignments. This level of agreement is not impressively high, but considering the problems posed in accurately identifying separate reasons, the ambiguities on some of the students' statements, and the fact that the rater had no training or practice with the coding scheme, the results are rather reassuring, suggesting that the coding process was neither arbitrary nor substantially unreliable.

Having classified all the responses, I examined how frequently each of the 6 primary kinds of reasons were mentioned and how many times each reason was identified as most important (when only one reason was listed, I considered it first in importance).

Rating explanations. The second section of the questionnaire provided students with 5 explanations of why students should avoid plagiarism, and asked them to rate each explanation using a 5-point scale to indicate "how closely it comes to expressing your own view of why students shouldn't plagiarize" (5=expresses my views very well, 4=expresses my views fairly well, 3 = expresses my views to some extent, 2=expresses my views only slightly, and 1=does not express my views). My aim in this part of the questionnaire was simply to obtain supplementary information about students' conceptions of plagiarism. The students' own explanations, in their own words, constituted the primary data for the study, but I also wanted to get students' responses to several different kinds of explanations for why it is wrong to plagiarize.

Each of the 5 explanations was designed to reflect a particular orientation that a person could adopt toward plagiarism: Self Respect, Fairness, Consequences for the Academic Community, Obedience to Rules, and Teacher-Student Relationship. In choosing these orientations I was guided by work in moral-development theory, particularly by Kohlberg's (1976, p. 40) notion of four "moral orientations" that focus on "one of four universal elements in any social situation." Thus my first explanation (Self-Respect) was modeled on Kohlberg's orientation to "ideal self," or one's image of oneself as a person of conscience and virtue; the second explanation (Fairness) was based on Kohlberg's orientation to "justice or fairness"; the third (Consequences for the Academic Community) drew on Kohlberg's orientation to "utility consequences", especially the sense of bad consequences for the college community; and the fourth (Obedience to Rules) expressed a view consistent with Kohlberg's orientation to "normative order", or an ethic based on prescribed rules. For my fifth explanation (Teacher-Student Relationship) I was influenced by Gilligan's (1977) arguments concerning a contextual and relational ethic based on respect and care for other persons—an orientation that, according to Gilligan, is particularly salient for women. Thus I wrote 5 explanations of plagiarism that were intended to reflect 5 different moral orientations, attempting to keep the explanations parallel in form and equal in length (all are about 65 words long).

The first explanation expressed an orientation toward Self Respect, the idea that a person shouldn't plagiarize because of the consequences for one's self-esteem.

(A) College students owe it to themselves to try always to act in a way that they can feel proud about. Plagiarizing, however, is nothing to feel proud of because it is an admission of carelessness, laziness, or (most seriously of all) dishonesty. Plagiarizing a paper ultimately diminishes one's own sense of integrity, honor, and self-esteem. If you want to keep your self-respect, don't plagiarize.

The second explanation focused on the concept of Fairness to the other students in the class.

(B) It is simply not fair when students get credit for work they didn't do themselves. By copying, the plagiarist is likely to produce a paper that makes other students' work look weak by comparison. Thus the plagiarist cheats those students in the class who are attempting, on their own, to do their best work. If you want to be fair to other students, don't plagiarize.

The third explanation reflected an orientation to the Consequences for the Academic Community if plagiarism were to be tolerated.

(C) When students go to college they join a community whose members value original thinking and believe that new ideas flourish only in an atmosphere of integrity and trust. Plagiarism violates this atmosphere, thereby destroying the conditions that are necessary for independent thinking and original research, If you want to preserve the university as a place where students and scholars can work productively, don't plagiarize.

The fourth explanation entailed the idea of Obedience to Rules, motivated by a desire to avoid the penalties for disobedience.

(D) All universities have strict rules against cheating. An act of plagiarism is an offense against these rules, and as such it merits penalties, some of them rather severe (including expulsion). Students have to learn to obey the rules of the institution, and if they get caught plagiarizing they should expect to pay the price. If you want to avoid failure or expulsion, don' t plagiarize.

Finally, the fifth explanation presented plagiarism as a violation of the ideal Teacher-Student Relationship.

(E) Most college teachers care a great deal about students and work hard to help them learn. These teachers expect their students to be equally caring and hard-working. It is therefore quite insulting and upsetting when a student acts deceitfully and plagiarizes a paper. Plagiarism violates a teacher's trust in students. If you respect your teachers and want them to respect you, don't plagiarize.

In a small pilot study, I found that students tended to give high ratings (4 or 5) to any explanations they felt were reasonable, sometimes resulting in identical ratings for all the explanations. Since I wanted to focus on differences in students' reactions to various kinds of explanations, I tried, in the directions, to encourage them to express distinctions in their responses. Thus the directions stated, "You may find that you agree with several (perhaps even all) of these explanations. But please try to differentiate between those explanations that express your own views quite well and those that express your views only slightly (even though you might agree with them)." In addition, I asked students to rank the 5 explanations from the one that best expressed their own view to the one that least expressed it. In my analyses, I focused only on the students' top-ranked explanation, the one they chose as best expressing their own view of plagiarism.

Rating statements about plagiarism. In the third part of the questionnaire, students were asked to use a 5-point rating scale (5=strongly agree, 4=agree to some extent, 3=neutral or undecided, 2=disagree to some extent, and 1=strongly disagree) to rate 8 statements about plagiarism:

(A) I would be angry and feel it was unfair if I discovered that another student in the class had plagiarized a paper.
(B) I don't care if other students want to plagiarize; it's their business, not mine.
(C) I don't think plagiarism is right, but there are still some situations in which a student might be forced to plagiarize in order to get a decent grade in a course.
(D) If I knew that another student in the class was planning to plagiarize a paper, I'd try to persuade him or her not to plagiarize.
(E) If I discovered that a student had plagiarized, I'd try to persuade him or her to confess.
(F) If I discovered that a student had plagiarized, I'd report him or her to the instructor.
(G) Plagiarism is always wrong, regardless of circumstances.
(H) If a student in this class got caught plagiarizing a paper, he or she would deserve to fail the course.

These statements focus on three issues that I was interested in exploring: students' feeling about a situation in which other members of a class were plagiarizing (statements A, B, and H), students' propensity to take some personal action against plagiarists (statements D, E, and F), and students' judgments about whether plagiarism was situationally relative (statements C and G).

Results and discussion

Why is plagiarism wrong?

Students' responses to the question "Why is plagiarism wrong?" were classified according to 6 primary reasons (plus Miscellaneous and Unclassifiable). Table 1 shows the percentages of students that mentioned each of the 6 reasons (the section of the table labeled "frequency") and also how often each of these reasons was rated as the most important reason plagiarism was wrong (the section labeled "importance"). The table shows clearly that, in terms of both frequency and importance, three of the categories—Individual Responsibility, Fairness, and Ownership—account for a large percentage of the students' responses. (To simplify the discussion, I will focus on the results for "frequency", or the percentage of students that mentioned each reason.)

Almost half of the freshmen (47%) said that students have a responsibility not to plagiarize, either because plagiarism involves cheating oneself (usually out of learning or improving as a writer), or because it violates the duty to do one's own work (and thus to use one's own mind or creative capacity). Below are some typical responses.

Plagiarizing is only cheating yourself.
It is wrong because everyone should use their own imaginative resources to the fullest

potential. If you are relying on someone else for your thoughts then you are cheating yourself. It is wrong because it doesn't expand the mind of the person doing it. The reason for writing your own thoughts is to increase your writing ability. If someone writes someone else's thoughts or ideas they are not increasing their ability to write .

It is wrong because you are not using your own ideas and mind. Your own creativity is being deprived its fullest attention.

Table 1. Students' reasons that plagiarism is wrong

Category of Reasons	Frequency (Percent of Students Who Mentioned Each Reason)			Importance (Percent of Students Who Chose as Most Important)		
	Total (n=150)	Men (n=75)	Women (n=75)	Total (n=150)	Men (n=75)	Women (n=75)
Individual Responsibility	47	39	55	28	24	32
Ownership	36	39	33	25	25	24
Fairness	46	47	45	27	27	27
Honesty	11	11	12	07	08	05
Laziness	11	13	09	04	05	04
Crime and Punishment	07	09	04	01	01	00
Miscellaneous	17	12	21	06	04	08
Unclassifiable	11	16	07	02	05	00

Note: The figures in the columns labeled "Frequency" indicate the percentage of students who mentioned a reason in a particular category; these percentages sum to more than 100% because students could mention reasons from more than one category in their explanations. The figures in the column labeled "Importance" show what percentage of students indicated that a reason in a particular category was the sole or most important reason that plagiarism is wrong; since students could indicate only one reason as most important, these columns sum to 100%.

While statements of Individual Responsibility were mentioned by the largest number of students, nearly as many (46%) listed reasons that were classified as Fairness, a category that included statements about the just distribution of the "credit" due to an author. Two major concepts were included in these responses: that an injustice occurs when an author doesn't get the credit he or she deserves, and that an injustice occurs when a person gets undeserved credit by plagiarizing. These concepts are clear in the following examples.

It is wrong to plagiarize because one should always give credit where credit is due.

It is wrong for people to take credit for other people's work because the original writer put a lot of hard work in his or her piece of writing and they want and deserve the credit for it.

One is using another's ideas which is not fair to the one who originally created the idea. It just would not be fair.

Plagiarism is wrong because one should not take due credit on someone else's hard work.

Plagiarism is wrong because it is taking credit for something someone else should get credit for. Not only are you claiming the credit for yourself, you are denying the real owner the recognition.

More than a third (36%) of the students gave reasons that were classified as Ownership, because they focused on the idea that plagiarism involves the theft of someone else's property or possessions, a crime analogous to stealing a car or stereo. This approach to plagiarism is clear in the following examples.

Plagiarism is wrong because it is like "stealing" something from someone-something that is not rightfully yours.

It's wrong to plagiarize because that is stealing. It is stealing the hard work that another person had to do.

It is wrong to plagiarize because you are stealing the thoughts and conclusions of someone else. That person spent a great amount of time to form the ideas he has so therefore they are his.

Plagiarism is a form of stealing. If you take someone else's words it's just like taking something that belongs to them.

It is immoral because you are stealing. It is just like if you were to steal a book from a bookstore.

Students gave other reasons that plagiarism is wrong, but none was mentioned by large numbers of freshmen. Of the three remaining categories of reasons, perhaps the most important is Honesty. Statements in this category focus on the notion that plagiarism is wrong because it involves such acts as lying, deceit, or fraud. Some sample responses illustrate the kinds of statements included in this category.

It is wrong because it is dishonest.

The main reason plagiarizing is wrong is because you are taking someone else's work and claiming it as your own.

Plagiarizing is also lying; when you hand in someone else's work as your own, you are lying to your instructor.

Plagiarism is wrong because it is not your own work and you are lying if you say it is.

Because it is simply dishonest .

Laziness was another response that occurred infrequently in the students' explanations:

Plagiarism is just a cop out for one's dullness and laziness.

People who plagiarize aren't using their brain. They are just looking for a lazy way out.

Plagiarism is too easy and therefore wrong.

Plagiarism is simply the easy way out.

People also plagiarize when they are too lazy to take the time to sort out their own ideas and pick the most important to write about.

Finally, only a small number of students mentioned reasons that could be classified under Crime and Punishment. This category included any statements that referred to plagiarism as a crime, as a violation of a rule or law, or as an act that risked punishment for the offender. Statements classified as Crime and Punishment included the following:

> Plagiarism is a type of crime.
> Because it is against the law .
> It is also wrong because many authority figures tell us that it is wrong.
> I don't want to get caught and kicked out of school.
> It can get a person expelled, or cause him to fail a class.

The men and women in the study gave rather similar reasons that plagiarism is wrong, but there were a few gender-related differences in the frequency with which particular reasons were mentioned. The largest difference—and the only one to approach statistical significance—was in the percentage of women (55%) and men (39%) who mentioned reasons oriented toward Individual Responsibility.

Fisher's Exact Test (applied to a 2×2 contingency table with the number of women and men who did and did not mention Individual Responsibility) produced a z-score of 1.72, p=.07 (two-tailed test). It thus seems to be the case that the women in this study attached somewhat more importance to an ethic of Individual Responsibility—to issues of doing one's own work for one's own good—than did the men.

Rating explanations

Students also responded to 5 short explanations of why a person shouldn't plagiarize, both rating these explanations according to how well they expressed the students' own views and then ranking the explanations in the order in which they expressed the students' views of why a person shouldn't plagiarize. Table 2 shows the mean ratings of explanations and the percentage of students that ranked each explanation as first in importance.

A one-way within-subjects analysis of variance was performed to compare mean ratings for the 5 explanations. The observed F ratio was statistically significant, $F_{(4, 596)}=17.92$, p.<.0001. An HSD (Tukey's Honestly Significantly Different) test, alpha level .05, revealed that the mean rating for the Fairness explanation (4.17) was significantly higher than mean ratings for the other 4 explanations. The only other statistically significant differences were between mean ratings for Self-Respect (3.69) and Consequences for Academic Community (3.36), and between mean ratings for Teacher-Student Relationship (3.67) and Consequences for Academic Community(3.36). The strength of the relationship between type of explanation and students' ratings (of concordance with their own views) was .89, as indexed by eta squared.

Interpreting these results in the light of the percentage of students who ranked each explanation as first in importance, it seems clear that the majority of students preferred the explanation based on an orientation to Fairness: This explanation received a significantly higher mean rating than any other and it was ranked first in importance by 44% of the students. Next in importance to the students were explanations based on Self-Respect (ranked first by 23%)and Teacher-Student Relationship (ranked first by 13%), followed by explanations oriented to Obedience to Rules (11%) and Consequences for the Academic Community (9%).

Table 2. Ratings and ranking of explanations of plagiarism

Explanation Based on	Mean Ratings			Percent Ranking First		
	Total (n=150)	Men (n=75)	Women (n=75)	Total (n=150)	Men (n=75)	Women (n=75)
Self-Respect	3.69 (1.02)	3.52 (0.99)	3.85* (1.02)	23	23	24
Fairness	4.17 (0.99)	3.99 (1.06)	4.36* (0.88)	44	44	44
Consequences for Academic Community	3.36 (1.11)	3.25 (1.12)	3.47 (1. 11)	11	11	11
Obedience to Rules	3.51 (1.12)	3.47 (1.28)	3.56 (0.95)	09	12	06
Teacher-Student Relationship	3.67 (1. 14)	3.59 (1.21)	3.75 (1.07)	13	11	15

Note: Standard deviations printed in parentheses below means.
*Difference between mean ratings for men and women significant at $p<.05$.

Responses to the 5 explanations of plagiarism were, in general, rather similar for men and women. Although the women's mean ratings were significantly higher than the men's for Self-Respect($F[1,148]=4.11$, $p<.05$) and for Fairness ($F[1,148]=5.52$, $p<.05$), Table 2 shows that an identical percentage of men and women chose these two explanations as the statements that best expressed their own views of plagiarism, suggesting that men and women had fairly similar positions on the importance of these explanations.

Rating statements about plagiarism

In Section III of the questionnaire, I asked students to rate (in terms of strength of agreement) a series of 8 statements about plagiarism. The mean ratings for all students (and for men and women separately) are shown in Table 3.

Items A, B, and H all involve students' feelings about a situation in which other students are plagiarizing. The relatively high mean ratings on A and H, and the low rating on B, indicate that these students do care about plagiarism, that they are angry when it occurs, and that they believe plagiarists should be punished. Items D, E, and F all focus on the students' propensity to take some personal action against plagiarists. The ratings on these items suggest that the students are reluctant to take action when it involves reporting plagiarism to an authority, somewhat more willing to persuade a student to confess, and most willing to talk another student out of plagiarizing. Finally, items C and G involve the issue of whether plagiarism is always wrong. The students' high rating of item G and relatively low rating of item C indicate a tendency to reject statements reflecting a relativistic position on the morality of plagiarism.

These ratings of statements about plagiarism reveal rather consistent differences between men and women. First, the women in the study appear to be somewhat less relativistic in their view of plagiarism, because they agreed more strongly than the men with the statement that plagiarism is always wrong (item G) and gave a significantly lower rating to the statement that there are situations in which a student might be forced to plagiarize (item C). Second, the women expressed a stronger reaction to plagiarism, giving significantly higher mean ratings to the statement about feeling angry if another student plagiarized (item A) and to the statement that if a student got caught plagiarizing he or she would deserve to fail the course (item H). Women also gave a slightly lower rating to the statement that they didn't care if other students want to plagiarize (item B), although the difference between mean ratings for men and women on this item was not statistically significant. Finally, the women's ratings suggest that they are more likely than the men to consider taking some action against plagiarizing: The women gave a higher mean rating to the statement that they would try to persuade a student not to plagiarize (item D), a higher rating to the statement that they would try to persuade a plagiarist to confess (item E), and a slightly higher (although still quite low) rating to the statement that they would report a plagiarist to the instructor (item F). If these ratings are an accurate indication of moral attitudes, it's difficult to escape the conclusion that the women in this study are less sympathetic to plagiarism than are the men.

Table 3. Ratings of statements about plagiarism

Statement	Total (n=150)		Men (n=75)		Women (n=75)	
	M	SD	M	SD	M	SD
A. Angry	3.79	(1.02)	3.59	(1.13)	3.99*	(0.86)
B. Don't care	2.62	(1.22)	2.80	(1.29)	2.44	(1.13)
C. Situations forced to plagiarize	2.37	(1.27)	2.57	(1.34)	2.16*	(1.16)
D. Persuade another not to plagiarize	3.23	(1.08)	3.04	(1.18)	3.41*	(0.95)
E. Persuade another to confess	2.16	(1.04)	1.92	(1.08)	2.40**	(0.94)
F. Report student	1.78	(1.02)	1.65	(1.05)	1.91	(0.99)
G. Plagiarism always wrong	3.77	(1.22)	3.51	(1.31)	4.04**	(1.06)
H. Plagiarist should fail	3.11	(1.30)	2.88	(1.40)	3.33*	(1.14)

*Difference between mean ratings for men and women significant at $p < .05$; **difference between mean ratings for men and women significant at $p < .01$.

Summary and implications

My aim in this study was to investigate, by means of a questionnaire, how beginning college freshmen at a large, public university view plagiarism. One section of the questionnaire addressed students' attitudes toward plagiarism. From their responses to statements about plagiarism, it appears that these freshmen—especially the women— take plagiarism seriously: They tend to be concerned when it occurs, to condemn it as nearly always wrong, and to endorse punishment for offenders.

Other parts of the questionnaire explored the reasons college students use to explain why it is wrong to plagiarize. In the first section of the questionnaire students were instructed to write an explanation of why plagiarism is wrong, and then to identify and rank the reasons they had given. Since these explanations contain the student's own reasons, in their own words, I believe they provide the best evidence for how these freshmen view plagiarism. In the second section of the questionnaire, students indicated how well 5 explanations—each designed to reflect a different moral orientation— expressed their own views on plagiarism. Ideally, of course, the results from these two methods—students' own statements and their ratings of explanations—would complement and support one another. And, in part, they do. But it is also clear that the students' statements and the 5 explanations do not always correspond in a way that affords easy comparisons. For example, some explanations conflate several issues that were regarded as separate reasons in the students' statements (e.g., the explanation based on Self-Respect incorporates elements of dishonesty and laziness, as well as responsibility to oneself—elements that were coded as separate reasons in analyses of the students' own explanations of plagiarism).

Despite these difficulties, results from the students' statements as well as their ratings of the 5 explanations indicate that, for these college freshmen, plagiarism involves three major ethical issues: fairness, individual responsibility, and ownership. These issues dominate the students' explanations of why plagiarism is wrong, and they are also reflected in the students' responses to the explanations they were asked to rate.

Issues of fairness and individual responsibility seem to be most important to these students. In their own accounts, 46% of the students mentioned the idea that plagiarism is unfair to authors (and 27% identified this idea as their sole or primary reason that plagiarism is wrong). Moreover, in their responses to the five explanations, students gave their highest mean ratings to the passage that focused on being "fair to other students", and 44% of them ranked this explanations as the one that best expressed their own views. It seems clear, therefore, that the desire for a just and fair system of rewards—for authors and students alike—is a fundamental issue for these college freshmen. Plagiarism is wrong because it is unfair.

But plagiarism is also wrong because it violates students' individual responsibilities to do their own work and make the most of their educational opportunities. In their accounts of plagiarism, 47% of the students referred to such responsibilities as working creatively and independently, or trying to improve their writing through hard work and practice (28% identified these concepts as the sole or most important reasons that plagiarism was wrong). And in their responses to the five explanations, the students gave their second highest ratings to the passage that focused on keeping one's self-respect through fulfilling a student's responsibilities and acting honestly.

Finally, quite a few students (36%) mentioned concepts of ownership in their explanations, identifying "stealing" as the major moral issue involved in plagiarizing. Of the students in this study, 25% ranked concepts of ownership as the sole or most important reason that plagiarism is wrong.

Because this study was small in scale and exploratory in nature, it would be imprudent to generalize its findings too broadly. But the study does suggest two general implications for teaching students about plagiarism. On the one hand, the results of the study suggest that while not all college freshmen construe plagiarism in exactly the same way, many freshmen—certainly the majority in this study—explain it in terms of a small number of familiar ethical issues: fairness to authors and other students, the responsibility to learn through independent work, and respect for ownership rights. If that is the case, then as teachers we can begin our discussions of plagiarism with those issues that are familiar and salient for our students, taking account of their moral frames of reference when we ask them to examine the ethics of plagiarism. On the other hand, the study also reveals how infrequently certain moral principles—such as truthfulness, fidelity, and trust—occurred in the students' explanations. If our students do not use these concepts to think about plagiarism, perhaps we need to encourage them to explore new lines of moral reasoning, broadening and deepening their understanding of why it is wrong to plagiarize.

References

Baird, J. S. (1980). Current trends in college cheating. *Psychology in the Schools*, 17, 512–522.

Bjaaland, P. C., & Lederman, A. (1973). The detection of plagiarism. *Educational Forum*, 37, 201–206.

Carroll, J. A. (1982). Plagiarism: The unfun game. *English Journal*, 71, 92–94.

Daniels, E. F. (1960). The dishonest term paper. *College English*, 21, 403–405.

Dant, D. R. (1986). Plagiarism in high school: A survey. *English Journal*, 75, 81–84.

Drum, A. (1986). Responding to plagiarism. *College Composition and Communication*, 37, 241–243,

Gilligan, C. (1977). In a different voice: Women's conceptions of self and of morality. *Harvard Educational Review*, 47, 481–517.

Hawley, C. S. (1984). The thieves of academe: Plagiarism in the university system. *Improving College and University Teaching*, 32, 35–37.

Kohlberg, L. (1976). Moral stages and moralization: The cognitive-developmental approach. In T. Likona (ed.), *Moral development and behavior* (pp. 31–52). New York: Holt, Rinehart & Winston.

Martin, R. G. (1971). Plagiarism and originality: Some remedies. *English Journal*, 60, 621–625, 628.

Nuss, E. M. (1984). Academic integrity: Comparing faculty and student attitudes. *Improving College and University Teaching*, 32, 140–144.

Sauer, R. (1983). Coping with copiers. *English Journal*, 72, 50–52.

Schab, F. (1980). Cheating among college and non-college bound pupils, 1969–1979. *Clearing House*, 53, 379–380 .

Waltman, J. (1980). Plagiarism: (II) Preventing it in formal research papers. *ABCA Bulletin*, 43, 37–38.

Barry M. Kroll is Associate Professor of English at Indiana University (Bloomington), where he teaches undergraduate and graduate courses in composition and directs the writing center. His research has focused on developmental and psychological dimensions of writing. He is currently working on studies of college students intellectual and ethical orientations.

Dictionary Use in English Learning

Anticipating the Issue

Discuss your answers to the following questions.

1. The following table illustrates some possible ways of classifying dictionaries. One example has been given for each category. Discuss with your partners and give more examples. Add more classifications if they are not listed in the table.

Classification of Dictionaries

Criterion	Examples of Dictionaries
the number of language involved	monolingual dictionaries
the nature of entries	linguistic dictionaries
the prospective reader	native speakers
semantic focus	collation dictionaries
lexical items	dictionaries of idioms
size	abridged dictionaries
medium	paper dictionaries

2. What kind of dictionaries have you used?

3. Fill in the table below with the advantages and disadvantages of paper dictionaries and computer dictionaries.

	Advantages	Disadvantages
Paper Dictionaries	familiarity	large size
Computer Dictionaries	fast retrieval	computer-needed

4. What kind of dictionary do you think language learners should use: a monolingual dictionary or a bilingual one?

5. How often do you use a dictionary when reading a passage in another language? Do you think dictionary use will have a more positive effect on an individual's vocabulary learning?

Selections

Dictionary Use and Vocabulary Choices in L2 Writing

Dictionary Use and Vocabulary Choices in L2 Writing

Idoia Elola, Vanessa Rodriguez-Garcia, Katherine Winfrey

Texas Tech University, U. S. A.

idoia.elola@ttu.edu

vanessa.rodriguez-garcia@ttu.edu   katherine.m.winfrey@ttu.edu

*In second language (L2) writing research it is essential to focus on the learners' writing processes to understand their L2 vocabulary use; namely, limitations, choices, and misunderstandings. This article offers an overview of learners' Spanish-English online dictionary use in relation to L2 writing tasks, the strategies being used, and the limitations encountered while on task. The diverse data collection techniques—written texts, verbal **protocols** and interviews—provide a **holistic** view of students of Spanish as a foreign language in their online dictionary use, as well as information about the learners' reflections on their dictionary use. Results do not only indicate that learners use the dictionary to find a word they did not know, to check their spelling, or to **ascertain** the meaning of a word, but also to express themselves better or translate the complexity of their English thoughts into Spanish. However, the texts they produced result also from their limited ability in the*

*dictionary use and inability to transfer known strategies from their first language (L1) to their L2. Finally, certain **pedagogical** implications are discussed to help learners achieve a better command of the dictionary.*

Keywords: *online dictionary use, vocabulary learning strategies, vocabulary acquisition, dictionary strategies and second language writing.*

1. Introduction

The **burgeoning** use of online dictionaries reflects the worldwide population's need to access multiple **lexical** sources rapidly. Language learners, who are generally technologically well informed, are motivated to **tap into** these resources and take an active approach toward their learning. However, regardless of the accessibility of these online tools, most can probably recount anecdotes about learners' misuse of the dictionary, both in oral and written productions: '*Tomar un chaparrón*' instead of '*ducharse*' (to take a shower); '*yo cuelgo afuera con mis amigos*' instead of '*paso tiempo con mis amigos*' (I hang out with my friends); and '*fechar*' instead of '*salir con alguien*' (to date someone). Learners' inability to use this tool effectively stems from a lack of knowledge of how the L1 and L2 mental **lexicon** functions as well as a lack of familiarity with the dictionary itself.

At present, the majority of the research studies related to dictionary use have focused on its relationship to L2 reading, such as the use of bilingual or monolingual dictionaries, dictionary use versus glossaries, and the impact of dictionary use on the learners' reading processes. Although this body of research offers insights into learners' behavior in relation to dictionary use, it is also essential to observe students' ability to use the dictionary as a tool for written production and to teach them to use it more effectively. It is important, as Scholfield (1982) suggested, to view the use of a dictionary not as a straightforward technical and passive activity, but rather as a complex process of hypothesis testing that involves the active participation of the learner. Within the **realm** of L2 writing, this article explores issues of dictionary use in relation to foreign language (FL) writing, more specifically in terms of Spanish.

2. Literature review

Research in the field of vocabulary acquisition and learning has shown the advantage of equipping learners with specific strategies to enhance and further the learner's lexical acquisition process. Several **taxonomies** have included dictionary use as an important learning strategy (Oxford, 1990; Gu & Johnson, 1996; Schmitt, 1997; Nation, 2001). Gu and Johnson (1996) and Schmitt (1997) consider dictionary use as a **cognitive** strategy that occurs **in conjunction with** guessing and note-taking strategies. Similarly, Nation's division (2001) of strategies describes dictionary use as a source strategy that provides information about a specific item.

Furthermore, studies on the use of vocabulary strategies have revealed that active strategy users are more successful vocabulary learners than those learners with a poor knowledge of strategy use, emphasizing the need to provide learners with conscious strategies (Ellis, 1994; Sanaoui, 1995; Lawson & Hogben, 1996; Chamot, 2001; Fan, 2003; Gu, 2005; Macaro, 2005; Peters, 2007). Moreover, most studies conducted on the use of dictionaries as a vocabulary learning strategy conclude that dictionary use has a positive influence on the learner's acquisition process (Hulstijn, 1993; Luppescu & Day, 1993; Knight, 1994; Jones, 1995; Laufer & Hadar, 1997; Bruton & Broca, 1997, 2004; Laufer & Hill, 2000; Bruton, 2007). Primarily, research on dictionary use has focused on exploring the benefits of monolingual (Ard, 1982; Scholfield, 1982; Meara & English, 1987; Thompson, 1987; Hartmann, 1991; Summers, 1995) and/or bilingual dictionaries (Baxter, 1980; Laufer & Hadar, 1997; Asher, Chambers & Hall, 1999; Barnes, Hunt & Powell, 1999; Bishop, 1998, 2000; Tall & Hurnam, 2000). Studies have also discussed learners' intentions when consulting dictionaries, namely checking spelling, gender and word meaning (Bishop, 1998, 2000), or searching for additional grammatical, phonological and **pragmatic** information (Cano Ginés, 2004). However, researchers have also realized that the effectiveness of vocabulary learning strategies depends on the type of task, the learner's preferences, personal characteristics, and the learning context (Williams & Burdens, 1997; Cohen, 1998, 2001; Gu, 2003).

One limitation in the use of the dictionary stems from the learner's inability to separate lexical and **semantic** meanings. From a psychological perspective, as Vygotsky (1978) noted, the mind is related to the social context, and since language is related to the mind, language consequently depends on the social context. Vygotsky divides linguistic development into three stages: the object-regulation stage (learner's language ability is controlled by the object); the other-regulation stage (learner is influenced by others in making his/her linguistic choices); and the self-regulation stage (learners are able to control their own lexical choices). When applied to dictionary use and vocabulary choice, learners appear to follow the same stages of regulation; it is not until the self-regulation stage that they develop their semantic knowledge (Lantolf; Labarca, & den Tuinder, 1985; Jiang, 2004). Studies indicate that semantic development is a slow process in which L2 learners learn a word at the lexical level and then at the semantic level. Hence, L2 learners need to have an idea of the form and meaning of the word in their L1 in order to find its **equivalent** in their L2 in a dictionary. Thus, a learner's specific stage of development influences the types of strategies used when looking up words: at a lower level of development, a learner will only be able to apply a lexical strategy, whereas at a more advanced level, a learner will engage in semantic lookup strategies (Hartmann, 1983; Laufer & Hadar, 1997). Different stages of development also make certain grammatical categories more difficult to acquire, such as prose words, domain-specific words, and **inflectional** words (González,1999).

Apart from L2 proficiency limitations, certain learners are unable to perform a successful search due to their inability to use the dictionary correctly. Christianson (1997) indicates that successful FL dictionary users, regardless of their level of English proficiency, are able to employ more **sophisticated** lookup strategies. Dictionary users may benefit from using efficient dictionary strategies (Graves, 1987; Summers, 1988), attending to all of the information in an entry before making conclusions about the meaning of a word (Laufer & Hadar, 1997; Hunt & Beglar, 1998), working with activities in which vocabulary is practiced in various contexts (Schmitt, 1997), and from being instructed not to take the first word that appears in the entry in the dictionary, so as to reduce the notion of a one-to-one equivalency between their L1 and L2 (Barbe, 2001).

Finally, it is important to note that new technological and computer developments have **facilitated** learning with tools such as electronic and online dictionaries, online translators, and thesaurus features available in Microsoft Word. The advantages that these new technologies offer to learners, teachers and researchers include: electronic dictionaries with multimedia **annotations** (Chun & Plass, 1996; Hulstijn, Hollander, & Greidanus, 1996), computer logs, trackers of learner behavior and online vocabulary **glosses** (Gu, 2003), and interactivity, **hypertextuality**, quick access, and multimedia effects, as well as other extra features such as video, audio materials, **corpus** examples, interactive exercises, and games (Pérez Tortes & Sáinchez Ramos, 2003). Most studies about electronic dictionary use have offered similar conclusions to those of studies on traditional dictionaries (Aust, 1993; Knight, 1994; Segler, 2002; Hill & Laufer, 2003; Pérez Torres & Sánchez Ramos, 2003; Fan, 2003; Loucky, 2005; Brnton, 2007; Peters, 2007).

Nevertheless, within the realm of online dictionary research, this article intends to further investigate issues and concerns about learners' inability to use online dictionaries effectively, select the correct information about certain words and employ strategies to search successfully for the appropriate meaning of the word. Although the **overarching** aim was to understand how learners use online dictionaries for L2 writing purposes, this idea was further explored in the following questions:

1. In what instances do FL learners consult online dictionaries while writing in Spanish?

2. What kinds of lexical items are problematic for FL learners while using online dictionaries?

3. What strategies do FL learners employ in their search for the appropriate meaning of lexical items?

Furthermore, this article presents some pedagogical suggestions for online dictionary use that can be incorporated in L2 classrooms.

3. Methodology

Setting, participants and tasks

Two studies were conducted at a Southwestern university with undergraduate students ranging from 19- to 22-years-old, majoring in fields other than Spanish. The first study was conducted with six learners at the intermediate level who were revising, editing, and creating new texts. The learners' think-aloud protocols[1] (TA) were video recorded while they were working on a revision task. Then, the learner's stimulated-recall protocol (SR) was triggered by the video of his/her performing the revision of the essay. Finally, the researcher set interviews (I) with the learners to obtain further information not observed in the stimulated-recall protocol[2] (see Table 1). The second study, which involved a translation task (English to Spanish), consisted of four participants at varying levels: beginner (1), intermediate (2) and advanced (1). A software program known as Camtasia recorded the learners' translation work; this program can capture and record images from a learner's computer desktop. This allows the researcher to see what the learner worked on and the sources consulted. After completing the task, the researcher watched the recording with each learner, which triggered the learner's comments as part of a stimulated-recall protocol. The participant's responses were also recorded by the audio mode of the Camtasia program. The **triangulation** of the data provided a more holistic perspective of the learners' problems, their strategy use, and their success or lack thereof when working with online sources.

Table 1. Tasks and data collection techniques

Studies	Tasks	Data Collection Techniques
First study (N=6)	Revision and editing tasks: Learners revised an essay related to games of chance based on teacher feedback on content and form.	Revision of essay Think-aloud protocols Stimulated recall protocols Interviews
Second study (N=4)	Translation task: Learners translated a paragraph from English to Spanish.	Translated texts Stimulated recall protocols Post-test

4. Results

All of the collected data from both studies were analyzed in relation to learners' online dictionary use. The oral data from the think-aloud protocols, stimulated-recall protocols and interviews were transcribed and categorized. The translation tasks and essays were also categorized in the same manner. Once the results were gathered, they were grouped following the **parameters** set by the research questions. Although the tasks were different and **entail** different degrees of difficulty, the studies yielded identical results regarding dictionary use. Thus, the results of both studies will be presented indistinctively. The analyses of the data offered interesting insights into: (1) learners' uses of online sources, (2) learners' lexical difficulties and (3) learners' strategy usage.

4.1 Learners' uses of online dictionaries

From the information collected, six categories emerged. Each category illustrates the moments in which learners made use of the online dictionary: (1) correction of grammatical errors, (2) clarification of verb **conjugation**, (3) spell checking, (4) looking up unknown words, (5) verification of meaning, and (6) consideration of style.

Correction of grammatical errors: The learner's purpose was to revise the grammatical aspects of the word: "I looked at words to help me with my grammar errors, to help me clarify what was wrong" (I). In the following excerpt the learner had an idea that the word for 'these' was *estos* but decided to consult the dictionary to reinforce his intuition. He realized that 'benefits' (*beneficios*) was a **masculine** word in Spanish and therefore chose 'estos' to agree both in gender and number.

> The casinos bring benefits to the state but these benefits estos, estos? [looks it up] estos/as, masculine or feminine? Beneficios, masculine, then **estos beneficios**[3], they are...(TA)

Clarification of verb conjugation: Although bilingual dictionaries do not provide verb conjugations in conjunction with the word entry, certain online dictionaries such as www.wordreference.com provide a link to a verb conjugator. One learner stated that she used the link within the dictionary to find the different verb conjugations for the verb '*poder*' (to be able to).

Spell checking: In some instances, online dictionaries were used to verify spelling when doubts surfaced: "Oh, yeah, I looked at 'responsible' to see how to spell it, which I didn't do correctly" (I).

Unknown words: A common use of the online resources was to look up words to find their equivalents in Spanish: "How do you say 'to become'? [Looks it up in the translator] OK, 'become'. I don't know. '*Hacerse*' (TA). Furthermore, one learner highlighted that an advantage of the online dictionary is that "[it] has the English to Spanish and Spanish to

English right on the side, below, and you can easily go back and forth" (SR).

Verification of meaning: The learners frequently showed signs of prior knowledge of a specific word, but decided to look it up to confirm its meaning: "Double check 'pay', 'pagar' [dictionary online]. It may not be right, 'pagar'. OK, it's right" (TA).

Style considerations: Certain learners were not only interested in achieving a more precise translation of their thought or idea from the L1 to the L2, but also in **refining** the writing style: "I was trying to find another word besides *destruir* since I had used it like 20 times in my paper" (I).

4.2 Problematic lexical items

Data analyses show that problematic lexical items can be classified into four main categories: abstract and domain-specific words, collocations and fixed expressions, lexical items of multiple grammatical categories, and discourse markers (see Table 2).

The difficulty when dealing with problematic lexical items depended on the learners' proficiency levels: learners at the beginner and intermediate-low stages relied on lexical lookup strategies and had more difficulty when consulting the dictionary for abstract and multi-word expressions. In contrast, learners in the intermediate-mid and advanced levels were able to apply semantic lookup strategies and were more successful when confronting the same items.

Abstract and domain-specific words: Slight variations of meaning caused by the abstract nature of an item or by the specificity of its use **confounded** the choice between various **denotations** of the same lexical item. In the case of 'widowhood', which is translated as '*viudez*' or '*viudedad*' in the bilingual dictionary, learners were unable to distinguish the difference between the two, basing their choice on intuition or previous knowledge: "I chose '*viudedad*' [because] I know similar words like '*edad*'... it is kind of familiar" (SR).

Similarly, lack of familiarity with a specific domain resulted in learners' random word selection: "How do you say 'county'? OK, [translator] '*provincial*', '*municipio*', '*comarca*', I'll use '*comarca*'" (TA).

Table 2. Categories of problematic lexical items

	Lexical Items of the Greatest Difficulty
Abstract & domain-specific words	wicker, fan, widowhood, flashes, turquoise, jumpsuits, squabbles, stools, nursemaids, gambling, thrill, county, finance
Collocations & fixed expressions	**flipping** open, **snapping** shut, far end, call away, make money
Lexical items of multiple grammatical categories	lounge, dress, change, flashes, reach, track, chance
Discourse markers	therefore, while, who, although, furthermore, in addition

Collocations and fixed expressions: The semantic relationships between the elements of a collocation (e.g., an old flame) or a fixed expression (e.g., the spitting image) cannot be fully transmitted into the L2 with a literal translation. These expressions may have a corresponding semantic unit in the target language, but learners are not able to identify it:

> [Student is searching for 'to call away'] I knew 'llamar' is to 'call'...and I knew 'afuera'...so I was OK...Oh, yeah, I will do that. (SR)

Lexical items of multiple grammatical categories: Items that fulfill different grammatical categories—noun, verb, adjectiv—in the L1 without a spelling change tend to confuse learners when looking up the corresponding entry in the L2. In the case of 'lounge', which in English can be both a noun and a verb, a learner recognized that: "I looked it up as a noun, and was given the option *'sala'*, [but] it was supposed to be a verb, ...so I kind of had to redo that one" (SR). Similarly, another subject was also confused about the word 'chance':

> I want to say something about winning, have a chance of winning. [Writes] **Todas las personas tienen** chance? I'll look that up. [Translator] **'Oportnnidad.'** Just for a quick reference, I'm going to look up the word 'azar', because I thought that meant 'chance' but it may not be the 'chance' that I want. (TA)

Discourse markers: Discourse markers—linking elements in a sentence or paragraphs in a discourse—are easily forgotten and confused due to their limited use and limited function.

> I always like to use transition words when I'm writing, but I don't know what they are by heart, or, from memory, so I have to look up in my dictionary. So [looking in dictionary] 'therefore' is 'por lo tanto'. Um, I hope I can remember that, [writes] **por lo tanto**. (TA)
> I'm going to go to the Spanish dictionary online, and look at 'although' because this is one of the words that i always get confused. 'Although' and 'furthermore', is 'además' or 'aunque'. And it's 'aunque'. (TA)

4.3 Learners' strategy use

Learners' vocabulary search in online sources is normally assessed by its outcome; that is, whether they have successfully found or chosen the right word. In looking at the final product, however, teachers do not grasp the problems learners encounter, attributing their failure to linguistic limitations. Observing learners' dictionary use through verbal protocols and interviews, two types of strategies emerged: a) strategies related to vocabulary choice; and b) strategies related to dictionary use. Learners' individual stage of development and their familiarity with and knowledge of the dictionary influenced the type of lookup strategies learners used. Learners at the beginner and intermediate-low levels relied on lexical lookup strategies focusing on the form; in higher levels, they applied semantic lookup strategies considering the context of a word. Similarly, learners with a higher knowledge of dictionary features were more successful when employing lexical or semantic lookup strategies.

Strategies related to vocabulary choice

As in L2 vocabulary acquisition, there are two dimensions that need to be considered: the form of a lexical entry in the mental lexicon and its context. In other words, learners display two strategies when choosing vocabulary by focusing on lexical form and/or the semantic value of the words.

A number of learners only paid attention to the lexical form without making a connection to the semantic value of the word, as evidenced when learners were working with collocations (e.g., flipping open). They looked up the words in the collocation as if they were separate entities, without understanding they needed to search for the combination of the words to obtain its equivalent in the L2. This is seen in the incorrect literal translation of 'flipping open and snapping shut' to *'voltean abierto y se rompen cerrado'*, instead of the appropriate translation of the text, *"abrian y cerraban"*. Other learners showed the capacity to move beyond the lexical form of the word, considering the context in which the word appeared: "I didn't know how to say 'flipping open,' so I just decided to say 'they open and close their fans'" (SR). However, in the case of single, **monosemic** (e.g., red/*rojo*) words, attention to lexical form resulted in a successful search.

Strategies related to dictionary use

Apart from vocabulary choice, learners displayed other strategies that pertained to the use of the online resources. Data analyses revealed the following dictionary strategies.

Second Word Strategy: Researchers identified that by examining multi-word lexical items, learners not only focused on the first content (i.e., communicative value) word, but relied on the second or third word to get the meaning of an expression. During a writing revision, a learner reflected on why the expression 'to make money' was not accepted as *'hacer dinero'* and decided to check the second word 'money' to make a more appropriate choice.

> As a result, government makes a lot of money because casinos make money. Ok, to 'make' is 'hacer'. I just don't understand [the teacher's comment]. Government makes money, um. Ok, I'm going to look up 'hacer' in my dictionary. [reads] *'Fabricar' 'producir'*, *'to make'*, *'to construct'*, *'to build'*, ok, *'to make him leave'*, *'to have something done'*, *'hacer algo'*, *'hacer que otro haga.'* What? *'To move'?* No, *'hacerse de'*, is that what I need to use? I'm going to go to freetranslation.com, which I feel bad, just to see if I can

go anywhere here. English to Spanish and then I'm going to write [writes] the government makes a lot of money because the casinos make a lot of money. Hit translations. [reads] *El gobierno hace dinero porque los casinos hacen dinero*. That's exactly what I wrote [laughs].

...I'm going to go back to 'to make' [looking it up 'money']. It can also be 'ganar' money, so I'm going to change 'hacer' to 'ganar', so that's what I'm going to do. (TA)

Online Translator Strategy: Free online translators became a tool to search for a combination of words, sentences, or parts of a text. Learners would type their search with the purpose of obtaining feedback on their performance in the L2 or an immediate translation of their words in the L1.

I usually write it first and do the best I can...and then, I put it into a translator to see if it understands what I've written...I do that at the end too ... and I use freetranslation.com for my accents. (SR)

Category Strategy: Familiarity with dictionary abbreviations and structure facilitated decisions about vocabulary choices. Knowing word categories helped a learner find the right L2 word, as in the case of 'entertaining,' which may be an adjective or a gerund in Spanish:

[Writes] it's true, **es verdad** that los casinos and juegos de azar son muy divertidos [sighs] are very fun, and entretenimiento, entre...Let's see 'entertainment'. The games are fun and entertaining, [looks it up] OK, [sighs] 'entertaining', OK, 'entreteniendo' but, OK, casinos and games of chance are very fun and entertaining [...] Synonyms? OK, 'entretenido'. (TA)

Context-based Strategy: Learners with developed or sophisticated dictionary-use skills paid attention to the examples provided for a particular word. These examples facilitated the recognition of the appropriate lexical item :

Some people are not able to control their gambling habits. Maybe their habits of gambling? Yeah, I'm going to look up 'habits' because I do not know how that is in Spanish. 'Costumbres'? Oh, 'costumbres', 'hábito' 'tener la costumbre de.' I'm going to use 'hábito', to be the habit of. That sounds better than 'costumbre' because it's not. Ok, did I look this up right'? Because religion is 'hábit' so I'm going to use 'costumbres.' (TA)

Familiarity Strategy: A number of students were influenced by the familiarity of the form (e.g., **cognates**), or by the ending of the word when it reminded them of other words that share similar endings: "I liked '*ventilador*' [for 'fan']...like ventilation is close to a cognate" (SR). Another student also reported:

Usually when I look up a word in my dictionary, I read the first one to see if it sounds familiar to me. Because if it sounds familiar then it's more likely that I'd use it. (I)

5. Discussion

The results of both studies support the notion that the use of online dictionaries has a positive effect when making vocabulary choices in L2 writing, since learners were more successful in their choices if they consulted the dictionary (Hulstijn, 1993; Knight, 1994; Hill & Laufer, 2003; Loucky, 2005; Brnton, 2007; Peters, 2007). The researchers also observed learners' tendency to take advantage of online dictionary features such as inter-activity and quick access (Pérez Torres & Sánchez Ramos, 2003), and hypertextuality in the form of links to online translators and verb conjugators (Chun & Plass, 1996; Hulstijn, Hollander, & Creidanus, 1996; Pérez Torres & Sánchez Ramos, 2003). A more extensive examination of the results led to a greater understanding of the three questions that framed both studies: (1) In what instances do FL learners consult online dictionaries while writing in Spanish? (2) What kinds of lexical items are problematic for FL learners while using online dictionaries? (3) What strategies do FL learners employ in their search for the appropriate meaning of lexical items?

First, the insight gained from the writing tasks and follow-up procedures **corroborates** the observations of learners' dictionary use suggested by Bishop (1998, 2000) with respect to L2 reading, and Cano Ginés (2004) with respect to monolingual dictionaries for FL learners. That is, learners did not employ the online dictionary for the sole purpose of finding the meaning of a concrete word, but instead referred to the dictionary with diverse intentions: (1) correction of grammatical errors, (2) clarification of verb conjugation, (3) spell checking, (4) looking up unknown words and (5) verification of meaning. In addition, learners in the present studies relied on the online dictionary when considering issues of precision and style in their L2 writing.

Second, our FL learners displayed diverse stages of regulation (Vygotsky, 1978) while writing in their L2. The application of lexical and semantic lookup strategies, therefore, seemed to depend on their proficiency level: learners in the self-regulation stage exhibited a greater ability to use both strategies. The learners' choice of strategies and ability to use them were clearly observed when the learners were coping with lexical items that presented greater difficulty, such as collocations and fixed expressions, and lexical items of multiple grammatical categories (González, 1999). Hence, the general trend among the Spanish beginners and lower-intermediate learners confirmed their tendency to look more frequently at the lexical rather than the semantic level of the word. However, as Lantolf; Labarca and den Tuinder (1985) and Jiang (2004) have suggested, learners with a higher-intermediate and advanced proficiency level engaged in semantic lookup strategies when challenged by more complex L2 lexical items.

Finally, this article also aimed at exploring the strategies that FL learners employ in their search for the appropriate meaning of lexical items. The results agreed with previous research (Oxford, 1990; Gu & Johnson, 1996; Schmitt, 1997; Nation, 2001), which found that using a dictionary is an effective learning strategy, since learners who did so were more successful using appropriate vocabulary in their L2 writing assignments. However, a need to further investigate the particular dictionary strategies learners used in these assignments led the researchers to identify five main strategies, some of which support the findings in previous studies: (1) *second word strategy*, learners relied on the content word of multi-word expressions (Christianson, 1997; Barbe, 2001); (2) *online translator strategy*, learners used free online translators to search for word combinations; (3) *category strategy*, familiarity and knowledge of the dictionary facilitated vocabulary selection; (4) *context-based strategy*, learners paid attention to contextualized examples (Laufer & Hadar, 1997; Hunt & Beglar, 1998); and (5) *familiarity strategy*, word selection was based on familiarity with known words in the L1 and L2. Nevertheless, learners often failed to use lookup strategies effectively. Therefore, teaching learners specific dictionary use strategies would not only improve their ability to complete writing tasks, but also **foster** their vocabulary acquisition processes.

6. Pedagogical implications

Understanding the difficulties that learners confront in their use of online dictionaries informs teachers of ways to modify their approach to teaching L2 writing. The teachers should focus on raising learners' awareness of the complex nature of the L2 lexicon (i.e., the form as well as semantic knowledge of a word) and helping learners familiarize themselves with online reliable sources. Teachers, therefore, need to develop activities that target learners' problematic areas and that guide them to (1) discover the semantic layers of a word, (2) understand the notion of collocations and fixed expressions, (3) identify word categories, (4) increase knowledge of dictionary features and (5) select appropriate lookup strategies. Online sources, then, become a resource tool where the main purpose can be "to prevent or at least reduce communication conflicts which may arise from lexical deficit" (Hartmann, 1987, p. 21). Following Barbe's (2001) suggestions for traditional dictionaries and Pérez Torres and Sánchez Ramos's recommendations for electronic dictionaries, the researchers designed various sample activities to achieve the **aforementioned** objectives:

Activity 1: Exploring abbreviations

<u>Objective</u>: To familiarize students with commonly used abbreviations in an online dictionary.

Instructions: Students access an online dictionary and search for a specific entry (i.e. echar). In groups, students analyze and comment on the abbreviations used. Then, they make a list of common abbreviations and provide their meaning and an example.

Activity 2: One word, how many categories?

Objective: To help students distinguish different parts of speech and identify items that may fulfill various categories.

Instructions: First, students are given a list of sentences and asked to distinguish every part of speech. Then, they search for the same words in the sentences and check whether these words can fulfill different categories.

    e.g. Happy people like to whistle while they work.
        a. Happy (adjective), people (noun), like (verb), to(preposition), whistle (verb), while
           (conjunction),they (pronoun), work (verb)
        b. like (verb/preposition), whistle (verb/noun), work(verb/noun)

Activity 3: Idiomatic equivalents

Objectives: To help students understand how to translate and search for specific idioms or fixed expressions by using the information that dictionaries provide with respect to word combinations.

Instructions: Students access an online dictionary and work to translate several sentences which contain idiomatic and/or fixed expressions. After the activity, class discussion focuses on (1) how idioms can be correctly identified in each sentence; (2) where idioms appear in the online dictionary; and (3) which option provides a closer equivalent in the L2.

    e.g. My girlfriend <u>drives me up</u> the wall.
        <u>In the twinkling of an eye</u>, he disappeared.
        <u>Look out</u> the window! It's <u>raining cats and dogs</u>.

7. Conclusion

We hope that the present article, together with the previous studies on dictionary use, will become a valuable contribution to future research; more specifically, to research regarding web tools that can foster learners' L2 vocabulary acquisition. The aim of our contribution was to observe the extent to which learners are able to use online dictionaries for L2 writing purposes. The overall picture emerging from the data illustrates that our findings corroborate those of dictionary use in L2 reading practices. The varied data collection techniques (i.e., verbal protocols and interviews) and the use of the Camtasia software provided information that was not based only on the text

produced, but also on the processes observed and reflections made by the learners when on task.

In addition, targeting translation and revision tasks facilitated the identification of the situations that led learners to look up words, the types of lexical items that are problematic (especially for beginners and intermediate-low proficiency level learners) and the strategies learners utilize to solve a problem. Although the results cannot be generalized due to the small number of participants in both studies, they support other studies' findings on the use of dictionaries in L2 reading tasks as a cognitive strategy. However, it is essential to point out that using only two types of writing tasks is also a limitation; thus, future studies need to examine more closely the relationship between vocabulary learning strategies such as online dictionary use and L2 vocabulary acquisition during L2 writing tasks. The use of pre- and post-tests will enable researchers to measure whether any vocabulary gain has taken place during the experiment.

While the overall results are encouraging, we see the need for language instructors to instruct L2 learners explicitly in the effective use and selection of reliable web sources through the development of activities **tailored** to learners' needs. It is through this teaching approach that learners will fully benefit from these online resources and become more independent in their own learning. In sum, this article has provided three types of taxonomies: uses, difficulties and strategies regarding online dictionaries for L2 writing purposes. Although these findings are limited by the small-scale nature of the studies, they are a step toward understanding L2 vocabulary acquisition processes, the mapping of L2 vocabulary learning strategies and the inclusion of online resources in the classroom.

Notes

[1]Think-aloud protocol: a verbal protocol that takes place while the participant is performing a task; that is, the participant talks aloud while completing a task.

[2]Stimulated-recall protocol: a verbal protocol that is prompted by a stimulus such as viewing a video of the participant's performance of the task or an essay written by the participant.

[3]In the think-aloud protocols, bold text means that the learner wrote these words in the document; italics means that the learner was reading the document or the teacher's comments; and normal font means that the learner was speaking aloud while he/she was thinking.

References

Ard, J. (1982). The use of bilingual dictionaries by ESL students while writing. *ITL Review of Applied Linguistics, 58*, 1–27.

Asher, C., Chambers, G., & Hall, K. (1999). Dictionary use in MLF examinations in the GCSE: How schools are meeting the challenge. *Language Learning Journal, 19*, 28–32.

Aust, R., Kelley, M. J., & Roby, W. (1993). The use of hyper-reference and conventional dictionaries. *Educational Technology Research & Development, 41*, 63–73.

Barbe, K. (2001). Learning to use bilingual dictionaries successfully. *Teaching German, 34*, 66–75.

Barnes, A., Hunt, M., & Powell, B. (1999). Dictionary use in the teaching and examining of MLFs at GCSE. *Language Learning Journal, 19*, 19–27.

Baxter, J. (1980). The dictionary and vocabulary behavior: A single word or a handful? *TESOL Quarterly, 14*, 325–336.

Bishop, G. (1998). Research into the use being made of bilingual dictionaries by language learners. *Language Learning Journal, 18*, 3–8.

Bishop, G. (2000). Dictionaries, examinations, and stress. *Language Learning Journal, 21*, 57–65.

Bruton, A. (2007). Vocabulary learning from dictionary referencing and language feedback in EFL translational writing. *Language Teaching Research, 11*, 413–431.

Bruton, A., & Broca, A. (1997). Dictionary use and feedback in composition writing, and learning. In J. Field, A. Graham, E. Griffiths, and K. Head (eds.), *Teachers Develop Teachers' Research II* (pp. 194–207). Whitstable: IATEFL.

Bruton, A., & Broca, A. (2004). Acquiring and using dictionaries in state secondary schools. *English Teaching Professional, 31*, 16–17.

Cano Ginés, A. (2004). El tratamiento del léxico en los diccionarios de ELE. *Monográfico: la enseñanza de léxico en español como segunda lengua/lengua extranjera, 56*, 69–97.

Chamot, A. U. (2001). The role of learning strategies in second language acquisition. In M. P. Breen (ed.), *Learner Contributions to Language Learning* (pp. 24–44). Essex: Pearson Education.

Chun, D. M., & Plass. J. L. (1996). Effects of multimedia annotations on vocabulary acquisition. *Modern Language Journal, 80*, 183–212.

Cohen, A. D. (1998). *Strategies in learning and using a second language.* London: Longman.

Cohen, A. D. (2001). *The learner's side of foreign language learning: Where do styles, strategies, and tasks meet?* Unpublished manuscript, University of Minnesota.

Christianson, K. (1997). Dictionary use by EFL writers: What really happens. *Journal of Second Language Writing, 6*, 23-43.

Ellis, R. (1994). *The study of second language acquisition.* Oxford: Oxford University Press.

Fan, M. Y. (2003). Frequency of use, perceived usefulness, and actual usefulness of second language vocabulary strategies: A study of Hong Kong learners. *Modern Language Journal, 87*, 222–241.

González, O. (1999). Building vocabulary: Dictionary consultation and the ESL student. *Journal of Adolescent and Adult Literacy, 43*, 264–270.

Graves, M. (1987). The roles of instruction in fostering vocabulary development. In M. G. McKeown & M. E. Curtis (eds.), *The Nature of Vocabulary Acquisition* (pp.167–184). Hillsdale: Lawrence Erlbaum.

Gu, P. Y. (2003). Vocabulary learning in a second language: Person, task, context and strategies. *TESLEJ, 7*. Retrieved December 20, 2005, from http://tesl-ej.org/ej26/a4.html.

Gu, P. Y. (2005). Learning strategies: Prototypical core and dimensions of variation. Retrieved December 12, 2005, from http://www.crie..org.nz/research_aper/Peter_Gu.pdf.

Gu, P. Y., & Johnson, R. K. (1996). Vocabulary learning strategies and language learning outcomes. *Language Learning, 46*, 643–679.

Hartmann, R. R. K. (1983). *Lexicography: Principles and practice.* London: Academic Press.

Hartmann, R. R. K. (1987). Four perspectives on dictionary use: A critical review of research methods. In A. Cowie (ed.), *The Dictionary and the Language Learner* (pp. 11–28). Tubingen: Max Niemeyer Verlag.

Hartmann, R. R. K. (1991). What's the use of learners' dictionaries? *Institute of Language in Education Journal, 8*, 73–83.

Hill, M., & Laufer, B. (2003). Type of task, time-on-task, and electronic dictionaries in incidental vocabulary acquisition. *IRAL, 41*, 87–106.

Hulstijn, J. H. (1993). When do foreign-language readers look up the meaning of unfamiliar words? The influence of task and learner variables. *The Modern Language Journal, 77*, 139–147.

Hulstijn, J. H., Hollander, M., & Greidanus, T. (1996). Incidental vocabulary learning by advanced foreign language students: The influence of marginal glosses, dictionary use, and reoccurrence of unknown words. *The Modern Language Journal, 80*, 327–339.

Hunt, A., & Beglar, D. (1998). Current research and practice in teaching vocabulary. Retrieved December 20, 2005, from http://www.jalt- publications.org/tlt/files/98/jan/hunt.html

Jiang, N. (2004). Semantic transfer and development in adult L2 vocabulary acquisition. In P. Bogaards & B. Laufer (eds.), *Vocabulary in a Second Language* (pp. 101–26). Amsterdam: John Benjamins, B. V.

Jones, F. R. (1995). Learning an alien lexicon: A teach-yourself case study. *Second Language Research 11*, 95–111.

Knight, S. (1994). Dictionary use while reading: The effects on comprehension and vocabulary acquisition for students of different verbal abilities. *The Modern Language Journal, 78*, 285–299.

Lantolf, J. P., Labarca, A. & den Tuinder, J. (1985). Strategies for accessing bilingual dictionaries: A question of regulation. *Hispania, 68*, 858–864.

Laufer, B., & Hadar, L. (1997). Assessing the effectiveness of monolingual, bilingual, and 'bilingualised' dictionaries in the comprehension and production of new words. *The Modern Language Journal, 81*, 189–196.

Laufer, B., & Hill, M. (2000). What lexical information do L2 learners select in a CALL dictionary and how does it affect word retention? *Language Learning & Technology, 3*, 58–76.

Lawson, M. J., & Hogben, D. (1996). The vocabulary-learning strategies of foreign-language students. *Language Learning, 46*, 101–135.

Loucky, J. P. (2005). Combining the benefits of electronic and online dictionaries with CALL web sites to produce effective and enjoyable vocabulary and language learning lessons. *Computer Assisted Language Learning, 18*, 389–416.

Luppescu, S., & Day, R. R. (1993). Reading, dictionaries, and vocabulary learning. *Language Learning, 43*, 263–287.

Macaro, E. (2005). Fourteen features of a language learner strategy. Retrieved May 12, 2005, from http://www.crie.org.nz/research_paper/1Ernesto_Macaro_WP4.pdf

Meara, P., & English, F. (1987). *Lexical errors and learners' dictionaries*. London: Birkbeck College.

Nation, P. (2001). *Learning vocabulary in another language*. Cambridge: Cambridge University Press.

Oxford, R. L. (1990). *Language learning strategies: What every teacher should know*. Boston: Newbury House.

Pérez Torres, I., & Sánchez Ramos, M. M. (2003). Fostering vocabulary acquisition through self-learning tools and electronic dictionaries. *The GRETA Magazine, 10*, 41–49.

Peters, E. (2007). Manipulating L2 learners' online dictionary use and its effect on L2 word retention.

Language Learning & Technology, 11, 36–58.

Sanaoui, R. (1995). Adult learner's approaches learning vocabulary in second languages. *The Modern Language Journal, 79*, 15–28.

Schmitt, N. (1997). Vocabulary learning strategies. In N. Schmitt & M. McCarthy (eds.), *Vocabulary: description, acquisition and pedagogy* (pp. 199–228). Cambridge: Cambridge University Press.

Scholfield, P. (1982). Using the English dictionary for comprehension. *TESOL Quarterly, 16*, 185–194.

Segler, T. M., Pain, H., & Sorace, A. (2002). Second language vocabulary acquisition and learning strategies in ICALL environments. *Computer Assisted Language Learning, 15*, 409–422.

Summers, D. (1988). The role of dictionaries in language learning. In R. Carter & M. McCarthy (eds.), *Vocabulary and language teaching* (pp. 111–125). London: Longman.

Summers, D. (1995). Vocabulary learning: Do dictionaries really help? *The Language Teacher, 19*, 25–28.

Tall, G., & Hurnam, J. (2000). Using a dictionary in a written French examination: The students' experience. *Language Learning Journal, 21*, 50–56.

Thompson, G. (1987). Using bilingual dictionaries. *ELT Journal, 41*, 282–286.

Vygotsky, L. S. (1978). *Mind in society. The development of higher psychological processes.* Cambridge: Harvard University Press.

Williams, M., & Burden, R. L. (1997). *Psychology for language teachers.* Cambridge: Cambridge University Press.

 **New Words**

aforementioned	[ə.fɔː'menʃənd]	a.	前面提及的，上述的
annotation	[ˌænə'teiʃn]	n.	注解，注释
ascertain	[ˌæsə'tein]	vt.	查明，弄清，确定
burgeoning	['bɜːdʒəniŋ]	a.	增长迅速的，发展很快的
cognate	['kɔgneit]	n.	同源词，同根词；同系语言
cognitive	['kɔgnitiv]	a.	认知的，认识能力的
confound	[kən'faund]	vt.	使混淆，使混乱
conjugation	[ˌkɔndʒu'geiʃn]	n.	词形变化；结合，配合
corpus	['kɔːpəs]	n.	全文，文集，语料库
corroborate	[kə'rɔbəreit]	vt.	确证
denotation	[ˌdiːnəu'teiʃn]	n.	（明示的）意义；指示
entail	[in'teil]	vt.	使承担，使成为必要，需要
equivalent	[i'kwivələnt]	a.	相等的，相当的
		n.	等价物，意义相同的词
facilitate	[fə'siliteit]	vt.	使变得（更）容易，使便利
flip	[flip]	vt.	快速翻动；轻抛；轻拍
foster	['fɔstə]	v.	培养，促进；收养
gloss	[glɔs]	n.	注解

holistic	[həu'listik]	*a.*	全部的
hypertextuality	[ˌhaipə'tekstʃuə'æləti]	*n.*	超文本性
inflectional	[in'flekʃənl]	*a.*	有屈折变化的；弯曲的
lexical	['leksikl]	*a.*	词汇的，词典的
lexicon	['leksikən]	*n.*	词典；语汇；词素
masculine	['mæskjulin]	*a.*	阳性的，雄性的，男子气概的
monosemic	[ˌmɔnəu'si:mik]	*a.*	单意（词）的
overarching	[ˌəuvə'ɑ:tʃiŋ]	*a.*	支配一切的，包罗万象的
parameter	[pə'ræmitə]	*n.*	（常 pl.）界限，范围；参数
pedagogical	[ˌpedə'gɔdʒikl]	*a.*	教育学的；教学法的
pragmatic	[præg'mætik]	*a.*	实际的，实用主义的
protocol	['prəutəkɔl]	*n.*	协议；外交礼节
realm	[relm]	*n.*	界，领域，范围；王国，国度
refine	[ri'fain]	*vt.*	精制，提纯；使优美，使完善，使文雅
semantic	[si'mæntik]	*a.*	语义的；语义学的
snap	[snæp]	*v.*	突然拉断，咔嚓折断；拍快照
sophisticated	[sə'fistikeitid]	*a.*	复杂的，精致的，富有经验的
tailor	['teilə]	*vt.*	调整使适应
taxonomy	[tæk'sɔnəmi]	*n.*	分类学
triangulation	[traiˌæŋgju'leiʃn]	*n.*	三角测量；三角剖分

Phrases

tap into	开发；挖掘；接近
in conjunction with	与……共同，连同

Discussion Ideas

1. Identify the research topic and the issues of this paper.

2. Is it proper to say a literature review is just a summary of the sources? Why or why not?

3. How did the researchers synthesize the previous research in this paper?

4. Compare the moves in research paper introductions illustrated in Unit 2 and this unit. Can you find some common points?

5. What research instruments (data-collection methods) were employed in this study? What are the advantages of such methods?

6. What does data triangulation refer to? What do you think might be its benefits?

7. Discuss the possible limitations of the present study and the implications for future research.

8. Is this study qualitative or quantitative? Use evidence to support yourself.

Vocabulary and Language Learning Skills

1. Word Building

In this paper, you read the word 'translate', 'transition', 'transfer', 'transmitted' and 'transcribe'. These words use the prefix '**trans-**', which means 'across', 'change', or 'move from place to place'. 'Trans-' comes at the beginning of many words to form nouns, verbs, adjectives, and adverbs in English.

Write down the word beside the definition to which it corresponds. Give three more words started with 'trans-'.

Word Prefixed with 'trans-'	Definition
	to use a skill, idea, etc in the new situation
	to represent speech sounds with phonetic symbol
	to change written or spoken words into another language
	to send or pass something from one person, place or thing to another
	change or passage from one state or stage to another

2. Recognizing Word Meanings

Match the definitions in Column B with vocabulary items in Column A.

Column A	Column B
1. essential	a. very different from each other
2. overview	b. of or relating to items of vocabulary in a language
3. diverse	c. an occasion when you meet or experience something
4. encounter	d. extremely important and necessary

(continued)

Column A	Column B
5. implication	e. a note added in explanation to a piece of writing
6. semantic	f. a record of data or observations on a particular experiment
7. lexical	g. to confirm or support
8. annotation	h. relating to the meanings of words
9. protocol	i. a general survey
10. corroborate	j. a possible future effect or result of an action, event, etc

3. Making a Collocation

Use the vocabulary items in the box to complete the sentences. Make changes if necessary.

holistic	highlight	pedagogical
stem	burgeoning	access
take advantage of	in conjunction with	tap into

1) It contrasts favourably with the arid _____ methods of our own childhoods.

2) In China, medical journals from 1400 BC refer to the use of massage _____ acupuncture.

3) Your resume should _____ your skills and achievements.

4) This project is aimed at helping people _____ training opportunities.

5) _____ ecology views humans and the environment as a single system.

6) Over recent years, researchers have reported a _____ increase in the incidence of the eating disorders.

7) The file can _____ many users at the same time.

8) Our interest in his ideas _____ a general concern with the nature of human consciousness.

9) A great many people would _____ the sports facilities while they are here.

Writing Focus

Literature Review

Function

A literature review surveys published scholarly information in a particular subject, or area of research within a certain time period. It may be a self-contained paper on a topic, or, most of the time, it constitutes an essential chapter of an academic writing. Not only a simple summary of the sources, a literature review should also be a synthesis and have its organizational pattern.

The important idea to convey is that you really know and understand what others in your field have accomplished, provide the information as background information to your readers, and thus set the stage for you to demonstrate what your research contribution is going to be.

Style

Writing a literature review can be a time-consuming endeavor. The following moves will save you some time and facilitate the process.

Move 1 Problem formulation

- Establish your research topic and its component issues

Move 2 Literature search

- Go to the library or go on the internet
- Find materials relevant to the subject being explored
- Keep a bibliographical trail
- Mark the sources as primary, secondary and tertiary

Move 3 Note-taking

- Critically read each source
- Take notes on the key issues identified earlier

Move 4 Literature review construction

- Start with an introductory paragraph and establish your research topic
- Synthesize the body text of literature and divide it into sections and subsections if necessary
  - Organize the literature according to chronology, theories, methods, findings, authors, etc.
  - Begin each major section with a clear and explicit topic statement and end

them with a transition
  - Present the literature by quoting, summarizing and paraphrasing
- End with a conclusion paragraph
  - Summarize previous research
  - Shed lights on the gaps of previous research
  - Create a space for your research argument

Language Focus

Paraphrase: Write Things in Your Own Words

Quoting, summarizing, and paraphrasing are three ways to include literature. Quotations are identical to the original and can add weight to your research paper, but the overuse of quotations may suggest your inability to comprehend the literature, endanger your writing with inconsistent style, and lead to accusations of plagiarism. Summarizing involves putting the main idea(s) into your own words, including only the main point(s). Summaries are significantly shorter than the original and take a broad overview of the source material. While paraphrasing, "expressing the meaning of (something written or spoken) using different words, especially to achieve greater clarity" (Oxford English Dictionary), indicates your thorough understanding, makes the style of your writing consistent, and legitimizes you to borrow from a source. Although paraphrasing, like summarizing, restates the idea in your own words, it differs from the latter in the objective. A summary is aimed to condense source material into a shorter form. Paraphrasing, however, is not centrally concerned with length. Rather, paraphrasing is concerned primarily with the restatement of source material in a form that is different than the original.

Methods of Paraphrasing

1. Use different vocabulary with the same meaning

    1) Use synonyms

    2) Change parts of speech

    3) Give definitions

2. Use different grammar

3. Use different structure

    1) Change sentence order

    2) Combine sentences

    3) Split sentences

A good paraphrase should meet two requirements:

1. Cite the source of material

2. Differ adequately from the original in that it doesn't require quotation marks

Compare the following examples from Purdue Online Writing Lab (n.d.)

Original:

> Students frequently overuse direct quotation in taking notes, and as a result they overuse quotations in the final [research] paper. Probably only about 10% of your final manuscript should appear as directly quoted matter. Therefore, you should strive to limit the amount of exact transcribing of source materials while taking notes. Lester, James D. *Writing Research Papers*. 2nd ed. (1976): 46-47.

Plagiarism:

> Students often use too many direct quotations when they take notes, resulting in too many of them in the final research paper. In fact, probably only about 10% of the final copy should consist of directly quoted material. So it is important to limit the amount of source material copied while taking notes.

The paraphrase fails for two reasons:

1. It does not have a citation, which gives the readers the impression that this is the author's research knowledge.

2. The language of the paraphrase is too similar to the original.

The following paraphrase includes a citation and creates an original construction.

Not plagiarism:

> In research papers students often quote excessively, failing to keep quoted material down to a desirable level. Since the problem usually originates during note taking, it is essential to minimize the material recorded verbatim (Lester 46-47).

Following are two examples of paraphrases, one is plagiarism and one is not. The original is taken from Maguelone Toussaint-Samat's A History of Food (Cambridge: Blackwell, 1992. 263).

Original:

> Wines drunk at Greek tables did not always come from Greece itself. The wine snobbery of the time extolled the merits of wines from the slopes of Mount Lebanon, from Palestine, Egypt and Magna Graecia-Greater Greece, i.e., southern Italy. The ten litres a day drunk by the famous wrestler Milo of Croton was a wine famous in Calabria, where Milo lived: this wine, Ciro, is still made.

Plagiarism:

> Wines drunk by Greeks were not always made in Greece itself. The wine snobs of that period celebrated wines from Mount Lebanon, Palestine, and Egypt. The famous wrestler Milo of Croton, who consumed ten liters of wine a day, drank wine made in Calabria outside of Greece; this wine, Ciro, is still made.

This paraphrase fails for two reasons:

1. By having no citation, the paraphrase misleads readers into believing that the ideas, facts and sense of the passage are a result of the author's own research and knowledge.

2. The language of the paraphrase is too similar to the original. Even if the author had provided a citation, some instructors would consider this plagiarism.

Not plagiarism:

> Although Greeks were picky about their wine, they enjoyed wine from outside Greece. Upstanding Greeks enjoyed wine from many of Greece's local trading partners—including Palestine, Egypt and southern Italy. One story tells of the famous wrestler Milo of Croton, who consumed ten liters of foreign wine daily (Toussaint-Samat 263).

This paraphrase cites the original and rephrases its words to create an original construction.

Relevant APA Style

In-Text Citations: The Basics

Note: APA style requires authors to use the **past tense** or **present perfect tense** when using signal phrases to describe earlier research. For example, Jones (1998) **found** or Jones (1998) **has found**...

APA Citation Basics

When using APA format, follow the author-date method of in-text citation. This means that the author's last name and the year of publication for the source should appear in the text, e.g., (Jones, 1998), and a complete reference should appear in the reference list at the end of the paper.

If you are referring to an idea from another work but **NOT** directly quoting the material, or making reference to an entire book, article or other work, you only have to make reference to the author and year of publication in your in-text reference.

Short Quotations

If you are directly quoting from a work, you will need to include the author, year of publication, and the page number for the reference (preceded by "p."). Introduce the quotation with a signal phrase that includes the author's last name followed by the date of publication in parentheses.

> According to Jones (1998), "Students often had difficulty using APA style, especially when it was their first time" (p. 199). Jones (1998) found "students often had difficulty using APA style" (p. 199); what implications does this have for teachers?

If the author is not named in a signal phrase, place the author's last name, the year of publication, and the page number in parentheses after the quotation.

> She stated, "Students often had difficulty using APA style," but she did not offer an explanation as to why (Jones, 1998, p. 199).

Long Quotations

Place direct quotations **longer than 40 words** in a free-standing block of typewritten lines, and omit quotation marks. Start the quotation on a new line, indented five spaces from the left margin. Type the entire quotation on the new margin, and indent the first line of any subsequent paragraph within the quotation five spaces from the new margin. Maintain double-spacing throughout. The parenthetical citation should come after the closing punctuation mark.

> Jones's (1998) study found the following: Students often had difficulty using APA style, especially when it was their first time citing sources. This difficulty could be attributed to the fact that many students failed to purchase a style manual or to ask their teacher for help (p. 199).

Summary or Paraphrase

If you are paraphrasing an idea from another work, you only have to make reference to the author and year of publication in your in-text reference, but APA guidelines encourage you to also provide the page number (although it is not required.)

> According to Jones (1998), APA style is a difficult citation format for first-time learners.

or

> APA style is a difficult citation format for first-time learners (Jones, 1998, p. 199).

In-Text Citations: Author/Authors and Sources

APA style has a series of important rules on using author names as part of the author-date system. There are additional rules for citing indirect sources, electronic sources, and sources without page numbers.

Citing an Author or Authors

A Work by Two Authors: Name both authors in the signal phrase or in the parentheses each time you cite the work. Use the word "and" between the authors' names within the text and use the ampersand in the parentheses.

> Research by Wegener and Petty (1994) supports...
> The research showed that... (Wegener & Petty, 1994)

A Work by Three to Five Authors: List all the authors in the signal phrase or in parentheses the first time you cite the source.

> (Kernis, Cornell, Sun, Berry, & Harlow, 1993)

In subsequent citations, only use the first author's last name followed by "*et al.*" in the signal phrase or in parentheses.

> (Kernis *et al.*, 1993)

In *et al.*, *et* should not be followed by a period.

Six or More Authors: Use the first author's name followed by *et al.* in the signal phrase or in parentheses.

> Harris *et al.* (2001) argued...
> (Harris *et al.*, 2001)

Unknown Author: If the work does not have an author, cite the source by its title in the signal phrase or use the first word or two in the parentheses. Titles of books and reports are italicized or underlined; titles of articles and chapters are in quotation marks.

> A similar study was done of students learning to format research papers ("Using APA," 2001).

Note: In the rare case the "Anonymous" is used for the author, treat it as the author's name (Anonymous, 2001). In the reference list, use the name Anonymous as the author.

Organization as an Author: If the author is an organization or a government agency, mention the organization in the signal phrase or in the parenthetical citation the first time you cite the source.

> According to the American Psychological Association (2000), ...

If the organization has a well-known abbreviation, include the abbreviation in brackets the first time the source is cited and then use only the abbreviation in later citations.

> First citation: (Mothers Against Drunk Driving [MADD], 2000)
> Second citation: (MADD, 2000)

Two or More Works in the Same Parentheses: When your parenthetical citation includes two or more works, order them the same way they appear in the reference list, separated by a semi-colon.

> (Berndt, 2002; Harlow, 1983)

Authors With the Same Last Name: To prevent confusion, use first initials with the last names.

> (E. Johnson, 2001; L. Johnson, 1998)

Two or More Works by the Same Author in the Same Year: If you have two sources by the same author in the same year, use lower-case letters (a, b, c) with the year to order the entries in the reference list. Use the lower-case letters with the year in the in-text citation.

> Research by Berndt (1981a) illustrated that...

Citing Introductions, Prefaces, Forewords, and Afterwords

When citing an Introduction, Preface, Foreword, or Afterword in-text, cite the appropriate author and year as usual.

> (Funk & Kolln, 1992)

Citing Personal Communication

For interviews, letters, e-mails, and other person-to-person communication, cite the communicators name, the fact that it was personal communication, and the date of the communication. Do not include personal communication in the reference list.

> (E. Robbins, personal communication, January 4, 2001).
> A. P. Smith also claimed that many of her students had difficulties with APA style (personal communication, November 3, 2002).

Citing Indirect Sources

If you use a source that was cited in another source, name the original source in your signal phrase. List the secondary source in your reference list and include the secondary source in the parentheses.

> Johnson argued that...(as cited in Smith, 2003, p. 102).

Note: When citing material in parentheses, set off the citation with a comma, as above.

Citing Electronic Sources

If possible, cite an electronic document the same as any other document by using the author-date style.

> Kenneth (2000) explained...

Citing Sources Without Page Numbers

When an electronic source lacks page numbers, you should try to include information that will help readers find the passage being cited. When an electronic document has numbered paragraphs, use the abbreviation "para." followed by the paragraph number (Hall, 2001, para. 5). If the paragraphs are not numbered and the document includes headings, provide the appropriate heading and specify the paragraph under that heading. Note that in some electronic sources, like Web pages, people can use the Find function in their browser to locate any passages you cite.

> According to Smith (1997), ... (Mind over Matter section, para. 6).

Note: Never use the page numbers of Web pages you print out; different computers

print Web pages with different pagination.

Task One

Categorize the following sources into primary, secondary and tertiary.

dictionaries	conferences	computer programs	journals
guides	scale models	proceedings	handbooks
books	drawings	encyclopedias	data sets

Primary:	
Secondary:	
Tertiary:	

Task Two

Paraphrase the following sentences.

1. The way to a male's heart is through his tummy.

2. A penny saved is a penny earned.

3. You can't teach an old dog new tricks.

4. Haste makes waste.

5. You can't make a silk purse out of a sow's ear.

6. Although our human ability to communicate is genetically determined and hence is a part of our biological nature, speech development is importantly affected by the environment.

7. Natural languages follow various rules and it is reasonably clear that humans inherit an innate cognitive capacity to learn these rules. As a result of normal maturation, this capacity of language acquisition reaches a stage of "readiness" before the age of two, and continues on through the childhood years until puberty. The actual nature of this universal readiness for language is still unknown. Some scientists think that humans are preprogrammed with the basic rules of language, but others believe that humans are innately prepared to learn these rules.

Task Three

Identify the different parts of the Literature Review section of the study in Unit 3.

The Effect of the Computer Dictionary and the Paper Dictionary on L2 Learners' Vocabulary Acquisition

Unit 4

The Effect of the Computer Dictionary and the Paper Dictionary on L2 Learners' Vocabulary Acquisition

Najeong Kim

Seoul National University

This paper investigates the effect of the computer dictionary and the paper dictionary on L2 learners' vocabulary acquisition while reading. Thirty-seven Korean college students divided into a computer dictionary group and a paper dictionary group read a short text for comprehension with access to a dictionary and were tested on the **retention** of the 14 target words. The results show that (1) while L2 learners read a short text, they look up significantly more words using the computer dictionary than using the paper dictionary, (2) the computer dictionary has a more positive effect on learners' incidental vocabulary acquisition by drawing learners' attention to the words than the paper dictionary, and (3) there is no difference in the retention rate between the words looked up in the computer dictionary and those looked up in the paper dictionary.

(**Seoul National University**)

Keywords: paper dictionary, computer dictionary, vocabulary acquisition, attention

1. Introduction

1.1 Background and motivation

Within the literature of L1 and L2 acquisition research, it is a widely accepted principle that learners acquire a large number of words incidentally while they read the texts trying to comprehend the texts as a whole. This kind of acquisition, incidental vocabulary acquisition, has been supported by many teachers and researchers, who have argued that reading is an effective and natural way to acquire vocabulary (Krashen,1989; Nagy, Andersen, & Herman, 1987). However, many researchers have pointed out that reading does not automatically lead to vocabulary learning. It has been argued that in order to acquire vocabulary while reading, learners have to pay attention to a word's meaning and form (Huckin & Coady, 1999; Robinson, 1995; Schmitt, 1990, 2001). In this light, dictionary consultation was proven to be effective in the learners vocabulary acquisition by **inducing** the learners attention to the word looked up in the dictionary (Hulstijn, Hollander & Greidanus, 1996; Knight, 1994; Luppescu & Day, 1993).

Today, in addition to a traditional paper dictionary, the development of technology **brings forth** to an alternative consultation tool, a computer dictionary, to the language learners. Due to its convenience, the computer dictionary is gaining popularities among the students in the current L2 education environment. With the increased interest in this new method, many researchers have investigated its effect on L2 learners language learning. However, most of the studies were focused on the effectiveness of the multimedia annotations on vocabulary acquisition and reading comprehension and only a few studies have been conducted on comparing the paper dictionary and the computer **counterpart**. Yet, no studies were conducted on the effects of a computer dictionary on L2 learners incidental vocabulary acquisition in comparison with a paper dictionary. In this sense, the present study is motivated to explore this issue.

The main aim of this study is to investigate the effect of the two different types of dictionaries, the computer dictionary and the paper dictionary, on L2 learners vocabulary acquisition while they read a text for comprehension.

1.2 Previous research

1.2.1 Incidental vocabulary acquisition

It is widely agreed among language researchers that learners acquire most of their vocabulary while they read for comprehension. This secondary learning is referred to as incidental vocabulary acquisition because it occurs incidentally while learners try to understand the text rather than to acquire vocabulary (Krashen, 1989; Nagy, Andersen, & Herman, 1987). For the last few decades, incidental vocabulary learning has been supported by much evidence in L2 research field.

In spite of the evident role of reading on incidental vocabulary learning, however, many researchers and teachers have pointed out that learning vocabulary by reading has some limitations.

First of all readers often ignore unknown words while they read. Reporting a study on the lexical processing strategy training and the strategy use by L2 readers **confronting** an unfamiliar word, Fraser (1999) analyzed the **introspective** data from eight participants reading eight texts over 5 months and a recall **cued** task. From the analysis, she found that the subjects ignored 24% of the unknown words they **encountered** during reading. In a similar introspective study without strategy training, Paribakht and Wesche (1999) investigated how the readers dealt with the unfamiliar words while they read for meaning. They found that learners ignored 56% of the unknown words in the summary task and 52% in the question task.

Secondly, readers often make incorrect guesses of unfamiliar words and consequently **retain** incorrect meaning. Incorrect guessing is mostly due to the lack of clear clues in the context and the lack of learners' language proficiency (Huckin & Coady, 1999). Bensoussan and Laufer (1984, cited in Paribakht and Wesche, 1997) reported that many of the target words in a text for adult ESL readers provide no contextual cues to meaning, and that even when existing did not help guessing. Furthermore, learners need to have a large amount of vocabulary and various kinds of knowledge including semantic, **syntactic**, and **morphological** knowledge about the words and world knowledge as well.

Thirdly, vocabulary acquisition through reading is not the most efficient way to improve vocabulary under a foreign language learning environment. Learning vocabulary through reading is an **increment** process. From the first encounter to integration of new lexical knowledge to mental lexicon, learners require repeated exposure to the word. It is **presumed** that around 5–26.5% of the unknown words are learned by readers in the first encounter (Chun and Plass, 1996; Knight, 1994). For full acquisition, researchers found that learners need 5 to 16 exposures to the target words (Huckin & Candy, 1999). However, L2 learners usually have very limited exposure to the target language.

To overcome these limitations, L2 researchers have suggested some complementary methods to enhance vocabulary learning while reading. They found that provision of glosses and dictionary consultation are effective to promote incidental vocabulary acquisition (Hulstijn, Hollander, & Greidanus, 1996; Knight, 1994; Luppesku & Day, 1993). Of the two methods, provision of glosses is limited to materials specialized for L2 learners, and thus dictionary use remains a general and useful tool for effective vocabulary learning. Therefore, this study will focus on dictionary use as an effective strategy to improve incidental vocabulary acquisition.

1.2.2 Dictionary use while reading

1.2.2.1 The role of dictionary use on incidental vocabulary learning

A number of studies on dictionary use have been conducted to investigate the role of dictionary consultation on incidental vocabulary acquisition while reading. Many L2 researchers found that dictionary consultation enhances incidental vocabulary acquisition (Fraser, 1999; Hulstijn et al., 1996; Knight 1994; Laufer & Hill, 2000; Luppescu and Day, 1993).

Knight (1994) investigated whether access to the on-line bilingual dictionary affects vocabulary learning and reading comprehension of American students of Spanish while they read on-line texts. Under two conditions (dictionary and no dictionary), the subjects were asked to read two 250-word texts containing 24 unknown words and then to take a vocabulary test and a recall comprehension test. Two weeks later, a delayed vocabulary retention test was **administered**. Knight found that the subjects with access to a dictionary learned more words and achieved higher reading comprehension scores than those without access to a dictionary.

In a similar study, Luppescu and Day (1993) examined the effect of the bilingual dictionary on vocabulary learning while 293 Japanese university students of English read a 1,853-word text. After reading, the subjects were asked to take an immediate multiple-choice test on vocabulary. The result showed that the dictionary group scored 50% higher on the vocabulary test than the no-dictionary group. However, they found that using a dictionary decreases reading speed by almost half compared to not using a dictionary.

Hulstijn, Hollander, and Greidaus (1996) studied the influence of **marginal** glosses, dictionary use, and the re-occurrence of unknown words on incidental vocabulary learning. Seventy-eight Dutch advanced students of French under three separate conditions (Marginal Glosses, Dictionary Use and No Aid) read a short story. Researchers found that the Dictionary Group who had access to the dictionary while reading **yielded** much higher retention scores on a subsequent test than the same words in the marginal gloss.

In an introspective study, Fraser (1999) investigated L2 learners lexical processing strategies when they encounter unfamiliar words while reading and the impact of the strategies on vocabulary learning. After a lexical strategy training session, 8 subjects reported their strategy use on eight texts over 5 months and took a delayed recall test measuring vocabulary learning after each reading. It was found that the partcipants used productive strategies such as inferring, dictionary consulting, and inferring followed by dictionary consulting and that inferring followed by dictionary consulting resulted in more vocabulary learning than inferring or consulting alone.

1.2.2.2 Comparison of the computer dictionary use and the paper dictionary use while reading

With the **advent** of computer technology, the computer dictionary appeared as a new convenient consulting device for L2 readers. The computer dictionary provides a different way of consultation to the users. Without flipping through pages and without looking for the spelling in alphabetical order which accompanies traditional dictionary use, electronic dictionary users can access the information in an instant by typing or clicking. (Sharpe, 1995; Nasi, 1996, 1999, 2000b). The advent of the computer dictionary inspired some research on the comparison of look-up behaviors of the computerized dictionary and the paper dictionary.

Roby (1991, cited in Roby, 1999) examined dictionary and gloss use of American students of Spanish reading a biographical sketch. The subjects were divided into four groups: (1) paper dictionary, (2) paper dictionary and gloss, (3) computer dictionary, and (4) computer dictionary and gloss. The factors he measured were reading time, number of look-ups and comprehension. The findings indicate that the subjects with access to the gloss read the passage much faster than those with the dictionary alone. He also found that the subjects with an electronic dictionary looked up much more words than the subjects with a paper dictionary. However, there was no significant difference on reading comprehension.

In the same line with the comparison studies, Nesi's (2000a) introspective study also focused on look-up behavior, learners' attitude and reading comprehension. The subjects were asked to read two paper-based texts of 286 words each using Oxford Advanced Learner's Dictionary under two conditions: computer condition and paper condition. Data gathered from the subjects were reading time, a self-record sheet of look-up behavior, and a true/false test on comprehension. She found that although there is no significant difference in reading comprehension, the subjects looked up more words when they use a computer dictionary and reported their preference for the computer dictionary and were more satisfied with it.

1.2.3 Noticing hypothesis

It is widely accepted that incidental vocabulary learning takes place during reading. However, it seems thet not all the comprehensible input is likely to be available for further learning processes. In the field of L2 research, many researchers have explored how some parts of the input used for comprehension become **activated** to be processed further in language learning.

Regarding this issue, Schmidt (1990, 1995, 2001; Schmidt & Frota, 1986, cited in Schmidt, 1990) proposed noticing hypothesis that for learners to learn some aspects of language, they must consciously notice them for any subsequent processing. That is, for input to be intake he claimed that noticing on the part of the learner is necessary. Schmidt defined intake as what Chaudron (1985) called **preliminary** intake, which means converting speech input into stored data that can be used for the construction of language, distinguishing from those used to organize stored data into linguistic systems (Schmidt, 1990, p. 139). He argued strongly against any intake of input that the learner has not noticed. He meant the term noticing as one of the levels of awareness, at which stimuli are subjectively experienced and attention at the level of the availability of the verbal report. However, he admitted that **stimulus** events could be noticed even though it could not be describable. In addition, he emphasized the role of consciousness as crucial to all learning, adapting the view of psychology that conscious processing is necessary for permanent long term storage and anything not processed consciously is not stored in the long-term memory.

1.3 Research questions

The first aim of this study is to confirm that the computer dictionary would increase learners look-up behavior more than the paper dictionary as found in previous comparison studies. Secondly, this study aims to investigate the effect of the computer dictionary and the paper dictionary on incidental vocabulary learning. According to the previous studies, it was found that dictionary consultation is effective in incidental vocabulary learning (Fraser, 1999; Hulstijn, Hollander, & Greidanus, 1996; Knight, 1994; Luppesku & Day, 1993) and that the computer dictionary encourages the users to look up more words than the paper dictionary (Nesi, 2000a; Roby, 1991). Based on these foundings, it is hypothesized that if a computer dictionary increases learners look-up behavior more than its paper counterpart, this will, in turn, result in a more positive effect on incidental vocabulary learning than a paper dictionary. Finally, the third objective of this study is whether the words looked up in the computer dictionary will be retained in memory as well as the words looked up in the paper dictionary. It is hypothesized that learners access the information too quickly and the easily searched words will not be retained in long-term memory.

The research questions to be answered from this research are the following:

(1) Do the computer dictionary users look up more words than the paper dictionary users?

(2) Is the electronic dictionary more beneficial to L2 learners' incidental vocabulary acquisition than the paper dictionary?

(3) Is there any difference on the retention rate between the words looked up in the paper dictionary and the electronic dictionary?

2. Method

2.1 Participants

The participants of the study were 38 undergraduate students enrolled in two college English classes in the spring semester of 2003 at Seoul National University. All the participants had TEPS scores since they were required to take TEPS before entering the university. Their average TEPS score was 585.6, equivalent to TOEFL 519, TOEIC 640[1].

One class had 22 students and the other had 17. The class consisting of 22 students was assigned to the computer dictionary group and the other class of 17 students to the paper dictionary group. The two groups were not different in English proficiency level, $t=-1.512$, $p =.139$.

In the final statistical analysis, thirty-seven students' data were examined. Two students' data were excluded, for one student in the computer group was absent in one session and the other student in the paper group already knew the meaning of the five target words. Thus, 21 participants remained in the computer dictionary group and 16 in the paper dictionary group. They majored in agriculture and life sciences (18), plant science (1), statistics (1), French education (1), electronic & computer engineering (15) and education (1).

2.2 Materials and instruments

As for the dictionary, the first edition of the Sisa Elite English-Korean dictionary was selected since the definition contained in the paper dictionary was also provided identically through an Internet site, at http://dic.ybmsisa.co.kr/~ybmsisa/s7.php3. The dictionary provides pronunciation, the word category, the Korean equivalents, the tensed forms for the verb and the plural forms for the noun, a few simple examples.

As for the reading material, the text was chosen from a textbook for learners of English as a Second Language (see Appendix A). The following factors were taken into account when selecting the text: text difficulty, text length and familiarity of a topic. The overall difficulty of the text was proven to be adequate for the participants by a pilot test. As for text length, it was quite short, 239 words long, which was appropriate for the purpose of this study since learners tend not to consult the dictionary while reading a long text (Hultijn et. al., 1996).

As for the pre-test, which measures the participants pre-knowledge of the target words, a list of 30 words were made. 20 words were selected from the reading material and 10 words were distracters. The vocabulary items that most participants were

---

1 TOEFL and TOEIC scores were converted from the TEPS score according to the score correlation table provided by Language Education Institute at Seoul National University.

unlikely to know were chosen from the selected text. Participants were required to provide the Korean equivalents for the given items. Fourteen words that more than 90% of the participants did not provide the correct meaning for were selected as target words: *affliction, ailment, autopsy, bout, candor elude, insidious, lesion, malady, mammogram, polio, scourge, susceptibility, telltale* in the alphabetical order. All the target words appeared once in the text.

As for the post-tests, multiple-choice tests were prepared in which the participants were asked to choose a Korean equivalent among 4 alternatives (See Appendix B). A multiple-choice test which can measure the receptive knowledge of the words was considered appropriate to measure the retention of the words gained incidentally from reading, since the probability that the participants can gain word knowledge at the production level at one exposure is very low. The immediate test and the delayed test contained the same items, but in a **scrambled** order.

2.3 Procedure

The experiment consisted of the pretest, the main session and the delayed test. All the sessions were held during the regular class time and in the regular classrooms with the cooperation of an instructor in charge of the two classes in May 2003.

Before reading the text, the pretest was administered to measure the pre-knowledge of the target words in the presence of the researcher. Based on the result, 14 target words that more than 90% of the respondents did not know were chosen.

In the main session, the participants of the paper group were provided with Sisa Elite English-Korean dictionaries in the classroom. Meanwhile, the participants of the computer group participated in the experiment in a computer lab where they could access the same version of the dictionary through the computer. First, the students were instructed to read the printed text for a comprehension test. The vocabulary test was not announced so that the condition was conducive to incidental vocabulary learning. There was no time limit, but they were advised to read the text within 15 minutes. They were allowed to consult dictionaries as much as they needed. However, they were asked to underline the words they looked up in the dictionary. After they finished their reading, the reading comprehension test was administered. Then, an unannounced vocabulary test was given. Finally, the participants were asked to respond to the questionnaire. Two days after the main session, a delayed unannounced vocabulary test was given in the presence of the researcher.

2.4 Data scoring and analysis

Only the 14 target words in the vocabulary tests were scored by the researcher. With respect to the pretest, a correct answer for each vocabulary item received a score of 1.

A half point was given to the answer which reflected partial knowledge of the word and zero points were given to the obviously wrong answer or no response. As for the multiple-choice post vocabulary tests, one point was given to the correct answer and zero points were given to the wrong answer or no response. Thus, a maximum score per participant was 14 points (14 vocabulary items * 1 point).

For the statistical analysis, the Statistical Packages for the Social Sciences (SPSS) 10.0 window version was used. The two-tailed independent t-tests were conducted at the level of .05 to examine the difference between tire two groups with respect to all the dependent variables. In order to prevent confusion between the total words looked up and the target words looked up, it is necessary to confirm in advance that the words in this study are restricted to the 14 target words.

3. Results and Discussion

3.1 The number of the words looked up

The first aim of this study was to investigate the effect of the two types of dictionaries on the number of the words looked up. To explore this, the words looked up in the dictionary by the participants were analyzed. According to Table 1, the participants of the computer dictionary group looked up the mean number of 11.6 words (82.8% of the target words) while those in the paper dictionary group looked up the average 8.9 words (63.6% of the target words). An independent t-test revealed that the computer group looked up significantly more words than the paper dictionary group, $t=3.744$, $p=.001$.

This finding is in line with Roby's (1991, cited in Roby, 1999) and Nesi's (2000a) studies. The increased look-up behavior of the computer dictionary group can be explained as the followings: The learners can access the meaning of the words in an instance when they use the computer dictionary. This convenience of the computer dictionary may enhance the learners look-up activities during reading to the extent that the paper dictionary cannot. In contrast to the computer dictionary, the paper dictionary demands more effort and time from the users and often interrupts the flow of reading to a greater extent than the computer dictionary, which, in turn, discourages the readers consultation activities while they read the text.

Table 1. Mean numbers of the words looked up by group

Group	n	M	(%)	SD
Computer	21	11.6	(82.8)	1.9
Paper	16	8.9	(63.6)	2.4
Total	37	10.4	(74.8)	2.5

The maximum number of the words looked up = 14

Compared with other studies, the participants of this study looked up a higher percentage of the target words (63.6–82.8%) than those of a similar study by Hultijn *et al.* (1996) which showed that the subjects reading the text with the paper dictionary looked up 12% of the 16 target words. The higher percentage of the present study can be accounted for by such factors as text length, text genre and students proficiency level. It is possible that the text of this study was so short that the participants were more motivated to look up the unfamiliar words than the subjects of Hultijn *et al.*'s study (1996) who read much longer text (1,306 word long), as suggested by Hultijn *et al.* (1996). Moreover, the text in this study was an **expository** essay, whereas the text in Hultijn *et al.*'s study (1996) was a fictional text. With respect to this point, Hultijn *et al.* (1996) argued that this structural difference between the text genres may cause the words to be more or less relevant to the reading task; thus, can **elicit** different look-ups. Furthermore, the students with greater vocabulary knowledge look up fewer words than students with smaller vocabulary knowledge (Hultijn, 1993). Thus, it is possible that Hultijn *et al.*'s (1996) students who had high verbal ability might look up fewer words than the students of this study who are intermediate level learners.

3.2 The overall retention of the words

The second aim of this study was to explore whether the computer dictionary can be a better aid to L2 learners incidental vocabulary acquisition than the paper dictionary. To explore this issue, the participants score gains between the pretest and the two post vocabulary tests were calculated by **subtracting** the pretest scores from the post-test scores.

According to Table 2, in the immediate test the participants of the computer dictionary group achieved the mean gain score of 9.8 (70%) out of the target words while those of the paper dictionary group gained a mean gain score of 8.1 (57.9%) out of the target words. Later, in the delayed test, the mean gain score of the computer dictionary group was 10.1 (72.1%) of the target words and that of the paper dictionary group was 8.2 (59.3%) of the target words. The result of the independents t-test showed that there are significant differences between the two groups in the immediate and delayed tests, t=2.626, p=.014, and t=2.369, p=.023, respectively. In conclusion, the learners who used the computer dictionary acquired more vocabulary while they read than the learners who used the paper dictionary.

Table 2. Mean score gains on the immediate and the delayed vocabulary tests

Group	n	Immediate Test		Delayed Test	
		M (%)	Sd	M (%)	SD
Computer	21	9.8 (70)	1.6	10.1(72.1)	2.0
Paper	16	8.1 (57.9)	2.3	8.2 (59.3)	2.7
Total	37	9.1 (65)	2.0	9.3 (66.4)	2.5

The maximum score gain=14

Compared with Knights (1994) study, the retention of vocabulary of this study is higher than that of Knights study. Knight (1994) found that the students who read the on-line texts consulting the on-line dictionary acquired 51–55% out of the target words on the immediate test and 39–48% on the delayed test. The difference of the percentage between Knights study (1994) and this study might **be attributable to** the different exposure to the reading material. The participants of this study were allowed to access the reading material during reading comprehension test, whereas Knights participants were not. In addition, in Hulstijn, *et al.*'s study (1996), it was found that advanced level students who read the 1,306-word text with access to the paper dictionary retained 3% of the target words. The low percentage of Hulstijn *et al.*'s study (1996) may be accounted for by the fact that the participants seldom looked up the word (they looked up 12%, as mentioned above), ignoring unfamiliar words while reading, thus; little attention to the words resulted in the low retention of the words.

The following may be the possible explanation about the advantage of the computer dictionary over the paper dictionary on incidental vocabulary learning. In order for the new words to be acquired, the unknown words must be noticed by the learners. According to Schmidt (1990), for the input to be the intake, it must be noticed on the part of the learners. The input ignored is not available for the subsequent learning processes, and thus cannot be acquired. Only the words that the learners pay attention to can be intake which can be acquired through further processes. That is, for the learners to acquire the words, they have to pay attention to the words, but not ignore the words. In this light, the convenience of the computer dictionary decreases the frequency of ignoring the unfamiliar words and the frequency of deciding not to look up because of time and effort of consultation required for the paper dictionary, but increases the possibility of the learners paying attention to the words by providing the words meaning easily. As a result, this enhances vocabulary acquisition more than the paper dictionary.

Finally, of interest was an unusual finding that the participants of this study gained additional words between the immediate vocabulary test and the delayed test. One possible explanation is that after the immediate test, they were asked to report their look-up behavior in the questionnaire where they had to write down each word they looked up while reading and reported why they looked up. During that procedure, they were exposed to the text and the words once more, which might reinforce their vocabulary learning.

3.3 The retention rates of the words looked up

The third major aim of the study was to investigate whether there is any difference in the retention rate between the words looked up in the computer dictionary and those looked up in the paper dictionary. To explore this issue, it was examined how many words the participants in each group remembered among the words they looked up in each dictionary. For each group, the retention rate of the words was obtained by dividing the number of the words remembered among the words looked up by the total number of the target words looked up in the dictionary.

As illustrated in Table 3, in the immediate test, the participants in the computer group remembered 75.9% of the words looked up and those of the paper group retained 76.4% of the words looked up. In the delayed test, the retention rates of the computer group and the paper group were 76.7% and 74.1%, respectively. Independent t-tests showed no significant differences between the two groups both in the immediate test and in the delayed test, t=−.102, p=.921 and t=.930, p=.359, respectively.

Table 3. Mean numbers of the words looked up (LU) and the words retained from dictionary consultation (WR) and mean retention rates (RR) by group

Group	n	LU	Immediate Test		Delayed Test	
			WR	RR(%)	WR	RR(%)
Computer	21	11.6	8.8	75.9	8.9	76.7
Paper	16	8.9	6.8	76.4	6.6	74.1
Total	37	10.4	7.9	76.0	7.9	76.0

The maximum number= 14

This finding does not support the hypothesis that the words looked up in the paper dictionary would be retained better than those looked up in the computer dictionary. In addition to the finding that the learners acquire more words using the computer dictionary than using the paper dictionary, the finding that the target words looked up in the computer dictionary were not different in the retention rate from those looked up in the paper dictionary further supports the advantage of the computer dictionary over the paper dictionary.

In comparison with other studies, the retention rate of this study is higher than that of other studies. In Hultijn et al.'s study (1996), they found that the retention of the 38 words looked up by the students who read a 1,306 word text with access to the paper bilingual dictionary was 22.5 (59%) in the immediate post test which required the subjects to provide the meaning. Thus, the retention rate of the paper dictionary group in the immediate test of this study is comparable with that of Hultijn *et al.*'s (1996). The higher retention rate of this study might be due to the different test types and the students further exposure to the text. The test of the present study was a multiple-choice test while that of the Hultijn *et al.*'s (1996) was supply-definition test. Furthermore, the participants of the present study took the reading comprehension test with the reading text at their disposal before the vocabulary test, and thus were exposed to the text more than those of the Hultijn *et al.*'s study(1996)who did not take the reading comprehension test.

4. Conclusion

In the framework of incidental vocabulary acquisition, this paper aims to investigate the effect of the computer dictionary and the paper dictionary on L2 learners vocabulary acquisition while reading. The findings of this study indicate that the learners look up much more words when they use the computer dictionary than when they use the paper dictionary, and as a result, the computer dictionary has a more positive effect on incidental vocabulary learning while reading than the paper dictionary. That is, the convenience of the computer dictionary increases the chances of learners' paying attention to the unfamiliar words by encouraging learners' look-up behavior and consequently the chances of vocabulary acquisition. In addition, it was found that the words looked up in the computer dictionary seem to be remembered as well as the words looked up in the paper dictionary. Thus, it can be concluded that the computer dictionary is more beneficial to L2 learners incidental vocabulary learning than the paper dictionary.

Based on these findings, in order to enhance the students' vocabulary acquisition while reading, the teachers can encourage them to use the computer dictionary. Facing unfamiliar words while they focus on reading for meaning, students tend to ignore unknown words and infer the incorrect meaning, and thus retain the wrong meaning. Therefore, as one of the enhancement methods for vocabulary learning, the teachers can instruct the students to pay attention to unknown words **tactically** while they read and to use the dictionary critically. That is, the teachers should encourage their students to infer the meaning of the words first, which is the original concept of incidental vocabulary learning, and to consult the dictionary later, by which the learners can gain the correct meaning as a backup for incidental vocabulary learning.

Regarding some limitations of this study, further research is necessary.

First, this study investigated the effects of the computer dictionary on incidental vocabulary learning while reading a short text in an experiment setting. To confirm the conclusions of this study, further studies are needed to investigate the long-term effects of the computer dictionary on language learning compared to the paper dictionary in a natural environment.

Next, further investigations are needed to determine whether the conclusions of this study can be generalized to different types of texts, different types of dictionaries and different levels of students. In addition, it would be interesting to explore the impact of the pocket-size electronic dictionary on language learning compared to the computer dictionary and the paper dictionary.

Last, the **interval** between the treatment and the delayed test in this was somewhat shorter than that of the other research on incidental vocabulary acquisition. Thus, future studies need to administer the experiment in a longer span to confirm the conclusion of this study.

References

Bensoussan, M., & Laufer, B. (1984). Lexical guessing in context in EFL reading comprehension. *Journal of Research in Reading, 7*, 15–32.

Chaudron, C. (1985). Intake: On models and methods for discovering learners processing of input. *Studies in Second Language Acquisition, 7*, 1–14.

Chun, D. M., & Plass, J. L. (1996). Effects of multimedia annotations on vocabulary acquisiton. *The Modern Language Journal, 80*, 183–198.

Eraser, C. A. (1999). Lexical processing strategy use and vocabulary learning through reading. *Studies in Second Language Acquisition, 21*, 225–241.

Huckin, T., & Coady J. (1999). Incidental vocabulary acquisition in a second language: A review. *Studies in Second Language Acquisition, 21*, 181–193.

Hulstijn, J. H., Hollander, M., & Greidanus, T. (1996). Incidental vocabulary learning by advanced foreign language students: The influence of marginal glosses, dictionary use, and reoccurence of unknown words. *The Modern Language Journal, 80*, 327–339.

Knight, S. (1994). Dictionary use while reading: The effects on comprehension and vocabulary acquisition for students of different verbal abilities. *The Modern Language Journal, 78*, 285–299.

Krashen, S. (1989).We acquire vocabulary and spelling by reading: Additional evidence for the input hypothesis. *The Modern Language Journal, 73*, 440–464.

Laufer, B., & Hilt, M. (2000). What lexical information do L2 learners select in a CALL dictionary and how does it affect word retention? *Language Learning & Technology, 3*, 58–76.

Luppescu, S., & Day, R. R. (1993). Reading, dictionaries, and vocabulary learning. *Language Learning, 43*, 263–287.

Nagy, W. E., Andersen, R. C., & Herman, P. A. (1987). Learning word meanings from context during normal reading. *American Educational Research Journal, 24*, 23–270.

Nesi, H. (1996). Review article: For future reference? Current English learners' dictionaries in electronic form. *System, 42,* 537–557.

Nesi, H. (1999). A user's guide to electronic dictionaries for language learners. *International Journal of Lexicography, 12,* 55–66.

Nesi, H. (2000a). On screen or in print? Students' use of a learner's dictionary on CD-ROM and in book form. In Howarth, P. and Herington, R. (eds.), *EAP Learning Technologies.* Leeds: Leeds University Press, 106–114.

Nesi H. (2000b). Electronic dictionaries in second language vocabulary comprehension and acquisition: The state of the art. In Held, U., Evert, S., Lehmann, E. and Rohrer, C. (eds.), *Proceedings of the Ninth EURALEX International Congress, EURALEX 2000 Volume II.* Stuttgart: Euralex, 839–847.

Paribakht, T. S., & Wesche, M. (1997). Vocabulary enhancement activities, and reading for meaning in second language vocabulary development. In J. Coady & T Huckin (eds.), *Second language vocabulary acquisition: A rationale for pedagogy.* New York: Cambridge University Press, 174–203

Paribakht, T. S., & Wasche, M. (1999). Reading and incidental L2 vocabulary acquisition. *Studies in Second Language Acquisition, 21,* 195–224.

Robinson, P. (1995). Attention, memory, and the "noticing" hypothesis. *Language Learning, 45,* 283–331.

Roby, W. B. (1991). Glosses and dictionaries in paper and computer formals as adjunct aids to the reading of Spanish texts by university students. Unpublished doctoral dissertation, University of Kansas.

Roby, W. B. (1999). What's in a gloss? *Language Learning & Technology, 2,* 94–101.

Schmidt, R. (1990). The role of consciousness in second language learning. *Applied Linguisitics, 11,* 129–158.

Schmidt, R. (1995). Consciousness and foreign learning: A tutorial on the role of attention and awareness in learning. In R. Schmidt (ed.), *Attention and awareness in foreign language learning.* Honolulu: University of Hawaii Press, 1–63.

Schmidt, R. (2001). Attention. In P. Robinson (ed.), *Congition and Second Language Instruction.* Cambridge: Cambridge University Press, 3–32.

Schmidt, R. W., & From, S. N. (1986). Developing basic conversational ability in a second language: A case study of an adult learner of Portuguese. In R. Day (ed.), *Talking to learn: Conversation in second language acquisition.* Rowley: Newbury House, 237–326.

Sharps, P. (1995). Electronic dictionaries with particular reference to the design of an electronic bilingual dictionary for English speaking learners of Japanese. *International Journal of Lexicography, 8* (1) 39–54.

 **New Words**

acquisition	[ˌækwiˈziʃn]	*n.*	取得，获得，习得；获得物
activate	[ˈæktiveit]	*vt.*	使活动，起动，触发
administer	[ədˈministə]	*v.*	管理，治理，给予，执行
advent	[ˈædvent]	*n.*	出现，到来
confront	[kənˈfrʌnt]	*vt.*	面对，使面对面，碰到，遇到

counterpart	['kauntəpɑ:t]	n.	相对物，配对物
cue	[kju:]	vt.	向……发出信号，给……暗示
elicit	[i'lisit]	vt.	引出，探出，诱出（回答等）
encounter	[in'kauntə]	v.	不期而遇，遭遇，碰见
expository	[iks'pɔzitri]	a.	说明的，解释的
increment	['inkrəmənt]	n.	增值，增加
induce	[in'dju:s]	vt.	引诱，引起，归纳
interval	['intəvl]	n.	间隔，幕间休息
introspective	[ˌintrə'spektiv]	a.	反省的
marginal	['mɑ:dʒinl]	a.	边缘的，旁注的
morphological	[ˌmɔ:fə'lɔdʒikl]	a.	形态学，形态的
preliminary	[pri'liminəri]	a.	预备的，初步的
presume	[pri'zju:m]	v.	假定；擅（做）
retain	[ri'tein]	vt.	保留，保持
retention	[ri'tenʃn]	n.	保留，保持
scramble	['skræmbl]	v.	扰乱，搞乱
stimulus	['stimjuləs]	n.	促进（因素）；刺激（物）
subtract	[səb'trækt]	vt.	减去，扣除
syntactic	[sin'tæktik]	a.	句法的
tactically	['tæktikəli]	adv.	战术地，有谋略地，策略上地
yield	[ji:ld]	v.	生产，获利

Phrases

| bring forth | 产生，引起 |
| be attributable to | 把……归因于 |

Discussion Ideas

1. Identify the structure of this research paper. Pay attention to the subheadings.

2. In the paper, the author used both "participants" and "subjects" to refer to the individuals taking part in a research project. Another term is "sample". Differentiate them from one another.

3. What voice is frequently used in the Methods section? Why?

4. What is the main tense in Methods? Why?

5. The author mentioned the aim of the study more than once. Do you think it is

necessary?

6. What is a research question? Work out the steps to developing a research question.

7. What are the research questions for this study?

8. Which of the following research questions is better? Why?

1) What can be done to prevent substance abuse?

2) What is the relationship between specific early childhood experiences and subsequent substance-abusing behaviors?

Vocabulary and Language Learning Skills

1. Recognizing Word Meanings

Match the definitions in Column B with the vocabulary items in Column A.

Column A	Column B
1. target	a. urge on or encourage
2. complementary	b. different from each other but making a good combination
3. enhance	c. the complete duration of something
4. inspire	d. a result that you are trying to achieve
5. scrambled	e. strengthen or make more firm
6. confirm	f. improve its value, quality, or attractiveness
7. span	g. earlier
8. previous	h. thrown together in a disorderly fashion

2. Making a Collocation

Use the appropriate vocabulary items to complete the sentences.

1) In this sense, the present study is _____ to explore this issue.

2) The aim of this study is to _____ the effect of the two different types of dictionaries on L2 learners vocabulary acquisition while they read a text for comprehension.

3) To _____ these limitations, L2 researchers have suggested some complementary methods to enhance vocabulary learning while reading.

4) A number of studies on dictionary use have been _____ to investigate the role of dictionary consultation on incidental vocabulary acquisition while reading.

5) However, there was no _____ difference on reading comprehension.

115

6) Regarding this issue, Schmidt _____ noticing hypothesis that for learners to learn some aspects of language, they must consciously notice them for any subsequent processing.

7) The difference of the percentage between these two studies might be _____ the different exposure to the reading material.

8) The low percentage of this study may be _____ by such factors as text length, text genre and students proficiency level.

Writing Focus

Methods

Function

In this section you explain clearly how you carried out your study. You need to give a completely accurate description of the equipment and the techniques used for gathering the data. You must also provide an explanation of how the raw data was compiled and analyzed.

Style

Whilst there are slightly different variations according to the exact type of research, the Methods can be divided into a few sections.

- Describe the materials and equipment used in the research.
- Explain how the samples were gathered, any randomization techniques and how the samples were prepared.
- Explain how the measurements were made and what calculations were performed upon the raw data.
- Describe the statistical techniques used upon the data.

A key concept is to keep this section as concise as you possibly can. Try to find the balance between keeping the section short, whilst including all of the relevant information.

Language Focus: Imperatives in Research Papers

In research papers, imperatives are less commonly used because they may be offensive. Compare the following sentences:

Imperative	Now compare the results in tables 1 and 2.
Passive	The results in tables 1 and 2 can now be compared.
Conditional	If we now compare the results in tables 1 and 2, we can see that…

However, one verb is widely used in many RP fields. Indeed, it may account for up to 50% of all the uses of the imperative in research writing. That verb is *let*.

Let *p* stand for the price-cost ratio.

Let *N* equal the number of consumers.

Task One

Read the following draft of the Methods section and answer the questions that follow.

Methods

In order to investigate the position of connectors, we examined their occurrence in academic papers published in three journals. The sample consisted of all the main articles appearing in the third issues of the 1999 volumes of *College Composition and Communication*, *English for Specific Purposes*, and *Research in Teaching of English*. (See Appendix A for a list of the articles studied.) The sample amounted to about 230 running pages of text, comprising 12 articles (four from each journal). Each occurrence of a connector was identified, highlighted, and then coded for one of three positions in a clause. If the connector was the first or last word in the clause, it was designated "initial" or "final" respectively. If it occurred in any other position, it was classified as "medial". The following examples illustrate the coding systems:

A t-test was run;

however, the results were insignificant.	Initial
the results, *however*, were insignificant.	Medial
the results were, *however*, insignificant.	Medial
the results were insignificant, *however*.	Final

For the purposes of this study, the category of sentence connector was interpreted quite broadly. We included items like *unfortunately* that are sometimes considered to be sentence adverbs. We included such items as *as it were* and *in turn*, which have an uncertain grammatical status. We also counted conjunctions like *but* as connectors when they occurred as first elements in sentences, because they seemed to be functioning as connectors in these contexts.

---

1. The main tense in the Methods section is the past. In one sentence, however, the

main verb is in the present. Which one is it and why?

2. Consider the following subject-verb combinations from sentences in the Methods section:

1) we examined…

2) each occurrence was identified…

3) it was designated…

4) it was classified…

5) the category was interpreted…

6) we included…

7) we counted…

In four cases we used the past passive, and in three cases we used *we* and the past active. APA guidelines suggest that you should use "I" and "We", but most researchers still prefer an impersonal passive tense. They believe the passive is used for standard procedures, while the use of *we* signals something new or unexpected. Do you think this might be true of your field?

3. In the Methods section, sentence 3 reads:

(See Appendix A for a list of the articles studied.)

Can you rewrite this sentence?

Task Two

John interviewed a student planning her first research paper in social work. Li said that the provisional title for her research paper was "Chinese Elderly Living in the United States: A Problem-free Population?" She said that she had chosen this topic because of some "prevailing myths" that the Chinese communities would always look after their elderly and that such elderly would not accept help from outsiders. She believed that certain traditional Chinese attitudes, such as "filial piety", were beginning to change in US communities. She added that all the research to date had been conducted in the large communities in big cities on the East and West Coasts. She wanted to study smaller communities in a Midwest town. John then asked her about methodology.

John: How are you going to collect your data?

Li: By face to face interviews. I want to do one-on-one interviews because I think if other family members are there the interviewees will not reveal their deep feelings and real problems.

John: How will you find your subjects?

Li: I'll use friends and acquaintance in the local Chinese community to introduce me.

John: Will you record the interviews?

Li: Yes, but of course, I'll ask permission first.

John: Will you use English?

Li: The interviewees can use any language they prefer—Mandarin, Taiwanese, or English. Whatever is most comfortable for them.

John: How long do you plan the interviews to last, and do you have a fixed list of questions?

Li: About an hour. I have a list of questions but I do not want to follow them very exactly. I'll use what sociologists call "semi-structures" interviews. Part planned, part "go with the flow", as the Americans say.

John: Finally, how many people will you interview?

Li: Because of limited time and contacts, only about ten. So I'll be doing a qualitative analysis. There will not be enough subjects for statistics.

Now write Li's Methods section for her. Assume that she has finished the work.

Task Three

Following are three examples of part of the Methods section of a research paper. Which one is better and why?

1. "The petri dish was placed on the turntable. The lid was then raised slightly. An inoculating loop was used to transfer culture to the agar surface. The turntable was rotated 90 degrees by hand. The loop was moved lightly back and forth over the agar to spread the culture. The bacteria were then incubated at 37 C for 24 hr."

2. "Each plate was placed on a turntable and streaked at opposing angles with fresh overnight E. coli culture using an inoculating loop. The bacteria were then incubated at 37 C for 24 hr."

3. "Each plate was streaked with fresh overnight E. coli culture and incubated at 37 C for 24 hr."

Task Four

Identify the structures of the Methods section of the research paper in Unit 4.

Supplementary Reading

Dictionary Use by EFL Writers: What Really Happens?

Kiel Christianson

University of Aizu

All of the words that 51 Japanese EFL university students had looked up in their dictionaries were identified in a 41,024-word corpus of student writing. Forty-two percent of these "dictionary words" were found to have been used incorrectly in some way. An analysis of the errors themselves and of interviews with more and less successful dictionary users was conducted in an attempt to better understand why these errors were committed and what can be done to assist students in avoiding such errors. The findings indicate that successful dictionary users, regardless of their level of English proficiency, employ a variety of sophisticated look-up strategies. Furthermore, this research brings into question some of the claims of previous studies into FL dictionary use.

Introduction

Dictionaries are ubiquitous in foreign language (FL) classrooms. While teachers may limit their use during class or dictate which kind of dictionary students may use (L1-L2, L2-L1, or L2-L2), there is little doubt that most FL teachers consider dictionaries to be useful for certain activities and that most FL learners consider them to be absolutely essential. Furthermore, both teachers and students can agree in principle that "the main purpose of a dictionary is to prevent or at least reduce communication conflicts which may arise from lexical deficit" (Hartmann 1987, p. 21). This research is an attempt to better understand what happens when for one reason or another "communication conflicts" occur despite dictionary use. Toward this better understanding, I offer an accounting and

Correspondence and requests for reprints should be sent to Kiel Christianson, 1422 F Spartan Village, E. Lansing, MI 48823.

This article is a revised version of an article presented at the 1995 JALT Conference, Nagoya, Japan, and the 1996 TESOL Conference, Chicago, IL. I thank the audiences of those two presentations, the *JSLW* editors, and two anonymous *JSLW* reviewers for their comments, which helped greatly to strengthen and clarify the article. Any remaining errors or omissions are solely my responsibility.

analysis of errors committed despite dictionary use and interviews with both more and less successful dictionary users.

Related research

A number of studies on dictionary use in the FL classroom have been conducted, all with somewhat different goals than the research presented here. Some authors have sought to classify dictionaries in terms of their intended use and intended audience (e.g., "reference" vs. "production" dictionaries, Summers, 1995; "decoding" vs. "encoding" dictionaries, Béjoint & Moulin, 1987; or "passive" vs. "active" dictionaries, Snell-Homby, 1987). Basically, reference, decoding, and passive dictionaries are ones the authors claim are best used for reading and listening tasks, while the production, encoding, and active dictionaries are for writing and speaking tasks.

Several researchers come out in support of either bilingual or monolingual dictionaries based on their research into the behavior of dictionary users. For example, Ard (1982) asserted that bilingual dictionaries "provoke errors" (p.5). Concurring opinions are found in Celce-Murcia and Rosenzweig, who stated that bilingual dictionaries "are often misleading" (1979, p. 254); Summers, who said, "bilingual dictionaries can cause problems and even errors" (1995, p. 25); and Meara and English, who quoted Nesi's findings that "[bilingual] dictionaries...were often ineffective, in that the entries either failed to prevent an obvious error, or actually reinforced error" (1987, p. 2). The most consistently cited drawback of bilingual dictionaries is that they "reinforce the belief in a one-to-one relationship at word level between two languages" (Thompson, 1987, p. 282; cf.Béjoint & Moulin, 1987; Hartmann, 1987; Snell-Homby, 1987; Summers, 1995).

Bilingual dictionaries also find some support in the literature. Although all authors offer extensive suggestions to bilingual lexicographers for ways to improve their dictionaries, several raise substantial arguments in favor of bilingual dictionary use (Baxter, 1980; Snell-Homby, 1987; Thompson, 1987). Still other researchers express no preference for either monolingual or bilingual dictionaries; they claim that errors can result from any dictionary whose headword definitions lack sufficient semantic, stylistic, syntactic, and collocational information (Maingay & Rundell, 1987).

Researchers have also sought to document how FL learners use their dictionaries, which is one of the goals of this study as well. A number of these have in turn attempted to describe the relationship between dictionary use and the errors made by FL learners in subsequent production (Ard, 1982; Béjoint & Moulin, 1987; Herbst & Stein, 1987; Maingay & Rundell, 1987; Meara & English, 1987; Tomaszczyk, 1987). On the whole, the authors of these studies make certain claims similar to, but perhaps not as grand as, Tomaszczyk's

(1987, p. 137): "[T]he vast majority of the errors would not have occurred if dictionaries had been used with skill." Meara and English (1987) "predicted" what errors would have been avoided through "effective" use of the *Longman Active Study Dictionary*. Herbst and Stein stated that 30% of the errors in their samples of student writing could have been avoided through "appropriate" use of a dictionary.

The main problem with studies such as these is that few authors are willing or able to describe exactly what "appropriate", "skillful" or "effective" dictionary use is. One finds tentative suggestions, as in Ard (1982) who proposed to "use both [bilingual and monolingual dictionaries] in tandem", but then concedes that this would only be of use where there are "no severe time constraints on composition" (p. 5). One also finds descriptions of various dictionary use strategies, as in Béjoint & Moulin (1987, p. 106ff), but without elaboration as to the types of learners or tasks for which they might be best suited.

The final area of research relevant to this study is that of dictionary use strategies. Dictionary training for both teachers and students is called for in several studies (cf. Ard, 1982; Béjoint & Moulin, 1987; Herbst & Stein, 1987). On the other hand, at least one study found that "[i]nstances of incompetent dictionary use were relatively few" (Tomaszczyk, 1987, p. 138) and posited that the main problem was that learners simply did not take time to consult dictionaries enough when writing.

Some studies suggest the most effective dictionary use strategies based on their research. For tasks on which there are no time constraints, Ard (1982) suggested using both a bilingual and monolingual dictionary as crossreferences (p. 5). Béjoint and Moulin (1987) listed a number of strategies, some of which they consider to be good, others bad (pp. 106-113). Obviously, however, the strategy that any given learner uses depends on the situation and on the learner's own learning and composition style.

I attempt to synthesize various aspects of all of these previous studies in order to reach the research goals listed below.

Research goals

Ultimately, the goal of this research is to describe what takes place when FL learners interact with dictionaries and by doing so, encourage teachers, in the spirit of Nunan (1991, p. xiv), to help students identify what works for them and why through the "collaborative exploration" of their dictionaries, the writing process, and their individual-writing and learning styles.

Three specific steps toward this primary goal are taken. These are:

1. Show that a significant number of writing errors were made by 51 Japanese EFL students

when they used dictionaries of all types by identifying such errors in a 41,024-word corpus of student writing.

2. Categorize all of these "dictionary word" errors occurring in the corpus to determine what aspects of English usage proved especially problematic to the dictionary users.

3. Interview four relatively more successful and four relatively less successful dictionary users as case studies in dictionary use behavior and strategies.

4. With reference to the knowledge gained in Steps 1 through 3, propose answers for a number of questions about some of the conclusions arrived at in previous studies dealing with FL writing and dictionary use.

Data collection

Throughout two academic semesters, two groups of Japanese university freshman EFL students majoring in computer science (51 students total) were asked to underline all of the words that they looked up in any dictionary (L1-L2, L2-L1,L2-L2) and then used in their in-class writing assignments. The topics for these writing assignments varied from week to week. Those given during the first weeks of the semester dealt with general topics (e.g., "My first impressions of the University of Aizu"), while later topics were more specifically related to the students' computer science studies (e.g., "The effects of computers on Japanese society").

The in-class writing sessions were timed, generally lasting 20 min. Group A(designated with A's in Table 2) wrote seven in-class writing assignments during the first 14-week semester. Group B (designated with B's in Table 2) wrote five during the 12-week second semester. The corpus for each student is composed of all in-class writings over the course of the semester. Students were urged to write as much as possible in the writing sessions; their grades depended on the length and development of the writing, not on the grammatical accuracy. However, all grammatical mistakes were later circled by the teacher, and students were asked in the following class period to correct all their mistakes. The students were allowed to use any type of dictionary they liked.

The writing sessions were structured in this way for two reasons. First, as using a dictionary involves "a considerable expenditure of time" (Ard, 1982, p. 15), the time constraint should have limited dictionary use to instances when students most pressingly felt a need for dictionary assistance. Thus, by analyzing the words which were looked up, we might gain some insight into the vocabulary level of these students, whose English education through at least 6 years of high-school English studies had been at least somewhat standardized by the Japanese Ministry of Education, and who had studied for and passed two rounds of rigorous university entrance exams containing sections on

English. Nevertheless, the levels of the students varied considerably, with TOEFL scores estimated at from approximately 248 to 542.

Second, although students might have used some dictionary words carelessly because they knew there was no penalty for grammar errors in the first draft, they also knew that they would be expected to correct all errors, including those made in connection with the underlined dictionary words, the following week. These errors were pointed out to the students, but they themselves were required to determine the exact error and the way to correct it. Furthermore, the time allotted for this correction process was limited, and the students' grades for the corrected and rewritten in-class writings depended solely on their error corrections. Therefore, there was incentive to get as much as possible right the first time and save work later. In this way I hoped the students' writings would reflect a realistic balance between fluency and accuracy.

Students were repeatedly reminded to underline their own dictionary words as they wrote. As a result, the vast majority of the students' dictionary words were accounted for accurately; the few that may have been missed would have no significant effect on the results. This straightforward method of data collection was also used by Ard (1982); however, Ard did not include the number of dictionary words, the number of incorrectly used dictionary words, or the number of total words written in that study.

Dictionary word-error categorization

The system used to categorize dictionary word errors was developed originally for purely pedagogical reasons. Thus, based on 3 years' experience teaching EFL writing to Japanese university students, I knew that all of the error categories (excluding *other*) would be readily identifiable in the students' compositions and would lend themselves to clear in-class explanations and student self-correction. (A description of the categories used and a full accounting of the data set can be found in Appendices A and B)

Whereas this approach is obviously not the most sophisticated, it is no less so than the categorizations used in the studies cited above. Meara and English's (1987) six error codes correspond roughly to the four categories of *wrong word*, *word form*, *spelling*, and *other* used in this article. Maingay and Rundell (1987)used just four categories: semantic, syntactic, collocational, and stylistic. These, however, are too broad and difficult to use in the classroom situation in which the data for this study were collected. Abraham, Matthies and Barratt (1994) discussed lexical-syntactic errors exclusively, thus omitting all errors described as *word form or wrong word*, two of the most common error types in this study. Their focus instead was on a number of errors which would fall into the categories of *preposition* and *other* (pp. 7-8).

The reliability of the error coding system used was not statistically measured—an obvious weakness in the data collection process. Nevertheless, after coding all dictionary word errors originally for classroom use, checking and grading the students' corrections of these errors, and then reevaluating each individual error another two times on separate occasions while preparing this study, apart from the slight difficulties described next, the coding was accurate. Even if one were to find fault with the categorization of a dictionary word error, there would be no doubt that it was indeed an error of some sort and as such still appropriate for inclusion in the study (i.e., not affecting the figures in Table 2).

Finally, a few notes of further explanation are necessary before moving on to Tables 1 and 2. Some of the dictionary words were actually phrases or idioms consisting of several words. Because these are often listed in dictionaries as one lexical unit and because students underlined them in one unit, such phrases have been counted as only one "word" (e.g., "Care killed the cat"; Student B3). In a few instances, there occurred multiple errors in one such phrase (e.g., *wrong word* and *spelling*) resulting in two errors counted for only one "word". Another slight difficulty experienced in the categorization of the dictionary word errors was that in approximately 10 instances sentences which students had written were not interpretable. Thus, the dictionary word included in the sentence was relegated to the *wrong word* category, possibly artificially inflating the category membership.

Table 1 contains the percentage of total dictionary word errors ranked by error type. For further discussion of these results, see the General Discussion section.

Table 1. Percentage of errors by error category

Error	No. of Errors	Percentage of All Dictionary Errors
Wrong word	77	27.2%
Other	46	16.3%
Preposition	38	13.4%
Article	34	12.0%
Plural	30	10.6%
Spelling	27	9.5%
Word form	20	7.1%
Tense	11	3.9%

Interviews

Hartmann (1987) reviewed the research methods of numerous studies of dictionary use. Only one of the articles included there, namely Ard (1982), used oral interviews to gather "students" recollections of how they use bilingual dictionaries" (Ard, 1982, p. 1). In this study, eight students were interviewed about the incorrect and correct dictionary words in their writings. These interviews were also tape recorded to supplement the notes taken during each interview (as suggested by Hartmann, 1987, p. 22).

The interviews were rather informal in order to, it was hoped, lower affective barriers and reduce the number of face-saving answers sometimes encountered in post hoc interviews. Nevertheless, the pattern of each interview was essentially the same. First, each student was given a very brief summary of the research data (see Table 2) and goals. Then each student and I proceeded word by word through all the dictionary words in the student's writings, those which constituted errors and those which did not. For each word, I began a series of questions aimed at determining what the student's thought process and look-up-strategy (Ard's "protocol") had been. Had they thought of a Japanese or English word first? Had they gone to a L1-L2, L2-L1, or L2-L2 dictionary first? What had they found and where? Had they read the example sentences? If there was more than one option (i.e., L2 translation of an L1 word) given in the dictionary, why had they chosen the one they did?

The students who were interviewed were selected according to the following criteria. First, students who had a higher or lower than average percentage of incorrect dictionary words were identified. Second, the percentage of overall dictionary words used was checked against the average of 1.6% dictionary word use (Table 2, Column 4) to eliminate students who had used, say, 66% of their dictionary words incorrectly but who had only looked up three words. Therefore, students such as A1, A10, and B14 (see Table 2) were not considered for interviews even though their incorrect percentages were above the average of 42%.

Only student B19 was chosen for an interview despite the fact that he had looked up only nine words, just 0.5% of his total words. The reason for this is that he presented a unique and perplexing case. B19 was perhaps the best writer of all of the students, having spent several years as a child in the United States, yet out of the nine words he looked up, seven (77.8%) were incorrect.

The eight students interviewed then consisted of four students who had a lower error percentage than average (A2, A20, A24, and B6), **Group L**, and four who had a higher error percentage than average (A21, B3, B5, and B19), **Group H**. This grouping brought with it an interesting dimension to the study. Group L did not exclusively contain students whom I would characterize as "relatively successful language learners" or "strong writers". Similarly, Group H did not contain only "relatively unsuccessful language learners" or "weak writers". Granted, these terms are extremely subjective; however, it was nevertheless somewhat of a surprise to find Students A2 and B6 in Group L and, as already mentioned, Student B19 in Group H. This suggests that efficient dictionary use does not necessarily correlate with overall FL ability or grades, and will be one of the issues raised in the discussion of the interviews.

Data analysis results

Table 2 gives the results of the error collection and categorization. It is rather striking that such a tiny fraction of words were looked up in a dictionary, only 674 (1.6%) of the total corpus of 41,024 words. Yet, more striking is the fact that of those 674 dictionary words, 283 (42%) were used incorrectly. These results are discussed in more detail below.

Interview results

The purpose of the interviews was to identify the dictionary strategies used by learners and then to try to determine why some of the students and strategies appeared to be successful although others did not. The students chosen to be interviewed were all paid minimum student-worker wage. Each interview (one session per student) lasted from 45 to 120 min. Space does not allow for a detailed analysis of all of the interviews, but the most salient parts of each will be discussed here.

Interviews of group L students (lower than average rate of dictionary word errors)

Student A24 (Group L)

Of the 51 students in the study, only A24 committed no errors. Student A24 used *Kenkyusha's Lighthouse English-Japanese Dictionary* (1990) and *Japanese-English Dictionary* (1990). She used the Japanese-English to look up 12 words, the English-Japanese for five, and both for one. She used both the Japanese-English and English-Japanese on different occasions to check spelling, usually of English loan words in Japanese, such as *resutoranto* (restaurant). She carefully read the example sentences provided, finding the one in each case which fit the context of her writing.

Table 2. Correct and incorrect dictionary word totals

St #	# of Total Words	# of Dict. Words	% of Dict. Words	# of Inc. Dict. Words	% of Inc. Dict. Words
A1	577	4	0.7	2	50.0
A2	500	9	1.8	1	11.1
A3	662	13	2.0	9	69.2
A4	576	22	3.8	11	50.0
A5	828	17	2.1	9	52.9
A6	1056	15	1.4	8	53.3
A7	882	16	1.8	9	56.3
A8	1110	39	3.5	15	38.5

(continued)

St #	# of Total Words	# of Dict. Words	% of Dict. Words	# of Inc. Dict. Words	% of Inc. Dict. Words
A9	882	20	2.3	7	35.0
A10	417	4	1.0	2	50.0
A11	689	17	2.5	8	47.1
A12	932	2	0.2	2	100.0
A13	676	15	2.2	5	33.3
A14	1056	26	2.5	10	38.5
A15	1355	11	0.8	6	54.5
A16	1221	19	1.6	7	36.8
A17	856	25	2.9	8	32.0
A18	926	15	1.6	5	33.3
A19	889	10	1.1	3	30.0
A20	1145	17	1.5	4	23.5
A21	548	15	2.7	12	80.0
A22	765	15	2.0	7	46.7
A23	914	2	0.2	1	50.0
A24	840	18	2.1	0	0.0
A25	725	34	4.7	13	38.2
A26	718	10	1.4	2	20.0
A27	719	33	4.6	14	42.4
B1	333	4	1.2	1	25.0
B2	605	2	0.3	1	50.0
B3	603	8	1.3	5	62.5
B4	795	10	1.3	5	50.0
B5	866	16	1.8	10	62.5
B6	817	23	2.8	4	17.4
B7	804	3	0.4	2	66.7
B8	729	18	2.5	8	44.4
B9	1257	10	0.8	4	40.0
B10	996	11	1.1	7	63.6
B11	596	6	1.0	2	33.3
B12	542	14	2.6	7	50.0
B13	730	17	2.3	8	47.1
B14	1042	2	0.2	1	50.0
B15	488	12	2.5	5	41.7
B16	1073	12	1.1	6	50.0
B17	458	6	1.3	3	50.0
B18	679	15	2.2	5	33.3
B19	1726	9	0.5	7	77.8
B20	786	6	0.8	3	50.0

(continued)

St #	# of Total Words	# of Dict. Words	% of Dict. Words	# of Inc. Dict. Words	% of Inc. Dict. Words
B21	743	3	0.4	1	33.3
B22	731	15	2.2	5	31.3
B23	714	3	0.4	1	33.3
B24	447	5	1.1	2	40.0
Totals	41,024	674	1.6	283	42.0

Note: The column headings refer to: student numbers, total number of words per student, total number of dictionary words per student, percentage of dictionary words per student, total number of incorrectly used dictionary words per student, and percentage of incorrectly used dictionary words per student.

For example, in one instance she knew the word *respect*, which she wanted to use, but was not sure of the preposition to go with it. In the English-Japanese she found, "She has great respect for her teacher." She went to the entry for the verb form of *respect* and found, "I respect Mr. Smith as our leader." When asked why she chose the verb construction, she said that she was influenced by the Japanese construction *sonkei suru* (to respect), so she had not really considered the entry for the noun form. She had not been able to construct an equivalent sentence to the example to fit her writing, so she used only, "I respect my mother".

One time she used both dictionaries in the manner suggested by Ard (1982). In the Japanese-English she looked under *katzukeru* and found the example sentence, "Shall I put [clear] away the tea cups on the table?" She then went to the English-Japanese to try to fit the example from the Japanese-English into her writing. In the English-Japanese she found, "She cleared the table", the sentence she finally incorporated into her writing as "I cleared the table". Her choice to cross-reference proved particularly fortunate as we see that the example from the Japanese-English is not completely correct and could easily lead to an inaccurate sentence such as, "I cleared the dishes on the table" rather than "I cleared the dishes from/off the table".

Finally, Student A24 displayed a high degree of sophistication in using her dictionaries as tools. At one point she had tried to find the English equivalent of *buraindo tacchi* (touch typing, literally, "blind touch"). First of all, she showed a great deal of linguistic maturity to recognize that even though *buraindo tacchi* is derived from English and is written in katakana, it might not be idiomatic English. So she went first to the Japanese-English but found nothing under that word. Her next step was to go to the table of contents and look under *kompyuuta* (computer). On page 586, she found a long list of computer-related terms, including *minai de* (touch type), the English translation, and the example sentence, "Can you touch type?"

A great deal of dictionary strategy training could be done by simply finding a student such as Student A24 in a class and then having her describe, in English or Japanese, step by step to her classmates the same look-up processes she related in this interview. However, it should also be noted that three times when she was presented with several possible translations of a Japanese word she had looked up, she chose the appropriate one simply because it was shorter, longer, or was listed first in the definition.

Student A2 (Group L)

Student A2 presented another fascinating case study in that he had serious difficulties expressing himself in written English, as evidenced by his low word count (see Table 2). His percentage of dictionary words was nominally above average, but the percentage of incorrect dictionary words was far below average at a mere 11.1%. The big question was: What was he doing right?

Student A2's dictionaries were *The New Anchor Japanese-English Dictionary* (1990) and *English-Japanese Dictionary* (1990). It was very surprising, however, to find that he had not used the Japanese-English for his writing. He had gone consistently and exclusively to the English-Japanese, thus casting a certain amount of doubt upon the validity of the dictionary typology of production, encoding, and active versus reference, decoding, and passive cited earlier. If Student A2's productive dictionary habits are used by even a small number of other FL learners around the world, this dichotomous typology would appear somewhat artificial. To be fair, though, it should be mentioned that Student A2 said that he does use a Japanese-English at home for completely unknown words, but when he is writing he prefers using an English-Japanese to double-check the appropriateness and spelling of words he has not had much experience using. While this strategy might have contributed to his low word count, it is well worth a brief analysis of his look-up procedures.

For all nine words, he first either translated the Japanese in his head or thought first of the English word and then proceeded to use the dictionary to check his translation, the usage, or both. In looking up the word, he was sure to read all of the example sentences provided. Student A2's strategy is described precisely in Béjoint and Moulin (1987, p. 106) when they asserted,"Writing should precede dictionary consultation. In other words, the result will be better if the learner first tries to express his thoughts by using the words and phrases which come spontaneously to mind."

The one error made by Student A2 was, "two slice of bread." The example sentences he read were all in the singular (e.g., "a slice of bread; a slice of luck"). Student A2 explained his mistake by saying that he simply had not thought of adding the plural "s". The fact that his dictionary contained no overt signal that "slice" is a countable noun may have contributed to the mistake.

Student A20 (Group L)

Student A20 displayed a high level of self-awareness and dictionary skills, but not to the extent of Student A24. By this I mean that Student A20 clearly remembered each step he had taken during the look-up process and displayed his familiarity with his dictionary's coding system for grammatical information. His lone dictionary was *Kenkyusha's New Collegiate Japanese-English Dictionary* (1983), demonstrating that a sophisticated dictionary user can be successful using a bilingual dictionary exclusively, contrary to some claims.

Student B6 (Group L)

Student B6's dictionary skills were equivalent to Student A20's; however, he had a tendency to ignore example sentences for the most part. Whether it was out of laziness or a rather too-optimistic feeling of knowing the language (also observed by Tomaszczyk, 1987), this habit appeared to have resulted in some errors. Student B6 used both Japanese-English and English-Japanese at various times for various words. He committed errors using both because, it seems, he either neglected the example sentences, or , when he used *Sanseido's Daily Concise Japanese-English Dictionary* (1990), there were none available. For instance, he wrote "had bought", using the wrong tense and omitting the direct object necessary in the causative construction he was attempting to use (i.e., "had someone buy something"). He translated the Japanese kau (to buy) in his head and then went to the English-Japanese for the tense formation, ignoring the example sentences, which in fact included a sentence exactly the same as the one he had been trying to write.

Interviews of group H students (higher than average rate of dictionary-word errors)

Student B19 (Group H)

As stated earlier, Student B19 was chosen for an interview because of his advanced English skills and his puzzling failure in using a dictionary effectively. The cause of his difficulties, it was discovered, was for the most part the dictionary he had chosen to use, namely XJDIC Version 1.1 (Breen, 1993), an online English-Japanese and Japanese-English dictionary for UNIX users. Actually, the dictionary is little more than a glossary with no example sentences or grammatical information, not even part of speech. A search for one of Student B19's errors, "situation," netted 20 different *kanji* choices, with only three of these containing even incomplete collocational information (e.g., "explosive situation"—no article).

If tools such as XJDIC were really useful in actual FL writing, as opposed to basic word-for-word translation (see also Ershov, Iizuka, Ryzhii, & Saito, 1995; Tung, 1993), one would predict that Student B19, an excellent student with a developed feel for English, would be able to use them correctly. The fact is, however, that six out of seven times he did not. All of his errors using XJDIC can be attributed to the lack of supporting grammatical and usage information. The one word from XJDIC he did use correctly, "tuition," netted only three glosses, one of which matched exactly the kanji of which B19 had been thinking. He was still, however, left with a choice of *tuition* and *school expenses* of which he chose the former just because it was shorter.

Interestingly, Student B19 also had only a 50% success rate (one out of two) with the *Collins Cobuild English Language Dictionary* (1987), an English-English learner's dictionary. After looking up "concern" he wrote, "The education doesn't concern with the difficulties." A correct version would be, "The education isn't concerned with." Examples containing the "is concerned with" and "doesn't concern itself with" constructions might have helped him avoid the error.

The word from the *Collins Cobuild* he did use correctly, *steal*, he found after first looking up *rob*. He saw *steal* in the definition of *rob*, went to *steal*, and chose it simply because it sounded better to him in the sentence. The choice was fortuitous, as *rob* would not have been appropriate for the context.

Students A21, B3, and B5 (Group H)

Students A21, B3, and B5 all used either one or both of the same dictionaries as Student A24, who made no errors (Student B3 used both *Lighthouse* dictionaries, Students A21 and B5 used the Japanese-English version in tandem with *Taishukan's Genius English-Japanese Dictionary*, 1988). This could be taken as anecdotal evidence that no matter which dictionary is used, its value depends on the user more than the dictionary itself (not including, perhaps, glossaries such as XJDIC). All three of these students reported consistently that they had almost never read any example sentences.

Students A21 and B3 used, in a few cases, both Japanese-English and English-Japanese in tandem and made errors. Student A21 in particular displayed no knowledge of the most basic grammar information coded in his dictionary, saying that he had thought the "C" after nouns such as *bottle* designated them as nouns; he did not realize that it meant they were countable nouns. When Student A21 did read the example sentences, he had mixed success, possibly because of his lack of practice using them. For instance, once he read a sample sentence under *remain*—"He remained silent." He reported that he had thought this sentence to be analogous to the sentence he then wrote, "I remained understand English." Once, however, he used an example sentence effectively. After reading the example sentence, "The plan was a great success [complete failure] as we had expected" in his dictionary, he wrote, "And I found the examination more difficult than I had expected."

Neither Students B3 nor B5 seemed to be able to easily recall what Japanese word they had in mind when they had used their dictionaries. This suggests that the initial dictionary consultation had been practically devoid of meaning for them, in no way connected to vocabulary learning or hypothesis building and testing. They appeared to have simply been looking for a word-for-word translation and then proceeded to forget the English word once they had written it. Glossaries which try to pass for dictionaries such as XJDIC and pocket dictionaries lacking example sentences undoubtedly foster in FL learners the false belief that the lexicons of two languages consist simply of lists of words with exact one-to-one translations. However, students B3 and B5 demonstrate that even adequately constructed dictionaries can be practically useless in the hands of unsophisticated, unobservant users, which is inconsistent with Tomaszczyk's (1987) observations quoted previously.

General discussion

At first glance, the tiny fraction of words in the corpus that were looked up in a dictionary, 1.6% (see Table 2), raises the question of whether or not this study of dictionary use is necessary or even worthwhile. The dictionary words identified here are obviously not a major part of the overall process of these students' FL writing production.

Nevertheless, dictionaries are basic tools for FL learners. Moreover, even if dictionaries are not used as much as might be expected for some tasks, such as timed in-class writing, they *are* used by most students. Only two students out of the 53 who contributed writings to this study never used any dictionary (their data was not included in Table 2). It is extremely important to remember that in the minds of many FL learners, their dictionaries are repositories of "all truth and guidance" (Abraham et al., 1994, p. 9), and at least at the beginner level a learner's first impulse is often to turn to a dictionary.

Furthermore, the errors analyzed are important, if for no other reason, because they were made despite dictionary use. Why use a dictionary at all if not to ensure that what you are writing is correct? From this perspective, the 42% error rate represents a dramatic failure.

Questioning the conclusions of previous studies

The fourth goal of this research, as stated earlier, is to suggest answers to some questions regarding FL dictionary use and to raise certain questions about the conclusions drawn in the studies previously cited.

1. Do bilingual dictionaries "provoke errors"?

Let us return to this statement of Ard's (1982) quoted above. The numerical data presented in Table 3 does not support such a claim. Table 3 is a random sampling of roughly 10% of the totals from Table 2, generated to more conveniently compare the number of dictionary word errors in the corpus to the number of all errors (dictionary word and non-dictionary word errors) made by the students.

Assuming this small sampling is anywhere near representative of the entire group of students, Table 3 shows a significantly higher percentage of total errors than of dictionary word errors (see Table 2). It also shows that dictionary word errors account for only 35 or 0.9% of the total words and 5.4% of the total errors. This suggests that these students make errors much more often than they use their dictionaries. So even if some dictionaries "provoked errors", it appears that they did not do so often enough to add significantly to the total error count.

Table 3. Errors and percents of errors

Total Words	Total Errors	Percent of Total
4105	644	15.7%
	dictionary word errors	percent of total
	35	0.9% (of total words)
		5.4% (of all errors)

Note: This table represents total words, all errors, dictionary word errors, and percentage of error from a five-student sampling.

Ard himself tempered his criticism of bilingual dictionaries by saying, "It has not been proven that the use of a bilingual dictionary leads to errors where no errors would otherwise occur" (1982, p. 17). Based on the data, trying to make such a claim would prove difficult. Furthermore, during the interviews not once did any students demonstrate or claim that they were planning to use an appropriate word or construction, but after looking in their dictionaries, made an error instead. It is also important to remember, however, that no evidence exists to refute the assumption that without the dictionaries, there could well have been 391 more total errors in the corpus (i.e., the 58% of dictionary words that were used correctly).

2. Can one predict what percentage or which types of errors could be avoided with "skillful" dictionary use?

Studies whose authors claim that a certain percentage of errors could have been avoided with "skillful" dictionary use must also be questioned (cf. Herbst & Stein, 1987; Tomaszczyk, 1987; Meara & English, 1987). Although the data suggest that about 60% of the lexical items looked up in dictionaries are used correctly, 40% are not. Add to this the

15% or so of all words which contained errors, and one is hard-pressed to believe that any FL writer could spend enough time with a dictionary to avoid, as Herbst and Stein claimed is possible, 30% of errors.

According to Table 3, such a process would entail the looking up of 644 words in order to avoid 193 errors (30% of the total errors). These numbers assume, of course, "skillful" use of the dictionary, which is neither defined nor described. If this level of skill were not present in the FL writer, another 40% of the 193 errors (77) would not be avoided, according to Table 2. Thus, we would have the average student looking up 644 words to avoid 116 errors. According to Ard (p. 15), each word would take very roughly 50 seconds to look up. So those 644 words alone, just 15.7% of the total words written, would cost the writer nearly 9 hours.

3. Can one predict which errors could be avoided by using a specific dictionary "skillfully"?

Predictions of what errors could have been avoided by using a certain dictionary (Meara & English, 1987) are highly specious, unless, perhaps, the learner has an unlimited amount of time, a number of dictionaries with which he or she is familiar, and a highly developed control of the FL. Table 1 shows that errors which even the most primitive dictionary should be able to prevent, namely spelling errors, still account for nearly 10% of errors committed by learners with six or more years of FL experience using a dictionary. If we could not predict that these errors would not occur, what can we reasonably predict? Furthermore, it is important to note that all of the students in Group H (those with a higher than average rate of dictionary word errors) used one or both of the same dictionaries as Student A24, who committed no errors at all, suggesting that accurate production relies more on the sophistication of the user than on that of the dictionary (glossaries such as XJDIC excluded).

4. Do grammatical information and example sentences really help users to avoid errors? If so, how?

Paikeday (1993) considered such "illustrative material" to be the most important part of a dictionary, "more important even than the definitions" (p. 240). Indeed, the one strong pattern that emerged in the interviews was that the students who read the example sentences and related them to the writing task at hand made fewer mistakes. With this in mind, Table 1 raises some practical issues for teachers and lexicographers. It is apparent that the errors which this group of students made most often are also the ones that are simplest to draw their attention to and to provide examples for in dictionary entries. *Wrong word* and *other*, the two most common errors, are also the most vague and often require the most complex explanations when it comes to telling the learner why an error is an error and how to correct it. Leaving these two categories aside for this reason, we are left with 56.5% of the dictionary errors. Whereas no one would assert that explaining English prepositions or articles is easy to do, it is not too optimistic to say that all of the students in this study group knew what these things were. They also knew some basic rules regarding their use and that these features of English grammar were especially difficult for them to use (as is illustrated in more than one of the interviews).

Therefore, a suggestion for teachers and lexicographers alike is to cover the basics first. Focus on what learners at a given level should know already (e.g., that there are some things called "articles" used with English nouns and that plurals are usually marked with an "[e]s"), on what is easiest to include in the examples found in entries, and on what is easiest to point out and explain in class.

Numerous authors have given some excellent suggestions as to what bilingual and monolingual learners' dictionaries should include (cf. Abraham *et al.*, 1994; Ard, 1982; Maingay & Rundell, 1987; Meara & English, 1987; Snell-Homby, 1987; Summers, 1995; Thompson, 1987). As helpful and necessary as these articles are, it should be stressed that the data here suggest that simply including examples with basic aspects of the entry's function and use (i.e., prepositional collocations, count-noncount, plural formation, and tense formation) should help reduce significantly the number of errors made when using a dictionary (as some of these authors also stress). Furthermore, this information should be provided in copious example sentences presented consistently and systematically throughout the dictionary for every entry.

5. Does the dictionary typology of production, encoding, and active dictionaries (generally L1-L2) versus reception, decoding, and passive dictionaries (generally L2-L1 or L2-L2) reflect actual dictionary use?

Not according to the interviews conducted. Several of the students interviewed, and Student A2 in particular, demonstrated how an L2-L1 dictionary can be used quite effectively for production.

6. Does a "more successful" or "more advanced" language learner necessarily use dictionaries more effectively than a "less successful" or "less advanced" language learner?

Student A2, a "less advanced" learner, used his dictionaries following sophisticated strategies, strategies that some researchers, in fact, have speculated to be optimal (see previous paragraphs). Student B19, on the other hand, despite his more advanced English skills, relied on a word-for-word translation strategy and made a number of dictionary word errors. These two students are counterexamples to Mochizuki's (1995) findings that the participants who took part in his study "benefitted from dictionary use according to the level of [their] proficiency in grammar" (p. 89).

7. Does one dictionary-use strategy suffice for all users in all situations?

The students in this study seem to employ various strategies during different tasks and for different words. For some students, their strategies were successful; for others, the same strategies were not. While teachers might be able to suggest a number of strategies that students may find helpful, the students themselves ultimately must choose based on the writing context and the given word or phrase being looked up.

Even though Student A24 made the fewest errors, I would not want to tell Student A2 that he should use Student A24's strategies; after all, Student A2's work fine, too. Likewise, I would not want to force Students A21, B3, or B5 to adopt Student A2's dictionary strategies, since these three students might not be able or ready to use such sophisticated strategies. Nevertheless, dictionary training, including strategy training, is obviously necessary, as demonstrated by the lack of familiarity with their dictionaries that the students with a higher than average rate of dictionary word errors (Group H) displayed.

8. Can university-level EFL teachers in Japan assume that incoming freshmen can use "basic" English vocabulary?

When analyzing all of the words the students in this study looked up, I was struck by the number of "basic" words (i.e., words contained in the General Service List of 2000 Words, as cited by Nation, 1990) that stu dents looked up in their dictionaries. These include words like wash, *hope*, *reason*, and *common*. In fact, of the 295 nonphrase words looked up, 128 (43%) can be found in the General Service List. It is odd that students who have passed long and difficult university entrance exam sections on English vocabulary would not know how to use such words or, more oddly, would not know how to use such words even after they had looked them up in a dictionary. This would be an interesting avenue of further research.

Conclusions and suggestions

In a recent article toward a "general theory of L2 writing" (Valdés, Haro, & Echevarriarza, 1992), there is a conspicuous and telling omission, namely the role of dictionaries in the writing process. Dictionaries are still considered by some to be no more of a language learning tool or aid than the pen or pencil with which the writing is done. Perhaps this is the reason that Béjoint & Moulin (1987) found that "most [secondary-school teachers] never use the simple and yet detailed syntactic information offered by learners' dictionaries and consequently never tell their pupils about it" (p. 110). We have seen here that FL learners do however need help using their dictionaries.

The quantitative and qualitative analysis presented here could serve as a model for FL teachers to use in their own classes. It seems that the dictionary habits of students, their strengths and weaknesses, can be much more clearly understood through similar scrutiny. If an FL teacher were to present similar data to his or her students, it would hopefully demonstrate to them the need for an increased self-awareness of their writing and dictionary use habits. This sort of conscious effort on their part might well improve both their dictionary skills and their overall FL writing ability.

References

Abraham, R., Matthies, B., & Barratt, M. (1994). *Beyond vocabulary: what's new in the lexicon.* Paper presented at the 28th Annual TESOL Conference, Baltimore, MD, March 8–12, 1994. (ERIC Document Reproduction Service No. ED 376 709).

Ard, J. (1982). The use of bilingual dictionaries by ESL students while writing. *ITL Review of Applied Linguistics, 58*, 1–27.

Baxter, J. (1980). The dictionary and vocabulary behavior: a single word or a handful? *TESOL Quarterly 14*(3), 325–336.

Béjoint, H., & Moulin, A. (1987). The place of the dictionary in an EFL programme. In A. Cowie (ed.), *The dictionary and the language learner: papers from the EURALEX seminar at the University of Leeds*, 1–3 April 1985 (pp. 97–114). Tübingen: Max Niemeyer Verlag.

Celce-Murcia, M., & Rosenzweig, F. (1979). Teaching vocabulary in the ESL classroom. In M. Celce-Murcia & L. McIntosh (eds.), *Teaching English as a second or foreign language* (pp. 241–257). Rowley: Newbury House.

Collins Cobuild English Language Dictionary. (1987). London: Collins Publishers.

Ershov, M., Iizuka, T., Ryzhii, V., & Saito, K. (1995). *English-Japanese mini-dictionary: semiconductors, microelectronics, and general physics.* Aizu-Wakamatsu: University of Aizu Computer Solid State Physics Lab/Computer Devices Lab.

Hartmann, R. R. K. (1987). Four perspectives on dictionary use: a critical review of research methods. In A. Cowie (ed.), *The dictionary and the language learner: papers from the EURALEX seminar at the University of Leeds*, 1–3 April 1985 (pp. 11–28). Tübingen: Max Niemeyer Verlag.

Herbst, T., & Stein, G. (1987). Dictionary-using skills: a plea for a new onentation in language teaching. In A. Cowie (ed.), *The dictionary and the language learner: Papers from the EURALEX seminar at the University of Leeds*, 1–3 April 1985 (pp. 115–27). Tübingen: Max Niemeyer Verlag.

Kenkyusha's Lighthouse English-Japanese Dictionary (2nd ed.). (1990). Tokyo: Kenkyusha.

Kenkyusha's Lighthouse Japanese-English Dictionary (2nd ed.). (1990). Tokyo: Kenkyusha.

Kenkyusha's New Collegiate Japanese-English Dictionary (3rd. ed.). (1983). Tokyo: Kenkyusha.

Maingay, S., & Rundell, M. (1987). Anticipating learners' errors: implications for dictionary writers. In A. Cowie (ed.), *The dictlonary and the language learner: papers from the EURALEX seminar at the University of Leeds*, 1–3 April 1985 (pp. 128–35). Tübingen: Max Niemeyer Verlag.

Meara, P., & English, F. (1987). *Lexical errors and learners' dictionaries.* Technical Report, Birkbeck College, London. (ERIC Document Reproduction Service No. ED 290 322).

Mochizuki, M. (1995). A relationship between learners' proficiency in grammar and their dictionary-using skills. *JACET Bulletin, 26*, 79–93.

Nation, I. S. P. (1990). *Teaching and learning vocabulary*. Boston: Heinle & Helnle.

The New Anchor English-Japanese Dictionary. (1990). Tokyo: Gakken.

The New Anchor Japanese-English Dictionary. (1990). Tokyo: Gakken.

Nunan, D. (1991). *Language teaching methodology: a textbook for teachers*. Englewood Cliffs: Prentice Hall Regents.

Paikeday, T. M. (1993). The Kenkyusha dictionaries: 50 years of shortchanging the Japanese. *JALT Journal, 15* (2), 239–244.

Sanseido's Daily Concise Japanese-English Dictionary (4th ed.). (1990). Tokyo: Sanseido.

Snell-Homby, M. (1987). Towards a learner's bilingual dictionary. In A. Cowie (ed.), *The dictionary and the language learner: papers from the EURALEX seminar at the University of Leeds*, 1–3 April 1985 (pp. 159–170). Tübingen: Max Niemeyer Verlag.

Summers, D. (1995). Vocabulary learning: do dictionaries really help? *The Language Teacher, 19*(2), 25–28.

Taishukan's Genius English-Japanese Dictionary (2nd ed.). (1988). Tokyo: Taishukan.

Thompson, G. (1987). Using bilingual dictionaries. *ELT Journal, 41*(4), 282–286.

Tomaszczyk, J. (1987). FL learners' communication failure: Implications for pedagogical lexicography. In A. Cowie (ed.), *The dictionary and the language learner: papers from the EURALEX seminar at the University of Leeds*, 1–3 April 1985 (pp. 136–145). Tübingen: Max Niemeyer Verlag.

Tung, L. W. (1993). *Japanese-English/English-Japanese glossary of scientific and techmcal terms*. New York: Wiley.

Valdés, G., Haro, P., & Echevarriarza, M. P. (1992). The development of writing abilities in a foreign language: contributions toward a general theory of L2 writing. *The Modern Language Journal, 76*(3), 333–352.

APPENDIX A: Heading and Category Explanations for the Full Data Set
(Expanded Version of Table 2)

st # (student number): The number assigned randomly to each student.

words: The total number of words written by each student in all of the students' inclass writings.

dicwords(dictionary words): The total number of words that the student underlined, thus marking them as dictionary words.

dic%: The percentage of the total number of a student's words that were underlined as dictionary words.

incorr (incorrect): The number of dictionary words that were used incorrectly.

inc%: The percentage of the dictionary words that were used incorrectly.

ww (wrong word): The number of the student's dictionary words marked as errors because they simply did not fit into the context of the student's writing. They may be morphologically related to the target word (paronyms), or words carrying unintended or inappropriate connotations, or nonsensical words in the context.

ww%: The percentage of all the student's incorrect dictionary words that were wrong words.

wf (word form): The number of the student's dictionary words marked as errors, incorrectly applying word formation principles, e.g. "bored/boring," or using a noun instead of a verb, adjective instead of an adverb, etc.

wf%: The percentage of the student's incorrect dictionary words that were word form mistakes.

art (article): The number of the student's dictionary words marked as mistakes because of either omitted, incorrect, or unnecessary article use.

art%: The percentage of the student's incorrect dictionary words that were article mistakes.

sp (spelling): The number of the student's dictionary words that were misspelled.

sp%: The percentage of the student's incorrect dictionary words that were spelling mistakes.

pl(plural): The number of the student's dictionary words marked as errors because of incorrect or malformed plural endings.

pl%: The percentage of the student's incorrect dictionary words that contained mistakes in the plural endings.

tns(tense): The number of the student's dictionary words marked as errors because of incorrect or malformed tense markers.

tns%: The percentage of the student's incorrect dictionary words that were mistakes in tense.

pr (preposition): The number of the student's incorrect dictionary words marked wrong because of an omitted, unnecessary, or wrong preposition.

pr%: The percentage of the student's incorrect dictionary words that were preposition mistakes.

o (other): The number of the student's incorrect dictionary words that did not fit into any of the other error categories.

o%: The percentage of the student's incorrect dictionary words that were "other" mistakes.

APPENDIX B: Full Data Set
(Expanded Version of Table 2)

st #	words	dic-words	dic%	incorr	inc%	ww	ww%	wf	wf%	art	art%	sp	sp%	p1	p1%	tns	tns%	pr	pr%	o	o%
A1	577	4	0.69	2	50.00		0.00		0.00		0.00		0.00	1	50.00		000	1	50.00		0.00
A2	500	9	1.80	1	11.11		0.00		0.00		0.00		0.00	1	100.00		0.00		0.00		0.00
A3	662	13	1.96	9	69.23	1	11.11	4	44.44	1	11.11	1	11.11		0.00		0.00		0.00	2	22.22
A4	576	22	3.82	11	30.00	6	54.55		0.00	1	9.09		0.00		0.00		0.00	2	18.18	2	18.18
A5	828	17	2.05	9	52.94	5	55.56		0.00		0.00		0.00	1	11.11	1	11.11	2	22.22		0.00
A6	1056	15	1.42	8	53.33	3	37.50		0.00	1	12.50		0.00		2.00	1	12.50	2	25.00	1	12.50
A7	882	16	1.81	9	56.25	2	22.22		0.00	1	11.11		0.00	2	22.22		0.00	2	22.22	2	22.22
A8	1110	39	3.51	15	35.46	7	46.67		0.00	3	20.00		0.00	1	6.67	1	6.67	2	13.33	1	6.67
A9	882	20	2.27	7	35.00	3	42.86		0.00	1	14.29	1	14.29	2	28.57		0.00		0.00		0.00
A10	417	4	0.96	2	50.00	2	100.00		0.00		0.00		0.00	0	0.00		0.00		0.00		0.00
A11	689	17	2.47	8	47.06	3	37.50		0.00	1	12.50	1	12.50	2	25.00		0.00	1	12.50		0.00
A12	932	2	0.21	2	100.00	2	100.00		0.00		0.00		0.00	0	0.00		0.00		0.00		0.00
A13	676	15	2.22	5	33.33	1	20.00		0.00	2	40.00		0.00	1	20.00		0.00		0.00	1	20.00
A14	1056	26	2.46	10	38.46	3	30.00	1	10.00	1	10.00	2	20.00		0.00		0.00	1	10.00	2	20.00
A15	1355	11	0.81	6	54.55	2	33.33		0.00	1	16.67		000		0.00	1	16.69		0.00	2	33.33
A16	1221	19	1.56	7	36.84		0.00	1	14.29	1	14.29		0.00		0.00		0.00	2	28.57	3	42.86
A17	856	25	2.92	8	32.00	2	25.00		0.00		0.00	2	25.00	1	12.50		000	2	25.00	1	12.50
A18	926	15	1.62	5	33.33	2	40.00	1	20.00		0.00		0.00		0.00		0.00	2	40.00		0.00
A19	889	10	1.12	3	30.00	1	25.00		0.00		0.00	2	66.67		0.00		0.00		0.00	1	33.33
A20	1145	17	1.48	4	23.53	1	25.00		0.00		0.00	1	25.00		0.00	1	25.00	1	25.00		0.00
A21	548	15	2.74	12	80.00	2	16.67		0.00	2	16.67		0.00	1	8.33	2	16.67	1	8.33	4	33.33
A22	765	15	1.96	7	46.67	1	14.29	1	14.29	1	14.29	1	14.29	2	28.57		0.00	1	14.29		0.00
A23	914	2	0.22	1	50.00		0.00		0.00		0.00		0.00		0.00		0.00		0.00	1	100.00
A24	840	18	2.14	0	0.00		0.00		0.00		0.00		0.00		0.00		0.00		0.00		0.00

(continued)

st #	words	dic-words	dic%	incorr	inc%	ww	ww%	wf	wf%	art	art%	sp	sp%	pl	pl%	tns	tns%	pr	pr%	o	o%
A25	725	34	4.69	13	38.24	4	30.77	1	7.69	1	7.69	1	7.69	2	15.38		0.00	2	15.38	2	15.38
A26	718	10	1.39	2	20.00		0.00		0.00		0.00		0.00		0.00		0.00	1	50.00	1	50.00
A27	719	33	4.59	14	42.42	2	14.29		0.00	1	7.14	4	28.57	2	14.29	2	14.29	2	14.29	1	7.14
B1	333	4	1.20	1	25.00		0.00		0.00	1	100.00		0.00		0.00		0.00		0.00		0.00
B2	605	2	0.33	1	50.00		0.00	1	100.00		0.00		0.00		0.00		0.00		0.00		0.00
B3	603	8	1.33	5	62.50	1	20.00		0.00		0.00	1	20.00	1	20.00		0.00		0.00	2	40.00
B4	795	10	1.26	5	50.00		0.00	1	20.00	2	40.00		0.00	1	20.00		0.00		0.00	1	20.00
B5	866	16	1.85	10	62.50	2	20.00	4	40.00	1	10.00		0.00		0.00		0.00	3	30.00		0.00
B6	817	23	2.82	4	17.39		0.00	1	25.00		0.00	1	25.00	1	25.00		0.00		0.00	1	25.00
B7	804	3	0.37	2	66.67		0.00		0.00		0.00	1	50.00		0.00		0.00		0.00	1	50.00
B8	729	18	2.47	8	44.44	2	25.00		0.00	2	25.00		0.00		0.00		0.00	1	12.50	3	37.50
B9	1257	10	0.80	4	40.00	2	50.00		0.00		0.00		0.00	1	25.00		0.00	1	25.00		0.00
B10	996	11	1.10	7	63.64	3	42.86		0.00	2	28.57		0.00	1	14.29		0.00	1	14.29		0.00
B11	596	6	1.01	2	33.33		0.00		0.00		0.00		0.00		0.00		0.00	2	100.00		0.00
B12	542	14	2.58	7	50.00		0.00	1	14.29	2	28.57	1	14.29	2	28.27		0.00	1	14.29		0.00
B13	730	17	2.33	8	47.06	3	37.50		0.00		0.00	2	25.00	1	12.50		0.00	1	12.50	1	12.50
B14	1042	2	0.19	1	50.00		0.00		0.00		0.00		0.00		0.00		0.00		0.00	1	100.00
B15	488	12	2.46	5	41.67	1	20.00		0.00	1	20.00	1	20.00		0.00	1	20.00		0.00	1	20.00
B16	1073	12	1.12	6	50.00	1	000		0.00		0.00	2	33.33	1	16.67		0.00		0.00	3	50.00
B17	458	6	1.31	3	50.00		0.00	1	33.33	1	33.33	1	33.33		0.00		0.00		0.00		0.00
B18	679	15	2.21	5	33.33	3	60.00		0.00		0.00	1	20.00		000		0.00		0.00	1	20.00
B19	1726	9	0.52	7	77.78	2	28.57	1	14.29	1	14.29		0.00	2	28.57		0.00		0.00	1	14.29
B20	786	6	0.76	3	50.00	2	66.67		0.00	1	33.33		0.00		0.00		0.00		0.00		0.00
B21	743	3	0.40	1	33.33	1	100.00		0.00		0.00		0.00		0.00		0.00		0.00		0.00
B22	731	16	2.19	5	31.25	1	20.00	1	20.00	1	20.00		0.00		0.00	1	20.00		0.00	1	20.00
B23	714	3	0.42	1	33.33		0.00		0.00		0.00		0.00		0.00		0.00		0.00	1	100.00
B24	447	5	1.12	2	40.00		0.00		0.00		0.00		0.00		0.00		0.00	1	50.00	1	50.00
totals	41024	674	1.64	283	41.99	77	27.21	20	7.07	34	12.01	27	9.54	20	10.60	11	3.89	38	13.43	46	16.25

Culture Adaptation

Topic Three

Anticipating the Issue

Discuss your answers to the following questions.

1. Do you agree with the following statement, "All communication is cultural"? Why or why not?

2. What is culture shock? What would you suggest to avoid or overcome culture shock?

3. What can we do to communicate effectively with people from other cultures?

Selections

Unit 5

Home-School Communication and Expectations of Recent Chinese Immigrants

Learning Objectives

- What are the functions and styles of Results and Discussion in a research paper?
- Sentence patterns in Results and Discussion
- How to write Results in a research paper?
- How to write Discussion in a research paper?

Home-School Communication and Expectations of Recent Chinese Immigrants

Lily L. Dyson

In this study, I investigated the nature of communication between home and school in families who recently immigrated to Canada. I used an open-ended questionnaire in interviews of 21 Chinese immigrant families and 19 non-immigrant European-Canadian families. The immigrant parents' pattern of communication differed from that of nonimmigrant parents: immigrant parents communicated less frequently, had more difficulty comprehending the communication, and were less satisfied with the communication. The immigrant parents especially emphasized the academic progress of their children and were concerned with the quality of teaching.

Home and school form the microsystems of a child's educational development. The connection between home and school is integral to a **cohesive** and effective learning environment (Bronfennbrenner,1979). Central to this connection is the communication between home and school. Scholars such as Epstein (1990) and Healey (1994) have stated that teachers' communication with parents increases many forms of parental involvement in school or at home; others (Norris, 1999; Watkins, 1997) have linked children's academic achievement and motivation to home-school communication. Watkins (1997) confirmed that the amount of teacher-initiated communication that parents perceive predicts parent involvement. Bowman (1989) suggested that effective home-school communication facilitates teachers' responsibility to **interpret** and relay the school's agenda to the parents. Bhattacharya (2000) identified a strong link between parents and teachers as a factor protecting children from dropping out of school.

Parental involvement in education is particularly important for elementary school children whose native language is not English (Constantino, Cui, & Faltis, 1995; Swap, 1990). Unfamiliar with the English language, these children need additional educational support, which in turn requires the involvement of the home. Yet cultural and linguistic differences may prevent effective home-school communication, and hence **hinder** parental involvement in school activities. Parents who have grown up in a culture outside North America may hold different views of schools and children than those of their children's teachers (Theilheimer, 2001). A study of Latin American families in Canada found that, despite parents' high **aspirations** for their children and despite the great value they attached to education, their children's teachers showed little awareness for their concerns (Bernhard & Freire, 1999). The language barrier also **deters** immigrant parents' communication with and involvement in the school (Bhattacharya, 2000; Gougeon, 1993). **Intimidated** by the linguistic barriers they face in the English-speaking school environment, such parents may be especially unable to participate actively in their children's education (Commins, 1992). Yet immigrant minority parents' lack of involvement is often misinterpreted by school personnel as a lack of interest in their children's academic work (Commins, 1992). Immigrant families' communication with their children's schools becomes a major educational concern, which **constitutes** the focus of the present study with recent Chinese immigrants.

Herrera and Wooden (1988) have suggested that miscommunication between home and school prompted minority children's failure in school. However, socio-economic disadvantages often associated with the minority and immigrant status may have confounded such a finding. Social class disadvantages provide parents with fewer resources for participating in their children's education (Lareau, 1987). Economic hardship, however, is not invariably the experience of immigrants. Immigrants with no socio-economic disadvantages would serve as a less **unbiased** sample for the study of home-school communication.

Even in the absence of economic disadvantages, Chinese immigrants who recently arrived in Canada or the U.S.A. may face barriers against effective communication with schools. Both parents and teachers in the study by Constantino et al. (1995) confirmed that language barriers caused Chinese parents' lack of communication with their children's school. Recent Chinese immigrants in Canada or the U.S.A. encountered another barrier: the gap between their native culture and that of mainstream North America. In general, Asians tend to value the needs of the group and emphasize duty and obligation (Hui & Triandis, 1986). In their communication style, Asian people are generally **succinct** whereas North Americans tend to favour **eloquence** of speech (Yang, 1993).

Moreover, Chinese culture emphasizes education (Ho, 1981). Grounded in a cultural belief in human **malleability** and effort (Chen & Uttal, 1988) and in education as a means for social advancement and the **procurement** of wealth (Ho, 1981; Stevenson, Lee, & Chen, 1994), Chinese parents value academic achievement (Lin & Fu, 1990) and set high expectations for their children (Ran, 2001). Chinese mothers also believed in direct **intervention** in their children's learning (Chao, 1996). Such an educational emphasis conflicts with the child-centred approach generally practised in Canada (Holmes, 1998) and hence might confound Chinese parents' communication with their children's schools.

North American schools have increasingly emphasized multicultural education, which Sleeter and Grant (1994) defined as "education policies and practices that recognize, accept, and affirm human differences and similarities related to gender, race, disability, and class" (p. 167). Governments and schools have introduced such a policy to reduce prejudice and **discrimination** toward ethnic and racial groups, and to promote ethnic identity and educational and career equity for minorities (Valencia, 1992).To achieve this policy, parents, especially those of an ethnic minority; need information about schools' policies and practices on multicultural education. Parents' knowledge of school practice of multicultural education depends on the effectiveness of home-school communication and thus constitutes a logical measure of such effectiveness.

Because of language barriers and their unique cultural values, recent Chinese immigrant parents would engage in a pattern of communication with their children's schools that differs from that of non-immigrant, European-Canadian parents, a basic pattern that includes frequency, method, and content of communication (Prescott, Pelton, & Dornbusch,1986). In practice, Chinese immigrant parents communicate less frequently with schools, have difficulty understanding the communication, and are less informed about school programs such as multicultural education. Moreover, because Chinese immigrant parents incline towards a cultural emphasis on group well-being and educational achievement, their communications with the school tend to focus on public affairs such as school events and benefits and on their children's academic achievement. However, these characteristics of Chinese immigrants' communication with schools are yet to be verified as a distinctive trait in relation to parents in general.

No Canadian researchers have studied recent Chinese immigrant families who are free from the confounding effect of socio-economic disadvantage. Such a study would be particularly timely because of the dramatic increase in recent years of Chinese immigration to Canada (Badets , 1993) and the U.S.A. (Zhou, 1997). The information would help schools develop effective communication with Chinese immigrant parents. To examine the home-school communication of recent Chinese immigrants, I investigated: (a) the pattern of communication in terms of frequency, method, and content; (b) parents' understanding of and satisfaction with the communication; and (c) parents' knowledge of the school's multicultural policies. In this paper, I refer to "recent Chinese immigrant" as "Chinese immigrant" or "Chinese", whereas "nonimmigrant European-Canadian" is interchangeable with "non-immigrant" or "Caucasian".[1]

Method

Participants

The participants were 40 parents: 21 recent Chinese immigrants and 19 non-immigrant Caucasian-Canadians, each from a different family. These families had a combined total of 46 children, 21 Chinese and 25 European-Canadian. Only one father took part in the interview and only one family involved both parents in the interview; mothers represented the rest of the families. The families lived in a medium-sized Canadian metropolitan city. The Chinese families, who originated from Taiwan, Mainland, and Hong Kong, had immigrated to Canada within the last 10 years, the majority (18) within the last 5 years. Members of the non-immigrant families were all Caucasian, having been born and having always resided in Canada.

On the basis of the Canadian socio-economic index for occupations (Blishen, Carroll, & Moore, 1987) and drawn on the major income earners, the majority of the Chinese (15 of 21) and non-immigrant (14 of 19) families obtained a socio-economic score of 50 and above, representing professional, technical, managerial, or small business categories. The rest of the Chinese and Caucasian families obtained a score of 25 to 49, which represented skilled and semi-skilled workers. Four families did not provide occupational data.

All the Chinese parents spoke some English; the most recent immigrants (one third of the group, immigrating within the last two years) spoke only limited English and had difficulty comprehending ordinary conversational English. Except for four parents who had completed high-school education, the Chinese parents had completed at least 14 years of formal education. All the Caucasian parents had at least a high-school education, the majority (13 of 19) having 14 or more years of education. Respect for privacy prevented the collection of the parents' specific ages. Estimates suggested that the majority of the mothers were in their mid-30s to early 40s, with only one non-immigrant father in his early 50s. All the children were attending elementary school in grades 2 to 7, with ages ranging from 7 to 13 years. According to the parents' reports, none of the children had any school difficulties. The schools involved were distributed throughout the city, the majority in middle socio-economic neighbourhoods.

Procedure

I recruited immigrant families from various sources: a local intercultural society; ethnic associations that included families originating from, China; English-as-a-second-language (ESL) classes for children; and a regular elementary class. Community members or participants also suggested other possible participants. I distributed a Chinese version of the recruitment letter to potentially **eligible** Chinese families through these recruitment sources. I also recruited nonimmigrant families from elementary schools and preschool, and through parents who had already participated in the study. These sources distributed letters to eligible families explaining the nature and requirements of the study. I also distributed the letter in preschool and elementary schools at their parent meetings. From this variety of sources, I obtained a broad representation of both the Chinese and Caucasian families in the city.

Using purposeful sampling (Coyne, 1997), I restricted the sample to families of Chinese origin who had immigrated to Canada within the 10 years prior to the collection of the data and who had children aged 7 to 14. I chose families not under any apparent economic stress. I also applied the same child and family **demographic** eligibility **criteria** to non-immigrant participants. In addition, I restricted non-immigrant families to those with a European background who had always lived in Canada. A total of 53 families gave their initial verbal consent; of them, 52 (27 immigrants and 25 non-immigrants) completed the study. I had to reduce the final sample to 40 families (21 immigrant families and 19 non-immigrant families) because of the target child's age (too old or too young) or the length of residence in Canada (over 10 years).After participants completed a written consent form, graduate research assistants in education and psychology and I interviewed families in their homes. Prior to the actual interview process, we practised interviewing to ensure our proficiency in interviewing.

Instrumentation

In this study, I used structured interviewing, with an open-ended questionnaire to allow variation in responses (Fontana & Frey, 2000). I developed the questionnaire on the model of communication proposed by Prescott et al. (1986), which included frequency, method, and content as the major elements. Additional questions regarded (a) the extent of understanding of and satisfaction with communication with the school, and (b) knowledge of multicultural education as practised by the school. I had the interview questions (see Appendix) translated into Chinese using the "back-translation" method (Bracken & Barona, 1991). Thus, the English questionnaire was translated into Chinese and then the Chinese text was translated back into English to examine its equivalency to the original English version. I adjusted the **discrepancies** before I finalized the Chinese version.

To ensure parents' comfort and understanding, Caucasian and Chinese interviewers interviewed the group corresponding to their racial origin. The Chinese interviewers were fluent in Mandarin and Cantonese, using the language of parents' choice. The interviewers audio-recorded participants' responses; Chinese interviews were later translated into English for analysis.

For the purpose of this study, I defined communication as: "speaking or interacting in person, by phone, by writing, or through shared activities, such as parent-teacher interviews, or school events." During the interview, the interviewers further **elaborated** communication for the participants as: "talking to or interacting with your child's teacher about your child, either in person, by phone or by note, attending school activities such as parent-teacher interviews and school fairs, or getting involved in school events such as fund-raising or sports." The interviewers also advised the respondents that the definition of communication included "interaction initiated by the teacher or the parents" and "parents' response to the school's communication, such as a note or newsletter".

Data analysis

A research assistant and I analyzed the data for each research question, using content analysis (Johnson & LaMontagne, 1993). Each word, phrase, or sentence that related to the topic being studied constituted a unit of analysis. Examples of units of analysis were: a word ("[I communicated with my child's school] in-person"); a phrase ("[the communication was about] peer pressure or decision-making, grades and achievement"); or a sentence ("I understood the communication with my friend's help"). Initially, we identified a small, randomly selected sample of the participants ($n=10$) and analyzed their responses for the basic idea within each unit of analysis. Through repeated comparisons, we integrated similar ideas until we identified the final, mutually exclusive, major themes. After we established major themes for each question, we used them for coding the rest of

the data. We repeated this procedure with each study question. To examine the reliability of coding, another coder independently coded all the families' responses to three of the questions. We then compared the two sets of themes generated for each question and the number of families who gave the response under each theme. When discrepancies in the wording or phrasing of a theme occurred, we discussed these differences; when coders reached **unanimous** agreement on the meaning, we then coded the theme. Otherwise, we left discrepancies as disagreements. We calculated a percentage score for the number of agreements by the sum of the number of agreements. The score for the three questions, respectively, was 76%, 90%, and 84%, with an average of 83%.

Results

Five themes emerged that corresponded to the research questions from the analysis of the coded data: (a) pattern of communication, (b) understanding of communication, (c) satisfaction with communication,(d) understanding of school's valuing of child's culture, (e) knowledge of the school's multicultural education.

Pattern of communication

Frequency of communication. Table 1 shows how Chinese and nonimmigrant parents communicated with the school. Chinese parents communicated infrequently: the majority one to four times a year, almost half of them one to two times a year, and two once. In contrast, almost all non-immigrant parents communicated with their children's schools at least once a month, and almost half of them one to three times a week. Chinese parents volunteered reasons for their infrequent communication:lack of time, no specific matters to discuss, unfamiliarity in communicating with the school, and the availability of school newsletters. The most common reason, however, was a lack of English speaking skills and hence the inconvenience of having to rely on interpreters. One mother explained:

I have gone to my child's school only once since we came here because I cannot speak English. I cannot talk with his teacher directly. I had to ask my friends to go with me and help me to communicate with the teacher. So I have not initiated any meeting with the school. (Chinese mother)

Method of communication. Table 1 also shows the various methods parents employed to communicate with their children's school. Both groups of parents used in-person communication most often. A combination of in-person contact, written messages, and telephone conversations was the second-most popular option, followed by an augmentation of this mixture with newsletters or formal interviews.

Table 1. Home-school communication by group: frequency and method

Category	Immigrant (n=21)	Non-immigrant (n=19)
Frequency of Communication		
Very often/1-3 times per week	0	9
1-3 times per month	0	9
3-4 times per year	7	1
1-2 times per year	10	0
Not often or rarely (once for all time)	2	0
Often before but now only at parent meeting	2	0
Method of Communication		
In person alone	8	6
In person plus message/telephone	6	5
Letters, notes, newsletters plus interview/telephone	4	4
Telephone	0	2
Newsletters	1	1
Others	2	1

However, unlike non-immigrant parents, immigrant parents did not use the telephone alone as a method for communicating with schools.

When asked about the best means for the school to communicate with them, one third of the Chinese parents did not show any preference. For another third of these parents, the most preferred method was in-person contact alone, followed by in-person contact combined with other means such as notes, newsletters, or phone calls. Non-immigrant parents shared this pattern of preference (seven for in-person contact alone and eight for in-person contact combined with other means, such as notes, newsletters, or phone calls). None of the immigrants desired newsletters as the only way of home-school communication.

Content of communication. Chinese parents communicated with their children's schools for reasons largely different than those of Caucasian parents. Table 2 shows that most Chinese parents communicated solely about their children's academic progress to determine what extra academic support to provide at home. Referring to communication with her son's teacher, one Chinese parent revealed, "We talked about my son's study, his progress in English. I want to make sure that my son is doing fine in school." Another Chinese parent elaborated on her communication with the school:

It is mostly about my son's learning attitudes, academic scores, and behaviour in school. I would also like to get advice from the teachers about how we, as parents, can help our child, about any good books for our son to read, and also about what we should emphasize at home to help our child learn more effectively at school. (Chinese parent)

Table 2. Content of communication by group

Category	Immigrant (*n*=21)	Non-immigrant (*n*=19)
Academic activities only (study, work, progress, report card)	17	0
School and relationship with others, general behaviour	4	4
General school activity and social events	0	5
School events plus child's progress	0	6
Others (school events plus fundraising or child attendance)	0	4

A smaller number of Chinese parents discussed both their children's general academic work and social relationships. A Chinese parent remarked, "We talked about my daughter's study and behaviours. I want to know whether my daughter is getting along with her classmates, whether she respects teachers, and how her study is going." One Chinese parent communicated only for the school's public events, such as fundraising.

In contrast to Chinese parents, none of the Caucasian parents communicated with schools about their child's academic progress alone. The same number (four) of Caucasian parents as the Chinese parents discussed their children's academic work and social relationships together. However, the Caucasian parents devoted much more of their communication to the school's public events and welfare (e.g., sports events, school concerts, and fundraising such as bake sales) or a combination of their children's academic progress and the school's public and social events. A Caucasian parent estimated her communication with the school to be "60% about the school activities and 40% about my daughter". Another Caucasian mother reported her communication with the school to be "two thirds about my daughter and one third about the Christmas hamper, Mustard Seed, and community issues". Several Caucasian parents communicated solely about school social events.

Understanding of communication

In response to the question, "Do you understand the communication from your child's school," most (18 of 21) Chinese parents responded that they did, although some required assistance. One mother reported, "Yes, because I have an interpreter, either my eldest son or my friend." Another parent reported a similar experience: "I understand because of the translator. It's good they [the school] have a translator." Still another Chinese parent explained, "I told the teacher at the very beginning that my English is not so good. So, he would use easy words to talk to me." Three Chinese parents reported not understanding the communication from the school. Some Chinese parents also reported difficulties with large group meetings because of a language barrier. A problem arose for another parent when the regular class teacher who, unlike the previous ESL (English as a Second Language) teacher, spoke too fast to be understood. As expected, all the Caucasians responded that they understood the communication with their children's school.

Satisfaction with communication

Table 3 summarizes the parents' responses by group to the question of whether they were satisfied with the communication they had with the school. Half of the Chinese parents responded **affirmatively**. One satisfied Chinese parent stated, "Yes, I was happy. The teacher was very nice and she pointed out my son's problem. I appreciated it because she cared about my son; she noticed his problem and told me in time." However, a few (three) happy Chinese parents requested more information about their children or more communication with the school. Two of these parents also suggested that the teachers and the school administration should use "easier words" in newsletters and initiate more meetings or other kinds of communication with parents.

Table 3 also shows that a number of Chinese parents expressed both satisfaction and dissatisfaction with their communication. They were satisfied with the teachers' availability for parent-teacher communication and the school's newsletters, which briefed them on school events and filled in the communication gap. However, these parents were also unhappy with the content of communication, which, to them, gave unrealistically positive reports of their children's academic progress. One parent remarked, "I am not happy with the content of the communication. There is too much good news. The reports were too good to be true. For example, the report cards seldom mention my son's mistakes."

Table 3. Parents' response by group to the question: Are you happy with the communication you have with the school?

Category	Immigrant (*n*=21)	Non-immigrant (*n*=19)
Happy (teacher cares, is open accessible)	8	15
Happy but would like more information or communication	3	0
Unhappy (due to lack of English-speaking skills and school's failure to provide real information on child's academic performance)	4	0
Happy and unhappy (happy with some aspects of communication but unhappy with teacher's not providing real progress of child; happy with teacher or with school only)	6	4

Of the few Chinese parents who felt completely unhappy, one said she lacked the English skills to communicate with the school. Other completely unhappy Chinese parents (3) were dissatisfied for other reasons. Tellingly, one parent regarded the school's information about children's school performance as **ambiguous** and superficial because it did not identify children's weaknesses. This parent argued that children and parents would not know how the children could improve and develop their skills for coping in the future in the more demanding world outside of school. This parent expressed her frustration, disappointment, and concern forcefully.

I would like to know whether my daughter is good at something or not so good at some subjects. I would like to know whether and how my daughter is progressing in learning and intelligence. But I really feel disappointed, even angry, about the comment from the school. The school will never tell me anything that I am really concerned about. I think it is because the philosophy of education here, the school seldom tells parents about their children's weakness. Even though a child does something not so good, not so perfect, the school still makes positive comments about his or her work. If children always hear the school talk about them positively, how can they encounter the society later on? In the real society, there is nothing that is always perfect. They will, of course, hear negative remarks about them. How can the children manage the contradiction between what they hear from the school and what they encounter in society? The school is not preparing them to face the reality outside school. (Chinese parent)

Non-immigrant parents did not share the dissatisfaction that some Chinese parents expressed. Instead, most of the non-immigrant parents were satisfied because of the open and prompt communication from the school. Satisfied European-Canadian parents commented that "the school philosophy encourages input from parents," and that "the school is always good with notices, returning phone calls, and quick chats in the school's hallway." Several non-immigrant parents indicated that they were both happy and unhappy with either the teacher or the administration. A Caucasian parent, unhappy with the teachers, expressed her frustration this way: "I find it difficult to explain my concerns in such a way as to ensure that the teachers understand and will take the appropriate steps if necessary." Other non-immigrant parents felt dissatisfaction with administrators when they failed to communicate ("the administrator was not very communicative.") or when administrators introduced funding cutbacks.

Understanding of school's valuing of the child's culture

To obtain specific information about the degree of effectiveness of home-school communication, I asked questions about parents' knowledge of the school's policies of multicultural education. The first question was, "From what you know, does your child's school value your child's race and culture? What evidence is there for your answer?" I defined valuing for the participants as, "showing respect in word or action" or "considering as important or valuable". Table 4 shows the participants' responses. Two thirds of the Chinese parents considered that their race and culture were valued at school. Two Chinese parents stated that their culture was not valued and that the school treated the child's culture just like traditional Canadian culture. Most Caucasian parents responded that schools valued their race and culture and treated their children equally. Only one such parent reported that individual children were not valued. A few Chinese and Caucasian-Canadian parents indicated that they did not know whether the school valued their race and culture because they saw no evidence.

Table 4. Response by group on the school's practice of multiculturalism: valuing of race and culture and practice of multicultural education

Category	Immigrant (*n*=21)	Non-immigrant (*n*=19)
Valuing of child's race and culture		
My child is treated equally and fairly; race, culture and language are respected.	14	16
Culture is treated fairly but child has been picked on by peers.	2	0
Culture is not valued, child is treated like a Canadian.	2	1
Don't know how	2	0
No/unclear answer	1	2
Practice of multicultural education		
Good multicultural education programs	4	15
Unaware of any multicultural education programs in school	13	0
Inadequate emphasis (could be more, lacks respect for Asian or other cultures)	3	0
Not emphasized	0	4
No clear answer	1	0

Knowledge of the school's emphasis on multicultural education

With the second question, related to multicultural education, I asked parents, "From what you know, does your child's school emphasize multicultural education? What evidence is there for your answer?" I defined multicultural education for the parents, using the definition presented earlier. Table 4 shows that four Chinese parents reported that their children's schools emphasized multicultural education as evidenced by a good multicultural education program. However, the majority reported that they were unaware of any multicultural education programs in their children's schools because the school either did not have such a program or did not communicate it explicitly to children or parents. One Chinese parent's remark typified the sentiment of the parents: "I have no idea about multicultural education. I don't know whether his school has this kind of

program or activity. I did not hear my son talk about it. Usually my son tells me everything that happened in school." Three of the Chinese parents responded that there was either inadequate or no emphasis on multiculturalism. One of these parents suggested that multicultural education was superficially practised with only token events, such as "a multicultural week", while history or social studies remained "very much European or North-American" with little Asian content.

Unlike immigrant parents, the majority of non-immigrant parents reported that their children's school emphasized multicultural education and had a good multicultural education program as evidenced by events celebrating international scenes or holidays. A non-immigrant parent answered:

Yes, lots are being done about other countries, foods, etc. The school also has flags from all over the world. I think schools are making good efforts despite the negative views in our society such as that about the RCMP—they were not allowed to wear turbans. (Nonimmigrant parent)

A few non-immigrant parents considered that multicultural education was not being emphasized in their children's schools. Referring to multicultural education, a non-immigrant parent remarked, "I have not really seen evidence of emphasis, even though the school is one-third Indo-Canadian." Both immigrant and non-immigrant parents indicated their wish for schools to balance their recognition of the main culture with that of minority cultures. Chinese parents especially desired to have their children integrated into the mainstream while maintaining their cultural heritage. A Chinese parent expressed this wish:

We would like our son integrated with the local culture as soon as possible. Our son also likes being integrated with the local people and local culture. But as parents, we would also like him to keep our Chinese culture—the values of Chinese culture. As overseas Chinese, we need, and have the responsibility, to pass our traditional values down to the next generation. (Chinese parent)

Other comments

The participants, especially the Chinese, volunteered additional comments during the interviews (30 by the Chinese and 21 by the non-immigrant parents). Their comments focused on curriculum, instructional methods, and student discipline in the school. In general, most parents perceived that the curriculum lacked **stringent** academic standards because students did little homework and much of it was unproductive or non-academic work. The curriculum especially did not teach critical thinking skills, which to some parents involved such exercises as analyzing a phenomenon and understanding its **underlying** causes and processes. The following quotation from a Chinese father provides a summary of these criticisms.

Students here are too relaxed because they do not have much schoolwork; students in Grade 5 still do not have much homework. Children also do not get sufficient teaching. Today my daughter brought home some insects because the teacher wants the class to observe the insects. That is all she has to do. A similar thing happened that my daughter's class spent several weeks blowing bubbles just to find out what kind of detergents can produce bigger bubbles. The teacher did not tell students [to find out] *why* and *how* detergent produces bubbles, which we think is more important for students to learn. (Chinese parent)

Parents who volunteered comments also criticized schools for their methods of instruction. Chinese parents were especially concerned about the lack of a well-defined instructional framework, guided by a systematic teaching model that co-ordinated with learning and that linked new knowledge to that previously learned. These parents further expressed their discontent with the weak mathematics instruction. Consequently, they were worried that their children would not be adequately prepared for future challenges in work and life. Referring to the lack of instructional framework, a Chinese father reported, "My son started learning French, but several weeks later, he switched to Italian since his teacher started teaching Italian. We don't know why." Another Chinese mother **articulated** a greater concern that the instruction at school limited children's future success.

Instruction is not systematic, for example, in mathematics. Mathematics is too easy, and sometimes what the school teaches is not relevant to what children have learned. There is no connection between new learning and old knowledge. It seems there is neither framework nor a systematic instructional plan... Students may not have much to do with their study now. But later, when they enter college or university, they will meet a big challenge. Since the school does not prepare students for the future, how can they adjust to the new and more challenging situation in universities and how can they adjust to competitive society in the future? (Chinese parent)

Both immigrant and non-immigrant parents considered the lack of discipline in school to be problematic. These parents were also concerned about unsatisfactory teaching practices, such as not marking students' assignments. A Chinese parent added another concern about school sports that did not accommodate Asian students' physical build.

Both groups of parents recommended greater emphasis on student discipline and academic learning. One Chinese parent recommended that "education administration should be more stringent and discipline should be better set [established]." Non-immigrant parents requested teacher models in which teachers are "well-disciplined" themselves and do not threaten to go on strike as a means of resolving conflicts. Chinese parents, in particular, advocated more homework, more interesting assignments, and more emphasis on basic skills such as reading, writing, and mathematics. Finally, Caucasian parents requested better-defined criteria for the evaluation of schoolwork and asked that there be no strike action in schools, thereby allowing greater attention to

children's learning.

Discussion

In this study, I examined the home-school communication of Chinese families who recently immigrated to Canada. As expected, even in the absence of socio-economic difficulties, cultural and linguistic uniqueness created a largely distinct pattern of parental communication with schools. Thus, in comparison with non-immigrants, immigrant parents communicated with schools less often, had more difficulty understanding the communication, and were less satisfied with the school's communication style and multicultural education program. However, immigrant parents also **circumvented** the language barrier by using an interpreter (e.g., their own children, friends, or school appointee) to facilitate their communication with schools.

The most distinctive feature of Chinese parents' communication was their high level of expectations for their children's academic achievement. Chinese parents communicated more for the sake of their children's academic progress than for the school's public events, such as fundraising, which was more the focus of communication for non-immigrant parents. Emphasis on education as a means for an individual's advancing in society(Stevenson et al., 1994) may have distracted the Chinese parents from their traditional valuation of group well-being, and hence from contributing to such public school events as fundraising. Real and perceived language barriers may also have reduced Chinese parents' involvement in school events. Researchers have observed that Asian-American parents often feel **reluctant** to participate in school functions because of their lack of confidence in English (Lee & Manning, 2001).

Drawing on their cultural philosophy and practices, Chinese parents expected teachers to communicate more factual **appraisal** of their children's school progress. These parents were thus dissatisfied when schools conveyed what they considered to be superficial and exclusively positive, "feel-good" generalizations about their children's performance. With their traditional belief in academic excellence as reflected in discipline and achievement (Mitchell, 2001), the Chinese parents also criticized schools for the lack of student discipline and the lower quality of curriculum and instruction in comparison to schools in China.

The Chinese parents' response to the issue of multicultural education further reflected ineffective home-school communication. Many Chinese parents were dissatisfied because the school did not value their race and culture; others were unaware of multicultural education at school. There were also Chinese parents who did not consider the multicultural education practised in schools adequate, especially to fulfil their desire to integrate their children into the mainstream Canadian life while preserving their ethnic distinction. The Chinese parents requested a multicultural education program that not only valued their ethnicity and culture but also contained substance that went beyond occasional, ceremonial festivals. Such a program would involve the ample inclusion of Chinese or Asian culture and history in the regular curriculum and the daily practice of multicultural education at school. However, Chinese parents' dissatisfaction may have been caused by their lack of knowledge about the school's existing multicultural education.

The present study clearly demonstrates the interplay between culture and home-school communication for immigrant parents. In their communication with the school, Chinese parents conveyed their educational expectations for their children, which were rooted in their culture of origin, and sought genuine information about their children's academic performance. Notwithstanding differences between immigrant and non-immigrant parents in the style and content of communication with the school, a common parental expectation for schools existed. Parents expected quality communication and education. Immigrant or not, parents valued the kind of home-school communication that readily responded to parental concerns and that showed care for meeting children's needs. Parents especially requested the type of education that emphasized academic excellence, critical thinking, practical skills, and behavioural discipline.

The results of this study corroborate previous research indicating that language differences may hinder immigrant families' effective communication and involvement with schools (Commins, 1992; Constantino et al., 1995; Gougeon, 1993). The results further highlight the impact of the language barrier and cultural differences on recently immigrated parents' communication with and expectations of their children's schools. Of interest, the discontent of immigrant parents with the school's curriculum and instruction **alludes** to the difference between Chinese parents and Canadian schools in pedagogical philosophy. The dissatisfaction also suggests that, perhaps for lack of adequate communication, immigrant parents fail to understand the school's philosophy.

The results indicate the need for improving home-school communication for Chinese immigrant families. Schools may meet this need by attending to parents' desire for responsive communication that shows care for children and for quality education that cultivates critical thinking and student discipline. Schools may also consider practising a style of communication with parents that is sensitive to their idiosyncratic linguistic and cultural heritage and to their educational expectations. Additionally, schools can **incorporate** multicultural education activities into the curriculum and daily life, while at the same time inform parents of school policy and practices related to multicultural education. Such practices would improve home-school communication, perhaps leading to greater involvement in school events by immigrant parents. Effective home-school communication, however, requires communication skills on the part of school administrators and teachers, which can be enhanced through inservice and pre-service teacher-education programs, focusing on cultivating respect for and understanding of cultural diversity. Teachers' educational institutions may provide such programs.

The inclusion of families mainly with socio-economic advantages delimits the results of this study. Parents with less economic resources may have different experiences in communicating with the school and should be included in future studies. Research may further involve teachers and children as informants to study the bi-directional process that characterizes home-school communication (Theilheimer, 2001). Future research may also consider the pedagogical orientation of schools and immigrant parents as a factor mediating the communication between home and school.

The present study has produced a preliminary set of interview data and new knowledge about home-school communication of recent immigrants such as Chinese. The results suggest other immediate research questions such as: (a) are these findings replicable in other urban centres and with other cultural minorities? and (b) what practices have been shown successful to improve home-school communication?

Acknowledgements

This study was funded by a general research grant from the Social Sciences and Research Council of Canada administered by the University of Victoria. I thank parents who kindly took part in the study.

Notes

1 I presented portions of this article at the International Conference of the Council for Exceptional Children, April 5–8, 2000, Vancouver, BC.

References

Badets, J. (1993). Canada's immigrants: Recent trends. *Canadian Social Trends, 29*, 8–11.

Bernhard, J. K., & Freire, M. (1999). What is my child learning at elementary school? Culturally contested issues between teachers and Latin American families. *Canadian Ethnic Studies, 31*(3), 72–95.

Bhattacharya, G. (2000). The school adjustment of South Asian immigrant children in the United States. *Adolescence, 35*, 77–86.

Blishen, B. R., Carroll, W. K., & Moore, C. (1987). The 1981 socioeconomic index for occupations in Canada. *Canadian Review of Sociology and Anthropology, 24*, 465–488.

Bowman, B. T. (1989). Educating language-minority children. *Phi Delta Kappan, 71*, 118–120.

Bracken, B. A., & Barona, A. (1991). State of the art procedures for translating, validating, and using psycho educational tests in cross-cultural assessment. *School Psychology International, 12*, 119–132.

Bronfenbrenner, U. (1976). Is early intervention effective? Facts and principles of early intervention: A summary. In A. M. Clarke & A. D. B. Clarke (eds.). *Early experience: Myth and evidence* (pp. 247–256). New York: The Free Press.

Chao, R. K. (1996). Chinese and European American mothers' beliefs about the role of parenting in children's school success. *Journal of Cross-cultural Psychology, 27*, 403–423.

Chen, C., & Uttal, D. H. (1988). Cultural values, parents' beliefs, and children's achievement in the United States and China. *Human Development, 31*, 351–358.

Commins, N. L. (1992). Parents and public schools. *Equity and Choice, 8*(2), 40–45.

Constantino, R., Cui, L., & Faltis, C. (1995). Chinese parental involvement: Reaching new levels. *Equity & Excellence in Education, 28*(2), 46–50.

Coyne, I. T. (1997). Sampling in qualitative research. Purposeful and theoretical sampling: Merging or clear boundaries. *Journal of Advanced Nursing, 26*, 623–630.

Epstein, J. L. (1990). School and family connections: Theory, research, and implications for integrating sociologies of education and family. *Marriage and Family Review, 15*, 99–126.

Fontana, A., & Frey, J. H. (2000). The interview: From structured questions to negotiated text. In N. K. Denzin & Lincoln, Y. S. (eds.), *Handbook of qualitative research* (2nd ed., pp. 645–671). Thousand Oaks: Sage.

Gougeon, T. D. (1993). Urban schools and immigrant families: Teacher perspectives. *The Urban Review, 25*, 251–287.

Healey, P. M. (1994, March). Parent education: Going from defense to offense. *Principal, 73*(4), 30–31.

Herrera, J. F., & Wooden, S. L. (1988). Some thoughts about effective parent-school communication. *Young Children, 43*(6), 78–80.

Ho, D. Y. F. (1981). Traditional patterns of socialization in Chinese society. *Acta Pspychologica Taiwanica, 23*(2), 81–95.

Holmes, M. (1998). *The reformation of Canada's schools: Breaking the barriers to parental choices.* (ERIC Document Reproduction Service No. ED439 495).

Hui, C. H., & Triandis, H. C. (1986). Individualism-collectivism: A study of cross-cultural researchers. *Journal of Cross-cultural Psychology, 17*, 229–244.

Johnson, L. J., & LaMontagne, M. J. (1993). Using content analysis to examine the verbal or written communication of stakeholders within early intervention. *Journal of Early Intervention, 17*(1), 73–79.

Lareau, A. (1987). Social class differences in family-school relationships: The importance of cultural capital. *Sociology of Education, 60*, 73–85.

Lee, G., & Manning, M. L. (2001). Treat Asian parents and families right. *Multicultural Education, 9*(1), 23–25.

Lin, C.-Y. C., & Fu, V. R. (1990). A comparison of child-rearing practices among Chinese, immigrant Chinese, and Caucasian-American parents. *Child Development, 61*, 429–433.

Mitchell, K. (2001). Education for democratic citizenship: Transnationalism, multiculturalism, and the limits of liberalism. *Harvard Educational Review, 71*, 51–78.

Norris, C. (1999). Parents and schools: The involvement, participation, and expectations of parents in the education of their children. *Education Quarterly Review, Statistics Canada–Catalogue no. 81-0003, 5* (4), 61–80.

Prescott, B. L., Pelton, C., & Dornbusch, S. M. (1986). Teacher perceptions of parent-school communication: A collaborative analysis. *Teacher Educational Quarterly, 13*(2), 67–83.

Ran, A. (2001). Travelling on parallel tracks: Chinese parents and English teachers. *Educational Research, 43,* 311–328.

Sleeter, C., & Grant, C. A. (1994). *Making choices for multicultural education: Five approaches to race, class, and gender* (2nd ed.). Englewood Cliffs: Prentice Hall.

Stevenson, H. W., Lee, S., & Chen, C. (1994). Education of gifted and talented students in Mainland China, Taiwan, and Japan. *Journal for the Education of the Gifted, 17,* 104–130.

Swap, S. M. (1990). *Parent involvement and success for all children: What we know now.* (ERIC Document Reproduction Service No. ED 321 907).

Theilheimer, R. (2001). Bi-directional learning through relationship building: Teacher preparation for working with families new to the United States. *Childhood Education, 77,* 284–288.

Valencia, A. A. (1992). Multicultural education: Contemporary perspectives and orientations for teachers and counselors. *Journal of Multicultural Counseling and Development, 20,* 132–142.

Watkins, T. J. (1997). Teacher communications, child achievement, and parent traits in parent involvement models. *The Journal of Educational Research, 91,* 3–14.

Yang, H. J. (1993). *Communication patterns of individualistic and collective cultures: A value based comparison.* (ERIC Document Reproduction Service No. ED 366 032).

Zhou, M. (1997). Growing up American: The challenge confronting immigrant children and children of immigrants. *Annual Review of Sociology, 23,* 63–95.

APPENDIX

The Questionnaire for the Interview

1. How often do you communicate with your child's school?

2. How is the communication carried out between you and your child's school?

3. What is the communication with your child's school mostly about?

4. Do you understand the communication given by your child's school?

5. What is the best way for the school to communicate with you?

6. Are you satisfied with the communication you have with the school?

7. From what you know, does your child's school value your child's race and culture? What evidence is there for your answer?

8. From what you know, does your child's school emphasize multicultural education? What evidence is there for your answer?

New Words

affirmatively	[əˈfɜːmətivli]	adv.	肯定地，赞成地，积极地
allude	[əˈljuːd]	vi.	暗指，提及
ambiguous	[æmˈbigjuəs]	a.	引起歧义的，模棱两可的，含糊不清的
appraisal	[əˈpreizl]	n.	估计，估量，评价
articulate	[ɑːˈtikjuleit]	v.	明确有力地表达
aspiration	[ˌæspəˈreiʃn]	n.	强烈的愿望
circumvent	[ˌsɜːkəmˈvent]	vt.	围绕，包围，避免
cohesive	[kəuˈhiːsiv]	a.	有黏着力的，紧密结合的
constitute	[ˈkɔnstitjuːt]	vt.	构成，组成
criteria	[kraiˈtiəriə]	n.	标准，准则
demographic	[ˌdeməˈgræfik]	a.	人口统计学的，人口统计的
deter	[diˈtɜː]	vt.	阻止
discrimination	[diˌskrimiˈneiʃn]	n.	歧视，辨别，区别，不公平的待遇
discrepancy	[disˈkrepənsi]	n.	不符合（之处），不一致（之处）
elaborate	[iˈlæbəreit]	v.	详述；详细制订
eligible	[ˈelidʒəbl]	a.	合适的，合格的，有资格当选的
eloquence	[ˈeləkwəns]	n.	口才，雄辩
hinder	[ˈhində]	v.	阻碍，妨碍
incorporate	[inˈkɔːpəreit]	v.	包含，加上，吸收；把……合并，使并入
interpret	[inˈtɜːprit]	v.	解释，理解，诠释
intervention	[ˌintəˈvenʃn]	n.	介入，干涉，干预，调解，排解
intimidate	[inˈtimideit]	vt.	恐吓，威胁
malleability	[ˌmæliəˈbiləti]	n.	有延展性，柔韧性，柔软
procurement	[prəˈkjuəmənt]	n.	获得，取得，采购
reluctant	[riˈlʌktənt]	a.	勉强的，不情愿的
stringent	[ˈstrindʒənt]	a.	严厉的；令人信服的
succinct	[səkˈsiŋkt]	a.	简明的，简洁的，简练的
unanimous	[juˈnæniməs]	a.	全体一致的，一致同意的，无异议的
unbiased	[ʌnˈbaiəst]	a.	无偏见的，不偏不倚的，公正的
underlying	[ˌʌndəˈlaiiŋ]	a.	潜在的，含蓄的

Discussion Ideas

1. What is "purposeful sampling"?

2. What is a "consent form"? Is it necessary for all the participants to sign consent forms?

3. What is "back-translation" method?

4. What is "content analysis"? What are the advantages and disadvantages of content analysis?

5. The researcher used "I" in this paper. How does that make you feel?

6. What do you do in the Results section?

7. What do you do in the Discussion section?

8. What do you think might be the limitations of the present study?

Vocabulary and Language Learning Skills

1. Recognizing Word Meanings

Match definitions in Column B with the vocabulary items in Column A.

Column A	Column B
1. conflict	a. embody the essential characteristics
2. affirmative	b. a strong effect
3. criterion	c. supporting an attitude
4. typify	d. a state of opposition
5. succinct	e. obstacle
6. eloquence	f. powerful and effective language
7. barrier	g. push for something
8. advocate	h. briefly giving the gist of something
9. impact	i. a factor on which you judge or decide something

2. Making a Collocation

A. Take one word from the box on the left and combine this with one from the box on the right to make a collocation. Then try to match the collocations with spaces in the sentences below.

distributed	total
corroborate	employed
randomly	the recruitment letters
combined	the discrepancies
provides	representation
dramatic	communication
methods	increase
adjusted	selected
broad	previous research
prompt	summary

1) I _____ _____ to potentially eligible Chinese families through these recruitment sources.

2) These families had a _____ _____ of 46 children, 21 Chinese and 25 European Canadian.

3) Such a study would be particularly timely because of the _____ _____ in recent years of Chinese immigration to Canada.

4) From this variety of sources, I obtained a _____ _____ of both the Chinese and Caucasian families in the city.

5) I _____ _____ before I finalized the Chinese version.

6) We identified a small, _____ _____ sample of the participants and analyzed their responses.

7) Table 1 shows the various _____ parents _____ to communicate with their children's schools.

8) The following quotation from a participant _____ _____ of these criticisms.

9) These results _____ _____ that was conducted in structured laboratory contexts.

10) The study established several expectations for online learners, including regular and _____ _____ with professors and clear expectations of the professors.

B. Finish the sentence. Choose the best ending of each of the sentence extracts below from the list underneath.

1) In one individual they may take the form of the desire to be an excellent parent, in another they may be expressed athletically, _____

2) In response to the first question, _____

3) A combination of in-person contact, written messages, and telephone conversations was the second-most popular option, _____

4) Notwithstanding differences between immigrant and non-immigrant parents in the style and content of communication with the school, _____

5) Such practices would improve home-school communication, _____

6) Even though it was expected that status appeals would be used more frequently in Chinese than in U.S. commercials, _____

7) Whereas this approach is obviously not the most sophisticated, _____

8) Their complex implicit knowledge enables 4 year olds to balance the blocks,

_____

a) most parents responded that they did, although some required assistance.

b) perhaps leading to greater involvement in school events by immigrant parents.

c) and in still another they may be expressed in painting pictures or in inventing things.

d) it is no less so than the categorizations used in the studies cited above.

e) even though they are sensitive only to observable data.

f) a common parental expectation for schools existed.

g) the statistical test result indicates otherwise.

h) followed by an argumentation of this mixture with newsletters or formal interviews.

Writing Focus

Results and Discussion

1. Results

Function

The purpose of a Results section is to present and illustrate your findings. Make this section a completely objective report of the results, and save all interpretation for the discussion. Use graphs and tables if appropriate, but also summarize your main findings in the text.

Style

Results Content
Summarize your findings in text and illustrate them, if appropriate, with figures and tables.
In text, describe each of your results, pointing the reader to observations that are most relevant.
Provide a context, such as by describing the question that was addressed by making a particular observation.
Describe results of control experiments and include observations that are not presented in a formal figure or table, if appropriate.

Language Focus: Figures and Tables

1. Either place figures and tables within the text of the result, or include them in the back of the report (following references)—do one or the other.

2. If you place figures and tables at the end of the report, make sure they are clearly distinguished from any attached appendix materials, such as raw data.

3. Regardless of placement, each figure must be numbered consecutively and complete with caption (caption goes under the figure).

4. Regardless of placement, each table must be titled, numbered consecutively and complete with heading (title with description goes above the table).

5. Each figure and table must be sufficiently complete that it could stand on its own, separate from text.

2. Discussion

Function

The objective here is to provide an interpretation of your results and support for all of your conclusions, using evidence from your experiment and generally accepted knowledge, if appropriate. The significance of findings should be clearly described. Interpret your data in the discussion in appropriate depth. This means that when you explain a phenomenon you must describe mechanisms that may account for the observation. If your results differ from your expectations, explain why that may have happened. If your results agree, then describe the theory that the evidence supported. It is never appropriate to simply state that the data agreed with expectations, and let it drop at that.

Overall, Results deal with *facts*, and Discussion deals with *points*; facts are *descriptive*, while points are *interpretive*. Effective Discussion sections are based on points, rather than on facts. Discussion should be more than summaries. They should go beyond the results. They should be more theoretical

or

more abstract

or

more general

or

more integrated with the field

or

more connected to the real world

or

more concerned with implications or applications

or

if possible, some combination of these

Style

Discussion can be viewed as presenting a series of points. Typically, they are arranged as in the following table.

Discussion Moves	
Move 1	Points to consolidate your research space (obligatory)
Move 2	Points to indicate the limitations of your study (optional but common)
Move 3	Points to identify useful areas of further research (optional but only common in some areas)

There are many options in opening a Discussion. Discussion sections can open with the main results, a discussion of the literature, a general conclusion, the original purpose, a summary, referring to theory, a comment about methodology, or the limitations of the data.

Language Focus: Generalization, Limitations and Values

Generalization

Overall, the results indicate that…

The overall results indicate…

The results indicate, overall, that…

In general, the experimental samples resisted…

With one exception, the experimental samples resisted…

Limitations

It should be noted that this study has examined only…

The findings of this study are restricted to…

This study has addressed only the question of…

The limitations of this study are clear:...

However, the findings do no imply...

The results of this study cannot be taken as evidence for...

Unfortunately, we are unable to determine from this data...

Values

Notwithstanding its limitations, this study does suggest...

Despite the preliminary character, the research reported here would seem to indicate...

However exploratory, this study may offer some insight into...

Task One

Survey and classify the openings of six discussion sections from a journal in your field.

Task Two

Read the following draft of the Discussion section. Identify the three moves of the Discussion section and summarize the linguistic characteristics of each move.

Discussion

The small sample sizes in these studies require great caution in drawing conclusions. However, several patterns were apparent in the results and these deserve some comment. At the very least, these studies offer two case-study views of the ways some students cope with studying in L2. We offer the following interpretations as speculations in need of further confirmation. Our comments concern what the students say they are doing during study and summarization, and what effect these processes have on performance.

In spite of their varying language difficulties, both groups of subjects employed deep processing. Both groups used more surface processing, with the more fluent subjects doing more appropriate surface processing. This supports the argument made earlier in this paper that a reasonable level of fluency provides a basis for higher level processes.

The results are not consistent with the suggestions of some (e.g. Kozminsky and Graetz, 1996) that L2 students are forced to rely solely upon surface processing, nor with those of others who conclude that L2 students tend to use deep processing as a "top-down" way of coping with ambiguous detail (e.g. Canwell and Biggs, 1988). Rather these results suggest that interlingua transfer and application of deep processing strategies is not automatic.

> We wish to suggest two general ways in which educators can facilitate their L2 students' learning. These suggestions derive largely from the literature, but are consistent with the results of these two studies. First, strategies that compensate for lack of fluency, reducing the cognitive load for L2 students and thereby freeing up their resources for higher-order activities, will be of value. The second approach is to ensure that students use their available processing capacity as effectively as possible.

Task Three

Based on your knowledge, can you guess from which of the sections the following sentences come, Results or Discussion?

1. Degree of misclassification for self-reported current smokers was minor (0–3%), regardless of cotinine cut-point used.

2. Second, the present study's use of nocturnal pancreatic emissions may not have been appropriate.

3. Their answers and comments show a very high degree of satisfaction, as reflected in the two bar charts below.

4. To test the hypothesis that hepatic secretions would be associated with self reports of small furry animal phobia, a series of correlations between Bile Production and scores on the ABIT self report were computed.

5. This unexpected result can be interpreted in several ways.

6. Future research should direct attention to both psychological and biological factors that influence small furry animal phobia.

An Exploratory Investigation of the Effects of a Cultural Orientation Programme on the Psychological Well-being of International University Students

Learning Objectives

• Title page: components and style
• Abstract: definition, style and language focus
• APA formatting and style: title page and abstract
• Revising

An Exploratory Investigation of the Effects of a Cultural Orientation Programme on the Psychological Well-being of International University Students

N. J. Mckinlay, H. M. Pattison & H. Gross

Department of Human Sciences, Loughborough University, Leicestershire, LE11 3TU,

U.K. (Requests for reprints)

Abstract 'Culture shock' has been identified as a psychological reaction to a change in cultural environment. The main symptoms of culture shock are reported to be psychological disturbance, a negative reaction to the new surroundings and a longing for a more familiar environment. Research has identified culture shock as a component, in the difficulties that international students face when studying in another country. One way that institutions of higher education have responded to these difficulties is to provide initial cultural orientation. In the study reported here, a group of post-graduate students who had participated in a study skills and cultural orientation course at a British university were compared with a group who had not. Contrary to the research hypothesis, the group that took part in the orientation course were significantly more homesick and reported more psychological difficulties. The overall findings **cast doubt on** the received view of culture shock as it affects international students. They suggest that culture shock is exacerbated by personal and social factors and this has implications for the way that international students may be helped through the experience.

'Culture shock' has been identified as a reaction to a change in cultural environment. The term was first used by Oberg (1960), who believed that the condition was "**precipitated by the anxiety that results from losing all our familiar signs and symbols of social intercourse**" (p.177). It has been described as an emotional reaction caused by an inability to understand, control or predict another person's behaviour (Bock, 1970). A major review of the literature on the psychological adjustment of short term visitors or **sojourners** was carried out by Church (1982). Church describes culture shock as a normal process of adaptation to cultural stress, which involves symptoms such as anxiety, **irritability** and a longing for a more predictable environment. However it has been suggested that the negative aspects of culture shock can be **ameliorated** through programmes of cultural orientation (see e.g. Bochner, 1982; Furnham and Bochner, 1986)

There have been a number of studies which suggest that international students are likely to experience culture shock when studying in a foreign country. Klineberg and Hull (1979) conducted a study of international students at foreign universities in eleven countries and identified problems such as language difficulties, homesickness, and adjusting to social customs and norms. Zwingman and Gunn (1983) reported case studies of individuals with severe psychological disturbance triggered by what they term **uprooting**. Attention has also been drawn to the negative effects of prejudice and discrimination on students' psychological health (Tajfel and Dawson,1965; Anumonye,1967; Singh, 1963). However Church (1982) reports that the majority of students cope with the change well.

It has been suggested that the problems that students report when studying abroad remain consistent but differ in degree between different cultures (Church, 1982). The 'culture distance' theory of Furnham and Bochner (1982) proposes that social difficulty cannot be predicted simply by a measure of geographical distance. One also must assess the degree of behavioural and cognitive change required by the move. Hofstede (1984) **maps out** absolute distances between countries on four dimensions which characterise particular cultures (power-distance, uncertainty-avoidance, individualism and masculinity), and proposes these may be used to predict the difficulties experienced.

Recent studies show that international students have more difficulty than home students in dealing with the new academic and social environment (Barker *et al.*, 1991; Cox, 1988; Furnham and Bochner, 1982; Furnham and Trezise, 1983). As a consequence there are numerous educational publications in the United Kingdom, directed at international students and people who work with them, that warn of the possible **sequelae** of culture shock when a student arrives for the first time in the host country (British Council, 1990 and 1991; Kinnell, 1990; Makepeace, 1989; UK Council for Overseas Student Affairs, 1992). The information on culture shock in the publications cited above is modelled on the *U curve hypothesis* (Lysgaard, 1955). This model proposes that a student experiences an initial 'honeymoon period', followed by a phase of 'feeling bad' which is finally **overtaken** by a period of 'recovery'. The final phase occurs when a person has

come to terms with, and has adjusted to, the new culture.

Bochner (1982) has highlighted the benefits of culture-learning for individuals who are adapting to a new cultural environment. Rather than adjusting to the new cultural environment the sojourner learns the **salient** characteristics, adapting to the new circumstances while keeping their own cultural behaviour intact. This is particularly important for visitors who will only spend a relatively short time in the new environment and are therefore more able to **assimilate** back into their own culture with as few problems as possible.

It has been suggested by Furnham and Bochner (1986) that practical culture learning experiences can relieve some of the distress experienced by individuals adapting to a new cultural environment. They believe that the distress suffered by many "culture travellers" is due to a lack of social skills of the new society. Barker *et al.* (1991) investigated the difficulties faced by visiting Asian students at Australian universities and suggest that schemes that help to provide friendship and informal skills training will be beneficial to the newly arrived student.

However one study (Selby and Woods, 1966) **runs counter to** the assessment of student adjustment being determined by the impact of the culture **at large**. In this study international students saw their primary problem as achieving academic excellence. The effect of cultural difference was that students found themselves on the outside of the culture of a 'high-pressure' academic institution. Their lack of contact with fellow students meant they were not **privy** to the process of learning about the internal system which governs which rules have to be obeyed and which may be broken with **impunity**. In this study psychological well-being did not follow a U shaped function but rather could be seen as being directly determined by academic crises such as examinations.

In the mid-eighties the overall international student numbers coming to study at British universities fell because of the introduction of full cost fees in 1980 (Kinnell, 1990). In response to this fall the government introduced the Education Counselling Service with the aim of promoting British higher education overseas. In 1991 there were 92,100 international students in the United Kingdom, an increase of 44% from 1981 (Department for Education, 1993). However research indicates that the failure rate for international students attending courses in this country is higher than that of U.K. students (Makepeace, 1989). Some universities are therefore looking for ways to provide adequate support for their international students.

In addition to providing English language support, a growing number of universities are attempting to focus more on cultural orientation, in line with recommendations from the studies and reports cited above. Kinnell (1990) asserted that pre-sessional orientation courses are especially worthwhile. The British Council Code of Practice advises institutions to provide an orientation programme for new overseas students (British Council, 1989, item no. 59). One example occurs at Loughborough University where the three week pre-sessional course is a mixture of language support, study skills, information and orientation to life in the United Kingdom, including practical matters such as opening a bank account and shopping in a supermarket.

The literature on international students clearly points to the benefits of pre-sessional information and orientation courses. Recent studies suggest that to some extent the distress experienced by individuals can be relieved by practical culture learning experiences. However there is no **empirical** evidence to suggest that university orientation courses for international students reduce the distress caused by culture shock. The aim of the study reported here was to measure the psychological effects of a cultural orientation course on postgraduate international students. It was hypothesised that a group that had attended the Loughborough University pre-sessional course would experience less cultural shock than a group that had not.

Method

Subjects

All subjects were postgraduate international students at Loughborough University. The criteria for selection for all subjects was that they had not previously lived in or visited the United Kingdom for more than two weeks; they were not nationals of the European Union; and they were not native English speakers. Subjects formed two groups: the 'pre-sessional group' (PSG), and the 'standard arrival group' (SAG), according to whether they had attended the pre-sessional course or not. The selection of subjects for the PSG was obviously limited to the number of people on the course who fitted the above criteria. It should be noted that international students could choose whether to take the pre-sessional course, but in practice the opportunity to attend the course is dependant on financial and time constraints placed on students by their sponsors rather than individual choice. The sample forming the SAG was selected to resemble as closely as possible the composition of the PSG.

A total of 74 subjects completed the initial stage of the study. Nineteen people were excluded as they did not meet the selection criteria. Of the 55 subjects who did meet the criteria, there were 29 in the PSG and 26 in the SAG.

The subjects in each group were predominantly male (87% in the PSG and 86% in the SAG), reflecting national statistics of international students. There were 19 different nationalities in the PSG and 16 in the SAG. To reflect historical and cultural differences the subjects were divided into the regions of Africa, Latin America, Middle East (including the Islamic Noah African countries), South Asia (India, Pakistan and Bangladesh), and the Far East (including Hong Kong, Singapore and Japan). Most subjects lived in a city in their own country (70%), with fewer coming from a town (26%) or rural area (4%).

All the university faculties were represented in each group, but the majority of students in both groups were members of the Engineering faculty (70% and 64%). A total of 89% of subjects were attending taught Masters degree courses and 11% were **enrolled** on research degree programmes. The mean age for subjects was 31.48 (sd = 5.23) in the PSG and 31.04 (sd = 6.59) in the SAG. There were 13 students living off campus, 7 from the PSG and 6 from the SAG.

The main symptoms of culture shock were identified, from the literature, as evidence of psychological disturbance, a negative reaction to the new surroundings and a longing for a more familiar environment. Therefore in this study three measures were used: a measure of mental health, the *Langner 22 item questionnaire*; an evaluation of experiences in the host country, the *International Students Questionnaire*; and a homesickness measure, the *Dundee Relocation **Inventory***.

The Langner 22 Index has been validated as a measure of psychological disturbance for groups from different cultures and has good statistics for reliability and validity (Cochrane *et al.*, 1977; Cochrane and Stopes-Roe, 1980). It has also been used in previous studies on the psychological problems of international students (Furnham and Trezise, 1983). The Dundee Relocation Inventory is a method of measuring homesickness and has been used on university students (Fisher, Murray and Frazer, 1985; Fisher and Hood, 1987).

An 'experiences' questionnaire, named the International Students Questionnaire (ISQ), was **devised** for this study (see Appendix). It was based on key, **recurrent** issues raised in the literature on international student support and cross-cultural counselling. The main part of the questionnaire consists of 13 'social questions', for example "Have you been invited to a British person's house?", and 13 'practical questions', for example "Have you had problems with the university administration?". The two types of question were included in **random** order and were presented in two sections, 'the UK' and 'the university' as appropriate. A low score would indicate a more negative experience and a high score would be more positive. There were 4 additional questions on using university services: Student Advice Centre; University Medical Centre; University Counselling Service; English Language Support Unit.

In order to **account for** possible confounding **variables** two additional measures were used. The first was an English language competence test, the *Nelson Quick Test*, to ensure that the levels of English of both groups were similar. The second was a questionnaire, devised for this study, to identify whether or not the expectations of students enrolled on the pre-sessional course were similar to those of students who did not enrol. This questionnaire had a second purpose of enabling a comparison to made of student expectations at the beginning of their time in the UK with their experiences after one term. The expectations questionnaire had the same format as the ISQ, but the questions were in the future tense e.g. "Do you expect to have an active social life?". The first part of this questionnaire was concerned with the collection of biographical information for the selection and categorisation of subjects. All subjects on the Loughborough University 1993 pre-sessional course were asked if they would like to take part in the study. At the beginning of the course the initial questionnaires, the Nelson Quick Test and the expectations questionnaire were completed with the co-operation of the Course Director.

At the beginning of the academic year, subjects for the SAG were found in a number of ways. The majority of subjects were contacted through the halls of residence, some subjects were obtained with the help of admissions tutors in various academic departments, and a few subjects were **recruited** through the University Mosque or the English Language Support Unit. Subjects forming the SAG were given the initial questionnaires. They completed the forms on their own and returned them within two days.

All subjects were informed that the study was looking at how international students adapt to life in the UK and were given an assurance that all information would be private and **confidential**. Each subject received a number for identification and therefore no names appeared on any of the forms or questionnaires.

Three months later, at the beginning of the spring term, all subjects were contacted and asked to complete the Langner 22 Index, the ISQ and the Dundee Relocation Inventory. Each subject was given a stamped addressed envelope and asked to complete and post the questionnaires within two days. They all **complied** with this request.

Finally, a representative sub-sample of 17 students (9 from the PSG and 8 from the SAG) took part in semi-structured interviews. These complemented the information received using the questionnaires. The interviews were structured around four questions on the most difficult time and methods of coping with that, extra support that would have helped with coping, and friendship networks whilst in the UK. Students who had attended the pre-sessional course were also asked if it had helped and, if so, how. Reference is made to material from these interviews in the discussion.

Results

All subjects

The mean scores for all subjects were calculated for the Langner 22 Index (m = 4.7, sd = 3.49) and the Dundee Relocation Inventory (m = 20.96, sd = 9.63). The mean score for the Langner 22 Index was typical of scores achieved by sojourner populations under stress, see Table 1, and was higher than the suggested cut off point (4.28) for identifying populations with high levels of **psychopathology** (Langner, 1962). The mean score for the Dundee Relocation Inventory was much higher than the **normative** scores recorded in home student populations. For example Fisher (1989) reports a mean score of 17.5 (sd = 3.9) for 51 self-reported 'homesick' students, and 5.3 (sd = 1.1) for 34 'non-homesick' students.

Table 1. Studies using the Langner 22 Index as a measure of psychological disturbance in immigrant and international student populations

Study	Subjects	Mean scores
Cochrane et al. (1977)	Indian immigrants	3.42
Furnham and Trezise (1983)	International students	4.21
Furnham and Shiekh (1993)	First generation Asian immigrants (female)	4.41
Present study	International students	4.7

The data for the subjects from the 'social questions' on the International Student Questionnaire revealed that a number of students (25%) had no friends to talk to about their problems and some students (28%) were never invited out by friends during the first three months. 37% reported that they had no British friends, but nearly half the students (47%) had been invited to a British person's house. 20% reported that they had experienced racism of one form or another. As far as the university was concerned, 38% of the subjects found British students unfriendly but only a small number (20%) had communication difficulties with lecturers.

The responses to the 'practical questions' revealed that a majority of students had no difficulty in practising their religion (89%), no difficulties shopping (92%), and no problems with British law (95%). 44% reported difficulties with coursework. 78% were satisfied with the university library and 89% had no problems with the university administration. The questions with the lowest number of positive responses were on the British weather (30%), followed by understanding British humour (41%).

Comparison of pre-sessional and the standard arrival groups

The measures that were taken to account for confounding variables showed no difference between the two groups. For the Nelson Quick Test, the measure of English language competence, the PSG mean score was 17.34, (sd = 5.34) and the SAG mean score was 17.65, (sd = 4.43). The mean score on the expectations questionnaire was 20.14, (sd = 4.57) for the PSG and 20.19, (sd = 3.78) for the SAG.

Table 2. The mean scores with standard deviations and Anova F ratios for the pre-sessional and standard arrival groups on the Dundee Relocation Inventory, the Langner 22 Index and the International Students Questionnaire

	Pre-sessional Group (N=29)		Standard Arrival Group (N=26)		F	
	Mean	Sd	Mean	Sd		
Dundee R.I.	23.14	9.47	18.23	9.23	4.21	p<0.05
Langner 22	5.24	3.27	4.07	3.70	1.54	n.s.
International Students Questionnaire	17.65	4.17	19.19	4.36	1.78	n.s

A series of one way **ANOVAs** was carried out between the PSG and the SAG. There was a significant difference on the Dundee Relocation Inventory $(F(1,53) = 4.21, p < 0.05)$ between the two groups with the PSG significantly more homesick than the SAG. (The criterion for statistical significance in this and all subsequent analyses was $p < 0.05$). The mean scores for the PSG were higher than the SAG on the Langner 22 Index, indicating more psychological distress, and lower on the International Students questionnaire, suggesting a more negative evaluation. However these differences did not reach significance on the Langner 22 index $(F(1, 53) = 1.54, n.s.)$ or the ISQ $(F(1, 53) = 1.78, n.s.)$. The mean scores for all measures for each group are given in Table 2.

On the ISQ, there was no difference between the mean scores on the overall responses to the 13 'social questions' for the PSG (m = 8.33, sd = 3.18) and the SAG (m = 8.92, sd = 3.03). However there was a significant difference between the mean scores of the two groups on the answers to the 13 'practical questions' $(F(1, 53) = 5.79, p < 0.05)$. The SAG (m = 10.34, sd = 1.65) responded with significantly more positive responses than the PSG (m = 9.27, sd = 1.65).

A large proportion of the PSG used the university medical centre (69%), half used the English language support unit (51%), and a smaller number used the student advice centre (24%) and the university counselling service (13%). In the SAG the same percentage of students used the student advice centre (24%), but fewer students used the medical centre (41%), the university counselling service (7%) and the English language support unit (7%).

Additional analyses

The relationship between expectations and experience mismatch, and homesickness and mental health was investigated by subtracting the score on the expectations questionnaire from the ISQ score for each subject. These scores were then **correlated** with the scores the subjects recorded on the Dundee Relocation Inventory and the Langner 22 index. There was a significant negative correlation, using Pearson's product-moment **coefficient**, between the difference between experiences and expectations and homesickness ($r(53) = -0.504$, $p < 0.001$). This indicates that if a subject's experience was worse than their expectations then they were more homesick. There was no significant correlation between the difference between experiences and expectations and mental health ($r(53) = -0.164$).

There was no significant correlation between level of English language and homesickness ($r(53) = -0.087$), and that with evaluation of experiences just failed to reach significance ($r(53) = 0.217$). However the negative correlation of English with mental distress was significant ($r(53) = -0.229$, $p < 0.05$). A significant negative correlation was found between age and the Langner 22 Index ($r(53) = -0.331$, $p < 0.025$), indicating younger students were more likely to suffer psychological distress. There was however no significant correlation between age and homesickness ($r(53) = 0.028$), experiences ($r(53) = 0.072$), or expectations ($r(53) = 0.127$).

One-way ANOVAs were carried out between all regional groups on the three primary measures, but no significant differences were found. One-way ANOVAs were also computed between students living on and off campus on all measures. On the homesickness measure, students living off campus ($m = 16.21$, $sd = 7.96$) were significantly less homesick ($F(1, 53) = 4.9$, $p < 0.05$) than students living on campus ($m = 22.58$, $sd = 9.69$). However the difference on the Langner 22 Index ($F(1, 53) = 1.96$, n.s.) between students living on campus ($m = 5.07$, $sd = 3.45$) or off campus ($m = 3.57$, $sd = 3.52$) did not reach significance. The ISQ score was also not significantly different ($F(1, 53) = 1.12$, n.s.) between the groups living on campus ($m = 18.02$, $sd = 4.4$) and off campus ($m = 19.43$, $sd = 3.9$). See Table 3.

Discussion

The pre-sessional group were significantly more homesick than the standard arrival group. They also had a higher level of psychological distress and reported a more negative evaluation of their experiences in the UK. The hypothesis that the PSG would experience less culture shock than the SAG after one academic term should therefore be rejected. Indeed the students who attended the pre-sessional course displayed more symptoms of culture shock than a group of students that arrived on their own and took no part in any cultural orientation. This could be explained in a number of different ways.

Table 3. The mean scores with standard deviations and Anova Fratios for students living off campus and students living on campus measured on the Dundee Relocation Inventory, the Langner 22 Index and the International Students Questionnaire

	Off Campus Students (N=13)		On Campus Students (N=42)		F	
	Mean	Sd	Mean	Sd		
Dundee R.I.	16.21	7.96	22.58	9.69	4.9	$p < 0.05$
Langner 22	3.57	3.52	5.07	3.45	1.96	n.s
International Students Questionnaire	19.43	3.9	18.02	4.4	1.12	n.s

It could be argued that the students who are attracted by, or are encouraged to participate in, the pre-sessional course are more likely to have difficulties when the academic term begins. However, as reported above, participation in the course is mainly determined by whether a student's sponsor is prepared to bear the cost, rather than by the student's individual wants and needs. Further, the SAG was selected to resemble the PSG as closely as possible on variables that might have been expected to affect the experience of culture shock e.g. age, country of origin, religion, place of residence.

Is it then realistic to suggest that the course made students more homesick? It could be argued that the orientation course creates a false sense of security and that students arriving on their own are more likely to make an effort to get to know people and to become familiar with their new environment.

It must be pointed out that the central aim of the pre-sessional course is not to prevent culture shock. The publicity surrounding the pre-sessional course promotes it primarily as a study skills course. No measures of academic achievement were taken in this study and therefore it is not known whether or not the course improved academic performance. In a recent assessment by the British Association of Lecturers in English for Academic Purposes, the course was recognised as being of "outstanding quality" and having "many strengths that could be profitably imitated by other institutions" (BALEAP, 1993). The pre-sessional course was also consistently praised by participants and regarded as a crucial part of their orientation to the university. Nevertheless, the literature would suggest that elements of the course would significantly help a student in the process of cultural adaptation.

There was a significant difference between the groups on the answers given on the ISQ for the 'practical questions', but not for the 'social questions'. There was no relationship between a high positive score on the 'social questions' and less psychological distress and homesickness as some studies would suggest there should be (Furnham and Bochner, 1986). However, this may be due in part to limitations of the ISQ. Each question was answered "yes" or "no" giving equal weight to a range of issues from experience of racism to being satisfied with the university library.

In their methods of coping the students adopted consistent strategies, turning to the familiar and maintaining contact with home and family. A striking feature throughout the interviews was that students did not turn to the structured support that was available at the university. Some students interviewed were not even aware of the existence of the University Counselling Service.

There were no significant differences on any of the measures between the five regional groups. These results do not provide support for the 'culture distance' theory (Furnham and Bochner, 1982). They also throw doubt on the relevance of Hofstede's (1984) four-**dimensional** model to the understanding of culture shock. This could be because these models somewhat simplify the dynamics taking place when a person from one cultural environment moves to another. For example Chinese Singaporean students will be culturally "Chinese" with the **commitments** to family and other traditions inherent in the Chinese culture, but they will also have had access to the same types of media and technology that students experience in the UK. Though culturally different, they may find more similarities between Britain and home than some European students.

A relationship was found between the degree of discrepancy between expectations and experiences, and homesickness. Students who had experiences that did not **match up to** their expectations, whether or not they were on the pre-sessional course, were more homesick than other students. This result supports work by Fisher (1990) on homesickness and expectations. It also has implications for the way that universities recruit international students. As competition increases for a share of student numbers marketing techniques could become more **aggressive**, but these should not **distort** expectations of living and studying in a foreign country. Accurate information before departure and on arrival at the university is obviously essential.

One consistent finding from the interviews is that there was not one isolated phase of feeling low. In the words of one student "Homesickness is something that comes and goes in waves". However nearly all subjects reported that the most difficult time for them was the first few days. Rather than experiencing an initial 'honeymoon period' many students were totally disoriented at the start of their time in the UK.

This information runs counter to the *U curve hypothesis*. Despite the fact that this model is still **replicated** in the research literature and literature for professionals working with international students, it is clear from the information in this study that the students' experience is much more complex and is related more to the personal and social factors affecting each individual. Importantly, the interviews indicate that academic concerns, over coursework assignments and examinations, caused considerable anxiety and restlessness. This **accords** with the work of Selby and Woods (1966).

There was no significant correlation between a subject's level of English language and homesickness or evaluation of their experience in the UK. However the correlation between level of English and level of psychological distress was significant, and these were all postgraduate students whose competence in English is comparatively high. Therefore it cannot be suggested that English language level has no **bearing** on potential difficulties in a new cultural environment.

It has been reported elsewhere that students themselves often falsely attribute social difficulties to language **deficiencies** (Barker *et al.* 1991). The information from the ISQ reveals that many students from the pre-sessional course continued to maintain contact with the English Language Support Unit. In interviews many students related that if they were able to speak better English then they would have fewer problems. However free English classes are available at the university and numbers attending them are very small.

Students living off campus were significantly less homesick than students living on campus. They also had a lower score on the Langner 22 Index, suggesting that they suffered marginally less psychological disturbance and reported a more positive evaluation of their experience in the UK, though the differences between the two groups on these last two measures did not reach significance. All students living off campus were living with their families, the students on campus were a mixture of married and single people, but all were living apart from their families. Current practice at the university is actively to discourage students from bringing their families with them to the U.K. in the belief that this will create more problems. Results from this study suggest that this is not the case. On the contrary, accompanied students reported a more positive experience of their time here and were less homesick and less psychologically troubled. All students reported that their closest friends were either co-nationals or students with a shared linguistic background. This is consistent with findings in other studies on international students and friendship networks (Bochner and Ohsako, 1977; Klineberg and Hull, 1979).

There was a relationship between age and psychological distress, with younger students scoring significantly higher on the Langner 22 Index. A common misconception is that older students will have more difficulty than younger students when studying abroad. One reason often cited by researchers for international students generally coping well with a cross cultural experience compared to other groups, is that they are younger. The evidence reported here runs contrary to that **assertion**.

Culture shock in the context of international students can be seen as an ongoing process. The psychological effects are **intermittent** and are intensified by personal and social factors affecting each individual. The student, unlike an immigrant, is a sojourner and will stay only temporarily in the host culture. The student is therefore preoccupied with the academic task in hand and outside cultural influences are regarded as a secondary factor. International students are not only adapting to the British culture, but perhaps primarily they are adapting to British university culture. Added to the difficulties of leaving home and family are the stresses brought on by academic study.

Furnham and Bochner (1986) state that for too long culture shock has been seen in the context of a 'disease' or clinical model. This is **reinforced** by the literature on working with international students. Current practice is **geared** towards arrival and orientation and neglects the follow up mechanisms needed to minimise the possible negative effects of cultural adaptation. Students are left to run the course of the 'culture shock cycle' and once 'adjusted' they 'recover' as if they have had a cold or the flu. This is not a helpful way to understand culture shock in this context.

The **stereotyping** of the members of different cultures is a common feature of material available to those working with international students. The use of a quote from Kardiner (1959) in a recently published manual, (Lago, 1990, p. 161), illustrates this approach, "Each culture tends to create and is supported by a basic personality type composed of complex personality characteristics...". Regarding members of a particular culture as homogeneous inevitably leads to inadequate blanket solutions to the problems of crossing cultural divides. It would be more helpful to treat people as individuals, while also being aware of their customs and beliefs.

There are a number of ways in which students could be helped through the experience. Fisher (1990) suggests that a way of helping people who are homesick is to encourage them to positively restructure the "qualities, opportunities and facilities offered by the new environment" (p. 307). Pennebaker et al. (1990) reveal in studies on university students, that writing about their experiences can significantly help the coping process. In Canada and Australia very promising results have emerged from peer-pairing schemes involving home and international students (Westwood and Barker, 1990).

On the basis of our findings we would recommend that the following could be considered by staff in higher education institutions, in addition to the provision of initial cultural orientation programmes:

– A more sophisticated analysis of the problems and needs of individual international students, relevant to the local higher education environment.

– The development of coherent management strategies to support international students. Support is often provided by several agencies within institutions in a relatively unco-ordinated and unstructured way. Communication between these agencies, and between them and students, tends to be poor.

– A support system that would address student needs all year round.

– A support system that reaches those who do not participate in initial orientation programmes. The assumption tends to be made that students not participating in initial programmes do not feel they need support. However many students are not able to participate in such programmes for reasons outside their control.

– The development of good documentation of the support system, so that international students know where to go for help and advice, and the provision of accurate information about the host environment.

– Less emphasis on the integration of international students, who will remain in a host country for a relatively short time, and an encouragement to maintain links with home, and form links with co-nationals in the host country.

In conclusion, this study suggests that the present model of culture shock used by the professionals at universities and colleges of higher education is unhelpful. The use of cultural orientation or 'culture learning' in a short course at the **commencement** of a student's visit, does not seem to be a solution to the difficulties faced by international students.

References

Anumonye, A. (1970). *African Students in Alien Cultures.* New York: Black Academy Press.

Barker, M., Child, C., Gallois, C., Jones, E. and Callan, V. J. (1991). Difficulties of overseas students in social and academic situations, *Australian Journal of Psychology* 43, 79–84.

Bochner, S. (1982). The social psychology of cross-cultural relations. In S. Bochner (ed.). *Cultures in Contact: Studies in Cross-cultural Interaction.* Oxford: Pergamon.

Bochner, S. and Ohsako, T. (1977). Ethnic role salience in racially homogeneous and heterogeneous societies, *Journal of Cross-cultural Psychology* 8, 477–92.

Book, P. (1970). *Culture Shock: A Reader in Modern Anthropology.* New York: A. A. Knopf.

British Association of Lecturers in English for Academic Purposes (1993). *Accreditation Report.* Manchester: BALEAP.

British Council (1989). *Code of Practice: Educational Institutions and Overseas Students.* London: British Council.

British Council (1990). *Studying and Living in Britain 1990.* London: British Council.

British Council (1991). *Feeling at Home.* London: British Council.

Church, A. T. (1982). Sojourner Adjustment, *Psychological Bulletin* 91, 540–72.

Cochrane, R., Hashmi, F. and Stopes-Roe, M. (1977). Measuring psychological disturbance in Asian immigrants to Britain, *Social Science and Medicine* 11, 157–164.

Cochrane, R. and Stopes-Roe, M. (1980). The mental health of immigrants, *New Community* 8, 123–8.

Cox, J. L. (1988). The overseas student: Expatriate, sojourner or settler?, *Acta-Psychiatrica-Scandanavia* 78, 179–184.

Department for Education (1993). *Students from Abroad in Great Britain 1981 to 1991*. London: Government Statistical Service.

Fisher, S. (1989). *Homesickness, Cognition and Health*. London: Lawrence Erlbaum.

Fisher, S. (1990). Helping the homesick: Attentional management strategy, commitment and adaptation. In S. Fisher and C. L. Cooper (eds.). *On the Move: The Psychology of Change and Transition*. London: Wiley.

Fisher, S., Murray, K. and Frazer, N. (1985). Homesickness and health in first-year students, *Journal of Environmental Psychology* 5, 181–195.

Fisher, S. and Hood, B. (1987). The stress of the transition to university: A longitudinal study of psychological disturbance, absent-mindedness and vulnerability to homesickness, *British Journal of Psychology* 78, 425–441.

Furnham, A. and Bochner, S. (1982). Social difficulty in a foreign culture: An empirical analysis of culture shock. In S. Bochner (ed.). *Cultures in Contact: Studies in Cross-cultural Interaction*. Oxford: Pergamon.

Furnham, A. and Bochner, S. (1986). *Culture Shock: Psychological Reactions to Unfamiliar Environments*. London: Routledge.

Furnham, A. and Sheikh, S. (1993). Gender, generational and social support correlates of mental health in Asian immigrants, *The International Journal of Social Psychiatry* 39, 22–33.

Furnham, A. and Trezise, L. (1983). The mental health of foreign students, *Social Science and Medicine* 17, 365–370.

Gunn, A. (1970). *The Privileged Adolescent*. Aylesbury: Medical and Technical Publications.

Hofstede, G. (1984). *Culture's Consequences: International Differences in Work Related Values*. California: Sage.

Kinnell, M. (1990). The marketing and managing of courses. In M. Kinnell (ed.). *The Learning Experiences of Overseas Students*. Milton Keynes: Open University Press.

Klineberg, O. and Hull, W. F. (1979). *At a Foreign University: An International Study of Adaptation and Coping*. New York: Praeger.

Lago, C. (1990). *Working with Overseas Students*. London: British Council and Huddersfield Polytechnic.

Langner, T. S. (1962). A twenty-two item screening score of psychiatric symptoms indicating impairment, *Journal of Health and Social Behaviour* 3, 269–276.

Lysgaard, S. (1955). Adjustment in a foreign society: Norwegian Fullbright grantees visiting the United States, *International Social Science Bulletin* 7, 45–51.

Makepeace, E. E. (1989). *Overseas Students: Challenges of Institutional Adjustment*. SCED Paper (56) Birmingham: Birmingham Polytechnic.

Oberg, K. (1960). Cultural shock: Adjustment to new cultural environments, *Practical Anthropology* 7, 177–82.

Pennebaker, J. W., Colder, M. and Sharp, L. K. (1990). Accelerating the coping process, *Journal of Personality and Social Psychology* 58, 528–537.

Selby, H. and Woods, C. W. (1966). Foreign students at a High Pressure University, *Sociology of Education* 39, 138–154.

Singh, A. K. (1963). *Indian Students in Britain*. Bombay: Asia Publishing House.

Tajfel, H. and Dawson, J. L. (1965). *Disappointed Guests*. Oxford: Oxford University Press.

United Kingdom Council for Overseas Student Affairs (1992). *Orientation within the Institution*. London: UKCOSA.

Willmuth, L., Weaver, L. and Donald, S. (1975). Utilization of medical services by transfered employees, *Archives of General Psychiatry* 2, 182–9.

Westwood, M. J. and Barker, M. (1990). Academic achievement and social adaptation among international students: A comparison of groups study of the peer-pairing program, *International Journal of Intercultural Relations* 14, 251–263.

Zwingmann, C. A. A. and Gunn, A. D. G. (1983). *Uprooting and Health: Psychological Problems of Students from Abroad*. Geneva: World Health Organisation.

Appendix: International Students Questionnaire

1. During your time of study at university have you:

1.1	Had problems with the university administration?	yes	no
1.2	Had communication difficulties with lecturers?	yes	no
1.3	Had any difficulties with the coursework?	yes	no
1.4	Been self disciplined for study?	yes	no
1.5	Been satisfied with the university library?	yes	no
1.6	Found British students friendly?	yes	no

Used any of the following agencies:

1.7	*The Student Advice Centre*	yes	no
1.8	*The University Medical Centre*	yes	no
1.9	*The University Counselling Service*	yes	no
1.10	*The English Language Support Unit*	yes	no

2. During the time that you have been in the UK have you:

2.1	Been invited out by friends?	yes	no
2.2	Been invited to a British person's house?	yes	no
2.3	Disliked British food?	yes	no
2.4	Disliked the British weather?	yes	no
2.5	Encountered problems with British law?	yes	no
2.6	Encountered racism?	yes	no
2.7	Enjoyed an active social life?	yes	no
2.8	Enjoyed your stay in the UK so far?	yes	no
2.9	Found the British polite and helpful?	yes	no

2.10	Made any British friends?	yes	no
2.11	Had difficulties when shopping?	yes	no
2.12	Had difficulties with accommodation?	yes	no
2.13	Had difficulties with social customs?	yes	no
2.14	Had difficulties with the English language?	yes	no
2.15	Had difficulty in practising your religion?	yes	no
2.16	Had financial difficulties?	yes	no
2.17	Had friends to talk to about problems?	yes	no
2.18	Participated in leisure activities?	yes	no
2.19	Travelled in the United Kingdom?	yes	no
2.20	Understood British humour?	yes	no

3. **Is there anything else about life in the United Kingdom or your time studying at university that you wish to share?**

New Words

accord	[ə'kɔːd]	v.	（with）相一致
aggressive	[ə'gresiv]	a.	侵犯（略）的，挑衅的；敢作敢为的
ameliorate	[ə'miːliəreit]	v.	改善
ANOVA	[ə'nəuvə]		方差分析
assertion	[ə'sɜːʃn]	n.	声称；主张；明确肯定
assimilate	[ə'siməleit]	v.	吸收，消化；使同化
bearing	['beəriŋ]	n.	关系，关联
coefficient	[ˌkəui'fiʃnt]	n.	系数
commencement	[kə'mensmənt]	n.	开始；毕业典礼，学位授予典礼
commitment	[kə'mitmənt]	n.	承诺，保证；信奉，献身；承担的义务
comply	[kəm'plai]	vi.	（with）遵从，依从，服从
confidential	[ˌkɔnfi'denʃl]	a.	秘（机）密的
correlate	['kɔrileit]	v.	（to, with）相关，关联；使相互关联
deficiency	[di'fiʃnsi]	n.	缺乏，不足；缺点，缺陷
devise	[di'vaiz]	vt.	想出，设计
dimensional	[di'menʃənl]	a.	空间的，维度的
distort	[di'stɔːt]	v.	歪曲，扭曲
empirical	[im'pirikl]	a.	以经验（或观察）为依据的

enrol	[in'rəul]	v.	注册；登记
gear	[giə]	v.	使适应；接上，调和
impunity	[im'pju:nəti]	n.	（惩罚、损失、伤害等的）免除
intercourse	['intəkɔ:s]	n.	交流，交往，交际
intermittent	[ˌintə'mitənt]	a.	间歇的，断断续续的
inventory	['invəntri]	n.	详细目录
irritability	[ˌiritə'biləti]	n.	易怒；过敏性；兴奋性
normative	['nɔ:mətiv]	a.	规范的，惯常的
orientation	[ˌɔ:riən'teiʃn]	n.	适应，（对新生的）情况介绍；方向，方位
overtake	[ˌəuvə'teik]	vt.	（overtook, overtaken）追上，超过
precipitate	[pri'sipiteit]	v.	促成；使沉淀
privy	['privi]	a.	知情的，秘密参与的
psychopathology	[ˌsaikəupə'θɔlədʒi]	n.	精神病理学
random	['rændəm]	a.	任意的，随机的
recruit	[ri'kru:t]	v.	招募，吸收；充实
recurrent	[ri'kʌrənt]	a.	重现，反复
reinforce	[ˌri:in'fɔ:s]	v.	增强，加强，增援
replicate	['replikeit]	v.	复制
salient	['seiliənt]	a.	显著的，突出的
sequelae	[si'kwi:li:]	n.	结果，后遗症
sojourner	['sɔdʒɜ:nə]	n.	旅居者；寄居者
stereotyping	['steriəˌtaipiŋ]	n.	定型；成见
uproot	[ʌp'ru:t]	v.	根除
variable	['veəriəbl]	n.	可变因素，变量

Phrases

cast doubt on	对……产生怀疑
map out	筹划
come to terms with	达成协议
run counter to	违反；与……背道而驰
at large	一般的，总的；详尽地
account for	解释，说明
match up to	比得上

Discussion Ideas

1. How many tenses were used in the Literature Review section and what are the possible differences of these patterns?

2. What is a research hypothesis? What is the nature of a research hypothesis?

3. A quantitative method was used in the study. Why is it appropriate for the present study?

4. In this study, the researchers formulated two groups—SAG and PSG, what is the underlying reason?

5. What is an inventory? What is the difference between an inventory and a questionnaire?

6. What is one way ANOVA? How to interpret an ANOVA test?

7. What do you think might be the limitaions of the present study and their implications for future research?

8. The format of the Abstract section varies according to different styles. What are the differences between the Abstract of this paper and that for the general APA style?

Vocabulary and Language Learning Skills

1. Recognizing Word Meanings

Match the definitions in Column B with vocabulary items in Column A.

Column A	Column B
1. affect	a. to become similar (to)
2. consistent	b. to become or cause to become a member; enlist
3. assimilate	c. spoken, written, or given in confidence; secret; private
4. orientation	d. a feeling of extreme worry, sadness or pain
5. empirical	e. to act upon or influence
6. enrol	f. a course, programme etc, introducing a new environment
7. national	g. always behaving in a similar, especially positive, way
8. confidential	h. to adjust to different conditions, a new environment, etc.
9. distress	i. based on experiment and observation rather than on theory
10. adapt	j.someone who is a citizen of a particular country but is living in another country

2. Making a Collocation

Use the vocabulary items in the box to complete the sentences. Make changes if necessary.

propose	replicate	validate
discrepancy	exclude	devise
in accordance with	at large	map out

1) A method _____ for quicker communications between offices.

2) This group is not representative of the population _____.

3) The government has issued a new document _____ its policies on education.

4) Researchers tried many times to _____ the original experiment.

5) This product can only be used _____ the manufacturer's instructions.

6) In his speech, he _____ a financial incentive for schools to take on poorer performing students.

7) Microbes must, as far as possible, _____ from the room during an operation.

8) There is a large _____ between the ideal image of motherhood and the reality.

9) The data is _____ automatically by the computer after it has been entered.

3. Text Completion

Complete the following paragraph with the help of the context. Write only one word for each blank.

'Culture shock' has been identified as a psychological reaction to a change in cultural environment. The main symptoms of 1)_____ are reported to be psychological disturbance, a negative reaction to the new surroundings and a longing for a more familiar 2)_____. Research has identified culture shock as a component, in the difficulties that international students face when 3)_____ in another country. One way that institutions of higher education have responded to these 4)_____ is to provide initial cultural orientation. In the study reported here, a group of post-graduate students who had participated in a study skills and cultural 5)_____ course at a British university were 6)_____ a group who had not. Contrary to the research hypothesis, the group that took part in the orientation course were significantly 7)_____ homesick and reported more

8)_____ difficulties. The overall findings cast doubt 9)_____ the received view of culture shock as it affects international students. They suggest that culture shock is exacerbated by personal and social factors and this has implications for the way that international students may be 10) _____ through the experience.

Writing Focus

Title Page and Abstract

1. Title Page

Function

The title page of a research paper lists the title of the work and the name of the author. However, depending on the format and nature of the work, the listed information may vary. It is the first thing your readers see so it makes a strong impression on them.

Style

Moves of Writing a Title Page:

Move 1 Finish writing your paper before starting to write the title page.

Move 2 Use the proper APA format.

- Begin the title page on Page one of your paper.
- Type the page header—"Running head:" and the title of your paper in uppercase letter flush left and the page number "1" flush right at the top of the page.
- Centre your title in upper and lowercase letters in the upper half of the page.
- Use one inch margins, 12 point font, and double spacing, which are consistent with the rest of the paper.

Move 3 Write the title page.

- Write your title of the paper with no more than 12 words in one or two lines; the title should not contain abbreviations or words that serve no purpose.
- Type the author's name in order of first name, middle initial(s), and last name; do not use titles (Dr.) or degrees (Ph.D.).
- Type the institutional affiliation, which should indicate the location where the author(s) conducted the research.
- (Optional) Include the course name, instructor name, and date of submission as required by instructors for undergraduate courses.

Sample of APA Title Page

Running Head: TITLE OF YOUR PAPER   1

The Title of Your Paper

Name

School Affiliation

Course Name

Instructor Name

Date of Submission

2. Abstract

Function

An abstract is a concise, comprehensive summary of the contents of the research paper; it allows readers to survey the contents of your paper quickly and is used by abstracting and information services to index and retrieve articles.

Style

Moves of Writing an Abstract:

Move 1 Finish writing your paper before starting to write the abstract.

Move 2 Use the proper APA format.

- Begin the abstract on Page two of your paper, after the title page.
- Include the page header, the text which is separated from the main body of text, and the page number "2" flush right at the top of the page.
- Centre the word "Abstract" on the first line (no bold, formatting, italics, underlining, or quotation marks).

- Use one inch margins, 12 point font, and double spacing, which are consistent with the rest of the paper.

Move 3 Compose the abstract.

- Write the abstract text with a single paragraph between 150 and 250 words with the block format.
- Compose a concise summary of the key points of your research, which contains your introduction, research questions, participants (optional), methods, results/findings, conclusions, and possibly implications (optional).
- Type the word "*Keywords*" (*italicized*) after the abstract text and list up to five keywords of your research.

Language Focus

1. **Introduction/Research topic**

   The purpose of the present paper is to provide…

   To investigate…, we examined…

   With the aim to provide…, we have…

   We examine the…issue in this study from a…perspective.

   The study is about a…survey/summary of the…issue.

   This paper presents a detailed analysis/methodology of…

   The present paper concerns itself with a…study of the…issue.

   The…issue(s) is/are examined in this research.

2. **Methods**

   We use…to investigate the…

   We present an analysis of…from…

   We study…with…

   We have developed a…to study/estimate/investigate the…

   Our research/study uses a(n)…approach…

   Our research/study is based on…

3. **Results**

   Our findings/results suggest/indicate/show…

   The results we obtained demonstrate that…

   We find in our research that…

   Based on these findings, we may conclude that…

   Some of our important findings include…

   And our conclusion(s) is/are…

4. **Conclusions/Value**

   The findings/results suggest/demonstrate that…

These results support the idea that…

…is of great…significance in…

In this study, we present/propose…

Here we provide evidence…

Our studies indicate that…

Different from previous research, this paper emphasizes the importance of…in the study of…

Different theories have been introduced in the field to solve…problem(s).

And in the present study, we attempt to use an alternative theoretic framework to examine…

The present experiment is designed to testify/challenge the validity of…

The results presented should be useful to…

5. **Implications (optional)**

It remains to be proved that…

However, …remains to be further studies.

Some useful implications obtained from this study include…

Some suggestions we would like to give to any further study of the same issue are… and…

Admittedly, what we have discussed in this study is far from complete. And some improvements we want to make in our further research include…

Task One

Study the following title page in APA format, and correct the inappropriate parts.

Running Head: Obesity in Children

Can Medication Cure Obesity in Children?

Zhang Xiaoyue

Psychology

Professor Yang

201X January 6

Task Two

*Study the following sentences from the abstract for the research paper entitled
"Effects and Student Perceptions of Collaborative Writing in L2" and work out
the tasks below.*

1. Below is a random list of sentences of an abstract, write down the names of the
elements of structure on the blanks.

_____ (1) In addition,most students in the CW condition found the experience
enjoyable and felt that it contributed to their L2 learning.

_____ (2) Results of the study showed that CW had an overall significant
effect on students' L2 writing; however, this effect varied from one
writing skill area to another. Specifically, the effect was significant
for content, organization, and vocabulary, but not for grammar or
mechanics.

_____ (3) This study investigated the effectiveness and students' perceptions
of collaborative writing (CW) in second language (L2).

_____ (4) A number of theoretical and pedagogical implications of the study,
and limitations and directions for further research, are presented.

_____ (5) The study involved 38 first year students in two intact classes at
a large university in the UAE (United Arab Emirates). One class
consisted of 18 students and was considered the experimental
group, and the second consisted of 20 students and was considered
the control group. In the control group, writing tasks were carried
out by students individually; in the experimental group, these tasks
were carried out in pairs.

_____ (6) Writing quality was determined by a holistic rating procedure
that included content, organization, grammar, vocabulary, and
mechanics.

_____ (7) Results of the study are discussed in light of the social constructivist
perspective of learning.

_____ (8) The study lasted 16 weeks and involved a pre- and post-test.

2. Work out the correct order of the above sentences for the abstract text.

3. List up to five keywords for the abstract text.

4. Use the APA format and the above information to complete the abstract page.

Task Three

Identify the elements of structure in the Abstract section of the study in Unit 6.

Supplementary Reading

The Relationship Between International Students' Cross-Cultural Adaptation and Dominant Language in Taiwan

Dr. Hsiaowen Huang (Corresponding author)

Assistant Professor

Department of Information Management

Chang Jung Christian University, 396, Sec 1, Chang Jung Rd

Kway Jen, Tainan, 71101, Taiwan

E-mail: victoria@mail.cjcu.edu.tw, Phone: 886-6-2785123

Chang, Yongsheng

133, Yu-Ying St, East District

Tainan, 70175, Taiwan

E-mail: hhuan004@hotmail.com, Phone: 886-6-2552500

Abstract

Higher education institutions of various "countries" have perceived the importance of international student recruitment, have studied the problems these students "encounter when they study abroad, and have searched for methods" and strategies to assist them in adapting to local culture and lifestyles. As current studies "on international students" have mainly focused on life adjustment, this study focused on the issue of cross-cultural adaptation. This study analyzed the relationship between international students' cross-cultural adaptation and the dominant language as Chinese of Taiwan, and put emphasis on the relationship between the linguistic competence acquired from studying abroad and the level of cross-cultural adaptation, as well as how they affect each other. It was found that international students' cross-cultural adaptation concerning the dimension of "studying and researching" was closely related to their Chinese proficiency, and that the level Chinese ability would affect the amount of cross-cultural adaptation.

Keyword: international student, cross-cultural adaptation, Chinese proficiency, Taiwan

I. Introduction

1. Research motives, purposes, and expected contributions

Ever since Taiwan joined the World Trade Organization (WTO) in 2002, in compliance with the WTO's General Agreement of Trade in Services (GATS), higher education in Taiwan has to face the impact of foreign higher education institutions being allowed to recruit students in Taiwan. Therefore, at present, the highest priority is to increase the international competitiveness of higher education in Taiwan.

"The Protocol for the Preliminary Work of Important Social Development" developed by the Ministry of Education in Taiwan in 2007 aggressively promotes and enhances academic exchanges between Taiwan and various countries in the world, in the hope that more international students will be attracted to study in Taiwan. International students can bring huge economic benefits to local regions and create business and trade opportunities. In addition, international student recruitment can further increase cultural exchanges, as well as stimulate and promote international interaction and reciprocity (Ministry of Education, 2007). Therefore, the higher education institutions and scholars in Taiwan both have perceived the importance of international student recruitment, and have studied the problems and challenge that are encountered by these students studying in Taiwan. In addition, they have sought methods to assist international students in adapting to local culture and lifestyles, which are also beneficial to international students' learning. Therefore, this study aimed to investigate international students' cross-cultural adaptation.

Language learning and cultural learning mutually support each other. Under the premise of language teaching, the purpose of cultural teaching is to increase the learners' understanding of the target language and to reduce cross-cultural conflicts in language and life. The key factor affecting cross-cultural adaptation is linguistic and cultural adaptation (Furnham & Erdmann, 1995). At present, the teaching materials for Chinese in Taiwan are mainly serial teaching materials, whereas short-term, practicable ones closely related to life and cultural in Taiwan have not been developed. To learners of Chinese, appropriate teaching materials can easily increase learning motivation and further trigger spontaneous learning to enable students to learn the language pleasantly and freely (Chang, 2007).

On the other hand, Chien (2008) suggested that in a cross-cultural environment, the teaching strategies of Chinese language teachers should take cross-cultural differences, which may affect international students' learning, into consideration. Huang (2007) indicated that the causes for international students' anxiety over learning Chinese are mainly from the teaching activities, the learning contents and the teaching materials. Moreover, because there are few studies on international students' cross-cultural adaptation and Chinese proficiency, the purposes of this study is to investigate the relationship between Chinese proficiency and international students' cross-cultural adaptation, and to further analyze the difference in the influence of various Chinese abilities on international students' cross-cultural adaptation in Taiwan. This study intended to clarify the relationship between international students' cross-cultural adaptation and Chinese proficiency, and to provide practical strategies and suggestions on international students' cross-cultural adaptation in order to assist them in facing the problems of cross-cultural adaptation more effectively. Moreover, the research results obtained from the analysis on the influence of Chinese proficiency on international students' cross-cultural adaptation can be used as a reference to the compilation and planning of Chinese teaching materials, and concrete suggestions can be proposed for both the training of Chinese language teachers and the policies for the instruction of international student affairs. The research results also address the current lack of studies on international students' Chinese learning and cross-cultural adaptation.

2. Definitions

2.1 International students: refers to students of other nationalities who are formally studying at colleges and universities in Taiwan.

2.2 Chinese proficiency: refers to the comprehensive abilities composed of the Chinese phonetic system usage ability, Chinese listening ability, Chinese speaking ability, Chinese literacy, Chinese character writing ability, Chinese language reading ability and Chinese composition ability.

2.3 Cross-cultural adaption: refers to the reconsideration and adjustment of behavior and ideological criteria to better match another culture. During the course of cross-cultural adaptation, individuals will experience various feelings or physical and psychological changes (Ward & Kennedy, 1996).

3. Literature review

3.1 Studies on language learning and cross-cultural adaption

Schumann (1978) proposed the Acculturation Theory and viewed the learning process of a second language as the gradual adaptation to the culture of target language from the perspective of the relationship between culture and language. In addition, Schumann also viewed the learning of an entire second language as a part of cross-cultural adaptation and suggested that a second language learner's level of adaptation to the culture of the target language can determine the level of understanding of the target language. Church (1982) indicated that the development of cross-cultural adaptation is triggered by individuals' sense of similarities and differences caused by exposure to strange environments, different languages, behaviors, regulations, eating habits and educational systems. Yeh (1999) mentioned that cross-cultural adaptation is the social and psychological combination between learners and the target language. Therefore, the social and psychological distances between learners and the culture of the target language become the main factors affecting the complete learning of the second language. Social distance refers to the equivalent social status shared by second language learners and members of the target language.

In addition, both second language learners and members of the target language hope that the second language can be assimilated into the society of the target language. Psychological distance refers to the influence of the factors affecting the learning of the second language on the learner's emotional state, including fear, intenseness, anxiety and culture shock caused by language barriers. The huge social and psychological distances impede language learning at the initial stage, and even when learners stay in the natural environment of the target language, they may not necessarily be able to learn the target language. Constantine (2004) suggested that cross-cultural adaptation is an adjustment process in which individuals intend to start to understand and integrate another new culture from their original cultural context. When individuals face the conflicts of different cultural standards, they will start to understand their cultural orientation. In general, people will expand their existing behaviors and habits to include more than two cultural orientations, and the larger the scope of the openness is, the higher the tolerability to their thinking being changed by external information will be.

3.2 Relevant dimensions of studies on international students' cross-cultural adaptation

Uehara (1988) investigated international students' cross-cultural adaptation in Japan using Baker's (1981) Freshmen Student Adjustment Scale.

The scale focuses on social and cultural aspects, and the dimensions of the scale include "studying and researching", "mind-body wellness", "interpersonal relationships", "culture and economics of the living environment". Sandhu and Asrabadi (1994) developed the Acculturative Stress Scale for International Students, which has been widely used in studies concerning international students. Sezrle and Ward (1990) indicated that cross-cultural adaptation includes two major dimensions, "psychological adjustment" and "socio-cultural adjustment". Psychological adjustment refers to the perceived levels of happiness and satisfaction. However, factors such as "pressure", "social support", "partners of the same nationality", "local friends", "life changes", "attitude towards interactions with local friends", and "other individual factors", will affect psychological adjustment. Moreover, the factors affecting socio-cultural adjustment are mainly based on social learning theory and thus include assessments on the bases and models of interactions, such as "cross-cultural contact", "cultural distance", "cross-cultural training", "previous cross-cultural experiences" and "length of residence". This study used the amended Cross-Cultural Scale adopted by Uehara (1988), as it is based on the socio-cultural model. This study mainly investigated the difficulties encountered by international students during their learning adaptation, and expanded the dimensions of cross-cultural adaptation from a psychological aspect to the interactions and relationships with local society. As a result, the scale comprehensively included all the factors that affect cross-cultural adaptation.

II. Research Method

1. Research scope and subjects

This study treated the international students of three universities, with Mandarin Chinese courses in the Tainan metropolitan area as subjects. According to the Ministry of Education in Taiwan (2009), international students in universities totaled to 459 of the Tainan metropolitan area. A total of 285 questionnaires were distributed, and 215 were returned. There were 204 valid questionnaires, for a return rate of 72%.

2. Research instruments

This study adopted a questionnaire survey, with analysis based on SPSS. Analytical approaches included descriptive statistics (mean, frequency distribution and standard deviation), and inferential statistics refer to t-test and one-way ANOVA. The questionnaire used in this quantitative study included two parts. Part one was the Scale of Cross-Cultural Adaptation for International Students, and the questions were developed based on amendments made to the questions concerning five dimensions in the Cross-Cultural Scale adopted by Uehara (1988). Therefore, the cross-cultural adaptation related problems encountered by international students could be analyzed based on these questions. A total of 39 items were used to measure international students' responses, upon a 5-point Likert Scale, ranging from 5, meaning "strongly agree" to 1, meaning "strongly disagree". The dimensions and contents of the scale are shown in Table 1. The Cronbach's α of the Scale of Cross-Cultural Adaptation for International Students was 0.929, and that of the questions ranged from 0.691 to 0.904. Therefore, the internal consistency of the scale was high, representing a high reliability of the scale. In order to test the appropriateness and representativeness of the contents and questions in the scale, it was important to conduct

a content validity analysis.

The value of the Kaiser-Meyer Olkin Measure of Sampling Adequacy (KMO), ranging from 0 to 1, can be used to determine the appropriateness. When the KMO value is greater than 0.50, the content validity is high and the scale is representative. The KMO value of the scale was 0.841, and that of the questions ranged from 0.770 to 0.910. Therefore, the content validity of the scale was high and the scale was representative. Part two of the questionnaire was the Chinese Proficiency Self-Assessed Scale. The questions were developed based on the Test of Chinese as a Foreign Language (TOCFL, 2009), which is a foreign language proficiency test for non-native speakers of Chinese those who wish to know about their level of Chinese proficiency, or those who want to study, work or do business in Chinese speaking countries (Steering Committee for the Test of Proficiency-Huayu, 2010). This test provides assessment on various Chinese abilities, including phonetic system usage ability, Chinese listening ability, Mandarin speaking skills, Chinese literacy, the ability to write Chinese characters, Chinese language reading ability and Chinese composition ability.

A 5-point Likert Scale, ranging from 5, meaning "very poor" to 1, meaning "excellent", was used to measure international students' responses. The lower the point score, the higher the ability is. A most of the subjects in this study did not take the TOCEL, therefore a self-assessed scale was used and international students were requested to check the boxes of the points for themselves in order to comprehensively assess their own Chinese proficiency. The Cronbach's α coefficient was used to test each factor and dimension to measure the internal consistency among all the questions. The Cronbach's a value of the Chinese Proficiency Self- Assessed Scale was 0.879, suggesting that the correlation among questions was high, as was the internal consistency of the scale. The validity of the scale could be determined by the value of the Kaiser-Meyer Olkin measure of sampling adequacy (KMO).

The KMO value of the Sell-Assessed Scale was 0.880, which was greater than 0.50, suggesting that the content validity of the Self-Assessed Scale was high and the scale was representative.

III. Research Results

1. Analysis on the difference in international students' phonetic system usage ability and cross-cultural adaptation

As shown in Table 2, international students' phonetic system usage ability in three dimensions of cross-cultural adaptation "studying and researching", "interpersonal relationship", and "living environment and financial conditions" showed significantly difference. The results (F=3.338, p=0.011<0.05) indicated that there is significantly difference between international students' phonetic system usage ability and the dimension of cross-cultural adaptation "studying and researching". According to the Scheffé method posteriori comparisons, regarding "studying and researching", the cross-cultural adaptation of international students whose phonetic system usage ability was "poor" was better than those whose phonetic system usage ability was "very poor". The ANOVA analysis (F=3.314, p=0.012<0.05) indicated there is significantly difference between international students' phonetic system usage ability and the dimension of cross-cultural adaptation "living environment and financial conditions". According to the Scheffé method posteriori comparisons, international students' phonetic system usage ability had a negative effect on "living environment and financial conditions". In other words, international students whose capability related to phonetic system usage is poorer can better adapt to life in Taiwan.

2. Analysis on the difference in international students' Chinese listening ability and cross-cultural adaptation

As shown in Table 3, the ANOVA analysis indicated that international students' Chinese listening ability in two dimensions of cross-cultural adaptation "studying and researching" (F=4.097, p=0.003<0.05) and "living environment and financial conditions" (F=3.412, p=0.010<0.05) showed significantly difference. Regarding "studying and researching", the cross-cultural adaptation of international students whose Chinese listening ability was "excellent" and "not bad" was better than those whose Chinese listening ability was "very poor". Regarding "living environment and financial conditions", the cross-cultural adaptation of international students whose Chinese listening ability was "excellent" was better than those whose Chinese listening ability was "good" in accordance with the Scheffé method posteriori comparisons.

3. Analysis on the difference in international students' Mandarin speaking skills and cross-cultural adaptation

As shown in Table 4, the ANOVA analysis indicated that international students' Mandarin speaking skills in two dimensions of cross-cultural adaptation "studying and researching" (F=3.402, p=0.010<0.05) and "living environment and financial conditions" (F=2.708, p=0.031<0.05) showed significantly difference. Regarding "studying and researching", the cross-cultural adaptation of international students whose Mandarin speaking skills was "excellent" was better than those whose Mandarin speaking skills was "very poor" in accordance with the Scheffé method posteriori comparisons.

4. Analysis on the difference in international students' Chinese literacy ability and cross-cultural adaptation

As shown in Table 5, the ANOVA analysis indicated that international students' Chinese literacy ability in the dimension of cross-cultural adaptation "studying and researching" ($F=5.473$, $p=0.000<0.05$) showed significantly difference. Regarding "studying and researching", the cross-cultural adaptation of international students whose Chinese literacy ability was "excellent" and "poor" was better than those whose Chinese literacy ability was "very poor" in accordance with the Scheffé method posteriori comparisons.

5. Analysis on the difference in international students' ability to write Chinese characters and cross-cultural adaptation

As shown in Table 6, the ANOVA analysis indicated that international students' ability to write Chinese characters in two dimensions of cross-cultural adaptation "studying and researching" ($F=7.743$, $p=0.000<0.05$) and "interpersonal relationship" ($F=4.682$, $p=0.001<0.05$) showed significantly difference. Regarding "studying and researching", the cross-cultural adaptation of international students whose ability to write Chinese characters was "good" and "poor" was better than those whose ability to write Chinese characters was "very poor" in accordance with the Scheefe's method posteriori comparisons. However, according to the Scheffé method posteriori comparisons, international students' ability to write Chinese characters had a negative effect on "interpersonal relationship".

6. Analysis on the difference in international students' Chinese language reading ability and cross-cultural adaptation

As shown in Table 7, the ANOVA analysis indicated that international students' Chinese language reading ability in two dimensions of cross-cultural adaptation "studying and researching" ($F=6.874$, $p=0.000<0.05$) and "interpersonal relationship" ($F=2.726$, $p=0.031<0.05$) showed significantly difference. Regarding "studying and researching", the cross-cultural adaptation of international students whose Chinese language reading ability was "good" and "not bad" was better than those whose Chinese language reading ability was "very poor" in accordance with the Scheffé method posteriori comparisons.

7. Analysis on the difference in international students' Chinese composition ability and cross-cultural adaptation

As shown in Table 8, the ANOVA analysis indicated that international students' Chinese composition ability in two dimensions of cross-cultural adaptation "studying and researching" ($F=5.78$, $p=0.000<0.05$) and "interpersonal relationship" ($F=2.886$,

p=0.024<0.05) showed significantly difference. Regarding "studying and researching", the cross-cultural adaptation of international students whose Chinese composition ability was "good", "not bad" and "poor" was better than those whose Chinese composition ability was "very poor" in accordance with the Scheffé method posteriori comparisons.

IV. Conclusions

In terms of the relationship between international students' Chinese proficiency and cross-cultural adaptation, international students' phonetic system usage ability had a negative effect on the "living environment and financial condition" dimension of cross-cultural adaptation. And Chinese characters writing ability also had a negative effect on the "interpersonal relationship" dimension of cross-cultural adaptation. In other words, international students' Chinese proficiency related to phonetic system usage and Chinese characters writing will neither affect their level of adaptation to social and interpersonal interactions in Taiwan nor their adaptation to local life in Taiwan. Therefore, international students' cross-cultural adaptation to "interpersonal relationships" and "living environments and financial conditions" is irrelevant to their Chinese phonetic apply and characters writing ability.

International students' phonetic system usage ability has a significant influence in the aspects of study and research of cross-cultural adaptation. However, the cultivation of international students' Chinese listening abilities and speaking skills, as well as the use of the Mandarin Phonetic Symbol or Hanyu Pinyin, does not initially rely on familiarity with the use of Mandarin Phonetic Symbol, but is based upon natural learning through imitation in environments and interpersonal interaction. In fact, the cultivation of the phonetic system usage ability relies on formal courses, which first requires students to memorize the Mandarin Phonetic Symbol, and then combine them with actual pronunciation. Some Chinese pronunciations are difficult, strange or had never been pronounced by international students. In other words, some international students cannot use phonetic symbols to speak more Chinese terms and sentences until they have memorized the symbols and constantly practiced. Although phonetic system usage ability is the foundation of Chinese learning, it is not required in daily life. Therefore, it has a negative influence in the aspect of the "living environments and financial conditions" of cross-cultural adaptation for international students. It is difficult to predict the actual pronunciation of words based on the Mandarin Phonetic Symbol used in Taiwan.

Therefore, while many international students enjoy the learning environment in Taiwan, they intend to learn the Hanyu Pinyin and reject learning the Mandarin Phonetic Symbol. In terms of the basic teaching materials, which mainly focus on Chinese listening and speaking, teaching of the Mandarin Phonetic Symbol only has already failed to meet international students' needs. Additionally, even though the Hanyu Pinyin learning system is adopted, it is preferable to integrate local life-related teaching materials into teaching curriculums. The result suggest that, in order to effectively improve and assist international students' cross-cultural adaptation, the actual difficulties in phonetic learning, the needs, and interests of international students learning in Taiwan, and their diversified cultural backgrounds, should be considered in the compilation of contents of Chinese phonetic teaching materials and the phonetic teaching strategies of Mandarin Chinese teachers. International students' Chinese ability in character writing has a significant influence regarding the aspect of "study and researching" of cross-cultural adaptation. Therefore, even though international students suggested that it is very difficult to write and learn Chinese characters, the Chinese characters writing ability remains an important factor affecting cross-cultural adaptation in Taiwan. The learning of Chinese character writing may enable international students to perceive, identify, and respect Chinese language and Chinese culture more profoundly, while further increasing their motivation and interests in continuous learning and studying Chinese. Chinese characters are the only ancient characters remaining from human history that are still in existence and continuously used.

They are a unique type of characters due to their historical value and unique characteristics. Moreover, Chinese characters writing ability is closely related to advanced Chinese language reading and Chinese composing abilities. Therefore, although international students suggested that it is difficult to learn writing Chinese characters, they must overcome the challenge and complete it. At present, traditional Chinese character is still the mainstream in Chinese characters teaching in Taiwan. However, in response to the global trend of use of simplified Chinese character, relevant educational authorities should carefully consider providing teaching resources and faculties for both traditional and simplified Chinese character systems in order to develop coping strategies that meet the needs of the competitive international market. Moreover, at present, it is important for Chinese teachers, scholars, and experts to determine the key factors affecting the success or failure of international students' learning of Chinese characters. The reason why international students' Chinese characters writing ability is negatively correlated to the aspect of "interpersonal relationship" of their cross-cultural adaptation may be that, most international students are poor in Chinese characters writing abilities. As a result, they seldom communicate or interact with others by writing Chinese characters, as only a small proportion of international students are proficient in Chinese characters writing ability.

However, they may not necessarily use Chinese characters as the only language for communication in the aspect of "interpersonal relationships" for cross-cultural adaptation. Moreover, international students' cross-cultural adaptation to "studying and researching" is closely related to their Chinese proficiency, and each of the Chinese abilities has a significant influence on it. In terms of the level of cross-cultural adaptation, the cross-cultural adaptation of international students with higher Chinese proficiency was better than that of those with lower proficiency. In other words, Chinese proficiency affects international students' status of cross-cultural adaptation. Furthermore, in terms of the cross-cultural adaptation to the "living environment and financial conditions", the level of adaptation of international students with excellent Chinese listening abilities and Chinese literacy was higher than that of students with good abilities. It could be inferred that the better the Chinese listening ability and Chinese literacy are, the higher the level of cross-cultural adaptation to the environment of the host country will be. Only when international students' language proficiency meets the basic threshold can they effectively increase their level of cross-cultural adaptation abroad.

References

Baker, R. W. (1981). *Freshman Transition Questionnaire*. Unpublished manual, Clark University .

Chang, Y. L. (2007). *A Study on the Teaching Materials for the Short-time Learning of Foreign Students in Taiwan*. Unpublished thesis, Taipei Municipal University of Education, Taiwan.

Chien, Y. H. (2008). An action research on the theories of intercultural communication theory for Chinese teaching practice abroad—Taking the teaching practice of Taipei Municipal University of Education in Thailand for example. *Chung Yuan Journal of Teaching Chinese as a Second Language*, 2, 243–269.

Church, A. T. (1982). Sojourner adjustment. *Psychological Bulletin*, 91(3), 540–572.

Constantine, M. G., & Okazaki, S. O. (2004). Sell-concealment, social sell-efficacy, acculturative stress and depression in African, Asian, and Latin American international college students. *American Journal of Orthopsychiatry*, 74(3), 230–241.

Furnham, A., & Erdmann, S. (1995). Psychological and socio-cultural variables as predictors of adjustment in cross-cultural transitions. *Psychologia*, 38(4), 238–251.

Huang, Y. H. (2007). *A Preliminary Investigation on the Status, Causes, and Coping Strategies for Learning Anxiety of Foreign Chinese Learners*. Unpublished thesis, National Taiwan Normal University, Taiwan.

Ministry of Education. (2007). *Protocol for the Preliminary Work of Important Social Development Projects for 2009*. Retrieved Oct. 16, 2009, from http://210.133/doc/423/plan 70 20080603230016.htm.

Ministry of Education in Taiwan. (2009). Retrieved Oct. 16, 2009, from http://www.edu.tw/edu web/edu mgt/statistics/ed722000 lgender/503-3.xls.

Sandhu, D. S., & Asrabadi, B. R. (1994). Development of an acculturative stress scale for international student: Preliminary finding. *Psychology Report*, 75, 435–448.

Schumann, J. H. (1978). The Acculturation model for second language acquisition. In R. Gingras (ed.). *Second Language Acquisition and Foreign Language Teaching*. Arlington: Center for Applied Linguistics.

Sezrle, W., & Ward, C. (1990). The prediction of psychological and socio-cultural adjustment during cross-cultural transitions. *International Journal of Intercultural Relations*, 14(4), 449–464.

Steering Committee for the Test of Proficiency-Huayu (2010). *Test of Chinese as a Foreign Language, TOCFL*. Retrieved June 15, 2010, from http://www.sc-top.org.tw/chinese/history.php.

Test of Chinese as a Foreign Language (TOCFL) (2009). Retrieved Oct. 17, 2009, from http://www.sc-top.org.tw/english/SP/testloverview.php.

Uehara, M. (1988). *International Students' Cross-Cultural Adaptation*. Hiroshima: Takahashi Press.

Ward, C., & Kennedy, A. (1996). Crossing cultures: The relationship between psychological and socio-cultural dimensions of cross-cultural adjustment. In Pandey, J., Sinha, D., & Bhawuk, D. P. S. (eds.). *Asian Contributions to Cross-Cultural Psychology*. New Delhi: Sage Publications.

World Trade Origination. (2009). *Economy Would Improve with More Flexibility and More Competitiveness*. Retrieved Oct. 16, 2009, from http:www.wto.org/english/tratop e/tpr_e/tp332_e.htm.

Yeh, T. M. (1999). *Regulations and Theoretical Basis of Chinese Teaching*. Taipei: NTNU Press.

Tables

Table 1. Dimensions and items of scale of cross-cultural adaptation

Dimensions		Numbers of items, and items
Studying and researching	1.	I feel happy in my studies recently.
	2.	I have been very happy since I began to study at the university.
	3.	My study attitude has been positive recently.
	4.	I have a clear goal in studying at the university.
	5.	I feel positive on the value of research or study at the university.
	6.	My research project or study has progressed very smoothly.
	7.	I have benefited from the curricula I am studying at the university.
	8.	I am satisfied with the courses of this semester.
	9.	I understand my chosen courses very well.
	10.	I feel easy reading books in the Chinese language for my chosen specific course.
	11.	Overall, I am satisfied with my study at the university.
Physical and mental health & emotions	1.	I have had a good health recently.
	2.	I have sleep very well recently.
	3.	I have felt homesick recently.
	4.	I have often felt pleasure recently.
	5.	My recent emotional ups and downs very smooth.
	6.	I am very active in the relationships recently.
	7.	I own psychological or spiritual satisfaction
Interpersonal relationship	1.	I have good Taiwanese friends at my university.
	2.	I have good international student friends.
	3.	I have good Taiwanese friends from outside the university.
	4.	I can communicate well with the professors or lecturers of my course.
	5.	I have had fairly good interpersonal relationship recently.
	6.	I have ample opportunities and Interactive for group activities with Taiwanese students at the university.
	7.	Overall I have good relationships at the university

(continued)

Dimensions		Numbers of items, and items
Local culture	1.	I understand and can integrate into Taiwanese culture in my daily life.
	2.	Although I am a foreigner, I feel I have integrated into the local life.
	3.	People in Taiwan do not discriminate strongly against foreigners; I can easily take part in group their group activities.
	4.	People in Taiwan are friendly, so communicating with them is easy.
	5.	I can understand the cultural identity of the Taiwan people.
	6.	I obtained a lot of information about Taiwan before I came.
Living environment and financial conditions	1.	My current living environment is comfortable and satisfactory.
	2.	The living environment and hygienic conditions are good in Taiwan.
	3.	The neighborhood is very safe around my residence.
	4.	I get along very well with the neighbors around my residence.
	5.	I can adapt to the local weather.
	6.	The rent charge of my residence is reasonable.
	7.	My current financial state is very good.
	8.	Overall, I am satisfied with the local life.

Table 2. Difference analysis of international students' phonetic system usage ability and cross-cultural adaptation (sd: standard deviation)

Variable	Mean	sd	F value	P value	Scheffé method
Studying and researching	42.57	7.10	3.338	0.011*	poor > very poor
Physical mental health & emotions	25.11	4.24	1.691	0.154	
Interpersonal relationships	26.56	4.78	3.307	0.018*	
Local culture	22.02	3.77	3.238	0.916	
Living environment and financial conditions	29.95	4.64	3.314	0.012*	poor > good

$p<.05*$ $p<.01**$ $p<.001***$

Table 3. Difference analysis of international students' Chinese listening ability and cross-cultural adaptation (sd: standard deviation)

Variable	Mean	sd	F value	P value	Scheflé method
Studying and researching	4257	710	4.097	0.003**	excellent, not bad > very poor
Physical mental health & emotions	25.11	4.24	0.681	0.606	
Interpersonal relationship	26.56	4.78	1.669	0.159	
Local culture	22.02	3.77	1.038	0.389	
Living environment and financial conditions	29.95	4.64	3.412	0.010*	excellent > good

$p<.05*$ $p<.01**$ $p<.001***$

Table 4. Difference analysis of international students' Mandarin speaking skills and cross-cultural adaptation (sd: standard deviation)

Variable	Mean	sd	F value	P value	Scheffé method
Studying and researching	42.57	7.10	3.402	0.010*	excellent > very poor
Physical mental health & emotions	25.11	4.24	1.365	0.247	
Interpersonal relationship	26.56	4.78	1.392	0.238	
Local culture	22.02	3.77	0.168	0.955	
Living environment and financial conditions	29.95	4.64	2.708	0.031*	

p<.05* *p*<.01** *p*<.001***

Table 5. Difference analysis of international students' Chinese literacy ability and cross-cultural adaptation (sd: standard deviation)

Variable	Mean	sd	F value	P value	Scheffé method
Studying and researching	42.57	7.10	5.473	0.000***	excellent, poor>very poor
Physical mental health & emotions	25.11	4.24	0.967	0.427	
Interpersonal relationship	26.56	4.78	1.290	0.275	
Local culture	22.02	3.77	0.570	0.685	
Living environment and financial conditions	29.95	4.64	0.274	0.894	

p<.05* *p*<.01** *p*<.001***

Table 6. Difference analysis of international students' ability to write Chinese characters and cross-cultural adaptation (sd: standard deviation)

Variable	Mean	sd	F value	P value	Scheffé method
Studying and researching	42.57	7.10	7.743	0.000***	good, poor>very poor
Physical mental health & emotions	25.11	4.24	0.972	0.424	
Interpersonal relationship	26.56	4.78	4.628	0.001*	poor > excellent
Local culture	22.02	3.77	1.244	0.293	
Living environment and financial conditions	29.95	4.64	1.473	0.212	

p<.05* *p*<.01** *p*<.001***

Table 7. Difference analysis of international students' Chinese language reading ability and cross-cultural adaptation (sd: standard deviation)

Variable	Mean	sd	F value	P value	Scheffé method
Studying and researching	42.57	7.10	6.874	0.000***	good, not bad>very poor
Physical mental health & emotions	25.11	4.24	1.660	0.161	
Interpersonal relationship	26.56	4.78	2.726	0.031*	
Local culture	22.02	3.77	1.828	0.125	
Living environment and financial conditions	29.95	4.64	0.906	0.461	

$p<.05*$ $p<.01**$ $p<.001***$

Table 8 Difference analysis of international students' Chinese composing ability and cross-cultural adaptation(sd: standard deviation)

Variable	Mean	sd	F value	P value	Scheffé method
Studying and researching	42.57	7.10	5.787	0.000***	good, not bad, poor>poor
Physical mental health & emotions	25.11	4.24	2.195	0.071	
Interpersonal relationship	26.56	4.78	2.886	0.024*	
Local culture	22.02	3.77	1.665	0.160	
Living environment and financial conditions	29.95	4.64	0.543	0.704	

$p<.05*$ $p<.01**$ $p<.001***$

Topic
Four

Anticipating the Issue

Discuss your answers to the following questions.

1. What constitutes good writing? What problems do you have with English writing? How can you improve your writing skills?

2. What processes do you usually go through when writing an essay in English?

3. What language do you use when planning and writing an essay in English? Can you think in English? When and to what extent?

Selections

Unit 7

EFL Writers' Perceptions of Portfolio Keeping

Learning Objectives

- References: function and style
- APA formatting: references
- Editing

EFL Writers' Perceptions of Portfolio Keeping[*]

Selami Aydin[*]

Balikesir University, Necatibey Education Faculty, ELT Department, 10100 Balikesir, Turkey

Received 4 February 2010; received in revised form 11 August 2010; accepted 20 August 2010

Available online 21 September 2010

Abstract:

Although **portfolios** in writing in English as a Foreign Language (EFL) learning are alternative tools, the portfolio process mainly concerns the decisions of language teachers rather than students' **perceptions** of portfolios. The present study aims to descriptively measure the perceptions of English as a Foreign Language (EFL) students towards portfolio keeping. The sample group in the study consisted of 204 EFL students. A portfolio contribution questionnaire and a portfolio problem questionnaire were used to collect quantitative data. Two results were obtained from the study: (1) portfolio keeping in EFL writing is beneficial to the improvement of vocabulary and grammar knowledge, reading, research, and writing skills; and (2) EFL students perceive some problems during the portfolio keeping process.

Keywords: English as a Foreign Language; EFL; writing; portfolio; students' perceptions

---

[*]All reported data that involve human participants are collected and analysed under appropriate ethical standards.

[*] Tel.: +90 266 241 27 62/533 626 17 41; fax: +90 266 249 50 05. E-mail addresses: saydin@balikesir.edu.tr, selami.aydin @yahoo.com.tr.

214

1. Introduction

In many disciplines, portfolios aid learning by providing **portraits** of students, offering **multidimensional** perspectives, encouraging students to participate, and linking teaching (O'Malley & Valdez Pierce, 1996; Genesee & Upshur, 1996). **In terms of** foreign language learning and teaching, they are an alternative assessment tool used to both offer opportunities for absorbing language **authentically** and actively, and for evaluating student progress (Delett, Barnhardt, & Kevorkian, 2001). The framework for the portfolio process, as Delett et al. (2001) underlined, involves seven steps: planning the assessment purpose, determining outcomes, matching classroom tasks to outcomes, establishing criteria, determining organisation, monitoring the portfolio, and finally, evaluating the process. However, it should be highlighted that the above-mentioned steps for assessing portfolios are mainly concerned with the decisions of language teachers rather than students' perceptions of portfolios. For instance, for Delett et al. (2001), during the process, teachers decide to use portfolios as a way to increase students' Involvement in the learning process; outcomes depend on teachers' instructional focus in terms of students' needs. Teachers also consider what types of materials will be used for portfolio products and develop criteria to assess students' progress towards the outcomes. Even though the portfolio process neglects students' perceptions of portfolios, Delett et al. (2001) emphasise that the use of portfolios creates an interactive assessment process that involves both teachers and students and forges a partnership in the learning process.

Studies indicate that portfolios make considerable contributions to foreign language writing. For instance, Cohen (1994) notes that portfolios are *"potentially beneficial... to the field of language assessment since the emphasis is on* **convergent** *and repeated measures over time rather than on single measures at one point in time"* (p. 361). On the other hand, Cohen (1994) also draws attention to the limitations of portfolio keeping. For example, portfolios require a lot of time from both teachers and students, and grading portfolios is difficult. Furthermore, as Hump-Lyons and Condon (1993) emphasise, assumptions and beliefs on portfolio evaluation should be **taken into account**, and the limitations and problems should be analysed systematically in terms of students' perceptions of portfolio keeping in foreign language writing. Thus, the purpose of the present study is to investigate the perceptions of EFL students towards portfolio keeping. Specifically, the present study focuses on the perceptions of EFL students towards portfolio keeping in terms of its contributions and the problems encountered during the portfolio keeping process.

The results of previous studies **chronologically** presented below indicate that beginning foreign language writers positively react to portfolio keeping in foreign language writing, and that portfolios make considerable contributions to the language learning process. To begin with, Kaminsky (1993) designed a **practicum** to address the needs of intermediate and upper grade-level English as a Second Language (ES L) students in becoming independent in the literacy process. He found that students learned to use the context of reading materials, dictionaries, or **encyclopaedias** to deter mine the correct spelling or meaning of a word. Further, teachers reported that these students wrote more than they did in previous classes and at a higher quality level. Research results also demon strated that portfolios help students become actively involved in their own learning (Newman, Smolen, and Lee, 1995), and improve the organisation, **exemplification**, and questioning of texts (Pally, 1998). In a quantitative study, Song and August (2002) compared the performance of two groups of advanced ESL students in a composition course. They found that students were twice as likely to pass into the second semester course when they were evaluated using portfolios rather than by writing assessment tests. In another study (Mathews & Hansen, 2004) aimed at examining a university foreign language department's process for developing a procedure to assess its curriculum using the ACTFL Proficiency Guidelines, the results indicated that students presented materials that documented their abilities to analyse literary texts, write in a variety of styles, and demonstrate an awareness of the target language culture. In an empirical study (Paesani, 2006) in which a writing portfolio project was presented, it was stated that portfolio keeping helps students integrate the development of proficiency skills, content knowledge, and grammatical competence. In Ozturk and Cecen's (2007) investigation on the effects of portfolio keeping on the writing anxiety of EFL students, the findings **revealed** that portfolio keeping is beneficial for overcoming writing anxiety. Finally, Burksaitiene and Tereseviciene (2008) examined students' perceptions of comprehensive learning. The findings of their study showed that an integrated approach to learning English was well received by the students for the following reasons: (a) the approach is effective and useful in promoting students' productive and receptive language skills, (b) it enhances students' satisfaction with their results, (c) it fosters one's motivation to learn a foreign language, and (d) it promotes students' development as independent students. **In conclusion**, prior research demonstrates that using portfolios in foreign language writing helps students develop writing skills, improves students' self-confidence, helps them learn actively, increases awareness in the target culture, integrates language skills, and motivates students.

Related research on the problems associated with portfolio keeping as a learning tool in foreign language writing is fairly limited. Among a limited number of studies, Pollari (2000) aimed to develop and use portfolios in foreign language teaching as a pedagogical innovation and to foster students' **empowerment**, i.e., their active and responsible role in learning. Findings obtained by the study suggest that a large majority of the students liked the portfolio approach and utilised it to **take charge of** their learning. However, though portfolios generally seemed to offer a means for student empowerment, some students disliked the portfolio course and found it uninspiring. In addition, students found the student-centred and self-directed approach to be inefficient, difficult, or unsuitable for them. Boyden-Knudsen (2001) investigated the effects of analytic corrections and revisions on college composition students working in a portfolio assessment setting. The results showed that even though analytical corrections helped students prepare for the mid-term and final evaluations by unknown instructors, some students did not understand these corrections entirely. In a study by Chang, Wu, and Ku (2005) examining the effects of introducing electronic portfolios in teaching and assessing English as a Foreign Language in Taiwan, the researchers found that some students felt intimidated by writing and speaking in English. Finally, Hirvela and Sweetland (2005) in their case study investigated students' experiences with portfolios in two ESL writing courses in which different portfolio pedagogies were employed. The findings indicated that although participants liked the idea of portfolios, they did not strongly endorse their use in courses that served as research settings. To conclude, the results showed that portfolios are found to be inefficient, difficult, or unsuitable by students, involve some confusion about error correction and grading, and make students concerned about their writing skills.

In conclusion, the present study is guided by certain reasoning. First, as the portfolio process is mainly concerned with the decisions of language teachers rather than students' perceptions of portfolios, it is necessary to investigate English as Foreign Language students' perceptions of portfolio keeping in their writing instruction in terms of the contributions of using portfolios in the language learning process and the problems encountered during the process of portfolio keeping. As a result, the present research aims to analyse descriptively the contributions of portfolios and the related problems. For this purpose, two research questions were asked:

1. What are perceptions of EFL writers towards the contributions of portfolio keeping in the EFL language learning process?
2. What problems do EFL writers encounter during the portfolio keeping process?

2. Method

The study consisted of two main procedures. The first part included a qualitative procedure used to design questionnaires that measure the perceptions of EFL students in terms of the contributions of portfolio keeping to the learning process and the problems encountered during the process. The second procedure was designed to gather and anal-

yse descriptive data. The details of these research procedures are presented below in two **subsections**.

2.1 Qualitative research

The sample group for the qualitative study consisted of 39 EFL students in the English Language Teaching Department (ELT) at Balikesir University, Turkey. They were all freshmen in the ELT department as writing classes are taught only during the first year of the teaching program; portfolio applications were administered during the same period. The group consisted of 23 (58%) females and 16 (42%) males whose mean age was 19.4.

The qualitative study used a three-step procedure: instruction, data collection, and data analysis:

1. *Instruction*: The content of writing instruction, which lasted for 24 weeks throughout two semesters of the academic year of 2007–2008, consisted of three main periods. In the first period, the structures of simple, complex and **compound** sentences, compositions and **punctuation**, unity, **coherence** and **conjunctives**, parts of a paragraph, and paragraph outline were introduced. The second period covered paragraph development methods and techniques, such as listing specific details, classification, using examples, definition, cause and effect, comparison and contrast, and problem solution. In the last period, parts of composition and methods such as **exposition**, **narration**, **argumentation**, and description were taught. During the second and third periods, the participants kept portfolios following a three-step procedure. In the first step, they produced the first draft of their portfolio including brainstorming, **clustering**, and outlining. In the second step, the participants gave and received **peer** feedback using a scale to evaluate the written pieces. After necessary revisions and corrections depending on the revision plans, students produced their second drafts. After receiving oral feedback from their instructor, students wrote their final drafts. In the last step, portfolios were completed with cover letters, tables of contents, entries, dates, drafts, reflections, and revision plans.

2. *Data collection*: To provide triangulation, and to ensure the validity of the obtained data, three instruments were administered: interviews, a survey, and essays. First, the participants were asked about the contributions of portfolio keeping and the problems encountered during the process. That is, they noted their responses in their cover letter, which included two survey questions and the background questionnaire, before **submitting** their portfolios. Second, two weeks later, the author interviewed the participants about the contributions of portfolio keeping and re-

lated problems individually, in small groups, and in a classroom environment. Finally, at the end of the semester, the instructor administered the final examination, which contained a question about the contributions of portfolio keeping and the problems encountered during the process.

3. *Data analysis*: The data obtained from each source were analysed separately. That is, the data obtained from each of the sources were transferred into three concept maps. After comparing the statements and numbers in the concept maps, it was observed that the triangulation indicated data validity. Finally, the data from the three maps were combined and presented in numbers and frequencies in percent in two tables, i.e., the numbers and frequencies in percentages were provided **in accordance with** the responses of the participants. At the end of the qualitative study, two questionnaires were developed for use in the descriptive research (Appendices A and B).

2.2 Descriptive research

The sample group in this part of the study consisted of 204 students studying in the English Language Teaching Department of the Necatibey Education Faculty at Balikesir University in Balikesir, Turkey. These students were chosen as the sample group because they had kept portfolios in their writing classes. Of the participants, 149 (73 %) were female students, whereas 55 students (27 %) were male. It should be noted that the gender distribution in the sample group was directly related to the general reflection of the overall population in the department. The participants' mean age was 19.96 falling within the age range of 18 and 22.

The data collection instruments consisted of a background questionnaire, the Portfolio Contribution Questionnaire (PCQ), and Portfolio Problem Questionnaire (PPQ). The background questionnaire **probed** the students about their gender and age. Both the PCQ and PPQ were designed using the data obtained from the qualitative research. The PCQ consisted of items examining the contributions of portfolio keeping to EFL learning, while the PPQ aimed to investigate problems experienced during portfolio keeping. The items were assessed on a scale ranging from one to five (never = 1, rarely = 2, sometimes = 3, usually = 4, always = 5).

After designing both questionnaires in accordance with the data obtained from the qualitative study, they were administered first to a group of ten senior students in the department to identify and correct any misconceptions and obtain **moderation** of the items in both questionnaires. Then, after obtaining written permission from the faculty administration, the background questionnaire, PCQ, and PPQ were administered to the participants at the end of the 2008–2009 academic year, following the completion of the portfolio keeping process. The data collected were analysed using the SPSS software. The reliability coefficient of the PCQ is .902, while the result for the PPQ is .865 in Cronbach's Alpha. That is, the reliability coefficients show that both questionnaires have high levels of reliability. Finally, in terms of the contributions of portfolios to EFL writing and the problems encountered during portfolio keeping, descriptive statistics were presented for both questionnaires. For this purpose, frequencies, mean scores, and standard deviations were computed.

3. Results

The findings obtained from the study can be divided into two subsections: the descriptive data regarding the contributions of portfolios in the EFL learning process and descriptive findings on the problems encountered during the portfolio process.

3.1 The contribution of portfolios to the EFL learning process

According to the findings presented in Appendix A, portfolio keeping in EFL writing con- tributes considerably to vocabulary and grammar knowledge, reading, research, and writing skills. In other words, it can be stated that portfolio keeping benefits EFL students' language skills and knowledge, and is useful in developing their **rhetorical** skills. First, EFL students believe that it improves their vocabulary knowledge. Specifically, they acquire more vocabulary, use it in context, and **are aware of** a variety of words. Second, students stated that portfolio keeping improves their grammar knowledge. This means that they can produce complex sentences, learn how to use signal words and to combine sentences, produce more fluent sentences, and use grammar in context. In other words, they believe that they use their grammar knowledge to write meaningful sentences. Third, students underlined that portfolio keeping contributes to their reading skills. That is, they believe that they acquire information about the topic they write about, learn to discover main ideas and details in texts, transfer the ideas in the texts to their written pieces, and improve their research skills. Fourth, they think that portfolio keeping contributes to their writing skills. Specifically, they stated that they acquire information about the or- ganisation of their paragraphs and compositions using brainstorming, clustering, and out- lining, they are informed about punctuation and compositions, and they learn about feed- back strategies. In other words, students state that portfolio keeping provides rhetorical gains. Moreover, they strongly believe that peer and teacher feedback help them identify their mistakes and correct them. Moreover, they also stated that they acquire informa- tion about paragraph and essay development methods and techniques. In this sense, they strongly believe that they learn the characteristics and parts of a paragraph and essay, coherence, unity, **originality**, and creativity. Conclusively, it can be highlighted that portfolios in EFL writing have positive effects on the foreign language learning process in terms of grammar, vocabulary, reading, writing, and research skills. Thus, the portfolio process in an EFL setting helps students advance in language acquisition and in the rhetoric of the target language's culture.

3.2 The problems in portfolio process

The values listed in Appendix B indicate that portfolio keeping in EFL writing is not without problems. To provide an example, students complain that portfolio keeping is boring, tiring, and takes too much time. In addition, EFL students have some difficulties providing feedback. In a narrower scope, they believe that it is difficult to use **checklists** and to analyse errors. Moreover, on a moderate level, they complain about pre-writing activities such as brainstorming, clustering, and outlining. Similarly, problems also arise while preparing revision lists, writing second and third drafts, using words in context, and sentence combinations. Finally, they stated that it is difficult to study with a peer although they have no fear of negative evaluations by their peers and teachers.

4. Conclusions and discussion

Two main results were drawn from the study. First, the descriptive data demonstrate that portfolio keeping in EFL writing is beneficial to the improvement of vocabulary and grammar knowledge, reading, research, and writing skills. Second, EFL students perceive some problems during the portfolio keeping process; they believe that it is boring, tiring, and takes too much time, and that they have difficulties in pre-writing activities, feedback, and rewriting processes. As a final note, the questionnaires are appropriate for examining the contributions of portfolios to foreign language learning and the problems encountered by EFL students during the portfolio keeping process. In other words, it can be stated that the instruments used in the study can be used or adapted to investigate EFL students' perceptions of the advantages and **drawbacks** of portfolio keeping.

Below is a summary of the study results. First, the results of the present study contribute to the related literature in terms of EFL students' perceptions of portfolio keeping in EFL learning as the portfolio process is mainly concerned with the decisions made by language teachers rather than students' perceptions of portfolios. In other words, given that, as Delett et al. (2001) underline, teachers decide to use portfolios as a way to increase students' involvement in the learning process, the outcomes depend on teachers' instructional focus **with regard to** students' needs; the teachers determine which types of materials will be used for portfolio products. The findings obtained from the present study are significant because they focus on students' perceptions rather than teachers' perceptions. Second, the results found in the study mainly support those obtained from previous studies. For example, similar to the previous findings, the results of the present paper indicate that portfolios contribute to using vocabulary in context, correcting mistakes and errors (Kaminsky, 1993), improving productive and receptive language skills (Burksaitiene & Tereseviciene, 2008), content knowledge, grammatical competence (Paesani, 2006), organisation, and exemplification (Pally, 1998).

On the other hand, it should be highlighted that, in addition to the previous findings, the results of the research show that students also improve their research skills and organisational knowledge of paragraphs and composition. Additionally, EFL students did not perceive any effects of portfolios on motivation and **autonomous** learning, contrary to the results found by Burksaitiene and Tereseviciene (2008). Third, as found by Hirvela and Sweetland (2005), Boyden-Knudsen (2001), and Cohen (1994), EFL students had some difficulties understanding corrections and perceived portfolio keeping as both tiring and boring. Moreover, contrary to the findings in the study by Ozturk and Cecen (2007), the present study revealed that during the portfolio keeping process, students do not experience anxiety. Additionally, the present study also demonstrated that students mainly have positive perceptions of portfolios, though Pollari (2000) found that some students disliked the portfolio course.

Given that portfolio keeping in the EFL learning process has considerable contributions to foreign language learning in spite of some problems, some practical recommendations can be noted. First, the questionnaires designed, tested, and analysed can be used to evaluate the perceptions of EFL students towards portfolio keeping. Second, portfolio keeping is a beneficial tool for improving vocabulary and grammar knowledge, reading, research, and writing skills, as well as organisational skills. Thus, EFL teachers and pre-service teachers can be instructed to use portfolios in foreign language teaching more efficiently. On the other hand, given that some students think that portfolio keeping is boring, tiring, and takes too much time, and that they have some difficulties in pre-writing activities, feedback, and rewriting processes, teachers should also be informed about motivational issues and autonomous learning to solve the above-mentioned problems.

As a final note on the limitations of the study, the participants of the descriptive research were restricted to 204 students studying English as a foreign language in the ELT Department at Balikesir University, Turkey. Moreover, the scope of the study was confined to the descriptive data obtained from the questionnaires designed in accordance with the qualitative data. Finally, further research should focus on the relationships between EFL students' perceptions of portfolio keeping and some independent variables such as demographic factors, **affective** states, and motivational issues. Another research area for further exploration is the comparison of EFL teachers' perceptions with students' perceptions.

Appendix A. Descriptives of the items in portfolio contribution questionnaire

Statements	Number	Frequencies (%)					Descriptives	
		Never	Rarely	Sometimes	Usually	Always	Mean	Std. deviation
I improved my vocabulary knowledge.	202	1.5	7.4	31.7	47.0	12.4	3.61	0.85
I learned new vocabulary.	201	1.5	5.5	39.3	42.8	10.9	3.56	0.82
I learned to use words in context.	196	0.5	7.1	32.2	48.08	12.2	3.64	0.81
I learned how to use a dictionary to find appropriate words.	203	4.5	11.3	17.2	29.6	37.4	3.84	1.18
I learned to use a variety of words.	203	1.5	9.4	34.0	43.3	11.8	3.55	0.87
I improved my grammar knowledge.	199	5.0	17.6	26.6	34.7	16.1	3.39	1.10
I learned to produce complex and compound sentences.	202	1.0	8.8	31.7	43.6	14.9	3.62	0.88
I learned to use signal words when I combine sentences.	203	1.5	8.9	31.0	38.4	20.2	3.67	0.95
I learned to write more fluent sentences.	204	0.5	2.5	26.5	54.9	15.6	3.83	0.73
I learned to use grammatical subjects in context.	203	2.4	9.9	37.4	35.0	15.3	3.51	0.95
I improved my reading skills.	195	0.5	8.2	26.7	33.8	30.8	3.86	0.97
I gained information on the topics I wrote about.	204	0.0	4.9	9.8	32.4	52.9	4.33	0.85
I learned to find main ideas in the texts.	204	0.0	1.5	12.3	42.6	43.6	4.28	0.73
I learned to see the details in the passages.	204	0.0	3.9	26.5	44.1	25.5	3.91	0.82
I learned to transfer the ideas in the texts to my papers.	204	0.5	2.9	26.5	51.0	19.1	3.85	0.77
I improved my research skills.	203	1.0	12.8	24.6	39.4	22.2	3.69	0.99
I learned how to organise a paragraph and composition.	204	0.0	1.0	9.8	46.6	42.6	4.31	0.69
I learned brainstorming before starting to write.	204	0.5	2.0	13.2	35.3	49.0	4.30	0.81
I learned clustering before starting to write.	204	1.5	2.5	12.7	33.8	49.5	4.27	0.88
I learned to prepare an outline before starting to write.	204	0.5	2.9	10.8	36.8	49.0	4.31	0.82
I learned how to use punctuation and capitalisation.	203	0.5	5.9	22.2	46.3	25.1	3.90	0.86

(continued)

Statements	Number	Frequencies (%)					Descriptives	
		Never	Rarely	Sometimes	Usually	Always	Mean	Std. deviation
I learned how to give feedback.	204	0.0	3.9	13.7	41.2	41.2	4.20	0.82
I learned to find the mistakes in a paper.	204	0.5	1.5	14.6	51.5	31.9	4.13	0.75
I learned to classify the mistakes in a paper.	202	1.0	5.0	25.2	39.6	29.2	3.91	0.91
I learned to use a checklist when I examine a paper.	200	1.5	6.2	16.0	44.0	32.0	3.99	0.94
Peer and teacher feedback helped me	194	1.5	4.2	14.9	37.6	41.8	4.14	0.93
To notice and correct my mistakes.	204	0.5	3.5	10.3	43.1	42.6	4.24	0.81
To revise my papers.	202	0.5	3.0	11.9	48.5	36.1	4.17	0.79
I acquired information about paragraph and essay development methods and techniques.	203	1.0	3.4	15.3	39.9	40.4	4.15	0.87
I learned the characteristics of a paragraph and essay.	204	0.0	1.0	22.6	48.0	28.4	4.04	0.74
I learned the parts of a paragraph and essay.	203	0.0	1.5	18.2	44.8	35.5	4.14	0.76
I learned to produce coherent paragraphs and essays.	203	0.0	2.5	23.2	50.7	23.6	3.96	0.75
I learned how to write a paragraph and essay in unity.	204	0.0	1.0	16.6	57.4	25.0	4.06	0.67
I learned how to produce original papers.	204	1.0	5.4	34.3	37.7	21.6	3.74	0.89
I began to write creatively.	204	0.5	5.9	36.3	38.2	19.1	3.70	0.86
I began to write in English without translating from Turkdsh.	204	1.4	6.4	21.1	37.3	33.8	3.96	0.97
I learned to reflect my ideas, feelings, and thoughts.	204	0.5	0.5	17.7	47.5	22.8	4.14	0.77

Appendix B. Descriptives of the items in portfolio problem questionnaire

Statements	Number	Frequencies (%)					Descriptives	
		Never	Rarely	Sometimes	Usually	Always	Mean	Std. deviation
It is boring to write every week.	202	5.9	11.4	32.7	18.8	31.2	3.58	1.21
Portfolio keeping takes too much time.	204	3.3	10.8	21.6	31.9	32.4	3.79	1.11
Portfolio keeping is thing.	203	5.4	7.9	28.6	26.6	31.5	3.71	1.15
Portfolio keeping prevents creative writing.	199	32.2	26.1	21.1	11.1	9.5	2.40	1.30
The most difficult part of portfolio keeping is To give feedback.	202	12.8	23.3	30.7	20.8	12.4	2.97	1.21
To find all the mistakes in a paper.	204	10.8	25.5	26.5	24.5	12.7	3.03	1.20
To check the paper using a checklist.	199	12.1	19.6	35.7	23.1	9.5	2.98	1.14
Pre-writing activities.	167	10.1	18.6	30.5	24.0	16.8	3.19	1.22

(continued)

Statements	Number	Frequencies (%)					Descriptives	
		Never	Rarely	Sometimes	Usually	Always	Mean	Std. deviation
To brainstorm.	203	10.9	22.2	31.5	24.6	10.8	3.02	1.16
To cluster.	203	11.8	22.7	37.4	21.7	6.4	2.88	1.08
To prepare an outline.	203	16.2	20.7	29.6	22.7	10.8	2.91	1.23
To prepare revision list.	202	9.8	22.8	31.2	21.8	14.4	3.08	1.19
To write the second and third drafts.	203	7.9	22.2	26.6	24.1	19.2	3.25	1.22
To find the appropriate words.	202	3.5	18.3	38.6	27.2	12.4	3.27	1.01
To combine the sentences.	203	9.8	26.6	34.5	22.7	6.4	2.89	1.07
To study with a peer.	202	21.9	28.2	26.2	16.3	7.4	2.59	1.21
To study with a teacher.	203	32.1	31.5	23.6	9.4	3.4	2.21	1.10
I hate negative comments from my partner.	204	56.3	19.6	17.2	4.9	2.0	1.76	1.03
I hate negative comments from my teacher.	204	51.0	23.0	19.6	5.4	1.0	1.82	0.99

References

Boyden-Knudsen, T. (2001). The effects of analytic corrections and revisions on college composition students in a portfolio assessment setting. Paper presented at the Annual Meeting of the American Educational Research Association, Seattle, WA.

Burksaitiene, N., & Tereseviciene, M. (2008). Integrating alternative learning and assessment in a course of English for law students. *Assessment and Evaluation in Higher Education, 33*(2), 155–166.

Chang, Y., Wu, C., & Ku, H. (2005). The introduction of electronic portfolios to teach and assess English as a foreign language. *TechTrends: Linking Research and Practice to Improve Learning, 49*(1), 30–35.

Cohen, D. (1994). *Assessing language ability in the classroom.* Boston: Heinle & Heinle.

Delett, J. S., Barnhardt, S., & Kevorldan, J. A. (2001). A framework for portfolio assessment in the foreign language classroom. *Foreign Language Annals, 34*(6), 559–568.

Genesee, E., & Upshur, J. (1996). *Classroom-based evaluation in second language education.* New York: Cambridge University Press.

Hamp-Lyons, L., & Condon, W. C. (1993). Questioning assumptions about portfolio-based evaluation. *College Composition and Communication, 44*, 176–90.

Hirvela, A., & Gweetland, Y. L. (2005). Two case studies of L2 writers' experiences across learning directed portfolio contexts. *Assessing Writing, 10*(3), 192–213.

Kaminsky, D. E. (1993). Helping elementary English as a second language students to become independent learners by improving their reading strategies (ERIC Document Reproduction Service No. ED36510).

Mathews, T. F., & Hansen, C. M. (2004). Ongoing assessment of a university foreign language program. *Foreign Language Annals, 37*(4), 630–640.

Newman, C., Smolen, L., & Lee, D. J. (1995). Implementation of portfolios in an ESL classroom. Paper presented at the Annual Meeting of the Eastern Educational Research Association.

O'Malley, M. J., & Valdez Pierce, L. (1996). *Authentic assessment for English language learners: Practical approaches for teachers.* New York: Addison Wesley Publishing.

Ozturk, H., & Cecen, S. (2007). The effects of portfolio keeping on writing anxiety of EFL students. *Journal of Language and Linguistic Studies, 3*(2), 218–236.

Pally, M. (1998). Film studies drive literacy development for ESL university students. *Journal of Adolescent and Adult Literacy, 41*(8), 20–28.

Paesani, K. (2006). Exercices de style: Developing multiple competencies through a writing portfolio. *Foreign Language Annals, 39*(4), 618–639.

Pollari, P. (2000). This is my portfolio: Portfolios in upper secondary school English studies (ERIC Document Reproduction Service No. ED450415).

Song, B., & August, B. (2002). Using portfolios to assess writing of ESL students: A powerful alternative? *Journal of Second Language Writing, 11*(1), 49–72.

New Words

affective	[ə'fektiv]	a.	情感的；表达感情的
argumentation	[ˌɑːgjumən'teiʃn]	n.	议论文；论证；争论；辩论
authentically	[ɔː'θentikli]	adv.	真正地，确实地；可靠地
autonomous	[ɔː'tɔnəməs]	a.	自治的；自主的；自发的
checklist	['tʃeklist]	n.	清单；检查表；备忘录；目录册
chronologically	[ˌkrɔnə'lɔdʒikli]	adv.	按年代地
clustering	['klʌstəriŋ]	n.	聚类，聚集
coherence	[kəu'hiərəns]	n.	一致；连贯性；凝聚
compound	['kɔmpaund]	a.	复合的；混合的
conjunctive	[kən'dʒʌŋktiv]	a.	连接的；结合的
		n.	连接词
convergent	[kən'vɜːdʒənt]	a.	收敛的；会聚性的；趋集于一点的
drawback	['drɔːbæk]	n.	缺点，不利条件；退税
empowerment	[im'pauəmənt]	n.	许可，授权
encyclopaedia	[enˌsaikləu'piːdjə]	n.	百科全书，大全
exemplification	[igˌzemplifi'keiʃn]	n.	范例；模范
exposition	[ˌekspə'ziʃn]	n.	说明文
multidimensional	[ˌmʌltidai'menʃənl]	a.	多维的；多面的
moderation	[ˌmɔdə'reiʃn]	n.	适度；自我节制
narration	[nə'reiʃn]	n.	叙述，讲述；故事
originality	[əˌridʒə'næləti]	n.	创意；独创性，创造力；原始
peer	[piə]	n.	同等的人
		vi.	凝视，盯着看；窥视
perception	[pə'sepʃn]	n.	知觉，觉察（力），观念
portfolio	[pɔːt'fəuliəu]	n.	公文包；文件夹

portrait	['pɔ:trit]	n.	肖像；描写
practicum	['præktikəm]	n.	实习课；实习科目
probe	[prəub]	v.	调查；（用探针）探测
		n.	探针；调查
punctuation	[ˌpʌŋktʃu'eiʃn]	n.	标点法，标点符号
reveal	[ri'vi:l]	vt.	显示；透露；揭露；泄露
rhetorical	[ri'tɔrikl]	a.	修辞学的；华丽的；夸张的
subsection	[ˌsʌb'sekʃn]	n.	分段，分部；细分；小部分
submit	[səb'mit]	v.	提交；顺从，服从

Phrases

in terms of	根据；按照；在……方面
take into account	考虑；重视
in conclusion	总之；最后
take charge of	接管，负责
in accordance with	依照；与……一致
be aware of	意识到；知道
with regard to	关于；至于

Discussion Ideas

1. What are portfolios in writing?

2. What are the seven steps involved in the portfolio process?

3. How many procedures were involved in this study? What are they?

4. Which three instruments were utilized in the qualitative study? What are they?

5. How was the sample chosen in the descriptive study? What factor was taken into consideration?

6. What is the term for the study administered to ten senior students before the formal questionnaire study?

7. The reliability coefficients are .902 and .865 in the descriptive study, claimed to show high levels of reliability. Do you know the benchmark for the reliability coefficient?

Vocabulary and Language Learning Skills

1. Word Building

Fill in the table with more words with the same affixes.

Affixes	Words Appeared in the Paper	Examples
em-/en-	encourage, empowerment, enhance, endorse, ensure	
-ize/-ise	emphasise, utilise, organise, revise	
-en	enable, enclose, encourage	
-ate	integrate, investigate, demonstrate, evaluate, indicate, motivate, associate, intimidate, evaluate	
-fy	classify, identify	
-ish	establish	

2. Recognizing Word Meanings

Match the definitions in Column B with vocabulary items in Column A.

Column A	Column B
1. affect	a. to become similar (to)
2. consistent	b. to become or cause to become a member; enlist
3. assimilate	c. spoken, written, or given in confidence; secret; private
4. orientation	d. a feeling of extreme worry, sadness or pain
5. empirical	e. to act upon or influence
6. enrol	f. a course, programme etc, introducing a new environment
7. national	g. always behaving in a similar, especially positive, way
8. confidential	h. to adjust to different conditions, a new environment, etc
9. distress	i. based on experiment and observation rather than on theory
10. adapt	j. someone who is a citizen of a particular country but is living in another country

3. Making a Collocation

Use the vocabulary items from the research paper in this unit to replace the italicized parts in the following sentences. Try and feel the differences of the two versions in style. You can refer to the words and phrases in the box below the sentences if you have any difficulties.

1) The portfolio process mainly *deals with*/_____ the decisions of language teachers rather than students' perceptions of portfolios.

2) Portfolio keeping is *helpful*/_____ for overcoming writing anxiety.

3) The use of portfolios involves both teachers and students and *sets up*/_____ a partnership in the learning process.

4) In one aspect, portfolios aid learning by providing *pictures*/_____ of students.

5) At the end of the semester, the instructor *gave*/_____ the final examination.

6) An *combined*/_____ approach to learning English was well received by the students.

7) The approach is effective in *improving*/_____ students' productive and receptive language skills.

8) *Finally*/_____, it can be highlighted that portfolios in EFL writing have positive effects.

9) The results found in the study mainly support those *got*/_____ from previous studies.

10) The present study *showed*/_____ that during the portfolio keeping process, students do not experience anxiety.

11) The scope of the study was *limited*/_____ to the descriptive data obtained from the questionnaires.

12) Further research should focus on the relationships between EFL students' perceptions of portfolio keeping and some independent variables such as demographic factors, *emotional*/_____ states, and motivational issues.

promoting	portraits	revealed
beneficial	affective	integrated
administered	concerns	confined
obtained	conclusively	forges

Writing Focus

References

Function

Citations are essential components of a research paper. Apart from citations in the

text (as introduced in Unit 3 of the book), they should also appear at the end of a paper on the reference list, which includes the information in correspondence to each source you cite in the text. Citations in a research paper serve to

- avoid plagiarism
- give credit where it is due
- help readers locate and retrieve sources
- give credentials to your research

The reference list is often entitled as References, but it is sometimes referred to as Works Cited. The terms mean the same thing. Each is an alphabetical list of works cited, or works to which you have made reference. The title References is used when citing sources using APA (American Psychological Association) style, while Works Cited is generally used when citing sources using MLA (Modern Language Association) style.

In some research papers, Bibliography is used in lieu of References. However, the two are not the same. In References you only list items you have actually cited. In a Bibliography you list all of the material you have consulted in preparing your essay whether or not you have actually cited the work.

Style

Moves of Writing a Reference List:

Move 1 Finish writing your paper before starting to write the reference list.

Move 2 Use the proper APA format.

- Begin the reference list on a new page.
- Centre "References" (do NOT bold, underline, or use quotation marks for the title) in upper and lowercase letters at the top of the page.
- Use one inch margins, 12 point font, and double spacing, which is consistent with the rest of the paper.

Move 3 Write the reference list.

- Use hanging indentation—indent all lines after the first line of each entry one-half inch from the left margin.
- Entries in reference list should be put in alphabetical order by last names of the first authors, editors, translators, etc., or by first words of titles.
- Start with the earliest year of publication if the same author(s) has/have more than one work.
- When referring to any work that is NOT a journal, such as a book, article, or Web page, capitalize only the first letter of the first word of a title and subtitle, the first

word after a colon or a dash in the title, and proper nouns. Do not capitalize the first letter of the second word in a hyphenated compound word.

- Capitalize all major words in journal titles.
- Italicize titles of longer works such as books and journals.
- Do not italicize, underline, or put quotes around the titles of shorter works such as journal articles or essays in edited collections.

Samples

Reference List: Author/Authors

The following rules for handling works by a single author or multiple authors apply to all APA-style references in your reference list, regardless of the type of work (book, article, electronic resource, etc.).

Single Author

Last name first, followed by author initials.

> Berndt, T. J. (2002). Friendship quality and social development. *Current Directions in Psychological Science, 11*, 7–10.

Two Authors

List by their last names and initials. Use the ampersand instead of "and".

> Wegener, D. T., & Petty, R. E. (1994). Mood management across affective states: The hedonic contingency hypothesis. *Journal of Personality & Social Psychology, 66*, 1034–1048.

Three to Seven Authors

List by last names and initials; commas separate author names, while the last author name is preceded again by ampersand.

> Kernis, M. H., Cornell, D. P., Sun, C. R., Berry, A., Harlow, T., & Bach, J. S. (1993). There's more to self-esteem than whether it is high or low: The importance of stability of self-esteem. *Journal of Personality and Social Psychology, 65*, 1190–1204.

More Than Seven Authors

> Miller, F. H., Choi, M. J., Angeli, L. L., Harland, A. A., Stamos, J. A., Thomas, S. T., ... Rubin, L. H. (2009). Web site usability for the blind and low-vision user. *Technical Communication 57*, 323–335.

Organization as Author

> American Psychological Association. (2003).

Unknown Author

> *Merriam-Webster's collegiate dictionary* (10th ed.). (1993). Springfield, MA:
> Merriam-Webster.

Note: When your essay includes parenthetical citations of sources with no author named, use a shortened version of the source's title instead of an author's name. Use quotation marks and italics as appropriate. For example, parenthetical citations of the two sources above would appear as follows: (*Merriam-Webster's*, 1993) and ("New Drug," 1993).

Two or More Works by the Same Author

Use the author's name for all entries and list the entries by the year (earliest comes first).

> Berndt, T. J. (1981).
> Berndt, T. J. (1999).

When an author appears both as a sole author and, in another citation, as the first author of a group, list the one-author entries first.

> Berndt, T. J. (1999). Friends' influence on students' adjustment to school. *Educational Psychologist, 34*, 15–28.
> Berndt, T. J., & Keefe, K. (1995). Friends' influence on adolescents' adjustment to school. *Child Development, 66*, 1312–1329.

References that have the same first author and different second and/or third authors are arranged alphabetically by the last name of the second author, or the last name of the third if the first and second authors are the same.

> Wegener, D. T., Kerr, N. L., Fleming, M. A., & Petty, R. E. (2000). Flexible corrections of juror judgments: Implications for jury instructions. *Psychology, Public Policy, & Law, 6*, 629–654.
> Wegener, D. T., Petty, R. E., & Klein, D. J. (1994). Effects of mood on high elaboration attitude change: The mediating role of likelihood judgments. *European Journal of Social Psychology, 24*, 25–43.

Two or More Works by the Same Author in the Same Year

If you are using more than one reference by the same author (or the same group of authors listed in the same order) published in the same year, organize them in the reference list alphabetically by the title of the article or chapter. Then assign letter suffixes to the year. Refer to these sources in your essay as they appear in your reference list, e.g.: "Berdnt (1981a) makes similar claims…"

> Berndt, T. J. (1981a). Age changes and changes over time in prosocial intentions and behavior between friends. *Developmental Psychology, 17,* 408–416.
>
> Berndt, T. J. (1981b). Effects of friendship on prosocial intentions and behavior. *Child Development, 52,* 636–643.

Introductions, Prefaces, Forewords, and Afterwords

Cite the publishing information about a book as usual, but cite Introduction, Preface, Foreword, or Afterword (whatever title is applicable) as the chapter of the book.

> Funk, R. & Kolln, M. (1998). Introduction. In E.W. Ludlow (Ed.), *Understanding English Grammar* (pp. 1–2). Needham, MA: Allyn and Bacon.

Reference List: Articles in Periodicals

Basic Form

APA style dictates that authors are named last name followed by initials; publication year goes between parentheses, followed by a period. The title of the article is in sentence-case, meaning only the first word and proper nouns in the title are capitalized. The periodical title is run in title case, and is followed by the volume number which, with the title, is also italicized or underlined.

> Author, A. A., Author, B. B., & Author, C. C. (Year). Title of article. *Title of Periodical, volume number* (issue number), pages.

Article in Journal Paginated by Volume

Journals that are paginated by volume begin with page one in issue one, and continue numbering issue two where issue one ended, etc.

> Harlow, H. F. (1983). Fundamentals for preparing psychology journal articles. *Journal of Comparative and Physiological Psychology, 55,* 893–896.

Article in Journal Paginated by Issue

Journals paginated by issue begin with page one every issue; therefore, the issue number gets indicated in parentheses after the volume. The parentheses and issue number are not italicized or underlined.

> Scruton, R. (1996). The eclipse of listening. *The New Criterion, 15*(30), 5–13.

Article in a Magazine

> Henry, W. A., III. (1990, April 9). Making the grade in today's schools. *Time, 135,* 28–31.

Article in a Newspaper

Unlike other periodicals, p. or pp. precedes page numbers for a newspaper reference in APA style. Single pages take p., e.g., p. B2; multiple pages take pp., e.g., pp. B2, B4 or pp. C1, C3-C4.

> Schultz, S. (2005, December 28). Calls made to strengthen state energy policies. *The Country Today*, pp. 1A, 2A.

Note: Because of issues with html coding, the listings below using brackets contain spaces that are not to be used with your listings. Use a space as normal before the brackets, but do not include a space following the bracket.

Letter to the Editor

> Moller, G. (2002, August). Ripples versus rumbles [Letter to the editor]. *Scientific American, 287*(2), 12.

Review

> Baumeister, R. F. (1993). Exposing the self-knowledge myth [Review of the book *The self-knower: A hero under control*]. *Contemporary Psychology, 38*, 466–467.

Reference List: Books

Basic Format for Books

> Author, A. A. (Year of publication). *Title of work: Capital letter also for subtitle.* Location: Publisher.

Note: For "Location", you should always list the city and the state using the two letter postal abbreviation without periods (New York, NY).

> Calfee, R. C., & Valencia, R. R. (1991). *APA guide to preparing manuscripts for journal publication.* Washington, DC: American Psychological Association.

Edited Book, No Author

> Duncan, G. J., & Brooks-Gunn, J. (Eds.). (1997). *Consequences of growing up poor.* New York, NY: Russell Sage Foundation.

Edited Book with an Author or Authors

> Plath, S. (2000). *The unabridged journals* K.V. Kukil, (Ed.). New York, NY: Anchor.

A Translation

> Laplace, P. S. (1951). *A philosophical essay on probabilities.* (F. W. Truscott & F. L. Emory, Trans.). New York, NY: Dover. (Original work published 1814).

Note: When you cite a republished work, like the one above, work in your text, it should appear with both dates: Laplace (1814/1951).

Edition Other Than the First

Helfer, M. E., Keme, R. S., & Drugman, R. D. (1997). *The battered child* (5th ed.). Chicago, IL: University of Chicago Press.

Article or Chapter in an Edited Book

Author, A. A., & Author, B. B. (Year of publication). Title of chapter. In A. Editor & B. Editor (Eds.), *Title of book* (pages of chapter). Location: Publisher.

Note: When you list the pages of the chapter or essay in parentheses after the book title, use "pp." before the numbers: (pp. 1–21). This abbreviation, however, does not appear before the page numbers in periodical references, except for newspapers.

O'Neil, J. M., & Egan, J. (1992). Men's and women's gender role journeys: Metaphor for healing, transition, and transformation. In B. R. Wainrib (Ed.), *Gender issues across the life cycle* (pp. 107–123). New York, NY: Springer.

Multivolume Work

Wiener, P. (Ed.). (1973). *Dictionary of the history of ideas* (Vols. 1–4). New York, NY: Scribner's.

Reference List: Electronic Sources (Web Publications)

Article from an Online Periodical

Online articles follow the same guidelines for printed articles. Include all information the online host makes available, including an issue number in parentheses.

Bernstein, M. (2002). 10 tips on writing the living Web. *A list apart: For people who make websites, 149*. Retrieved from http://www.alistapart.com/articles/writeliving

Newspaper Article

Parker-Pope, T. (2008, May 6). Psychiatry handbook linked to drug industry. *The New York Times*. Retrieved from http://www.nytimes.com

Online Encyclopaedias and Dictionaries

Feminism. (n.d.). In *Encyclopædia Britannica online*. Retrieved from http://www.britannica.com/EBchecked/topic/724633/feminism

Wikis

Please note that the *APA Style Guide to Electronic References* warns writers that

wikis (like Wikipedia, for example) are collaborative projects that cannot guarantee the verifiability or expertise of their entries.

> OLPC Peru/Arahuay. (n.d.). Retrieved April 29, 2011 from the OLPC Wiki: http://wiki.laptop. org/go/OLPC_Peru/Arahuay

Refer to <u>http://owl.english.purdue.edu/owl/resource/560/10/</u> for more information. Here is a complete sample paper using the APA style:

<u>http://owl.english.purdue.edu/media/pdf/20090212013008_560.pdf</u>

Task One

Identify the type of sources for the following items.

Evans, V., & Melanie, G. (2006).*Cognitive Linguistics: An Introduction.* Edinburgh: Edinburgh University Press.

(   )

Stern, B. (1997, March). Rising to the challenge. *Canadian Living*, pp. 68–71.

(   )

Wallace, A. (n.d.). *The new cost of the old economy.* Retrieved from http://www.quarryinstitute.org/articles/quarry.htm

(   )

Harrison, B. K. (2003). Mummy's curses: Methods of identifying, tracking, and categorizing. *The Interlake Egyptologist*, 7(8), 17–22.

(   )

Schwartz, J. (2005, February 13). Are organic vegetables really better for you? *The Gazette*, p. D6. Retrieved February 25, 2005, from Proquest database.

(   )

Task Two

Each of the following entries has one mistake, correct them and put the entries in correct order.

> Brady, J. T., and Brady, P. L. (2003, November). Consumers and genetically modified foods. *Journal of Family and Consumer Sciences*, 95(4), 12–18. Retrieved February 25, 2005, from Proquest database
>
> Parent, K. & Vandelac, L. (Directors). (1999). *THE GENETIC TAKEOVER, OR, MUTANT FOOD*. [Motion picture]. Canada: National Film Board of Canada.

Genetic engineering. (2002). In *The new encyclopaedia Britannica micropaedia* (Vol. 5, p.178). Encyclopaedia Britannica.

Health Canada. (2002, February). *The safety of genetically modified food crops.* March 22, 2005, from http://www.hc-sc.gc.ca/english/protection/biologics_genetics/gen_mod_foods/genmodebk.html.

Nottingham, S. (2003). *Eat your genes: How genetically modified food is entering our diet.* London: Zed Books Ltd.

SCOPE Forum (2000–2005). *Genetically modified food: Controversies surrounding the risks and benefits of genetically modified food.* Retrieved from: The SCOPE Research Group (UC Berkley, UW, AAAS): http://scope. educ.washington.edu/ gmfood/

Zheng, M. Y. (2004). *Genetically modified (GM) foods.* In B. D. Ness (Ed.) *Encyclopedia of genetics* (Vol.1, pp.366–370). Pasadena, Calif.: Salem Press.

Task Three

Browse the reference lists of other papers in this book to get a better understanding of writing references.

Unit 8

Writing in an Electronic Age: A Case Study of L2 Composing Processes

Learning Objectives

- EFL writing: approach and practice
- Presentation
- Proofreading

Writing in an Electronic Age: A Case Study of L2 Composing Processes

Paul Stapleton*

Department of English, Hong Kong Institute of Education, 10 Lo Ping Road, Taipo, Hong Kong

Abstract

Studies on second language (L2) learners writing in English have found that composing is a **recursive** process requiring planning, formulating and revising. Of particular note among the many studies that have explored the composing processes of L2 writers are two characteristics: 1) They examine the composing processes of writers in real time while they respond to a **prompt**. 2) They have been performed on writers who compose using pen and paper. While such research has been valuable for advancing the understanding of the processes taken by L2 writers, both the task (an immediate response to a prompt) and the instruments (pen and paper) do not reflect typical approaches **undertaken** by L2 university students. This exploratory case study follows the composing processes of "Andrea", a master's student, while she wrote a 4000-word essay. Using in-depth **logs**, a questionnaire and interviews, starting from her receipt of a prompt to the assignment submission, Andrea's composing processes were categorized and analyzed both qualitatively and **temporally**. Findings indicate **notable** differences between Andrea's time **allotment** to composing behaviors and that of other studies, suggesting that the cognitive resources used by

---

* Tel.:+852 2948 8823.

E-mail address: paulstapleton@gmail.com.

writers in an electronic environment may be different from those used when using pen and paper.

Keywords: Composing processes; Second language writing; Academic writing; Cognitive resources

1. Research on the composing process

Uncovering the processes taking place as a writer produces text, either via pen and paper or keyboard and screen is an extremely difficult **undertaking**. Writers have the complex task of taking raw ideas and representing them on screen as **a string of** words with syntax, i.e., an undertaking that recursively mixes thoughts and mechanics (Roca de Larios, Mancho'n, Murphy, & Marin, 2008). Researchers of writing processes have the even more complicated job of breaking down the processes into understandable components that accurately reflect this deeply cognitive behavior. Fortunately, understanding of this process advanced considerably beginning in the 1980s when models (e.g., Bereiter & Scardamalia, 1987; Flower & Hayes, 1981) were first developed for grasping what takes place in the minds of writers who were composing in their first language (L1). The Flower and Hayes model (1981), for example, outlined three writing processes—planning, translating and reviewing—each of which was also further sub-categorized (see discussion below). When a writer is composing in a second language, however, these processes are compounded because extra steps are needed to decode thoughts into language before text finally appears on the page or screen.

In order to understand the composing processes of both L1 and L2 writers as they construct prose, researchers have designed studies in which they ask writers to voice their thoughts in think-aloud protocols while being videotaped. During these sessions, participant writers usually complete their composing task **in a** single **sitting**, using pen and paper. However, while such an experimental set-up is both convenient and necessary for controlling the composing conditions and conducting the protocols, the actual task at hand, i.e., an immediate written response to a **generic** prompt, tends not to reflect the types of writing normally performed in real life. A much more common **scenario** among university students is the research paper, which is more likely to be completed over a period of weeks while requiring research. This paper is also written in an electronic environment rather than with pen and paper, **replete** with information from electronic sources. Because of these differences, the composing processes, including their associated time allotment, may be considerably different from those that have been investigated in highly controlled situations using think-aloud protocols. Accordingly, the present study seeks to both explore composing processes in a more naturalistic environment, as well as propose alternative methods for revealing their nature. Any

differences in the composing process exposed by a more naturalistic study have the potential to **shed light on** new writing behaviors, which **in turn** may suggest a need for change in pedagogy.

1.1 Understunding the composing process

Interest in the process of composing in a second language **grew out of** studies that explored the writing behavior of L1 students. Early studies by Emig (1971) and Perl (1980) revealed that the discovery of meaning through the act of writing was not a linear process, but a recursive one in which "writers go back in order to move forward" (Zamel, 1982, p. 197). The **seminal** model proposed by Flower and Hayes (1981) revealed composing as deeply cognitive behavior requiring many sub-processes within three main phases—planning, translating and reviewing. Planning includes the generation of ideas, organizing information and setting goals. Translating, not to be confused with translating from one language to another, requires writers to put their ideas into words and sentences including all that this task entails, from obeying rules of grammar to controlling motor skills for hand-writing text. The third phase, reviewing, covers the evaluation of the text and the subsequent reorganizing, deleting and adding.

Led by studies on the composing process in the native tongue, research on L2 composing processes followed. Such interest is understandable because of the significant extra steps involved, as L2 writers at most levels need to literally translate their ideas from their native tongue into a second language. However, Zamel (1982, 1983) found the same recursive process existed among the more experienced L2 writers she surveyed, with pre-writing, drafting and revising characterizing the progression through to the final product. In a later study, however, Raimes (1985) found that unskilled L2 writers displayed a more complex profile, with the implication that lower level writers also have sufficient ability to discover meaning as they write. Nevertheless, subsequent studies suggested that skilled writers are advantaged over the unskilled in terms of **metalinguistic** analysis, i.e., thinking about what language to use (Cumming, 1990), and their **allocation** of time to the various composing processes (Roca de Larios, Murphy, Mancho'n, 1999; Sasaki, 2000; Sasaki & Hirose, 1996).

Studies comparing L1 and L2 processes have tended to support the notion that fluency is negatively affected when composing in a second language (Silva, 1993) with fewer words written (Sasaki & Hirose, 1996) and more frequent interruptions in the formulation process (Roca de Larios, Mar'm, & Murphy, 2001). Similarly, Roca de Larios, Mancho'n, & Murphy (2006) found that twice as much time was lent to formulation in the L2 than the L1. In fact, Wang and Wen (2002) found that sentence construction occupied two-thirds of the composing time spent by their L2 subjects. Further, when Roca de Larios et al. (2008) examined how time was allocated to various composing processes, they identified three main practices that L2 writers typically perform when completing a writing task—planning, formulation, and revision—a result which appears to parallel the planning, translating and reviewing of the Flower and Hayes model (1981). Among these, formulation accounted for the bulk of time taken (from 62% for advanced writers to 81% for lower level writers) to complete the task at all proficiency levels. Meanwhile, "planning" accounted for a maximum of 13% of time for advanced writers, but only 1% for low level writers. Time allocation for revision ranged from 6% at the lowest level to 21% at the intermediate level, with the advanced writers using 16% of the time.

This finding is particularly important for the present study because it sets a clear **benchmark** for the types of processes used by L2 writers against which comparisons can be made for a much more common writing scenario—a research paper written over a period of weeks. Accordingly, the present exploratory study seeks to answer two questions:

1) How is time allocated to different composing processes in a research paper from receipt of prompt to submission of product written in an electronic environment over a period of weeks?

2) What behaviors characterize each of the processes in #1?

2. Methods

Data from studies on the composing processes of L2 writers found in the literature have been **derived from** instruments such as think-aloud protocols (Cumming, 1990; Raimes, 1985; Roca de Larios et al. 2006; Roca de Larioset al., 2008) interviews (Zamel, 1982), text analysis (Zamel, 1982), stimulated recall protocols (from video) (Sasaki,2000, 2004), and direct observation (Pennington & So, 1993; Zamel, 1983). See Table 1 for a sample summary.

While such instruments have proved effective for uncovering writing processes in highly controlled settings in a paper-and-ink environment, the present study, which operated in a more naturalistic setting, adopts a mixed methods approach principally employing qualitative methods (a student log, a **retrospective** questionnaire and interviews).Recording and **tabulating** the amount of time spent on each of the processes (see details below) accounted for the quantitative part of the study. The reason for using such instruments was related to the nature of the writing assignment which made real-time behavioral observation methods, such as think-aloud protocols, impracticable because the time between receiving the writing assignment and completing it took a period of weeks. Such a length of time and the variety of composing **locales** also **precluded** using other methods such as direct observation, keystroke logs (Miller, 2000), stimulated recall sessions (e.g., Lindgren & Sullivan, 2003) and videotaping because one of the distinctive requirements of the proposed study was to track the composing process as it took place in authentic situations, i.e., over a period of time, on multiple occasions and in multiple settings. In contrast, the type of writing tasks which lend themselves well to employing think-aloud and stimulated recall protocols as well as keystroke logs are those which set a prompt with learners completing the task within a limited period of time while recording takes place. Such a method, however, does not explore and analyze the much more common writing scenario faced by EAP (English for Academic Purposes) learners in which a writing assignment is received and a completed research paper is submitted several weeks later.

Table 1. Characteristics of selected studies on L2 composing.

Author/year	Mode	Time	# of ppts	Genre	Design	Purpose
Sasaki (2004)	Pencil and paper	30–60 min.	11	Argument	Videotaped writing behavior; stimulated-recall protocols (video) (retrospective account)	Comparing composing behavior of ESL and EFL writers
Roca de Larios et al. (2008)	Pen and paper	60 min.	21	Argument	Think-aloud protocols	Influence of proficiency on allocation of attentional resources
Cumming (1990)	Pen and Paper		23	Informal letter; argument	Think-aloud protocols	Allocation of composing behavior across levels of expertise
Roca de Larios et al. (2006)		60 min.	21	Argument	Think-aloud protocols	Influence of proficiency on allocation of attentional resources
Pennington and So (1993)	Pen and paper	30 min –5 h.	6	Narrative	Direct observation and retrospective interviews	Comparing L1 and L2 as well as skilled vs non-skilled
Zamel (1983)	Pen and paper	4–18 h.	6	Expository	Direct observation retrospective interviews	Describe composing processes
Raimes (1985)	Pen and paper	65 min.	8	Narrative	Think-aloud protocols and questionnaire	Composing low and high proficiency
Wang and Wen (2002)	Pen and paper	45 min.	16	Narrative/ argument	Think-aloud protocols and retrospective interviews	Comparing L1 and L2 composing processes
Roca de Larios et al. (2001)	Pen and paper	60 min.	21	Argument	Think-aloud protocols and questionnaire	Comparing L1 and L2 composing processes

2.1 Participant

In the studies noted above, as **delineated** in Table 1, sample sizes ranged from half a dozen participants to upwards of two dozen. While such numbers appear appropriate for using the methods described, the present study explores one student's behavior using different instruments which allow for the in-depth examination of composing processes more suited to case studies. The choice of this methodology was largely determined by the **logistical impediments** implied in the research questions, particularly the need to describe the writing process in a naturalistic environment (over a period of weeks in multiple settings). Duff (2008) notes, "choice of [research] method is...determined in large part by the questions one seeks answers to, the body of knowledge that already exists on that topic, the domain of inquiry and context, and the methods the questions lend themselves to" (p. viii). The present case study method also **dovetails** with an exploratory approach which examines the **feasibility** of the procedures used (Yin, 2003). Additionally, the somewhat burdensome log-keeping, although less cognitively **intrusive** during the composing task at hand than think-aloud protocols, demands a cooperative participant, which again suits the case study approach. Four previous case studies on L2 writers show that this methodology can generate useful findings: Spack's oft-cited **longitudinal** study (1997) of a Japanese graduate student's reading and writing strategies, Johns's case study of a Vietnamese science student (1991) who had repeatedly failed an English competency exam and Yi (2007) as well as Yi and Hirvela's studies (2010) of the non-school writing practices of a Korean high school student.

"Andrea" was 23 years old at the time the study took place. She had recently completed a Master's in TESOL ata Hong Kong **tertiary** institute and was about to **embark** on an English teaching career at a local primary school. Her IELTS score was 8.0 (equivalent to the mid-600 range on the TOEFL paper test). Andrea described herself as an **underachieving** student who disliked English during her high school years. She repeated her final year of high school as her grades were too low for university acceptance. When she entered university, she described herself as "below average" as a first year student; however, by fourth year, she was in the top 10 percent of her class as measured by her grades. As a Master's student, her grades were at the B+ level which she claimed was average in her class. Andrea's (average) profile along with her availability and willingness to participate were the three main criteria for her selection.

As for Andrea's composing experience, she noted that writing in English was always her worst subject in school; however, she felt that she had improved considerably as an undergraduate, "but I still do not enjoy writing essays in English." When Andrea was interviewed for the present study, she claimed that she felt more comfortable writing in

English than her native Chinese. Part of the reason for this was that for the past several years, all of her assignment writing was in English. Another reason was that she felt less than proficient in using a Chinese keyboard.

2.2 Writing prompt

The writing prompt was decided via negotiation between Andrea and the author in a way which would best reflect a typical assignment undertaken by master's-level students in the program she attended. Andrea collected several assignment prompts that she had received in courses, such as Second Language Acquisition, but for which she had not written any papers when studying for her master's degree. Among these, she was allowed to choose one which interested her. The chosen prompt "Write an essay supporting or critiquing Long's Interaction Hypothesis". Andrea later entitled her paper "Rethinking Long's Interaction Hypothesis (IH)".

Andrea was asked to write a 3000-word paper as if it were a term assignment for a credit-bearing course. She was told that both the researcher and one of her master's course teachers would read the paper and assign a grade to it and return it to her. She was also told to approach the assignment exactly as she would if she were taking a course for credit expending the same amount of time and effort. Andrea received financial compensation upon completing the task slightly after the three-weak deadline. She was also fully informed of the study's purpose and that her real name would not be used.

2.3 Log, retrospective questionnaire and interviews

Logs are a well-established tool used in education as effective learning aids (Dolmans, Schmidt, van der Beek, Beintema, & Gerver, 1999; McCarthy & Walvoord, 2008). McCarthy and Walvoord (2008), in particular, conducted a study of their students' composing processes using logs as the principle data-producing instrument supplemented by interviews and audiotapes. The author has also used logs in studies for generating useful data (Helms-Park, Radia, & Stapleton, 2007; Radia & Stapleton, 2008). Most recently, the participant student in Yi and Hirvela's case study (2010) produced useful data in an activity checklist similar to log entries. Logs, like diaries, bring access tothe cognitive processes undertaken by students as they make decisions about writing content and mechanics that they encounter over time. Unlike the use of think-aloud protocols and direct observation during immediate-response-to-prompt studies, the logs are relatively non-intrusive (see Dornyei, 2007; Gibson, 1995) and perhaps the only method of accessing composing behavior as students write an assignment over a period of time in multiple locales. However, log-keeping is a demanding activity, so both **rigorous** training, and motivation **on Andrea's part** were challenges that had to be overcome in order for her to accurately record her composing processes.

Before receiving the prompt, Andrea was shown a sample log to ensure she would include an appropriate level of detail and accuracy of her composing activities. Essentially, in her log she had to record all of her composing activities during each session in chronological order with an indication of the length of time taken for each, in as much detail as possible. Andrea was given the following sample framework in addition to the sample log:

1) Reading and Pre-writing, e.g., how you identify ideas and categories, library searches and searching for information on the Internet (keywords, search engine names, and links clicked on including non-textual information); sequencing information, goal-setting;

2) Selecting Information, e.g., copying hard copies and copying and pasting information from websites; reasons for including and eliminating information;

3) Drafting and Composing, e.g., comments on note-taking, vocabulary choice, sentence construction and organization; extent of use of electronic tools for composing; extent of use of copied electronic texts as models for composing;

4) Revising and Reviewing, e.g., comments on decisions about when idea generation was complete; comments on self-evaluation; extent of use of software, both prepackaged and Web-sourced for improving language mechanics.

After Andrea's first log-keeping session had finished, she viewed and rewrote her entries with the author for the purposes of recording her composing processes using language that accurately reflected the needs of the study. For example, Andrea was asked to elaborate on details of her online searching practices, her struggles with finding the right word, and the amount of text she deleted and rewrote, among many other composing activities. Although the log was the main data-gathering instrument, Andrea also completed an open-ended retrospective questionnaire and was interviewed three times, once each before, during and after her composing sessions.

2.4 Data analysis

Log entries were read through several times in an initial coding exercise (Richards, 2003). This entailed the development of **provisional** themes before the generation of codes, four of which were informed by categories in Rocade Larios et al. (2008 pp. 36–37). Three of the seven codes from Roca de Larios et al. were eliminated because they related to procedural elements of think-aloud protocols, e.g., meta-comments, prompt-reading and task interpretation. Examples from Andrea's log are below each of the four categories and **rubrics** as follows:

Planning: Those episodes which involve the **retrieval** and generation of ideas, the establishment of connections between them, and the setting of goals.

"Thinking what to write next. Thinking whether or not I should suggest some reasons for that observation."

Formulation: Those episodes which indicate that the writer is trying to convert thoughts and ideas into language, with or without having to engage in problem solving.

*1. ...using online **thesaurus** to search for words meaning 'good', picked 'desirable'*

2. Writing two versions of the sentence...deciding which I should use to describe the origin of the hypothesis

Evaluation: A process by which the writer assesses the **efficacy** of his/her pragmatic, textual, and linguistic decisions.

"Reading the part again before moving on...see if there are any better words I can use."

Revision: Those episodes in which the writer changes, adds to, or deletes previously written segments of different length.

1. Modifying and elaborating the transitions for each paragraph to make sure the organization is tightly hanged together.

2. Wrote "helped obtained"...Deleted it...not satisfied...not vivid...used "secure" instead.

A significant number of log entries could not be classified under these four categories however. These unclassified entries were first assigned to conceptual categories in an open coding process and then further passed through **axial** coding (Strauss & Corbin, 1998), whereby sub-categories were related to each other and **subsumed** into the following two core categories:

Research: Those episodes in which the writer sources, reads and/or copies information pertaining to the composing task at hand.

Searching for how Socio-interactionists view language learning among the journal articles I collected. Typing the keyword 'socio-interactionist, language learning' in Google search bar.

Collaboration: Those episodes in which the writer consults with others regarding the composing task at hand.

Talking to my friend online with yahoo messenger to discuss my introduction and what he thinks of it and how I can write it better.

Once categories were established, a second rater was trained to code a portion of the items (as per Smagorinsky, 2008) as a reliability check. Using the categories and definitions below, the inter-rater reliability between two raters was 80% (agreement on 112 of 140 entries).

The resulting categories above served as a guide for deciding how to code the questionnaire and interview data. Each questionnaire and interview response was also coded under one of the six categories based on the content in Andrea's responses. Subcategories under each of the six main composing activities above were then further generated using a similar coding process as above.

3. Results

Andrea spent a total of 49 and a half hours over a period of three weeks in three different **venues** (library, home and intransit) writing her paper of over 4000 words which included 18 sources. Her log comprised 216 entries delineating at least that number of separate composing behaviors. The author and one other faculty member teaching in the same program as Andrea's independently graded her paper as if it were submitted as a term paper for a Master's level course. Both awarded the paper a B+, an above-average grade in the program she had graduated from. Neither was a former teacher of Andrea.

3.1 Research question #1

The time she spent on each composing behavior (research question #1) is shown below in Table 2 and Fig. 1.

3.2 Research question #2

The behaviors that characterized each of the six processes outlined in #1 were the focus of research question #2. These are delineated under their **respective** tides below. Quotations below are taken from the log, questionnaire and interviews.

Table 2. Composing behavior measured in time and percent

Composing Behavior	Time (in hours)	%
Research	12:00	24
Planning	8:50	18
Formulation	16:15	33
Revision	5:25	11
Evaluation	3:10	6
Collaboration	3:45	8
Total	49:25	

3.2.1 Research

Log data revealed that Andrea's research behavior fell into three broad activities-searching, reacting and copying(either by copying and pasting or typing out). Andrea's searches were largely performed using yahoo. com with her institute library's database being her second choice. However, on advice from the author during an interview halfway through Andrea's composing process, she switched to Google Scholar. Her keyword searches were usually confined to two to three words and resulted in many false leads which she claimed wasted her time. The cause appeared to be Andrea's

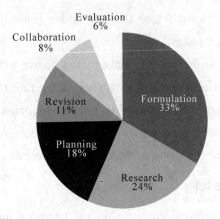

Figure 1. Composing behavior by time allotment

poor choice of search engine and keywords, e.g., failing to use advanced searches in scholarly engines. While Andrea's references reveal that most of her sources came from recognizable journals or book publishers, she cited two sites whose academic **rigor** was questionable. One of these was an EFL blog/forum in which teachers are invited to share their views. The other was a master's dissertation from a Chinese university. When the **dubious** academic rigor in these sites was pointed out to her, she claimed to be focusing on the content, without paying attention to the source of information, while believing them to be "journals".

Andrea's time spent reading had two main purposes: to gather information and ideas, i.e., the customary research task, and read for structural purposes, i.e., to better understand how to organize the sections of her paper and also how to express ideas at the sentence and word-level. Andrea's copying of materials was almost exclusively performed electronically with only one reference made to a session of paper copying.

3.2.2 Planning

The time that Andrea spent planning fell into three broad sub-categories: 1) generating ideas, 2) deciding how to organize ideas, and 3) **deliberating** over audience reaction. The following quotes are illustrative examples of the three types of planning:

Generating ideas. "Decided I should support the role of interaction in effective learning, and then argue against the universally assumed benefits." (log)

"There were times that I suddenly came up with an idea of how I write the literature review, or my arguments for my theory, and I would type it down in the same page and then cut and paste it on another page as another document." (questionnaire)

Deciding how to organize ideas. "Instead of writing straight ahead, I [**jotted down**] the things I wanted to write first. And then I made a 'landscape' for my entire essay, listing down the parts/the structure of the essay and the things that I would more or less include in it." (questionnaire)

"Thinking whether I should use my own words to summarize what Long found...or just quote what he said..." (log)

Deliberating over the audience reaction. "Thinking what the readers would argue, and my counter arguments." (log)

3.2.3 Formulation

Formulating thoughts into language encompassed several distinct behaviors for Andrea beyond the straight "translating" or "the process of putting ideas into visible language" (Flower & Hayes, 1981, p. 373). Andrea's formulation decisions at the word-level, beyond the typical "translation" included using online dictionaries and the **built-in** thesaurus as well as combing through published papers for parallel phrasings. Andrea spent a substantial amount of time **stuck with** writer's block, simply unable to come up with the word she wanted. This block also appeared when Andrea tried to form her sentences. One strategy she often used when forming her sentences was to write out multiple versions of the same idea and choose the best one. Another strategy she admitted to was borrowing sentences of published works and then changing a few of the words in order to avoid charges of plagiarism.

> "...for the introduction [and] the literature review, I copied and pasted several sentences from different journal articles, and then I first tried combining them together. I replaced the adjectives and the main verbs using Cambridge online dictionary...I rearrange the sentence structure and the word orders...simplified it a little bit so to make the sentence look more like my own. For some sentences I borrowed the adjectives and main verbs, and the sentence structures for some completely different sentences in my essay just to make it look more matured and better. (questionnaire)

A Turnitin check of Andrea's paper resulted in a "5%" match with no string of matched words longer than six, well within the **bounds** of acceptability.

Spell and grammar checkers acted as Andrea's constant composing assistant. Andrea claimed,

> When I was writing my essay, I kept correcting my spellings with the MS [W]ord spelling check (the red lines) since I usually rely on **phonics** to spell my vocabularies (and thus would have a lot of spelling errors). Whenever I see green lines, I would stop, right click the green lines to check what's wrong with my sentence, and then rephrase and restructure my sentences according to the suggestions or hints provided by the MS [W]ord until the green line's gone. (questionnaire)

Andrea added that she would go to considerable lengths to get rid of a green line even though she realized that the grammar checker was far from perfect as she sometimes noticed unmarked mistakes of her own. (Only four green lines appeared in her paper).

3.2.4 Collaborating

Roughly eight percent of Andrea's composing time (four occasions) was spent collaborating with a more experienced writer. This collaboration came in the form of advice following the electronic exchange of her drafts. Feedback from her collaborator on various versions of sentences helped Andrea decide which versions and wording to choose.

3.2.5 Evaluating

Andrea's log comments about her evaluative processes tended to focus on broader aspects of what she had written rather than specifics as **encapsulated** in the following remark: "Re-reading twice to confirm it gives the right feeling and good organization."

However, occasionally, Andrea expressed specific dissatisfaction upon reading a section as illustrated in the following quote:

"Reacting the part again...wanting to say it's finished...but feeling something's missing. Thinking it's too irresponsible just putting the quotation there without explanation...what is it that you want the reader to get from that quotation? Thinking what to do."

These evaluative comments tended to be more frequent when Andrea was finishing a section and especially towards the end of her paper.

3.2.6 Revising

At very frequent **intervals** throughout Andrea's entire composing process she made comments about her revisions which operated at all levels of detail from the word- to multi-paragraph-level. The examples below illustrate this.

"Reorganizing the sentence structure, finding synonyms to replace the adjectives and the verb. Corrected myspelling and sentence structure with the help of the MS [W] ord grammar check." (log)

"Reacting the sentence...adding 'descriptive' before 'statistics'. Replace 'regarding' with 'concerning,' replace' next' with 'succeeding'."(log)

In the retrospective questionnaire, Andrea wrote about her frustrations.

"I deleted a HUGE amount of text. The amount that I deleted was almost as many and as long as the length of the essay itself. This was actually the most frustrating part when writing an essay, because I kept deleting what I wrote. I tended to write several versions for each sentence (with different sentence structures/wordings) but I could not decide which one was better, I kept thinking there would a better way to link my ideas in that paragraph in a more organized, comprehensible and concise way, and that the language could be more academic or matured. It was like I could not really deliver what I meant. Sometimes I was very indecisive of what to write first, and what vocabularies l should use." (questionnaire)

4. Discussion

The purpose of this study was to describe how one L2 writer allotted time to composing processes as she wrote a research paper over a period of weeks largely in an electronic environment. Because studies of the composing processes of writers have almost exclusively taken place in highly controlled experimental environments with participants writing with pen on paper, the present case study attempts to set a benchmark as well as suggest a methodology for further studies in more naturalistic situations.

What appears significant, although perhaps not unexpected, is the remarkably different time allocations of composing behaviors in the present study compared with previous ones. The present study reveals a much reduced allocation of time to formulation (33%) when contrasted with other L2 studies, e.g., 62–81% (Roca de Larios et al., 2008), 69% (Roca de Larios *et al.*, 2001), two-thirds (Wang & Wen, 2002), and those in L1, about 50% (Kellogg, 1987) and 72% (Roca de Larios *et al.*, 2001). Given that Andrea was an advanced level user of English, her lower allotment of time to formulation is expected as per findings in the L2 studies above; however, such a low allotment suggests that in naturalistic contexts other composing behaviors take up substantial portions of time. Chief among these was "research" accounting for close to a quarter of Andrea's time. This behavior was not included in any of the other studies mentioned here due to the nature of their procedures. However, research, i.e., searching, reading and copying, are integral to the idea-generating process which leads to the planning and formulation of a written product. Such being the case, studies on composing processes need to integrate this major component into the composition formula.

The inclusion of 'research' as a category arouses the link with the macro-level processes explored by Prior (1998) and Tardy (2009) whose thick descriptions of graduate students taking part in longitudinal case studies uncover the complexities of the writing process over lengthy periods of time. These complexities, which include elements such as the writers' understanding of the genres in which they compose, are reminders that the writing processes described here account mostly for real-time composing, while there is an unseen wealth of **schema** behind the words, syntax, ideas and organization of any written text.

While it is clear that social factors interact with the production of texts (Riazi, 1997), electronic communication may be even further enhancing social influence. Another behavior unaccounted for in previous studies was "collaboration". On four occasions, Andrea consulted a person she deemed qualified to comment on her writing which **presumably** led to an improved product. Certainly, collaboration is not a new kind of behavior among L2 writers (deGuerrero & Villamil, 1994); however, electronic means of communicating and sharing files may have facilitated this activity to an extent where advice from peers and **mentors** is addting a new dimension within the socio-cognitive sphere of influence and is worthy of inclusion as an integral part of the composing process.

As for "evaluation," Andrea's time spent in this activity, (6%), as opposed to 14% in another study (Roca de Larios *et al.*, 2008) may have reflected her ability to better manage time over a period of weeks when compared to the severe time **constraints** dictated by experimental conditions in other studies. This flexibility of temporal management (over a period of weeks) probably accounts for the much greater amount of time given over to 'planning" as well. Other studies (see Table 1) which have used experimental procedures operating under time constraints leave little opportunity to plan, e.g., 1–13% (Roca de Larioset *et al.*, 2008). On the other hand, Andrea's 18% allotted to planning was such a significant portion of her composing that it could be broken into sub-categories. Two of the three of these (generating ideas and deciding how to organize ideas) bore a similarity to Flower and Hayes's seminal study (1981). The third, "deliberating over the audience reaction," likely reflected writing instruction received by Andrea during university highlighting discipline-specific genre approaches to writing.

Although 11 percent of Andrea's time was spent revising, this number is actually below the percentage (16) used by advanced level writers in the study by Roca de Larios et al. (2008). This lower percentage may be explained by the great frequency of occasions that Andrea used tools such as the grammar checker, thesaurus and online dictionaries, which could have increased the efficiency of her revising. In other words, new tools may have reduced the amount of time she spent in some processes leaving more time for others.

4.1 Electronic shortcomings, strengths and implications

Despite Andrea's frequent application of electronic tools, her occasional substandard use of new media and resources suggests that new tools and resources come with **caveats** which in turn points to several pedagogical implications. Beginning with researching skills, Andrea displayed only rudimentary knowledge of keyword searches, often using a poor choice of words. Her use of a generic engine, yahoo.com, was also particularly worrisome. Once told about Google Scholar mid-way through her composing, she switched to this engine and used it exclusively thereafter. Similarly, the lack of rigor at certain websites she had chosen escaped her notice resulting in citations in her paper that did not meet academic standards. Such substandard approaches to sourcing appear widespread among students (Stapleton & Helms-Park, 2006; Wang & Artero, 2005) indicating a need for basic researching skills built in both as part of the taught curriculum as well as the feedback.

Despite Andrea's sometimes casual acceptance of a dubious source, she also displayed a strategic use of web sources. In particular, she visited Wikipedia as a "first stop source" for getting a general idea about her chosen topic (but not citing it) during the early stages of her research. While even Jimmy Wales, the founder of Wikipedia, discourages the citing of Wikipedia articles by students in their papers, he does encourage its use for basic overviews of a subject (Wired Campus, 2006), and this strategy appears to have merit. Rather than the unmitigated condemnation of Wikipedia as an academic source often espoused in university classrooms, instructors may consider encouraging a strategic use of such online sites as first-stop sources.

Andrea's use of electronic tools while formulating text displayed some interesting contrasts with previous studies. Roca de Larios et al. (2001) discuss "lexical searches" (p. 516) referring to a cognitive hunt for a certain word to fill a slot in a sentence. In Andrea's case, this cognitive hunt was often replaced by her use of the electronic thesaurus. Likewise, Andrea was a heavy user of spell and grammar checkers to the extent that she may have overused the grammar checker given its tendency for false negatives (Buck, 2008; McGee & Ericsson, 2002). While it appears to be an overstatement to claim that the "grammar check confuses much more frequently than it helps" (Buck, 2008, p. 409), clear direction from teachers about the strengths and weaknesses of this tool appear necessary. Such a directive also applies to the textual borrowing or "paraphrasing" (Keck, 2006) or the patchwriting (Pecorari, 2003) employed by Andrea. Certainly, some of Andrea's sentences would fall under Keck's term "Near copy." Again, rather than instructors issuing blanket instructions condemning plagiarism, more **nuanced** advice that draws attention to borrowing strategies is needed which clearly delineates the difference between paraphrasing and plagiarism.

A larger point here is that the cognitive energy normally used in a non-digital environment for lexical searches and formulating spelling and grammar was at least partially replaced by Andrea's use of electronic tools and her manipulation of borrowed text. If Andrea's example is typical, the present electronic environment used by most writers may be creating a shift in how cognitive resources are allocated. The former raw "translation" of ideas into language (in the Flower and Hayes (1981) sense) is possibly being replaced by a more strategic process that has writers utilizing multiple tools and resources for reaching their textual goals. In fact, Andrea did not use all the tools available to her that have been shown to enhance L2 writing such as **concordancers**

(Gaskell & Cobb, 2004; Hafner & Candlin, 2007; Lee & Swales, 2006; Sun & Wang, 2003), corpora (Flowerdew, 2002; Liu & Jiang, 2009), corpus consultation (O'Sullivan & Chambers, 2006) and Add-Ins (Milton, 2006). As tools such as these become more powerful, composing processes may continue to shift with a **concurrent** need for instructors to **keep abreast**.

4.2 Limitations

As with any case study, the findings here cannot be generalized beyond the individual in question. It bears noting that writing is "locally situated, extensively mediated, deeply **laminated** and highly **heterogeneous**" (Prior, 1998, p. 275). Indeed, the context, level, native language, background and even character of the participant were all highly distinctive. Andrea was very **fastidious** about wording and phrasing and often labored over her choices for lengthy intervals. Such a characteristic is not possessed by all or even a majority of writers. Although this paper describes the methods used as naturalistic, in fact, Andrea wrote considerably more words in describing her composing processes in her log (in real time as she was composing) than she wrote in her paper. Such a heavy task certainly could have impacted Andrea's processes. Questions also remain about how accurately she described these processes. The level of detail in her logs sometimes varied as it is very difficult to describe every step and thought while one is composing. Indeed, any technique which imposes constraints on cognitive processes (in this case, interrupting the flow of normal behavior by requiring log-writing) is bound to influence the outcome. This issue is not unlike the concern brought up by Smagorinsky (2001) with regard to think-aloud protocols. Leaving aside whether thinking aloud interferes with composing processes, Smagorinsky points to Vygotsky's claim that "thought is never the direct equivalent of word meanings. Meaning mediates thought in its path to verbal expression" (Vygotsky, 1987, p. 282). Such a claim reveals that caution must be taken when interpreting and making hard conclusions about any composing processes revealed through language as this study and most others have done. In the end, in order to **bypass** the reliance on self-described efforts using logs and think-aloud protocols, perhaps only physiological techniques such as **neurological** measurements of blood flow (fMRI) can provide more accurate descriptions.

Another major concern was whether Andrea's composing accurately **emulated** the conditions experienced by students writing research papers. While it is true that her conditions were superficially different, Andrea did express feeling stress before the deadline as well as concern for her final grade and requested an extension of several days in order to improve the discussion and conclusion. Thus, Andrea, like most students, experienced both the stress of a deadline and motivation to get a high grade, arguably the two biggest issues for student writers. Moreover, in the end, she wrote 1000 more words than assigned.

The classification of data was another area of concern. While the categories and sub-categories described above may appear straightforward, the reality was much cloudier. In effect, distinguishing between formulating, evaluating and revising was challenging because the three often overlapped with two of the processes happening simultaneously. During Andrea's composing process she would sometimes suddenly stop composing, and delete, and then revise in the middle of a sentence; yet these behaviors had to be categorized differently. As noted by Roca de Larios *et al.* (2001), differentiating between processes is sometimes difficult and can best be overcome by a continuous refining of definitions. From a broader perspective, the difficulty experienced in distinguishing among processes only serves to **underscore** the complexity and **recursion** that exists as text is generated.

5. Conclusion

In ancient times, the transition from using bronze chisels for carving **hieroglyphs** on clay to **reed** brushes and ink for drawing characters on **papyrus** must have been **momentous**. Carving speciafists must have given way to new experts who could convey ideas in symbols much more quickly with fingers **deft** in different ways. The composing processes of the authors able to make the switch from clay to papyrus probably witnessed significant change. The few literati surely appreciated the efficiency and **portability**. As for the composing process, perhaps the increased speed at which symbols could be drawn cognitively taxed formulation when compared with the leisurely carving of clay. We can only speculate.

Likewise, the present decline in the teaching of **cursive** writing (Breen, 2009; Hallows, 2009) with the concurrent transition to an electronic composing environment may be equally momentous. As Microsoft announced upon the **demise** of their online encyclopedia, Encarta: "People today seek and consume information in considerably different ways than in years past" (Stross, 2009). A similar comment may be made about the cognitive processes used to generate and express ideas in written language.

The present study has taken the case approach using a log, questionnaire and interviews and demonstrated that such methods may be used for following the composing process over time. Future studies into the composing processes of writers may wish to employ larger samples using different methods. Whatever the methodology, efforts should be made to capture those processes in a way which best reflects how authors compose in real-life situations that appreciate the context, time and technology as they are presently used.

References

Bereiter; C., & Scardamalia, M. (1987). *The psychology of written composition.* Mahwah: Lawrence Erlbaum.

Bieen, T. (2009, Sept. 21). Caisive writing: a fading skill. *Discovery News.* Retrieved from http://dsc. discovery.com/news/2009/09/21/cursive-writing.html.

Buck, A. M. (2008). The invisible interface: MS word in the writing center. *Computers and Composition, 25,* 396–415.

Cumming, A. (1990). Met a linguistic and ideational thinking in second language composing. *Written Communication, 7,* 482–511.

de Guerrero, M. C. M., & Villamil, O. S. (1994). Social-cognitive dimensions of interaction in L2 peer revision. *The Modern Language Journal, 78,* 484–496.

Dolmans, D., Schmidt, A., van del Beck, J., Beintema, M., & Gerver, W. J. (1999). Does a student log provide a means to better structure clinical education? *Medical Education, 33,* 89–94.

Dornyei, Z. (2007). *Research methods in applied linguistics.* Oxford: Oxford University Press.

Duff, P. (2008). *Case study research in applied linguistics.* New York: Lawrence Erlbaum and Associates.

Emig, J. (1971). *The composing processes of twelfth graders.* Urbana: National Council of Teachers of English.

Flower, L., & Hayes, J. R. (1981). A cognitive process theory of writing. *College Composition and Communication, 32,* 365–387.

Flowerdew, L. (2002). Corpus-based analyses in EAP. In J. Flowerdew (ed.), *Academic discourse* (pp.95–114). Harlow: Longman.

Gaskell, D., & Cobb, T. (2004). Can learners use concordance feedback for writing errors? *System, 32,* 301–319.

Gibson, V. (1995). An analysis of the use of diaries as a data-collection method. *Nurse Researcher, 3,* 66–73.

Hafner, C. A., & Candlin C. N. (2007). Corpus tools as an affordance to learning in professional legal education. *Journal of English for Academic Purposes, 6,* 303–318.

Hallows, N. (2009, Feb. 26). The slow death of handwriting. *BBC News.* Retrieved from http://news.bbc. co.uk/2/ifi/7907888.stm.

Helms-Paik, R., Radia, P., & Stapleton P. (2007). A preliminary assessment of Google Scholar as a source of EAP students' research materials. *The Internet and Higher Education, 10,* 65–76.

Johns, A. (1991). Interpreting an English competency examination: the frusrations of an ESL science student. *Written Communication, 8,* 379–401.

Keck, C. (2006). The use of paraphrase in summary writing: a comparison of L1 and L2 writers. *Journal of Second Language Writing, 15,* 261–278.

Kellogg, R. T. (1987). Effects of topic knowledge on the allocation of processing time and cognitive effort to writing. *Memory and Cognition, 15,* 256–266.

Lee, D., & Swales, J. (2006). A corpus-based EAP course for NNS doctoral students: moving from available specialized corpora to self-compiled corpora. *English for Specific Purposes, 25,* 56–75.

Lindgren, E., & Sullivan, K. P. H. (2003). Stimulated recall as a trigger for increasing noticing and language awareness in the L2 writing classroom: a case study of two young female writers. *Language Awareness, 12,* 172–186.

Liu, D., & Jiang, P. (2009). Using a corpus-based lexicogrammatical approach to grammar instruaction in EFL and ESL contexts. *The Modern Language Journal, 93,* 61–78.

McCarthy, L. P., & Walvoord, B. E. (2008). Research methods and theory. In B. E. Walvoord, & L. P. McCarthy (eds.), *Thinking and writing in college: a naturalistic study of students in four disciplines* (pp.17–49). WAC Clearinghouse Landmark Publications in Writing Studies. Retrieved Sept. 28, 2009, from: http://wac.colostate.edu/books/thinkingwritnig/.

McGee, T., & Ericsson, P. (2002). The politics of the program: MS word as the invisible grammarian. *Computers and Composition, 19,* 453–470.

Miuer, K. S. (2000). Academic writers on-line: investigating pausing in the production of text. *Language Teaching Research, 4,* 123–148.

Milton, J. (2006). Resource-rich web-based feedback: helping learners become independent writers. In K. Hyland, & F. Hyland (eds.), *Feedback in second language writing: contexts and issues* (pp.123–139). Cambridge: Cambridge University Press.

O'Sullivan, I., & Chambers, A. (2006). Learners' writing skills in French: corpus consultation and learner evaluation. *Journal of Second Language Writing, 15,* 49–68.

Pecorari, D. (2003). Good and original: plagiarism and patchwriting in academic second-language writing. *Journal of Second Language Writing, 12,* 317–345.

Pennington, M., & So, S. (1993). Comparing writing process and product across two languages: a study of 6 Singaporean university student writers. *Journal of Second Language Writing, 2,* 41–63.

Perl, S. (1980). Understanding composing. *College Composition and Communication, 31,* 363–369.

Prior, P. A. (1998). *Writing disciplinarity: a sociohistoric account of literate activity in the academy.* Mahwah: Lawrence Erlbaum Associates.

Radia, P., & Stapleton, P. (2008). Unconventional Internet genres and their impact on second language undergraduate students' writing process. *The Internet and Higher Education, 11,* 9–17.

Raimes, A. (1985). What unskilled ESL students do as they write: a classroom study of composing. *TESOL Quarterly, 19,* 229–258.

Riazi, A. (1997). Acquiring disciplinary literacy: a social-cognitive analysis of text production and learning among Iranian graduate students of education. *Journal of Second Language Writing, 6,* 105–137.

Richards, K. (2003). *Qualitative inquiry in TENOL.* New York: Palgrave.

Roca de Larios, J., Mancho'n, R. M., & Murphy, L. (2006). Generating text in native and foreign language writing: a temporal analysis of problem-solving formulation processes. *The Modern Language Journal, 90,* 100–114.

Roca de Larios, J., Mancho'n, R. M., Murphy, L., & Marin, J. (2008). The foreign language writer's strategic behavior in the allocation of time to writing processes. *Journal of Second Language Writing, 17,* 30–47.

Roca de Larios, J., Marin, J., & Murphy, L. (2001). A temporal analysis of formulation processes in L1 and L2 writing. *Language Learning, 51,* 497–538.

Roca de Larios, J., Murphy, L., & Mancho'n, R. M. (1999). The use of restructuring strategies in EFL writing: a study of Spanish learners of English as a foreign language. *Journal of Second Language Writing, 8,* 13–44.

Sasaki, M. (2000). Toward an empirical model of EFL writing processes: an exploratory study. *Journal of*

Second Language Writing, 9, 259–291.

Sasaki, M. (2004). A multiple-data analysis of the 3.5-year development of EFL student writers. *Language Learning, 54,* 525–582.

Sasaki, M., & Hirose, K. (1996). Explanatory variables for EFL students' expository writing. *Language Learning, 46,* 137–174.

Silva, T. (1993). Toward an undertanding of the distinct nature of L2 writing: the ESL research and its implications. *TESOL Quarterly, 27,* 657–677.

Smagorinsky, P. (2001). Rethinking protocol analysis from a cultural perspective. *Annual Review of Applied Linguistics, 21,* 233–245.

Smagorinsky, P. (2008). The method section as conceptual epicenter in constructing social science research reports. *Written Communication, 25,* 389 411.

Spack, R. (1997). The acquisition of academic literacy in a second language: a longitudinal case study. *Written Communication, 14,* 3–62.

Stapleton, P., & Helms-Paik, R. (2006). Evaluating Web sources in an EAP course: introducing a multi-trait instrument for feedback and assessment. *English for Specific Purposes, 25,* 438–455.

Strauss, A. L., & Corbin J. (1998). *Basics of qualitative research: techniques and procedures for developing grounded theory* (2nd ed.). Thousand Oaks: Sage.

Stross, R. (2009, May 2). Encyclopedic knowledge: then vs. now. *The New York Times.* Retrieved from: http://www.nytimes.com/2009/05/03/business/03digi.html? ref=technology.

Sun, Y. C., & Wang, L. Y. (2003). Concordancers in the EFL classroom: cognitive approaches and collocation difficulty. *Computer Assisted Language Learning, 16,* 83–94.

Tardy, C. M. (2009). *Building genre knowledge.* West Lafayette: Parlor Press.

Vygotsky, L. S. (1987). Thinking and speech. N. Minick, Trans.. In R. Rieber, & A. Carton (eds.), *L.S. Vygotsky, Collected works, Vol. 1* (pp. 39–285). Retrieved from http://books.google.comllbooks?id=u8UTfKFWb5UC&pg=PA282&dp=PA282&dq="mediates+thought+in+its+path+to+ver-bal+expression."&source=bl&ots=VA-rtGZK5Y&sig=r4WF5hgfR6OiymcQS15PGZpX56s&l=en&ei=UKUgS9v9EsqGkAWT6OhiCg&sa=X&oi=book_result&ct=result&result&resmum=1&ved=0CAoQ6AEwAA#v=onepage&q=%22meAimes%20thought%20hl%20its%20path%20to%20vmbal%20expression.%22&f=false.

Wang, Y. M., & Artero, M. (2005). Caught in the web: university student use of web resources. *Educational Media International, 42,* 71–82.

Wang, W., & Wen, Q. (2002). L1 use in the L2 composing. *Journal of Second Language Writing, 77,* 225–246.

Wired Campus. (2006, June 12). Wikipedia founder discourages academic use of his creation. *The Chronicle of Higher Education.* Retrieved from http://chiolaicle.com/wirededcampus/milcle/1328/wikipediafounder-discounages-academic-use-of-his-creation.

Yi, Y. (2007). Engaging literacy: a biliterate student's composing practices beyond school. *Journal of Second Language Writing, 16,* 23–39.

Yi, Y. & Hirvela, A. (2010). Technology and "self-sponsored" writing: a case study of a Korean-American adolescent. *Computers and Composition, 27,* 94–111.

Yin, R. (2003). *Applications of case study research* (2nd ed.). Thousand Oaks: Sage.

Zamel, V. (1982). Writing: the process of discovering meaning. *TESOL Quarterly, 16,* 195–209.

Zamel, V. (1983). The composing processes of advanced ESL students: six case studies. *TESOL Quarterly, 17,* 165–187.

New Words

allocation	[ˌæləˈkeiʃn]	n.	配给，分配
allotment	[əˈlɔtmənt]	n.	分配；分配物；养家费；命运
axial	[ˈæksil]	a.	轴的；轴向的
benchmark	[ˈbentʃmɑːk]	n.	基准；标准检查程序
bound	[baund]	a.	有义务的；受约束的；装有封面的
		n.	范围
built-in	[ˈbiltˈin]	a.	嵌入的；固定的
		n.	内置
bypass	[ˈbaipɑːs]	vt.	绕开；忽视；设旁路；迂回
		n.	旁路；支路
caveat	[ˈkæviæt]	n.	警告；中止诉讼手续的申请
concordancer	[kənˈkɔːdənsə]	n.	语词检索；关键词排序的程式
concurrent	[kənˈkʌrənt]	a.	并发的；一致的；同时发生的
constraint	[kənˈstreint]	n.	约束；局促，态度不自然；强制
cursive	[ˈkɜːsiv]	a.	草书的；草书体的
deft	[deft]	a.	灵巧的；机敏的；敏捷熟练的
deliberate	[diˈlibərət]	v.	仔细考虑；商议
delineate	[diˈlinieit]	vt.	描绘；描写；画……的轮廓
demise	[diˈmaiz]	n.	转让；死亡，终止；传位
dovetail	[ˈdʌvteil]	v.	与……吻合
dubious	[ˈdjuːbjəs]	a.	可疑的；暧昧的；无把握的；半信半疑的
efficacy	[ˈefikəsi]	n.	功效，效力
embark	[imˈbɑːk; em-]	v.	从事，着手
emulate	[ˈemjuleit]	vt.	仿真；模仿；尽力赶上；同……竞争
encapsulate	[inˈkæpsjuleit]	v.	压缩；将……装入胶囊；将……封进内部
fastidious	[fæˈstidiəs]	a.	挑剔的；苛求的，难取悦的
feasibility	[ˌfiːzəˈbiləti]	n.	可行性；可能性
generic	[dʒəˈnerik]	a.	类的；一般的；属的；非商标的
heterogeneous	[ˌhetərəˈdʒiːniəs]	a.	不均匀的；由不同成分形成的
hieroglyph	[ˈhaiərəglif]	n.	象形文字；图画文字；秘密符号
impediment	[imˈpedimənt]	n.	口吃；妨碍；阻止

intrusive	[in'tru:siv]	a.	侵入的；打扰的
laminated	['læmineitid]	a.	层压的；层积的；薄板状的
locale	[ləu'kæl]	n.	场所，现场
log	[lɔg]	n.	记录；航行日志
longitudinal	[lɔndʒi'tju:dinl]	a.	经度的，纵向的
logistical	[lə'dʒistikl]	a.	后勤方面的；运筹的，逻辑的
mentor	['mentɔ:]	n.	指导者，良师益友
metalinguistic	['metəliŋgwistik]	a.	元语言的；纯理语言的
momentous	[mə'mentəs]	a.	重要的；重大的
neurological	[ˌnjuərə'lɔdʒikl]	a.	神经病学的，神经学上的
notable	['nəutəbl]	a.	值得注意的，显著的；著名的
nuanced	['nju:ɑ:nst]	a.	微妙的；具有细微差别的
papyrus	[pə'pairəs]	n.	纸莎草；纸莎草纸
phonics	['fɔniks]	n.	声学；声音基础教学法
portability	[ˌpɔ:tə'biləti]	n.	轻便；可携带性
preclude	[pri'klu:d]	vt.	排除；妨碍；阻止
presumably	[pri'zju:məbli]	adv.	据推测，大概，可能
prompt	[prʌmpt]	n.	提示
		vt.	提示；促进；激起；（给演员）提白
		a.	敏捷的，迅速的；立刻的
provisional	[prə'viʒənl]	a.	临时的，暂时的；暂定的
recursion	[ri'kɜ:ʃn]	n.	递归，循环；递归式
recursive	[ri'kɜ:siv]	a.	递归的；循环的
reed	[ri:d]	n.	芦苇；簧片；牧笛；不可依靠的人
replete	[ri'pli:t]	a.	充满的；装满的
respective	[ri'spektiv]	a.	各自的，分别的
retrieval	[ri'tri:vl]	n.	检索；恢复；取回；拯救
retrospective	[ˌretrə'spektiv]	a.	回顾的，怀旧的
rigor	['rigə]	n.	精确；严厉；苛刻；僵硬
rigorous	['rigərəs]	a.	严厉的；严格的；严密的；严酷的
rubric	['ru:brik]	n.	题目；红字标题；红色印刷
scenario	[si'neəri:ˌəu]	n.	（行动的）方案，剧情概要

schema	['ski:mə]	n.	模式；计划；图解；概要
seminal	['seminl]	a.	种子的
subsume	[səb'sju:m]	vt.	把……归入；把……包括在内
tabulate	['tæbjuleit]	vt.	把……制成表格
temporally	['tempərəli]	adv.	时间地，短暂地
tertiary	['tɜ:ʃəri]	a.	高等的；第三的；第三位的；三代的
thesaurus	[θi'sɔ:rəs]	n.	同义词词典，百科全书
underachieve	[ˌʌndərə'tʃi:v]	vi.	学习成绩不良，未能发挥学习潜能
underscore	[ˌʌndə'skɔ:]	vt.	强调；划线于……下
undertake	[ˌʌndə'teik]	vt.	承担，保证；从事；同意；试图
undertaking	[ˌʌndə'teikiŋ]	n.	事业；企业；保证；殡仪业
venue	['venju:]	n.	审判地；犯罪地点；发生地点；集合地点

Phrases

a string of	一系列，一串
in a sitting	一次
shed light on	阐明；使……清楚地显出
in turn	轮流，依次
grow out of	产生于
derive from	起源于，来源于
on one's part	就某人而言，在某人方面
jot down	草草记下，匆匆记下
be stuck with	突然产生
at intervals	时时；不时；相隔一定距离（或时间）
keep abreast	并行

Discussion Ideas

1. What do you think of the saying "Writing is rewriting"?

2. Process approach in writing holds that writing is a nonlinear process, which includes a string of processes such as pre-writing, drafting, revising, editing, and publishing. Whereas product writing focuses on writing tasks in which the learner imitates, copies and transforms (See Supplementary Reading in this unit). Which

approach are you more familiar with? What do you think of the advantages and disadvantages of each approach?

3. What is a case study? What are advantages and drawbacks of a case study?

4. In the first sentence of the second paragraph (Methods), the author mentions "highly-controlled settings", what do you think they are like? And what is the opposite of highly-controlled settings?

5. What instruments were used in this study?

6. Recount Andrea's research experience in 3.2.1, what can you learn from her experience?

7. What belong to the word- to multi-paragraph-level of writing, refer to Andrea's revising process (3.2.6) and use examples to illustrate them.

8. What practical implications can you draw from this study?

Vocabulary and Language Learning Skills

1. Word Building

Fill in the table with more words with the same affixes.

Prefix	Meaning	Words Appeared in the Paper	Examples
under-	under, beneath	undertake, understand, underscore, undergraduate, underachieving	
over-	above, across, beyond	overcome, overview, overstatement, overuse, overlap	

Use the information given above to guess the meaning of the words in the table.

Word	Meaning
underemployment	
underestimate	
underlie	
undermine	
underpin	
overcharge	
overcoat	
overcrowded	
overestimate	
overthrow	

2. Recognizing Word Meanings

For each group, underline the word or phrase that does not belong. The words in italics are vocabulary items from the paper.

1)	edit	*revise*	adapt	modify
2)	*undertaking*	task	operation	underline
3)	discover	*expose*	disclose	*reveal*
4)	following	later	*subsequent*	successive
5)	*sufficient*	enough	adequate	efficient
6)	contribute	assign	distribute	*allocate*
7)	major	*principal*	principle	main
8)	apply	supply	*employ*	use
9)	*dubious*	doubtful	questionable	certain
10)	consider	*deem*	think	redeem
11)	basis	primate	*rudimentary*	fundamental
12)	unnecessary	whole	full	*integral*

3. Making a Collocation

Use the vocabulary items in the box to complete the sentences. Make changes if necessary.

prompt	seminal	bound
accordingly	convert	tertiary
constrain	shed	eliminate
notable	embark	feasible

1) As an economist, he was able to _____ some light on the problem.

2) More than 60% of American high school graduates start some form of _____ education.

3) She's an expert in her field, and is paid _____.

4) They _____ the spare bedroom into an office.

5) They are conducting a study on new TOEFL CBT writing _____.

6) It has _____ differences from traditional CBT.

7) We're looking at the _____ of building a shopping centre there.

8) He _____ on a new career as a teacher.

9) She wrote a _____ article on the subject while she was still a student.

10) You're _____ to feel nervous about your interview.

11) This paper presents a new model for multi-issue negotiation under time _____ in an incomplete information setting.

12) We eventually found the answer by a process of _____.

Writing Focus

Presentation

Function

Presentation is the practice of showing and explaining the content of a topic to an audience. Presentations take many forms on academic occasions such as courses, seminars, workshops, conferences, and meetings, etc.

Style

Presentation involves skills and endeavor. The following strategies introduce some useful moves in this respect.

Move 1 Prepare your presentation

- Know four Ws—what, why, who, where, and an H
  - What—what is your subject
  - Why—why are you giving this talk
  - Who—who will be your audience
  - Where—Where will you be giving your presentation
  - How—how long do you have for the presentation
- Structure your presentation with opening, body and summary
  - Opening
    - Greet your audience
    - Briefly introduce yourself
    - Check everyone can see and hear you
    - State your purpose
    - Introduce the subject
    - Give an outline
  - Body
    - Explain the main points of your research: research questions, literature review, methods, results and discussion, etc.

- ■ Summary
  - ◆ Briefly summarize what you have said
  - ◆ Leave the audience a parting shot to stimulate their thoughts
- Write a script of your presentation if necessary
- Prepare visual aids (PowerPoint slides, handouts, video clips, etc.) to reinforce your presentation
- Use questions sparingly

Move 2 Practice your presentation

- Avoid reading from your script
- Use cue cards if necessary
- Rehearse on your own or with friends
- Time your presentation
- Dress properly
- Arrive before time and check the resolution, fonts, colors, transitions, animation, graphics, etc.
- Breathe slowly and deeply if you are nervous

Move 3 Give your presentation

- Pose yourself confidently
- Greet your audience heartily
- Maintain eye contact with your audience
- Avoid reading from your script or the PowerPoint slides
- Speak slowly, clearly, loudly and confidently
- Smile even if you make an error
- Ignore distractions
- Thank your audience for their interest and patience

Task One

Have you given a presentation before? If yes, what were your problems? If not, what are your major concerns?

Task Two

Identify the positive and negative features of the following slides using the results of Task One.

Some factors in European exploration of 15th and 16th centuries

- Much of the exploration by Europeans was motivated *by the desire to find faster trade routes*. Several governments negotiated <u>treaties so that their nations could trade in other countries</u>. In addition, the **population grew rapidly,** creating an increased demand for food. Among the workforce, there was a trend towards developing a particular expertise. With growing wealth, there was *a demand for gold and other precious metals,* some of which was turned into coins and used for buying and selling. Probably even more prized at this time were spices, which were used for preserving and flavouring meats.

Some factors in European exploration of 15th and 16th centuries

- desire to find better routes to use when trading
- need for states to sign treaties permitting trade
- need for food for increasing population
- necessity for increasing specialisation of workforce
- need for raw materials for production of coins
- need for various spices to use in cooking

Some <u>FACTORS</u> in European exploration of 15th and 16th centuries

- desire to find better routes to use when trading
- need for states to sign treaties permitting trade
- need for food for increasing population
- necessity for increasing specialisation of workforce
- need for raw materials for production of coins
- need for various spices to use in cooking

Task Three

Give a presentation on your research project, using a PowerPoint document to reinforce your presentation.

Integration of Process and Product Orientations in EFL Writing Instruction

Taeko Kamimura

Senshu University, Japan

Abstract

This study investigated whether product-oriented knowledge and composing process skills are both necessary or whether either one of the two is sufficient in order for EFL students to become skilled writers in EFL. Thirty-five Japanese college EFL students participated in the study as subjects. First, they wrote an argumentative essay, and immediately after finishing it, they were given a retrospective questionnaire designed to probe their composing process strategies. They also took a form-based test which assessed their knowledge of English academic texts. The students were classified into two groups, skilled and unskilled, according to the holistic scores given to their essays. The two groups were compared in terms of the behaviors shown in the questionnaire and the scores on the test. The results showed that the skilled writers possessed more developed knowledge of formal aspects of English academic writing as well as more sophisticated composing process strategies. It was also clarified that both the form-oriented knowledge and process-oriented skills are necessary to function as successful EFL writers. The study suggests that L2 writing instruction should maintain a balance between process and product orientations to meet the needs of various L2 writers who come from non-English discourse communities.

Introduction

With Emig's pioneering study in the composing processes of 12th graders in 1977, writing research in English as a first language (L1) shifted its focus from the product to the process approach, and since then several subsequent L1 researchers have attempted process-centered studies. Some of them focused upon a specific component of the composing process: for example, Sommers (1980), Bridwell (1980), and Faigley and Witte (1981) conducted research centered on the revising process. Others, such as Perl (1979)

and Pianko (1979), elucidated several characteristics of student writers' composing processes. By putting together the findings of various studies, Flower and Hayes (1980a, 1980b, 1981) established a comprehensive cognitive process model of writing.

Influenced by such a development in the L1 writing research field, ESL/EFL writing researchers also began to undertake studies from the process perspective. Zamel, for example, was representative of those process-oriented ESL writing researchers. In a series of case studies (1982, 1983), she examined the composing processes of ESL students and found that their processes were on the whole similar in nature to those of native English-speaking students. According to her (1983), ESL students' writing was not influenced by their linguistic proficiency nor by their L1 rhetorical conventions.

As the process orientation gained primacy in ESL/EFL writing, attention to product, including both linguistic and rhetorical forms, began to be criticized. The process and product orientations were often conceived of as a dichotomy, which led to a series of heated debates. Researchers who challenged the primacy of process orientations were mainly those who advocated contrastive rhetoric and EAP (English for academic purposes).

For instance, Reid (1984) argues that Zamel's implications in her 1983 study with heavy emphasis on writing as a meaning-making process could only account for her "advanced" students with sophisticated language proficiency, but not for inexperienced ESL writers who comprise the majority of the total ESL population. She also maintains that Zamel's criticism against contrastive rhetoric as "predictions that are hypothetical and consequently not necessarily accurate" is not justified, when considering the recent growing body of research in this field. She further insisted that inexperienced ESL writers need "rhetorical acculturation" by saying as follows:

> Inexperienced and unskilled ESL writers who have not been exposed to rhetorical analyses of American academic prose need to develop their understanding of the forms of academic prose, and they need to have the opportunity to practice those formats... [because] their approaches to rhetorical forms differ from the approach of native speakers (Reid, 1984: 151).

Another line of debate was initiated by Horowitz (1986a, b, c) from the viewpoint of writing in EAP. Horowitz argues that process proponents are so obsessed with the writer's internal mental processes involving the "psycholinguistic, cognitive, and affective variables" (1986b: 446) that they fail to "provide any clear perspective on the social nature of writing: the conventions, regularities, genres, requirements, typical task types, etc" (1986c: 788). According to Horowitz, Zamel's contention that "decisions about form and organization only make sense with reference to the particular ideas being expressed"

(1993: 181) is based on an "erroneous assumption" which holds that "writers work in a cultural vacuum" (1986b: 447). Horowitz further maintains that the process advocates' overemphasis on individual differences and creativity reduces teaching into "humanistic therapy". But the teacher's responsibility, says Horowitz, should lie in socializing students into the academic community which dictates "a specified range of acceptable writing behaviors" (1986c: 789).

The notion of "discourse community", as was introduced by Horowitz, became popular among L1 writing researchers during the 1980's (e.g., Bartholomae, 1982) and what was termed the "social constructivist approach" to writing (Connor, 1996) emerged. With the emphasis on the role of social context in composing, renewed interest in linguistic and rhetorical conventions in different discourse communities has grown. Such a socially-oriented approach to composing in L1 influenced L2 writing and gained popularity among ESL writing researchers and instructors (e.g., Swales, 1990). Classifying the process approaches into two categories, i.e., the "expressionist" and the "cognitive", Connor (1996: 74), as a contrastive rhetorician, states that "it seems safe to say that the expressionist approach to writing about oneself is not fruitful by itself." Also Grabe and Kaplan (1996: 173) claim that "it remains highly unlikely that the unmodified 'process approach' to teaching composition will prove to be sufficient." It seems, therefore, that in theory, the role of textual forms and conventions has been revitalized from a new perspective derived from the notion of discourse community.

The empirical ESL/EFL writing research, however, has presented controversial findings as to the relative importance of process-based composing skills and product-based textual knowledge in ESL/EFL students' writing development. Hirose and Sasaki conducted two studies (1994, 1996) to explore the explanatory variables for EFL students' expository writing. In their 1994 study, they found that their good Japanese EFL writers manifested writing strategies identified as those employed by the good writers in the past L1 and ESL/EFL process writing research. Those strategies involved "planning content, paying attention to content and overall organization while writing, and revising at the discourse level" (Hirose and Sasaki, 1994: 218). In their subsequent study (1996), however, they found that the composing processes of skilled Japanese EFL students differed from those of their unskilled counterparts only in terms of their concern with overall organization before and while writing. Concerning form, their 1994 study demonstrated the relatively negligible contribution of the students' metaknowledge of English texts in explaining the scores given to their expository essays in EFL, whereas in their 1997 study such metaknowledge exhibited a significantly explanatory power.

These mixed results suggest the need of "continued efforts to investigate issues of process and product in a variety of L2 contexts" (Pennington and So, 1993: 58) and to "search for a descriptive model which will allow us to reconcile the 'product approach' and the 'process approach'" (Hamp-Lyons, 1986: 794). The present study was conducted to probe if such reconciliation is possible in a context of EFL writing classrooms in Japan.

Purpose of the study

The purpose of the present study is to examine what roles Japanese EFL students' product-based metaknowledge of English academic texts and process-based composing skills in EFL play in their argumentative writing performance in EFL. More specifically, the study posed the following research questions:

1. What differences can be observed between skilled and unskilled Japanese EFL writers in terms of their knowledge of formal aspects of English academic text?
2. What composing strategies differentiate skilled from unskilled Japanese EFL writers?
3. In order for Japanese students to become skilled writers in EFL, are both the developed textual knowledge and sophisticated composing skills in EFL needed, or is either one of the two sufficient?

Method

Subjects

A total of 50 students in two classes of Composition I participated in the present study as subjects. They were college freshmen majoring in English at a four-year university in Japan. They had studied English for at least six years through formal English instruction provided at Japanese secondary schools, and none of them had lived in English-speaking countries. The students participated in two sessions, as described below. Their English proficiency level was considered as intermediate, ranging from 273 to 141 points as assessed by *CELT* (*A Comprehensive English Language Test for Learners of English*) (Harris and Palmer, 1986). Some of the students missed one of the two sessions, and those students were excluded from the study. The remaining 35 students served as final subjects.

Procedure

Two sessions were conducted, with a two-week interval between the two sessions. Figure 1 shows the experimental design.

First Session (Text-Knowledge Test)

↓   2 weeks

Second Session (Argumentative Essay Writing & Retrospective Composing Process Questionnaire)

Figure 1. Experimental design

The first session was designed to assess the students' metaknowledge of formal aspects of English academic writing. The second was conducted to collect their writing samples as well as data on their writing processes.

a) First session

In the first session, the students were given a "Text-Knowledge Test" (henceforth called a TK Test). This test was devised by consulting several ESL/EFL writing textbooks, such as *Introduction to Academic Writing* and *Academic Writing* by Oshima & Hogue (1988), *Paragraph Development* by Arnaudet & Barrett (1990). Sample questions are presented in Appendix A.

The test consisted of five different sections, each of which had a specific target to be assessed. The first section had questions asking some general characteristics of an English paragraph and essay. For instance, the students were given a statement such as "A paragraph consists of sentences which state one main idea", and asked if the statement was true or false.

The second section examined the students' knowledge of the concept "unity". In this section, they were told to read a paragraph and delete a sentence that would break the unity of the entire paragraph.

The questions in the third section asked the students to rearrange scrambled sentences into a logical order and to choose one sentence as an appropriate topic sentence. This section aimed at testing the students' knowledge of "coherence".

The target point in the fourth section was "cohesion". The students were told to provide appropriate transition words to make a logical tie between sentences or clauses.

In the last section, the students were given a pair of passages and told to choose the one which would be more appropriate as an English paragraph and to state the reason for their choice. This section was more comprehensive than the other four, in that it was designed to assess the students' ability to integrate the individual skills covered in the preceding four sections.

b) Second session

In the second session, the students were first told to write an argumentative essay in 40 minutes without using a dictionary. The writing prompt was as follows:

> Mr. Brown, a teacher at ABC High School in the U.S., has been wondering if his school should adopt school uniforms. Since most American high schools are not familiar with school uniforms, he asked for your opinion from the viewpoint of a student in Japan, where school uniforms are very popular. Your job is to write a report to Mr. Brown. The question he asked you was: "What do you think of school uniforms? Are you for or against them?"

Immediately after writing the essay, the students were given a "Retrospective Composing Process Questionnaire" (henceforth called the questionnaire) to investigate their composing processes in this specific task. In devising the questionnaire, the present study consulted Hirose and Sasaki (1994) and Sasaki and Hirose (1996), but expanded their idea and developed a more detailed version.

Like the studies by Hirose and Sasaki (1994, 1996), this study used a questionnaire consisting of three parts: "pre-writing", "while-writing", and "post-writing" (see Appendix B). Admitting that composing, as Flower and Hayes (1981) point out, is actually a recursive process where idea-generating, translating and revising constantly appear and reappear, the three-part division was posed for the sake of convenience to probe the students' planning, writing, and revising behaviors.

The section "pre-writing" asked the students whether they planned before actually beginning to write, and if so, what and how they planned. The section "while-writing" asked them whether they relied on Japanese, tried to write a lot, and hesitated while writing. It also asked them while writing, what textual features they paid attention to, ranging from content to spelling/punctuation. The "post-writing" section asked them whether they reread and revised their essay, and if so, on what textual features they reread and revised.

Scoring

Each student's score on the TK test was calculated, with 100 points as perfect scores. Also, each student's essay was rated holistically by two experienced EFL writing instructors on a scale from one to six, with six being the highest score. One rater had taught EFL composition at a four-year university in Japan for nine years, while the other had taught EFL writing at Japanese high school for two years. The interrater reliability was r=81. When disagreement occurred, the two raters discussed their judgements until they reached full agreement.

The data on the retrospective composing questionnaire were analyzed by assigning a numerical value to each item by referring to the criteria established by the findings of the past process-oriented studies in L1 and ESL/EFL. For instance, composing strategies such as planning before writing and paying attention to content, audience, and organization throughout the entire composing process have been judged to be higher-order skills by most previous process studies in L1 (Pianko, 1979) and ESL/EFL (Zamel, 1983, 1984). On the other hand, the heavy focus on surface features like spelling and mechanics while writing and revising have been regarded as characteristics of unskilled writers (Perl, 1979; Pianko, 1979; Zamel, 1983, 1984). Therefore, if the students marked "Yes" in Question 8A in the "post-writing" section, that is, if they answered, "I paid attention to content when rereading my composition," they were given 3 points. On the other hand, if the students said "Yes" in Question 8F by saying "I paid attention to spelling/punctuation", they were given only 1 point. The present researcher and one of the raters who conducted holistic scoring held thorough discussions until they reached full agreement about how many points should be assigned to each question. The point assigned to an affirmative answer to each question is presented in Appendix C.

Data analysis

The students were classified into two groups, skilled and unskilled, according to the holistic scores given to their essays. Sixteen students whose essays scored 5 or 6 points were categorized as "skilled", while 19 students whose essays scored 1 or 2 points were classified as "unskilled". The two groups were compared in respect to the scores on the TK test and the questionnaire.

Results and discussion

TK Test

Table 1 shows the mean scores on the TK test total and each section in the test. *T-tests* were administered to examine whether there were any statistically significant differences between the skilled and unskilled writers.

Table 1. Mean scores on the TK Test

Section	Group		
	Skilled (n=16)	Unskilled (n=19)	
	Mean	Mean	t
Section 1	24.00	19.47	2.89**
Section 2	8.75	6.32	1.91
Section 3	9.50	3.47	4.55**
Section 4	15.19	6.00	4.84**
Section 5	8.56	6.37	1.47
Total	66.00	41.63	5.03**

*p<.05, **p<.01

Statistically significant differences between the two groups were observed for the scores on Section 1, 3, 4, and the test total, but not for the scores on Section 2 and Section

5. These results suggest that the skilled writers had much more developed textual knowledge of English academic writing than the unskilled writers. The skilled writers superseded their unskilled counterparts in the knowledge of various characteristics of an English paragraph and essay (as assessed in Section 1), coherence (as assessed in Section 3), and cohesion by the use of transition words (as assessed in Section 4). It was anticipated that the good writers would score high on Section 5 which asked the students to choose a more appropriate English paragraph and thus required more comprehensive, integrated textual knowledge. However, the two groups did not differ in this section. This might indicate that it is rather difficult for intermediate Japanese EFL students to apply such separate textual concepts as unity, cohesion and coherence in an integrated manner in judging an English paragraph of better quality.

Retrospective composing process questionnaire

Table 2 displays the mean scores of the skilled and unskilled writers on the questionnaire and the results of a t-test employed to see whether there was any statistical difference between the two groups.

Table 2. Mean score on the questionnaire

Group		
Skilled (n=16)	Unskilled (n=19)	t-value
42.50	17.89	2.16*

The results showed that compared with the unskilled writers, the skilled group used composing strategies identified as more sophisticated in the past process-oriented studies.

To observe more detailed differences between the two groups of writers, they were compared in terms of each question in the questionnaire. Table 3 shows the percentage of the subjects in each group who answered "Yes" on each of the questions.

Chi-square tests were used to examine whether there were any statistically significant differences between the two groups.[1] As Table 3 indicates, the results of the tests showed significant differences in questions 1A ($x = 7.296$, $p <.01$), 1B ($x = 4.804$, $p <.05$), and 2B ($x = 4.610$, $p <.05$) in the "pre-writing" section, and 8A ($x = 6.302$, $p <.05$), 8B ($x = 6.909$, $p <.01$), 8C ($x = 6.408$, $p <.05$), and 8F ($x = 6.239$, $p <.05$) in the "post-writing" section." That is, a greater number of the skilled writers planned content (87.5%) and organization (68.75%) before actually beginning to write than the unskilled writers (36.84% for content and 31.58% for organization). The skilled writers also tended to make outlines (31.25%), whereas none of the unskilled writers did.

The two groups did not differ in terms of behaviors while actually writing. However,

they differed in four categories in post-writing activities: a larger number of skilled
writers reread their essays by paying attention to content, audience, organization, and
spelling/punctuation. The better writers, therefore, tended to consider simultaneously
both high-order textual features such as content, audience and organization and lower-
order features such as spelling and punctuation (68.75% of the skilled writers vs. 26.32%
of the unskilled writers for content, 50% vs. 5.26% for audience; 75% vs. 26.32% for
organization, and 68.75% vs. 21.05% for spelling/punctuation). Thus, it seems that planning
and rereading behaviors are important factors which could differentiate skilled from
unskilled writers.

**Table 3. Number of skilled and unskilled writers who demonstrated each composing
behavior in the questionnaire**

Composing behavior		Skilled (n=16)	Unskilled (n=19)	x^2
Pre-writing	1A	14 (87.5 %)	7 (36.84%)	7.296**
	1B	11 (68.75%)	6 (31.58%)	4.804*
	1C	6 (37.5 %)	3 (15.79%)	1.157
	2A	10 (62.5 %)	10 (52.63%)	0.345
	2B	5 (31.25%)	0 (0%)	4.610*
	2C	5 (31.25%)	1 (5.26%)	2.502
	2D	2 (12.5 %)	4 (21.05%)	0.048
While-writing	3	7 (43.75%)	7 (36.84%)	0.173
	4	0 (0 %)	5 (26.32%)	1.657
	5	7 (43.75%)	5 (26.32%)	1.172
	6	4 (25 %)	3 (15.79%)	0.065
	7A	16 (100 %)	17 (89.47%)	0.367
	7B	10 (62.5 %)	8 (42.11%)	1.108
	7C	14 (87.5 %)	15 (78.95%)	0.048
	7D	12 (75 %)	13 (68.42%)	0.003
	7E	14 (87.5 %)	15 (78.95%)	0.048
	7F	12 (75 %)	12 (63.16%)	0.149
Post-writing	8A	11 (68.75%)	5 (26.32%)	6.302*
	8B	8 (50 %)	1 (5.26%)	6.909**
	8C	12 (75 %)	5 (26.32%)	6.408*
	8D	8 (50 %)	4 (21.05%)	2.073
	8E	8 (50 %)	4 (21.05%)	2.073
	8F	11 (68.75%)	4 (21.05%)	6.239*
	9A	2 (12.5 %)	1 (5.26%)	0.024
	9B	1 (6.25%)	0 (0 %)	0.008
	9C	2 (12.5 %)	2 (10.53%)	0.123
	9D	4 (25 %)	1 (5.26%)	1.386

(continued)

Composing behavior	Skilled ($n=16$)	Unskilled ($n=19$)	x^2
9E	5 (31.25%)	1 (5.26%)	2.503
9F	5 (31.25%)	3 (15.79%)	0.464

$*p < .05, **p < .01$

Combined effects of textual metaknowledge and composing skills in EFL

The preceding sections examined the respective roles of students' product-based textual knowledge and process-based composing skills in their writing performance by considering the two factors independently. The following section will investigate whether these two factors are both required or either one of the two is sufficient in order to become a skilled EFL writer. For this purpose, the skilled and unskilled student writers were further classified into four categories by combining the two factors. Table 4 displays this categorization.

First, the average scores of the entire subjects in the present study on the TK test and the questionnaire were calculated respectively. Those average scores (54 points for the TK test and 25 points for the questionnaire) were set as demarcation lines between high and low, as shown in Table 4.

Table 4. Further classification of the students

		TK test	
		High 54	Low<54
Questionnaire	High 25	A	C
	Low<25	B	D

Thus, Group A was defined as the students who scored high on both the TK test and the questionnaire. Group B scored high on the TK test but low on the questionnaire. On the contrary, Group C scored high on the questionnaire but low on the TK test, and Group D scored low on both. Table 5 shows the number of skilled and unskilled students who fell into each category, and Figure 2 indicates the percentage of the students in each group.

Table 5. Number of the students in the four groups

	Group A	Group B	Group C	Group D
Skilled writers	9 (56.25%)	1 (6.25%)	4 (25 %)	2 (12.5 %)
Unskilled group	1 (5.26%)	2 (10.53%)	4 (21.05%)	12 (63.16%)

As Table 5 shows, clear differences between the skilled and unskilled writers were found in Groups A and D, while none was observed in Groups B and C. That is, more than half of the skilled writers (56.25%) fell into Group A with more developed formal metaknowledge as well as more sophisticated composing skills, whereas only one unskilled writer (5.26%) fit into this category. On the other hand, the majority of the unskilled writers (63.16%) were found in Group D with undeveloped textual metaknowledge and composing process strategies, while only 2 skilled writers (12.5%) belonged to this group. As to Groups B and C, there were only slight differences between the percentages of the skilled and unskilled writers (6.25 % of the skilled writers vs. 10.53% of the unskilled writers for Group B, and 25% vs. 21.05% in the Group C). These results suggest that the students need both sufficient knowledge of English academic writing and sophisticated EFL composing skills to become skilled writers of EFL.

Analysis of sample writings

This section will discuss the differences between the above-mentioned groups in more detail by showing sample writings which represent each group respectively. Samples are shown with all errors left intact.

a) Sample 1 (Group A)

Sample 1 was written by a skilled writer in Group A with developed textual knowledge and sophisticated composing skills. This sample was given 6 points in the holistic scoring.

Sample 1 by Subject 9 in Group A

I am against school uniforms. In fact, in the case of my high school, more than half of the students didn't like school uniforms very much. There are some reasons for this.

First of all, if we have school uniforms, we have also many school rules about school uniforms. For example, the day when we can change from the summer school uniforms to winter ones is set. So even if I catch a cold in June and want to wear more clothes, I can't wear anything besides the uniform because of the school rules. It is natural that we wear suitable clothes on suitable occasions. But school uniforms don't allow this.

Second, if we wear the same uniform everyday, it gets dirty. We have school five days a week. It means we wear same clothes five days a week. It is strange.

Third, after we graduate school, we never wear the school uniforms although the cost of them are very high.

Lastly, if there are school uniforms, we can't enjoy fashion. If we cut the skirt a little shorter, maybe the teachers scold us. They think the shorter the skirt is, the lazier we are. I don't think so. It is strange to judge the people by what type clothes they wear.

In conclusion, if we have school uniforms, the relationship between the teachers and the students will get worse. Teachers want to regulate us in the same way, while the students don't want to be regulated and want to have freedom, that is, we want to wear our favorite clothes. Therefore, I don't agree to have the school uniforms and I think school uniforms should be abolished as fast as possible. (282 words)

This sample writing was the second longest composition of all the essays written in this study. This suggests Subject 9's fluency in writing, which is characteristic of the efficient composing process. Her writing is well organized, clearly showing her argumentative position at the outset by saying, "I am against school uniforms." This position is repeated in the conclusion as well. Her anti-school-uniform position is also substantiated by four specific reasons: many rules about school uniform, dirtiness, high cost, and a lack of enjoyment in fashion. Those four reasons are introduced by such transition words as "first of all," "second", "third", and "lastly", and thus create cohesion in writing. Although several grammatical errors are found, this sample is both substantially developed and well structured, which attests to Subject 9's sophisticated composing skills and textual knowledge.

b) Sample 2 (Group B)

Sample 2 was written by an unskilled writer in Group B who scored high in terms of textual knowledge but low in the composing process.

> **Sample 2 by Subject 39 in Group B**
>
> I heard you asked me for my opinion about school uniforms from the viewpoint of a student in Japan. I am for them. Because they are good price. I don't need to choose some clothes and they are reasonable everyday. I think women's uniforms are like attendants'. Because they are very cute, nice and popular. I think men's uniforms are like pillots'. (62 words)

Clearly, Sample 2 is extremely short; indeed, it was the shortest essay of all. Subject 39 sadly lacks fluency in writing. Her first sentence is almost a copy of the instructions in the writing prompt. In the second sentence, she argues for school uniforms and attempts to support this position in the rest of the essay. She tries to say that school uniforms help us save our money and time and that the uniforms look nice on students. However, her writing skills are so immature that she fails to develop her ideas in full sentences.

c) Sample 3 (Group C)

Sample 3 represents Group C who were rated low in terms of textual knowledge but high in composing skills. It was written by Subject 14, one of the unskilled writers.

> **Sample 3 by Subject 14 in Group C**
>
> I agree school uniforms. But I don't like them because I want to wear clothes which I like. And there is only one pattern of school uniform, at least my high school was so. I think this don't allow us to show our characters. If there are some patterns, we can enjoy our different styles and we guess someone's character from her fashion each other. If not, I think a little arrange should be allowed. Next, I had only one set school uniform. Though I had a few skurts, I want to wash them more often. I could wash them only spring, winter and summer bacation and when I chang summer version and winter version. But I think it is useful, when I am bothered I put on which clothes. And it was a little expensive for me, taking another clothes' cost into consider, it was economistic. That is why I agree school uniforms. (154 words)

Sample 3 is rather long, compared with the other students' compositions. Thus, Subject 14 wrote rather fluently, but her composition was rated low and given only 1 point. She starts her essay by supporting school uniforms. But immediately in the next sentence, she says, "But I don't like them because I want to wear clothes which I like." The following sentences explain why she does not like school uniforms. But suddenly, she starts to argue for school uniforms and concludes her writing with this position. She alters argumentative positions several times; therefore, the readers are left confused wondering which position she really takes. What is lacking in this sample is logical consistency based upon a solid overall organization.

d) Sample 4 (Group D)

Sample 4 was produced by an unskilled student writer in Group D whose composing strategies and textual knowledge were judged to be both insufficient.

> **Sample 4 by Subject 5 in Group D**
> The school uniforms are very popular in Japan. I weared it in Junior school and high school. I liked school uniforms very much. I never thought that I don't want to wear it. I go to college now. I hope I want to wear college uniforms. I have to think about the cloth every morning. I don't know that why we need school uniforms. But I think the school uniforms are important for Japanese student. Almost Japanese student probably say they need it. (83 words)

Sample 4 is also a short essay, which suggests Subject 5's lack of fluency in her composing process. It is poor both in content and textual organization. She simply says, "I think the school uniforms are important for Japanese students," and never attempts to substantiate her position throughout the essay. What she offers is just anecdotal comments on her junior and high school days as well as an overgeneralized statement which says that almost all Japanese students probably say they need school uniforms.

Conclusion

This study investigated the roles of process-based composing skills and product-based textual knowledge in Japanese EFL students' argumentative writing. The results of the study uncovered the following tendencies:

1. Skilled Japanese EFL writers possess more developed knowledge of formal aspects of English academic writing than unskilled writers;

2. Skilled Japanese EFL writers demonstrate more sophisticated composing process strategies, especially in planning and rereading processes, than unskilled writers; and

3. To become skilled Japanese EFL writers, both efficient process-based composing skills in EFL and sufficient product-based knowledge of English academic texts are necessary.

The findings of the present study offer several implications for EFL writing classrooms in Japan. First of all, the present results suggest that instructors need to integrate both process-based skills and product-based knowledge in their writing instruction. Both are important and necessary, and a lack of either of the two factors leads to unsuccessful EFL writing performance. It is necessary to create a balance between the "linguistic form and cognitive processing in [EFL] writing (Grabe & Kaplan, 1996, p. 113).

As to composing process skills, students need to pay more careful attention to planning and rereading processes. Especially, they need to be more actively engaged in idea generation and revision exercises. Also, it might be effective to use a retrospective questionnaire like the one used in this study in order to raise the students' consciousness of their own composing processes and of what writing strategies they lack.

Form-oriented exercises, like the TK tests employed in the present study, might also be useful. Japanese students need to learn how to organize an English paragraph and essay as well as how to create coherence and unity in English writing. Product-based or form-oriented perspectives have often been criticized as prescriptive in nature (Zamel, 1983). The instructional approach with the emphasis on rhetorical forms is often a target of criticism in the L1 writing pedagogy. However, what is true in L1 writing instruction is not necessarily so in L2, and especially in EFL contexts, because EFL students come from cultural and linguistic backgrounds where non-English discourse conventions and audience expectations are operating. Grabe and Kaplan (1996) state as follows:

> L1 students have some implicit knowledge of rhetorical plans, organizational logic, and genre form in their native language; it is not at all clear that students have the same implicit knowledge with respect to L2 (p. 142).

The present study suggests that formal instruction on written discourse form might be effective at least for Japanese EFL writing classrooms.

This study is limited in research instruments and in the number of subjects involved. Future studies are called for in order to further investigate the issues of process-based skills and product-based knowledge and to probe ways for keeping a balance between these two orientations in ESL/EFL writing.

Acknowledgements

I would like to thank Dr. Joyce James and anonymous reviewers of *RELC Journal* for their helpful comments on earlier versions of this paper.

This study was conducted with an individual research grant from Senshu University, 1999.

Notes: For each question, a chi-square test was performed to a 2 (skilled writers and unskilled writers) x 2 (those answered "yes" and those answered "no") table consisting of the following four cells: (1) the skilled writers who answered "yes", (2) the unskilled writers who answered "yes", (3) the skilled writers who answered "no", and (4) the unskilled writers who answered "no". Thus, for instance, for Question 1, the data placed in the four cells were (1) 14, (2) 7, (3) 2, and (4) 12 respectively. A chi-square test was administered to this set of data to determine if the observed difference between the skilled and unskilled writers for Question 1 was statistically significant. Similarly, chi-square tests were performed for the rest of the questions.

References

Arnaudet, Martin, L., and Barrett, Mary E. 1990. *Paragraph development: a guide for students of English*. Englewood Cliffs: Prentice Hall.

Bartholomae, David. 1985. Inventing the university. *When a Writer Can't Write*. Edited by Mike, Rose. 134–165. New York: The Guilford Press.

Berkenkotter, Carol, and Huckin, Thomas, N. 1993. Rethinking genre from sociocognitive perspective. *Written Communication* 10. 475–509.

Blanchard, Karen, and Root, Christine. 1994. *Ready to write* (2nd ed.). Reading: Addison-Wesley.

Bridwell, Lillian, S. 1980. Revising processes in twelfth grade students' transactional writing. *Research in the Teaching of English* 14: 3. 197–222.

Connor, Ulla. 1996. *Contrastive rhetoric: cross-cultural aspects of second-language writing*. Cambridge: Cambridge University Press.

Emig, Janet. 1971. *The composing processes of twelfth graders*. Urbana: National Council of Teachers of English.

Faigley, Lester, and Witte, Stephen. 1981. Analyzing revision. *College Composition and Communication* 32. 400–414.

Flower, Linda, and Hayes, John. 1980a. The cognition of discovery: defining a rhetorical problem. *College Composition and Communication* 31. 21–32.

Flower, Linda, and Hayes, John. 1980b. The dynamics of composing: making plans and juggling constraints. *Cognitive Processes in Writing*. Edited by Lee, W. Gregg, and Erwin, R. Steinberg. 31–50. Hillsdale: Lawrence Erlbaum.

Flower, Linda, and Hayes, John, R. 1981. A cognitive process theory of writing. *College Composition and Communication* 32. 365–387.

Grabe, William, and Kaplan, Robert. 1996. *Theory and practice of writing*. London: Longman.

Hamp-Lyons, Liz. 1986. No new lamps for old yet, please. *TESOL Quarterly* 20: 4. 790–796.

Harris, David, E, and Palmer, Leslie, A. 1986. *CELT (A comprehensive English language test for learners of English)*. New York: McGraw-Hill Book Company.

Hinds, John. 1983. Contrastive rhetoric: Japanese and English. *Text* 3: 2. 183–196.

Hinds, John. 1987. Reader versus writer responsibility: a new typology. *Writing Across Languages: Analysis of L2 Text*. Edited by Ulla Connor, and Robert B. Kaplan.141–152. Reading: Addison-Wesley.

Hinds, John. 1990. Inductive, deductive, quasi-inductive: expository writing in Japanese, Korean, Chinese, and Thai. *Coherence in Writing: Research and Pedagogical Perspectives*. Edited by Ulla Connor, and Ann, M. Johns. 87–110. Alexandria : TESOL.

Hirose, Keiko, and Sasaki, Miyuki. 1994. Explanatory variables for Japanese students' expository writing in English: an exploratory study. *Journal of Second Language Writing* 3: 3. 203–229.

Hogue, Ann. 1996. *First steps in academic writing.* New York: Longman.

Horowitz, Daniel. 1986a. Process, not product: less than meets the eye. *TESOL Quarterly* 20: 1. 141–144.

Horowitz, Daniel. 1986b. What professors actually require: academic tasks for the ESL Classroom. *TESOL Quarterly* 20: 3. 445–462.

Horowitz, Daniel. 1986c. The author responds to Liebman-Kleine. *TESOL Quarterly* 20: 4. 788–790.

Kamimura, Taeko, and Oi, Kyoko. 1997. Contrastive rhetoric in letter writing: the interaction of linguistic proficiency and cultural awareness. *JALT Journal* 19: 1. 58–76.

Kaplan, Robert, B. 1966. Cultural thought patterns in intercultural education. *Language Learning* 16: 1. 1–20.

Kitao, S. Kathteen, and Kitao, Kenji. 1993. *From paragraphs to essays: improving reading and writing skills.* Tokyo: Eichosha.

Kobayashi, Hiroe. 1984. Rhetorical patterns in English and Japanese. *TESOL Quarterly* 18: 40. 737–738.

Leki, Illona. 1991. Twenty-five years of contrastive rhetoric: text analysis and writing pedagogies. *TESOL Quarterly* 25: 1. 123–143.

McEloy, Jane. 1997. *Write ahead.* Tokyo: MacMillan Language House.

Oi, Kyoko. 1986. Cross-cultural rhetorical patterning: a study of Japanese and English. *JACET Bulletin* 17. 23–48.

Oshima, Alice, and Hogue, Ann. 1988. *Introduction to academic writing.* Reading: Addison-Wesley.

Oshima, Alice, and Hogue, Ann. 1991. *Writing academic English.* Reading: Addison-Wesley.

Pennington, Martha. C., and So, Sufumi. 1993. Comparing writing process and product across two languages: a study of 6 Singaporean university student writers. *Journal of Second Language Writing* 2: 1. 41–63.

Perl, Sondra. 1979. The composing process of unskilled college writers. *Research in the Teaching of English* 13: 4. 317–336.

Pianko, Sharon. 1979. A description of the composing processes of college freshman writers. *Research in the Teaching of English* 13: 1. 5–22.

Reid, Joy. 1984. Comments on Vivian Zamel's "The composing processes of advanced ESL students: six case studies." *TESOL Quarterly* 18: 1. 149–157.

Sasaki, Miyuki, and Hirose, Keiko. 1996. Explanatory variables for EFL Students' expository writing. *Language Learning* 46: 1. 137–174.

Sommers, Nancy. 1980. Revision strategies of student writers and experienced writers. *College Composition and Communication* 31. 378–388.

Spangler, Mary. S., and Werner, Rita. R. 1990. *Paragraph strategies.* Fort Worth: Holt, Rinehart and Winston.

Swales, John. 1990. *Genre analysis: English in academic and research settings.* Cambridge: Cambridge University Press.

Zamel, Vivian. 1983. The composing processes of advanced ESL students: six case studies. *TESOL Quarterly* 17: 2. 165–187.

Zamel, Vivian. 1982. Writing: the process of discovering meaning. *TESOL Quarterly* 16: 2. 195–209.

APPENDIX A   Examples of Questions for the Product-Knowledge Test

Section 1: [General characteristics of an English paragraph and essay]

Read the following statements. If the statement is true, circle "T"; if it is false, circle "false". (Adapted from Kitao & Kitao, 1993)

1) (T F) A paragraph is a group of sentences that has one main idea.

2) (T F) A paragraph is longer than an essay.

3) (T F) Paragraphs are usually made of an introduction, discussion, opinion, and conclusion.

4) (T F) In a paragraph, each sentence starts on a new line.

5) (T F) The conclusion may repeat the main idea of the paragraph.

Section 2: [Unity]

Read the following paragraph and underline (an) irrelevant sentence(s).(Excerpted from Oshima & Hogue, 1991)

The convenience and economy of small cars account for their popularity. They are easy to park quickly and take smaller parking spaces. Small cars are also a means of conserving energy because they use less gas than big cars. Small cars are inconvenient and uncomfortable on long trips, however, because of their limited passenger and trunk space. They are also more economical to operate and maintain, and they cost less. Because of all these advantages, the demand for small cars remains high.

Section 3: [Coherence]

The following sentences are in a scrambled order. 1) Decide which of the sentences is the topic sentence of the paragraph and write "TS" on the line next to the sentence.

2) Rearrange the sentences into a logical order and number them 1, 2, 3, and so on. (Excerpted from Oshima & Hogue, 1991)

_____ (   ) a. Furthermore, researchers are continuing to work on the development of an official, electrically powered automobile.

_____ (   ) b. Researchers in the automobile industry are experimenting with different types of engines and fuels as alternatives to the conventional gasoline engines.

_____ (   ) c. One new type of engine, which burns diesel oil instead of gasoline, has been available for several years.

_____ (   ) d. Finally several automobile manufacturers are experimenting with methanol, which is a mixture of gasoline and methyl alcohol, as an automobile fuel.

_____ (   ) e. A second type is the gas turbine engine, which can use fuels made from gasoline, diesel oil, kerosene, other petroleum distillates or methanol.

Section 4: [Cohesion]

Fill in the blanks with appropriate transition words. (Excerpted from Spangler & Werner, 1990; McElroy, 1997)

1. A puzzle is a group of pieces that fit together to create a unified picture. (   ), a paragraph is a group of sentences that work together to convey a single idea.

2. Some animals are frightened by sudden, loud noises. (   ), a dog jumps a fence or hides under the bed when it hears thunder.

3. The hotel accommodations in my small town were very poor; (　), the facilities in the city where I now live are excellent.

Section 5: [Integration of the skills and concepts covered in the preceding four sections]

Read the following two paragraphs. Decide which one is more appropriate as an English paragraph and state the reason. (Based on Frydenbert & Boardman, 1990)

A) Alcohol is harmful for your health. It primarily damages the liver. A long period of alcohol abuse can cause cirrhosis of the liver, and it has recently been determined that even cancer of the liver can be caused by excessive drinking. Too much alcohol may also cause insomnia and loss of control of the body. In fact, it may permanently damage the nervous system. In many ways, alcohol brings a lot of effects on your body.

B) Alcohol primarily damages the liver. A long period of alcohol abuse can cause cirrhosis of the liver, and it has recently been determined that even cancer of the liver can be caused by excessive drinking. Too much alcohol may also cause insomnia and loss of control of the body. In fact, it may permanently damage the nervous system.

APPENDIX B　Retrospective Composing-Process Questionnaire

Read the following statements on how you have written the composition.

Answer "Yes" or "No."

Pre-Writing

1　A. I thought about content before beginning to write.:　　Yes　　No

　　B. I thought about organization before beginning to write:　　Yes　　No

　　C. I thought about audience before beginning to write:　　Yes　　No

2　A. I read the instructions in the task several times:　　Yes　　No

　　B. I wrote an outline:　　Yes　　No

　　C. I listed ideas:　　Yes　　No

　　D. I jotted down words:　　Yes　　No

While-Writing

3　I thought and wrote in English from the beginning.:　　Yes　　No

4　I avoided writing whatever idea came into my mind:　　Yes　　No

5　I tried to write as much as possible:　　Yes　　No

6　I seldom stopped in the middle:　　Yes　　No

7　While I wrote my composition, I paid attention to the following aspects of writing:

　　A. Content　　Yes　　No

　　B. Audience:　　Yes　　No

　　C. Organization:　　Yes　　No

　　D. Vocabulary:　　Yes　　No

　　E. Grammar:　　Yes　　No

　　F. Spelling/punctuation:　　Yes　　No

8.　After I wrote my composition, I reread it by paying attention to the following aspects of writing:

　　A. Content　　Yes　　No

　　B. Audience:　　Yes　　No

C. Organization:	Yes	No
D. Vocabulary:	Yes	No
E. Grammar:	Yes	No
F. Spelling/punctuation:	Yes	No

9. I revised my composition by paying attention to the following aspects of writing:

A. Content	Yes	No
B. Audience:	Yes	No
C. Organization:	Yes	No
D. Vocabulary:	Yes	No
E. Grammar:	Yes	No
F. Spelling/punctuation:	Yes	No

APPENDIX C   Points Assigned to an Affirmative Answer for Each Question in the Questionnaire

Question Items	Points
Pre-Writing	
1A	3
1B.	3
1C.	3
2A.	1
2B.	1
2C.	1
2D.	1
While-Writing	
3.	1
4.	1
5.	1
6.	1
7A.	3
7B.	3
7C.	3
7D.	2
7E.	2
7F.	1

Post-Writing	
8A.	3
8B.	3
8C.	3
8D.	2
8E.	2
8F.	1
9A.	3
9B.	3
9C.	3
9D.	2
9E.	2
9F.	1

abstraction	[æb'strækʃn]	n.	抽象化；抽象过程	U2
accord	[ə'kɔ:d]	v.	（with）相一致	U6
acquisition	[ˌækwi'ziʃn]	n.	取得，获得，习得；获得物	U4
activate	['æktiveit]	vt.	使活动，起动，触发	U4
administer	[əd'ministə]	v.	管理，治理，给予，执行	U4
advent	['ædvent]	n.	出现，到来	U4
affective	[ə'fektiv]	a.	情感的；表达感情的	U7
affirmatively	[ə'fɜ:mətivli]	adv.	肯定地，赞成地，积极地	U5
aforementioned	[əˌfɔ:'menʃənd]	a.	前面提及的，上述的	U3
aggravate	['ægrəveit]	vt.	加重（剧），使恶化；激怒，使恼火	U1
aggressive	[ə'gresiv]	a.	侵犯（略）的，挑衅的；敢作敢为的	U6
alienate	['eiliəneit]	vt.	使疏远，离间；使转移，放弃	U2
allegation	[ˌælə'geiʃn]	n.	（无证据的）指控	U1
allocation	[ˌælə'keiʃn]	n.	配给，分配	U8
allotment	[ə'lɒtmənt]	n.	分配；分配物；养家费；命运	U8
allude	[ə'lju:d]	vi.	暗指，提及	U5
ambiguous	[æm'bigjuəs]	a.	引起歧义的，模	U5
			棱两可的，含糊不清的	U5
ameliorate	[ə'mi:liəreit]	v.	改善	U6
annotation	[ˌænə'teiʃn]	n.	注解，注释	U3
anomie	['ænəmi]	n.	社会的反常状态，混乱	U1
ANOVA	[ə'nəuvə]		方差分析	U6
appraisal	[ə'preizl]	n.	估计，估量，评价	U5
apprenticeship	[ə'prentiʃip]	n.	学徒身份，学徒期	U1
argumentation	[ˌɑ:gjumən'teiʃn]	n.	议论文；论证；争论；辩论	U7
articulate	[ɑ:'tikjuleit]	v.	明确有力地表达	U5
ascertain	[ˌæsə'tein]	vt.	查明，弄清，确定	U3
ascription	[ə'skripʃn]	n.	归属	U2
aspiration	[ˌæspə'reiʃn]	n.	强烈的愿望	U5
assertion	[ə'sɜ:ʃn]	n.	声称；主张；明确肯定	U6
assimilate	[ə'siməleit]	v.	吸收，消化；使同化	U6
augment	[ɔ:g'ment]	vt.	增强，加强，增加	U1
authentically	[ɔ:'θentikli]	adv.	真正地，确实地；可靠地	U7
autonomous	[ɔ:'tɒnəməs]	a.	自治的；自主的；自发的	U7
axial	['æksil]	a.	轴的；轴向的	U8
bearing	['beəriŋ]	n.	关系，关联	U6
benchmark	['bentʃmɑ:k]	n.	基准；标准检查程序	U8
bound	[baund]	a.	有义务的；受约束的；装有封面的	U8
		n.	范围	U8

breach	[bri:tʃ]	n./vt.	破坏，破裂，违反	U1
built-in	['bilt'in]	a.	嵌入的；固定的	U8
		n.	内置	U8
burgeoning	['bɜ:dʒəniŋ]	a.	增长迅速的，发展很快的	U3
bypass	['baipɑ:s]	vt.	绕开；忽视；设旁路；迂回	U8
		n.	旁路；支路	U8
caveat	['kæviæt]	n.	警告；中止诉讼手续的申请	U8
checklist	['tʃeklist]	n.	清单；检查表；备忘录；目录册	U7
chronologically	[ˌkrɔnə'lɔdʒikli]	adv.	按年代地	U7
circumvent	[ˌsɜ:kəm'vent]	vt.	围绕，包围，避免	U5
clustering	['klʌstəriŋ]	n.	聚类，聚集	U7
coefficient	[ˌkəui'fiʃnt]	n.	系数	U6
cognate	['kɔgneit]	n.	同源词，同根词；同系语言	U3
cognitive	['kɔgnitiv]	a.	认知的，认识能力的	U3
coherence	[kəu'hiərəns]	n.	一致；连贯性；凝聚	U7
cohesive	[kəu'hi:siv]	a.	有黏着力的，紧密结合的	U5
collaboration	[kəˌlæbə'reiʃn]	n.	合作，协作；勾结	U2
collusion	[kə'lu:ʒn]	n.	勾结，串通	U1
commence	[kə'mens]	v.	开始	U1
commencement	[kə'mensmənt]	n.	开始；毕业典礼，学位授予典礼	U6
commitment	[kə'mitmənt]	n.	承诺，保证；信奉，献身；承担的义务	U6
comply	[kəm'plai]	vi.	（with）遵从，依从，服从	U6
compound	['kɔmpaund]	a.	复合的；混合的	U7
concordancer	[kən'kɔ:dənsə]	n.	语词检索；关键词排序的程式	U8
concurrent	[kən'kʌrənt]	a.	并发的；一致的；同时发生的	U8
confidential	[ˌkɔnfi'denʃl]	a.	秘（机）密的	U6
confound	[kən'faund]	vt.	使混淆，使混乱	U3
confront	[kən'frʌnt]	vt.	面对，使面对面，碰到，遇到	U4
conjugation	[ˌkɔndʒu'geiʃn]	n.	词形变化；结合，配合	U3
conjunctive	[kən'dʒʌŋktiv]	a.	连接的；结合的	U7
		n.	连接词	U7
consent	[kən'sent]	n./vi.	准许，同意，赞成	U1
constitute	['kɔnstitju:t]	vt.	构成，组成	U5
constraint	[kən'streint]	n.	约束；局促，态度不自然；强制	U8
construe	[kən'stru:]	vt.	分析，解释	U2
contentious	[kən'tenʃəs]	a.	好辩的，喜争吵的	U2
contingent	[kən'tindʒənt]	a.	视条件而定的	U1
contravene	[ˌkɔntrə'vi:n]	vt.	违反	U2
convergent	[kən'vɜ:dʒənt]	a.	收敛的；会聚性的；趋集于一点的	U7
corpus	['kɔ:pəs]	n.	全文，文集，语料库	U3
correlate	['kɔrileit]	v.	（to, with）相关，关联；使相互关联	U6
corroborate	[kə'rɔbəreit]	vt.	确证	U3
counterpart	['kauntəpɑ:t]	n.	相对物，配对物	U4
criteria	[krai'tiəriə]	n.	标准，准则	U5
cue	[kju:]	vt.	向……发出信号，给……暗示	U4
cursive	['kɜ:siv]	a.	草书的；草书体的	U8
daunting	['dɔ:ntiŋ]	a.	令人畏惧的，令人气馁的	U2

debrief	[ˌdiːˈbriːf]	vt.	向……询问情况，汇报情况	U1
deem	[diːm]	v.	认为，视为	U1
deficiency	[diˈfiʃnsi]	n.	缺乏，不足；缺点，缺陷	U6
deft	[deft]	a.	灵巧的；机敏的；敏捷熟练的	U8
deliberate	[diˈlibərət]	v.	仔细考虑；商议	U8
delineate	[diˈlinieit]	vt.	描绘；描写；画……的轮廓	U8
delve	[delv]	v.	深入探究，钻研	U1
demise	[diˈmaiz]	n.	转让；死亡，终止；传位	U8
demographic	[ˌdeməˈgræfik]	a.	人口统计学的，人口统计的	U5
denotation	[ˌdiːnəuˈteiʃn]	n.	（明示的）意义；指示	U3
deter	[diˈtɜː]	vt.	阻止	U5
deterrent	[diˈterənt]	a.	威慑的，制止的	U1
detrimental	[ˌdetriˈmentl]	a.	有害的，不利的	U2
deviant	[ˈdiːviənt]	a.	越出常规的，反常的	U1
devise	[diˈvaiz]	vt.	想出，设计	U6
dimensional	[diˈmenʃənl]	a.	空间的，维度的	U6
dire	[ˈdaiə]	a.	可怕的	U1
discern	[diˈsɜːn]	v.	看出，理解，了解	U1
discrepancy	[disˈkrepənsi]	n.	不符合（之处），不一致（之处）	U5
discrete	[diˈskriːt]	a.	分离的，不相关联的	U2
discrimination	[diˌskrimiˈneiʃn]	n.	歧视，辨别，区别，不公平的待遇	U5
disillusion	[ˌdisiˈluːʒn]	vt.	使不再抱幻想，使理想破灭	U2
disjuncture	[disˈdʒʌŋktʃə]	n.	分离，分裂	U1
distort	[diˈstɔːt]	v.	歪曲，扭曲	U6
dovetail	[ˈdʌvteil]	v.	与……吻合	U8
draconian	[drəˈkəuniən]	a.	严峻的，苛刻的	U1
drawback	[ˈdrɔːbæk]	n.	缺点，不利条件；退税	U7
dubious	[ˈdjuːbjəs]	a.	可疑的；暧昧的；无把握的；半信半疑的	U8
duplication	[ˌdjuːpliˈkeiʃn]	n.	复制；副本	U2
efficacy	[ˈefikəsi]	n.	功效，效力	U8
elaborate	[iˈlæbəreit]	v.	详述；详细制订	U5
elicit	[iˈlisit]	vt.	引出，探出，诱出（回答等）	U4
eligible	[ˈelidʒəbl]	a.	合适的，合格的，有资格当选的	U5
eloquence	[ˈeləkwəns]	n.	口才，雄辩	U5
embark	[imˈbɑːk; em-]	v.	从事，着手	U8
empirical	[imˈpirikl]	a.	以经验（或观察）为依据的	U6
empowerment	[imˈpauəmənt]	n.	许可，授权	U7
emulate	[ˈemjuleit]	vt.	仿真；模仿；尽力赶上；同……竞争	U8
encapsulate	[inˈkæpsjuleit]	v.	压缩；将……装入胶囊；将……封进内部	U8
encompass	[inˈkʌmpəs]	vt.	包围，包含或包括某事物	U1
encounter	[inˈkauntə]	v.	不期而遇，遭遇，碰见	U4
encyclopaedia	[enˌsaikləuˈpiːdjə]	n.	百科全书，大全	U7
endorse	[inˈdɔːs]	vt.	赞同；签名于……背面	U1
enrol	[inˈrəul]	v.	注册；登记	U6
entail	[inˈteil]	vt.	使承担，使成为必要，需要	U3
equitably	[ˈekwitəbli]	adv.	公正地	U2

equivalent	[i'kwivələnt]	a.	相等的，相当的	U3
		n.	等价物，意义相同的词	U3
espouse	[i'spauz]	vt.	支持，拥护	U2
exacerbate	[ig'zæsəbeit]	vt.	加重，恶化	U1
exemplification	[ig,zemplifi'keiʃn]	n.	范例；模范	U7
exhortation	[,egzɔ:'teiʃn]	n.	敦促，极力推荐	U1
expel	[ik'spel]	vt.	把……开除；驱逐，放逐；排出，喷出	U1
exposition	[,ekspə'ziʃn]	n.	说明文	U7
expository	[iks'pozitri]	a.	说明的，解释的	U4
facilitate	[fə'siliteit]	vt.	使变得（更）容易，使便利	U3
fastidious	[fæ'stidiəs]	a.	挑剔的；苛求的，难取悦的	U8
feasibility	[,fizə'biləti]	n.	可行性；可能性	U8
flip	[flip]	vt.	快速翻动；轻抛；轻拍	U3
forensic	[fə'rensik]	a.	法庭的，辩论的	U1
foster	['fɔstə]	v.	培养，促进；收养	U3
fraternity	[frə'tɜ:nəti]	n.	兄弟会，大学生联谊会，友爱	U1
gear	[giə]	v.	使适应；接上，调和	U6
generic	[dʒə'nerik]	a.	类的；一般的；属的；非商标的	U8
gloss	[glɔs]	n.	注解	U3
haphazard	[hæp'hæzəd]	a.	偶然的，随意的，任意的	U1
heterogeneous	[,hetərə'dʒi:niəs]	a.	不均匀的；由不同成分形成的	U8
hieroglyph	['haiərəglif]	n.	象形文字；图画文字；秘密符号	U8
hinder	['hində]	v.	阻碍，妨碍	U5
holistic	[həu'listik]	a.	全部的	U3
homogeneous	[,hɔmə'dʒi:niəs]	a.	同种类的，同性质的，有相同特征的	U1
hypertextuality	[,haipə'tekstʃuə'æləti]	n.	超文本性	U3
impediment	[im'pedimənt]	n.	口吃；妨碍；阻止	U8
implementation	[,implimen'teiʃn]	n.	生效，履行，实施	U2
impose	[im'pəuz]	vt.	强加于	U2
impunity	[im'pju:nəti]	n.	（惩罚、损失、伤害等的）免除	U6
inadvertent	[,inəd'vɜ:tənt]	a.	非故意的	U1
incongruent	[in'kɔŋgruent]	a.	不一致的	U1
incorporate	[in'kɔ:pəreit]	v.	包含，加上，吸收；把……合并，使并入	U5
increment	['inkrəmənt]	n.	增值，增加	U4
induce	[in'dju:s]	vt.	引诱，引起，归纳	U4
inflectional	[in'flekʃənl]	a.	有屈折变化的；弯曲的	U3
intercourse	['intəkɔ:s]	n.	交流，交往，交际	U6
intermittent	[,intə'mitənt]	a.	间歇的，断断续续的	U6
interpret	[in'tɜ:prit]	v.	解释，理解，诠释	U5
interval	['intəvl]	n.	间隔，幕间休息	U4
intervention	[,intə'venʃn]	n.	介入，干涉，干预，调解，排解	U5
intimidate	[in'timideit]	vt.	恐吓，威胁	U5
introspective	[,intrə'spektiv]	a.	反省的	U4
intrusive	[in'tru:siv]	a.	侵入的；打扰的	U8
inventory	['invəntri]	n.	详细目录	U6
irritability	[,iritə'biləti]	n.	易怒；过敏性；兴奋性	U6
judicious	[dʒu:'diʃəs]	a.	明智的	U1

laminated	['læmineitid]	a.	层压的；层积的；薄板状的	U8
leniency	['li:niənsi]	n.	宽大，仁慈	U1
lexical	['leksikl]	a.	词汇的，词典的	U3
lexicon	['leksikən]	n.	词典；语汇；词素	U3
locale	[ləu'kæl]	n.	场所，现场	U8
log	[lɔg]	n.	记录；航行日志	U8
logistical	[lə'dʒistikl]	a.	后勤方面的；运筹的，逻辑的	U8
longitudinal	[lɔndʒi'tju:dinl]	a.	经度的，纵向的	U8
malleability	[ˌmæliə'biləti]	n.	有延展性，柔韧性，柔软	U5
marginal	['mɑ:dʒinl]	a.	边缘的，旁注的	U4
masculine	['mæskjulin]	a.	阳性的，雄性的，男子气概的	U3
massification	[ˌmæsifi'keiʃn]	n.	扩大化，大规模化	U2
mediate	['mi:dieit]	vt.	经调停解决	U2
mentor	['mentɔ:]	n.	指导者，良师益友	U8
metalinguistic	['metəliŋgwistik]	a.	元语言的；纯理语言的	U8
moderation	[ˌmɔdə'reiʃn]	n.	适度；自我节制	U7
moderator	['mɔdəreitə]	n.	调解人，仲裁人	U1
momentous	[mə'mentəs]	a.	重要的；重大的	U8
monosemic	[ˌmɔnəu'si:mik]	a.	单意（词）的	U3
morale	[mə'rɑ:l]	n.	士气，斗志	U2
morphological	[ˌmɔ:fə'lɔdʒikl]	a.	形态学，形态的	U4
multidimensional	['mʌltidai'menʃənl]	a.	多维的；多面的	U7
narration	[nə'reiʃn]	n.	叙述，讲述；故事	U7
neurological	[ˌnjuərə'lɔdʒikl]	a.	神经病学的，神经学上的	U8
normative	['nɔ:mətiv]	a.	规范的，惯常的	U6
notable	['nəutəbl]	a.	值得注意的，显著的；著名的	U8
nuanced	['nju:ɑ:nst]	a.	微妙的；具有细微差别的	U8
obliterate	[ə'bli:təreit]	vt.	涂去，擦掉，使消失	U1
onus	['əunəs]	n.	义务，责任	U1
orientation	[ˌɔ:riən'teiʃn]	n.	适应，（对新生的）情况介绍；方向，方位	U6
originality	[əˌridʒə'næləti]	n.	创意；独创性，创造力；原始	U7
overarching	[ˌəuvə'ɑ:tʃiŋ]	a.	支配一切的，包罗万象的	U3
overlap	[ˌəuvə'læp]	n.	重叠部分，相交	U2
overtake	[ˌəuvə'teik]	vt.	(overtook, overtaken) 追上，超过	U6
panel	['pænl]	n.	面，板；专门小组	U1
papyrus	[pə'pairəs]	n.	纸莎草；纸莎草纸	U8
parameter	[pə'ræmitə]	n.	(常 pl.) 界限，范围；参数	U3
paramount	['pærəmaunt]	a.	最重要的，主要的	U2
pedagogical	[ˌpedə'gɔdʒikl]	a.	教育学的；教学法的	U3
peer	[piə]	n.	同等的人	U7
		vi.	凝视，盯着看；窥视	U7
penalty	['penəlti]	n.	处罚，惩罚，罚金	U2
perception	[pə'sepʃn]	n.	知觉，觉察（力），观念	U7
perpetuate	[pə'petʃueit]	vt.	使永存，使不朽	U2
pertain	[pə'tein]	vi.	(to) 从属，有关	U1
pertinent	['pɜ:tinənt]	a.	有关系的，相关的	U1
phonics	['fɔniks]	n.	声学；声音基础教学法	U8

piecemeal	['pi:smi:l]	a.	逐渐的，零碎的	U1
plagiarise	['pleidʒəraiz]	vt.	剽窃，抄袭（别人学说、著作）	U1
portability	[ˌpɔ:tə'biləti]	n.	轻便，可携带性	U8
portfolio	[pɔ:t'fəuliəu]	n.	公文包；文件夹	U7
portrait	['pɔ:trit]	n.	肖像；描写	U7
practicum	['præktikəm]	n.	实习课；实习科目	U7
pragmatic	[præg'mætik]	a.	实际的，实用主义的	U3
precipitate	[pri'sipiteit]	v.	促成；使沉淀	U6
preclude	[pri'klu:d]	vt.	排除；妨碍；阻止	U8
preliminary	[pri'liminəri]	a.	预备的，初步的	U4
presumably	[pri'zju:məbli]	adv.	据推测，大概，可能	U8
presume	[pri'zju:m]	v.	假定；擅（做）	U4
privy	['privi]	a.	知情的，秘密参与的	U6
probe	[prəub]	v.	调查；（用探针）探测	U7
		n.	探针；调查	U7
procrastination	[prəuˌkræsti'neiʃn]	n.	耽搁，拖延	U1
procurement	[prə'kjuəmənt]	n.	获得，取得，采购	U5
prompt	[prʌmpt]	n.	提示	U8
		vt.	提示；促进；激起；（给演员）提白	U8
		a.	敏捷的，迅速的；立刻的	U8
propensity	[prə'pensəti]	n.	癖好	U1
protocol	['prəutəkɔl]	n.	协议；外交礼节	U3
provisional	[prə'viʒnl]	a.	临时的，暂时的；暂定的	U8
pseudonym	['sju:dənim]	n.	假名，笔名	U1
psychopathology	[ˌsaikəupə'θɔlədʒi]	n.	精神病理学	U6
punctuation	[ˌpʌŋktʃu'eiʃn]	n.	标点法，标点符号	U7
punitive	['pju:nətiv]	a.	处罚的	U1
qualitative	['kwɔlitətiv]	a.	（性）质上的，定性的	U1
ramification	[ˌræmifi'keiʃn]	n.	结果，后果	U1
random	['rændəm]	a.	任意的，随机的	U6
rationale	[ˌræʃə'nɑ:l]	n.	理论的说明，基本原理，依据	U2
realm	[relm]	n.	界，领域，范围；王国，国度	U3
recidivism	[ri'sidəˌvizəm]	n.	再犯，累犯（行为或倾向）	U1
reconcile	['rekənsail]	vt.	使和解，调停，排解	U2
recruit	[ri'kru:t]	v.	招募，吸收；充实	U6
recurrent	[ri'kʌrənt]	a.	重现，反复	U6
recursion	[ri'kɜ:ʃn]	n.	递归，循环；递归式	U8
recursive	[ri'kɜ:siv]	a.	递归的；循环的	U8
reed	[ri:d]	n.	芦苇；簧片；牧笛；不可依靠的人	U8
refine	[ri'fain]	vt.	精制，提纯；使优美，使完善，使文雅	U3
reinforce	[ˌri:in'fɔ:s]	v.	增强，加强，增援	U6
reluctant	[ri'lʌktənt]	a.	勉强的，不情愿的	U5
reminiscent	[ˌremi'nisnt]	a.	（of）使人想起……的；怀旧的	U1
repercussion	[ˌri:pə'kʌʃn]	n.	（不良的）影响，反响，后果	U2
replete	[ri'pli:t]	a.	充满的；装满的	U8
replicate	['replikeit]	v.	复制	U6
respective	[ri'spektiv]	a.	各自的，分别的	U8

retain	[ri'tein]	vt.	保留，保持	U4
retention	[ri'tenʃn]	n.	保留，保持	U4
retrieval	[ri'tri:vl]	n.	检索；恢复；取回；拯救	U8
retrospective	[ˌretrə'spektiv]	a.	回顾的，怀旧的	U8
reveal	[ri'vi:l]	vt.	显示；透露；揭露；泄露	U7
rhetoric	['retərik]	n.	修辞学	U2
rhetorical	[ri'tɔrikl]	a.	修辞学的；华丽的；夸张的	U7
rigmarole	['rigmərəul]	n.	冗长无聊的废话	U1
rigor	['rigə]	n.	精确；严厉；苛刻；僵硬	U8
rigorous	['rigərəs]	a.	严厉的；严格的；严密的；严酷的	U8
rubric	['ru:brik]	n.	题目；红字标题；红色印刷	U8
salient	['seiliənt]	a.	显著的，突出的	U6
sanction	['sæŋkʃn]	n.	批准；约束力	U1
scant	['skænt]	a.	不足的，缺乏的	U1
scenario	[si'neəri:əu]	n.	（行动的）方案，剧情概要	U8
schema	['ski:mə]	n.	模式；计划；图解；概要	U8
scramble	['skræmbl]	v.	扰乱，搞乱	U4
semantic	[si'mæntik]	a.	语义的；语义学的	U3
seminal	['seminl]	a.	种子的	U8
sequelae	[si'kwi:li:]	n.	结果，后遗症	U6
snap	[snæp]	v.	突然拉断，咔嚓折断；拍快照	U3
sojourner	['sɔdʒɜ:nə]	n.	旅居者；寄居者	U6
sophisticated	[sə'fistikeitid]	a.	复杂的，精致的，富有经验的	U3
sorority	[sə'rɔrəti]	n.	妇女联谊会，女学生联谊会	U1
stereotyping	['steriəˌtaipiŋ]	n.	定型；成见	U6
stimulus	['stimjuləs]	n.	促进（因素）；刺激（物）	U4
stringent	['strindʒənt]	a.	严厉的；令人信服的	U5
submit	[səb'mit]	v.	提交；顺从，服从	U7
subsection	[ˌsʌb'sekʃn]	n.	分段，分部；细分；小部分	U7
subsidiary	[səb'sidiəri]	a.	辅助的，附设的	U2
subsume	[səb'sju:m]	vt.	把……归入；把……包括在内	U8
subtract	[səb'trækt]	vt.	减去，扣除	U4
succinct	[sək'siŋkt]	a.	简明的，简洁的，简练的	U5
synonymous	[si'nɔniməs]	a.	同义的，同义词的	U2
syntactic	[sin'tæktik]	a.	句法的	U4
tabulate	['tæbjuleit]	vt.	把……制成表格	U8
tactically	['tæktikəli]	adv.	战术地，有谋略地，策略上地	U4
tailor	['teilə]	vt.	调整使适应	U3
tarnish	['tɑ:niʃ]	v.	（使）失去光泽；玷污，败坏	U1
taxonomy	[tæk'sɔnəmi]	n.	分类学	U3
temporally	['tempərəli]	adv.	时间地，短暂地	U8
tertiary	['tɜ:ʃəri]	a.	高等的；第三的；第三位的；三代的	U8
thesaurus	[θi'sɔ:rəs]	n.	同义词词典，百科全书	U8
transcribe	[træn'skraib]	vt.	抄写，转录	U1
transgression	[træns'greʃn]	n.	违反，违法，罪过	U2
trawl	[trɔ:l]	vt.	查阅（档案等）	U1
triangulation	[traiˌæŋgju'leiʃn]	n.	三角测量；三角剖分	U3

unanimous	[ju'nænimǝs]	a.	全体一致的，一致同意的，无异议的	U5
unbiased	[ʌn'baiǝst]	a.	无偏见的，不偏不倚的，公正的	U5
underachieve	[ˌʌndǝrǝ'tʃi:v]	vi.	学习成绩不良，未能发挥学习潜能	U8
underlying	[ˌʌndǝ'laiiŋ]	a.	潜在的，含蓄的	U5
underpin	[ˌʌndǝ'pin]	vt.	加固（墙等）的基础，加强……的基础	U2
underscore	[ˌʌndǝ'skɔ:]	vt.	强调；划线于……下	U8
undertake	[ˌʌndǝ'teik]	vt.	承担，保证；从事；同意；试图	U8
undertaking	[ˌʌndǝ'teikiŋ]	n.	事业；企业；保证；殡仪业	U8
uproot	[ˌʌp'ru:t]	v.	根除	U6
utilise	['ju:tilaiz]	vt.	利用	U1
variable	['veǝriǝbl]	n.	可变因素，变量	U6
venue	['venju:]	n.	审判地；犯罪地点；发生地点；集合地点	U8
verbatim	[vɜ:'beitim]	a.	（完全）照字面的，逐字的	U1
yield	[ji:ld]	v.	生产，获利	U4